THE GLASS CEILING IN THE 21ST CENTURY

THE GLASS CEILING IN THE 21ST CENTURY

UNDERSTANDING BARRIERS TO GENDER EQUALITY

EDITED BY
MANUELA BARRETO,
MICHELLE K. RYAN,
AND MICHAEL T. SCHMITT

AMERICAN PSYCHOLOGICAL ASSOCIATION · WASHINGTON, DC

Published by
American Psychological Association
750 First Street, NE
Washington, DC 20002
www.apa.org

To order
APA Order Department
P.O. Box 92984
Washington, DC 20090-2984
Tel: (800) 374-2721; Direct: (202) 336-5510
Fax: (202) 336-5502; TDD/TTY: (202) 336-6123
Online: www.apa.org/books/
E-mail: order@apa.org

In the U.K., Europe, Africa, and the Middle East, copies may be ordered from
American Psychological Association
3 Henrietta Street
Covent Garden, London
WC2E 8LU England

Typeset in Goudy by Circle Graphics, Inc., Columbia, MD

Printer: McNaughton & Gunn, Inc.
Cover Designer: Mercury Publishing Services, Rockville, MD
Technical/Production Editor: Tiffany L. Klaff

The opinions and statements published are the responsibility of the authors, and such opinions and statements do not necessarily represent the policies of the American Psychological Association.

Library of Congress Cataloging-in-Publication Data

The glass ceiling in the 21st century : understanding barriers to gender equality / edited by Manuela Barreto, Michelle K. Ryan, and Michael T. Schmitt.
    p. cm. — (Psychology of women book series)
    Includes bibliographical references and index.
    ISBN-13: 978-1-4338-0409-0
    ISBN-10: 1-4338-0409-3
    1. Glass ceiling (Employment discrimination) 2. Sex discrimination in employment. 3. Women executives—Promotions. I. Barreto, Manuela da Costa. II. Ryan, Michelle K. III. Schmitt, Michael T.

    HD6060.G63 2009
    331.4'133—dc22

                                                            2008021600

British Library Cataloguing-in-Publication Data

A CIP record is available from the British Library.

Printed in the United States of America
First Edition

PSYCHOLOGY OF WOMEN
BOOK SERIES

v

CONTENTS

CONTRIBUTORS

Marisol Arroyave, MBA, EMC Corporation, Hopkinton, MA

Manuela Barreto, PhD, Centro de Investigação e Intervenção Social, University of Lisbon, Lisbon, Portugal

Gargi Bhattacharya, PhD, University of Birmingham, Birmingham, United Kingdom

Stacy Blake-Beard, PhD, School of Management, Simmons College, Boston, MA

Nyla R. Branscombe, PhD, Department of Psychology, University of Kansas, Lawrence

Eleanor Chin, Clarity Partners Coaching & Consulting, Boston, MA

Sezgin Cihangir, PhD, Social and Organizational Psychology, Leiden University, Leiden, the Netherlands

Mina Cikara, Department of Psychology, Princeton University, Princeton, NJ

Faye J. Crosby, PhD, Psychology Department, University of California, Santa Cruz

Kelly Danaher, University of Kansas, Department of Psychology, Lawrence

Alice H. Eagly, PhD, Department of Psychology, Northwestern University, Evanston, IL

Naomi Ellemers, PhD, Social and Organizational Psychology, Leiden University, Leiden, the Netherlands

Susan T. Fiske, PhD, Department of Psychology, Princeton University, Princeton, NJ

Chad Forbes, Department of Psychology, University of Arizona, Tucson

S. Alexander Haslam, PhD, School of Psychology, University of Exeter, Exeter, United Kingdom

Mette D. Hersby, PhD, School of Psychology, University of Exeter, Exeter, United Kingdom

Laurie Hunt, CPCC, Laurie Hunt & Associates, Toronto, Ontario, Canada

Aarti Iyer, PhD, School of Psychology, University of Queensland, St. Lucia, Australia

Clara Kulich, PhD, School of Psychology, University of Exeter, Exeter, United Kingdom

Gina LaRoche, MBA, INSPIRITAS Corporation, Cambridge, MA

Floor Rink, PhD, Department of Economy and Business Administration, University of Groningen, Groningen, the Netherlands

Michelle K. Ryan, PhD, School of Psychology, University of Exeter, Exeter, United Kingdom

Laura Sabattini, PhD, Catalyst, New York, NY

Toni Schmader, PhD, Department of Psychology, University of Arizona, Tucson

Michael T. Schmitt, PhD, Department of Psychology, Simon Fraser University, Burnaby, British Columbia, Canada

Maureen Scully, PhD, College of Management, University of Massachusetts, Boston

Sabine Sczesny, PhD, Institute of Psychology, University of Bern, Bern, Switzerland

Jennifer R. Spoor, PhD, School of Psychology, University of Queensland, St. Lucia, Australia

Margaret S. Stockdale, PhD, Department of Psychology, Southern Illinois University, Carbondale

Katherine Stroebe, MSc, Department of Social and Organizational Psychology, Leiden University, Leiden, the Netherlands

M. Dana Wilson-Kovacs, PhD, Department of Sociology, Exeter, United Kingdom

Shen Zhang, Department of Psychology, University of Arizona, Tucson

SERIES FOREWORD

Contemporary society is marked by a great number of critical challenges: The number of children and families living in poverty is rising. High school dropouts from our nation's schools are increasing, and high-stakes testing is changing the way our students are being educated. We are living with the effects of welfare reform and need to look critically at how these reforms have affected children, youth, and families. Head Start programs, long celebrated for being scientifically based educational interventions, are at risk for losing funding.

Since September 11, 2001, we have lived with new restrictions on our freedoms, new costs for wars launched in the Middle East, and constant fear. How is this new anxiety affecting women who have long been the transmitters of culture and community? Mental health problems in this age of anxiety are enormous even as managed care and federal policies reduce support for mental health services. How can prevention programs be developed in an age of drastic budget cuts and removal of basic social and health services? New neurological research and the genome project are revealing individual differences that require careful thought regarding the implications for education, socialization, and remediation. While our country is becoming more diverse, tolerance and celebration of diversity are decreasing and reproductive choices are becoming more restricted. How are individual rights preserved while we balance human rights and the welfare of others? How can women and other minorities thrive when they face invisible glass ceilings?

Feminist psychologists have claimed they have a moral imperative to improve society. This book, and others to follow in the Society for the Psychology of Women Series (Division 35) of the American Psychological Association, draws on the expertise of psychologists who have been working on social issues using the lens of feminist consciousness. Forthcoming books in the series will present invited monographs and edited volumes that address critical issues facing our society. These volumes will be based on current scholarship but will be written in a way that is accessible to laypersons who are not knowledgeable in a given field. Longer than a journal article but shorter than a full text, invited monographs in the series will not just tell the readers *what we know* on a topic, but also what we as a society (as professionals, parents, researchers, policymakers, and citizens) *need to do* regarding the issue. Authors will synthesize the literature and make recommendations for action. Edited volumes will present state-of-the-art research on issues that bear on women, gender, and public policy.

Arnold S. Kahn, PhD
Series Editor
James Madison University

ACKNOWLEDGMENTS

Putting a volume like this together is not something one does in isolation. Several people have made this possible, whether by actually writing the various chapters or by providing valuable help in the various stages through which the volume passed. First we wish to thank Alex Haslam, who first suggested that we embark together on a similar project. Alex's intuition about how much we would enjoy working together was right on target. We wish to thank the authors of all chapters for their willingness to join this project; for their enthusiasm; for their work, patience, and perseverance; and for their positive response to all of the reviewers' comments. We also wish to thank all of our colleagues who offered to review chapters in this volume (some of whom even offered to review several chapters): Aarti Iyer, Alex Haslam, Belle Derks, Clara Kulich, Elianne van Steenbergen, Jessica Salvatore, Katherine Stroebe, Mette Hersby, Naomi Ellemers, and Norann Richards. Several of these reviewers had the double work of coauthoring a chapter for this book as well as reviewing a chapter authored by someone else—double thanks to them. We thank Naomi Ellemers also in particular for reviewing the introductory chapter. Chris Robus is thanked for his help in formatting some of the chapters. We thank Arnie Kahn, editor of the Psychology of Women Series, for his support, careful reading of the entire book, and helpful suggestions. We are also thankful to the Society for the Psychology of Women (Division 35) of the American Psychological Association (APA) for agreeing to publish this book, and to Lansing Hays, Maureen Adams, Judy Nemes, and Tiffany Klaff, at APA Books, for their patience and valuable advice.

THE GLASS CEILING IN THE 21ST CENTURY

1

INTRODUCTION:
IS THE GLASS CEILING STILL
RELEVANT IN THE 21ST CENTURY?

MANUELA BARRETO, MICHELLE K. RYAN,
AND MICHAEL T. SCHMITT

The glass ceiling is arguably one of the most familiar and evocative metaphors to emerge from the 20th century. The publication of Rosabeth Moss Kanter's 1977 book, *Men and Women of the Corporation*, brought to the fore the notion that experiences within the workplace are clearly gendered. Indeed, since that time, explaining the existence of the glass ceiling and other forms of discrimination leading to the underrepresentation of women in the upper echelons of organizations has become a primary question for employers and researchers alike. The importance placed on diversity is, at least in part, a response to the growing number of women in the workplace and the need to make full use of a changing labor market. Organizations are also attempting to access the competitive advantage that is purportedly gained from having a diverse workforce (K. Y. Williams & O'Reilly, 1998).

However, despite continued political lobbying, legislative reform, and the almost 50 years that have passed since the second wave of the feminist social and political movement, the extent of women's advancement is unclear. Certainly the media's and the public's opinions are mixed. Newspapers, the popular press, and social commentators offer a different story each day about whether gender discrimination is a problem faced by women today. Whereas some report on the persistence of the glass ceiling (e.g., "Women Still Face

Glass Ceiling," BBC, 2004), others herald the shattering of the glass ceiling (e.g., "Women Atop IT Ladder Say Glass Ceiling Not Apparent," Ferris, 2005) and others offer suggestions on how it can be overcome (e.g., "Glass Ceiling? Get a Hammer," Holstein, 2006). The nature of such claims is not depen-dent on time frame or in which country the claims are made. Indeed, in a single fortnight the U.K. newspaper the *Guardian* printed three stories on the glass ceiling: the first argued that it was "still firmly in place" (Parker, 2002), the second reported that "Britain leads glass ceiling breakers" (Macalister, 2002), and the third maintained that "women struggle to shatter glass ceiling" (Adams, 2002, n.p.).

Such uncertainty also resonates in the available statistics on women's representation in the workplace. Indeed, as many of the chapters in this volume attest, the statistics may be interpreted as showing great gains or a frustrating status quo. On the one hand, there have been clear advances, with women progressively moving into spheres that had long been all-male preserves. For example, women's participation in work outside of the home has risen dramatically in recent years. In the United States, it rose from 20% to 59% between 1900 and 2005 (U.S. Census Bureau, 2007), and in the United Kingdom, between 1971 and 2004, it rose from 42% to 70% (Women and Work Commission, 2005). Moreover, a growing number of women have achieved senior positions within organizations (Equal Opportunities Commission, 2006; U.S. Bureau of Labor Statistics, 2005). In particular, the proportion of women managers rose from only 18% in 1972 to 42% in 2005 (U.S. Bureau of Labor Statistics, 2006), with such gains echoed in European and other Western nations.

On the other hand, women continue to be underrepresented in the most powerful positions of society. This is particularly the situation in the corporate world, in which women are a minority among those in power. For example, within the European Union, women make up, on average, just over 10% of the top executives in the top 50 publicly quoted companies (European Commission, 2005). In the United States, women make up less than 16% of corporate officers and less than 15% of members of boards of directors within Fortune 500 companies (Catalyst, 2007).

These raw statistics can give some indication of change over time, and they certainly make dramatic headlines, but their message is mixed and their interpretability is contestable. The purpose of this volume is to go beyond social commentary, anecdotal evidence, and raw statistics. We have gathered a group of experts on gender discrimination to set the record straight and provide scientific insight into the real situation of women in organizations. We move beyond the numbers and provide an in-depth examination of the experiences of women in the workplace. In this way we can get an idea of the current situation, in which advances have been made, and what the real barriers are at this point in time. The fundamental question that this volume asks is "Is the glass ceiling still relevant in the 21st century?" By providing an answer to this question, this volume targets all who are interested in understanding the barriers women face in today's organizations. This volume should thus be of interest to academics working in social psychology, women's studies, or organizational psychology, but it should also be of use to practitioners whose practice is grounded in a deep understanding of how organizations function, as well as of what motivates individuals to function at their best in organizational contexts.

THE GLASS CEILING

Researchers, journalists, and the general public alike have for more than 20 years drawn on the metaphor of the glass ceiling to depict the experience of women in the workplace. It is most commonly used to refer to the phenomenon whereby men dominate the upper echelons of management. The word *ceiling* implies that women encounter an upper limit on how high they can climb on the organizational ladder, whereas *glass* refers to the relative subtlety and transparency of this barrier, which is not necessarily apparent to the observer. The barrier denoted as the glass ceiling can be distinguished from other, more formal or even some more legitimate obstacles to advancement, such as those based on education or past experience. Although the notion of the glass ceiling is metaphorical, for those women who encounter it, it is an all-too-real impenetrable barrier.

The first documented use of the phrase, by magazine editor Gay Bryant (Frenkiel, 1984), still resonates with the experience of women in the workplace today:

> Women have reached a certain point—I call it the glass ceiling. They're in the top of middle management and they're stopping and getting stuck. There isn't enough room for all those women at the top. Some are going into business for themselves. Others are going out and raising families. (n.p.)

The term became popularized and moved into more general usage after it was the focus of an article in the *Wall Street Journal* (Hymowitz & Schellhardt, 1986). The U.S. Department of Labor acknowledged the existence of the glass ceiling in 1991 when it defined it as "artificial barriers based on attitudinal or organizational bias that prevent qualified individuals from advancing upward in their organization into management-level positions" (U.S. Department of Labor, 1991, p. 1). In an effort to address these barriers and level the playing field, the U.S. Department of Labor established the Glass Ceiling Commission. The Commission extended the notion of the glass ceiling to incorporate members of other marginalized groups. The Commission concluded that

> Equally qualified and similarly situated citizens are being denied equal access to advancement into senior level management on the basis of gender, race, or ethnicity. At the highest levels of corporations the promise of reward for preparation and pursuit of excellence is not equally available to members of all groups. (U.S. Glass Ceiling Commission, 1995, pp. 10–11)

In the 2 decades since the phrase was coined, the status of women in the workplace has continually improved, with growing numbers of women obtaining senior positions (Equal Opportunities Commission, 2006; U.S. Bureau of Labor Statistics, 2005). However, it is clear that the notion of the glass ceiling is still reflected in the experiences of many women. Indeed, the power of the metaphor has resulted in an explosion of new research (and new metaphors) to explain the underrepresentation of women at the top. By means of *escalators* men are accelerated through the organizational ranks, especially in female-dominated professions (C. L. Williams, 1992); because of *glass walls* women are concentrated in certain sectors, such as human resources or marketing, that do not lead to senior positions (Miller, Kerr, & Reid, 1999); the *glass slipper* refers to women's reduced aspirations for power (Rudman & Heppen, 2003); and the *glass cliff* describes the precariousness of women's leadership positions (Ryan & Haslam, 2005).

One could mistakenly conclude that these metaphors have arisen because the notion of the glass ceiling is outdated and a corresponding need arose to characterize women's situation differently. However, in our view, the proliferation of metaphors is better viewed as a reflection of the need to provide a more specific analysis of the variety of barriers that women currently face. Indeed, this is precisely what we aim to do in this volume. In what follows, we provide a summary of the chapters included in the volume, while reflecting on how the different contributions inform us about the situation of women in the workplace.

STRUCTURE OF THE VOLUME

This volume includes contributions from scientists who examine the social psychological factors that shape women's position in the workplace. For the reader's convenience, these contributions are structured into four parts. The first provides an analysis of both positive and negative developments in women's workplace experiences since the term *glass ceiling* was first coined, with a special focus on the role of stereotypes. The second part offers an examination of some of the ways women respond to the subtle barriers with which they are confronted in the work domain. The third part addresses how gender shapes the way in which people experience the workplace. The fourth and final part includes chapters that examine the feasibility and efficacy of some of the solutions that have been proposed to improve women's position at work. Although we believe that these parts are meaningful and provide structure, it is important to note that they are interconnected. Indeed, each chapter informs and speaks to the chapters that are included in other parts and chapters. The cross-referencing within these chapters can guide readers through their own personal structure, providing links between what remains at the surface in one chapter and what is analyzed in depth in other chapters.

OVERVIEW OF THE CHAPTERS IN THE VOLUME

This volume opens with an analysis of the developments in workplace gender equality over the past 20 years, since the term *glass ceiling* was first coined. This analysis leads fairly directly into a discussion of whether the glass ceiling is still relevant as a metaphor reflecting the existence of impenetrable but subtle barriers to women's advancement in the workplace. The first chapter to address this issue is the one authored by Alice H. Eagly and Sabine Sczesny, titled "Stereotypes About Women, Men, and Leaders: Have Times Changed?" This chapter focuses on one of the most important (and persistent) hurdles for women in organizations and in management: the close association between stereotypes of managers and stereotypes of men. The authors examine how the "think manager–think male" association has changed over time and how these stereotypes relate to a social role analysis of women in the workplace. Eagly and Sczesny observe that although concrete changes in women's position in the workplace are modest, several emerging tendencies offer a promise of further improvement. For example, the authors observe some decrease in the think manager–think male association, albeit only for some samples and only in some studies. Moreover, the authors suggest that the increasing representation of women in nontraditional roles and in leadership positions may provide a basis for change in stereotypes and reduce the incongruity between the stereotype of women and the stereotype of leaders. Moreover, perceptions of what it means to be a good leader have changed in a direction favorable to women, as they now tend to include more stereotypically female characteristics. However, Eagly and Sczesny also observe that the incongruity between what it means to be a woman and what it means to be a good leader still exists, and that the pace of change is slow and is unlikely to lead to the complete elimination of this incongruity in the near future.

The extent to which the situation of women has changed continues to be examined in the chapter authored by Michael T. Schmitt, Jennifer R. Spoor, Kelly Danaher, and Nyla R. Branscombe. However, in this chapter, titled "Rose-Colored Glasses: How Tokenism and Comparisons With the Past Reduce the Visibility of Gender Inequality," the authors examine the changes in women's position in organizations from quite a different angle and at a different level of analysis. The authors are not so much concerned with the notion of stereotype change per se as with what changes in the representation of women in the workplace mean for women and men. Indeed, the modesty of these changes raises the question of whether they should be regarded as stimulating or as discouraging. Although the direction of these developments is clearly positive, the authors propose that considering improvement in women's position across time has important consequences for gender relations. Indeed, the authors demonstrate that when people focus on the reduction of gender inequalities over time, or the advancement of even a small number of women to high-status positions, they come to see contemporary gender relations as more egalitarian. Furthermore, these perceptions of relatively fair and harmonious gender relations lower women's collective identification while making them feel more satisfied with the treatment of women in general. The arguments put forth in this chapter and the evidence reviewed somewhat paradoxically suggest that the increased representation of women in leadership positions results in psychological consequences that can undermine perception of current inequalities and the motivation to work toward more substantial reductions in inequality. Thus, this chapter suggests that as long as this representation remains modest, its effects appear more negative than positive for women individually and as a whole.

The chapter by Mina Cikara and Susan T. Fiske provides yet another perspective on the issue of how stereotypes have developed. In the chapter titled "Warmth, Competence, and Ambivalent Sexism: Vertical Assault and Collateral Damage," the authors examine how women's gains in terms of vertical mobility within organizations are accompanied by important losses. This research demonstrates that to truly understand what has changed with regard to gender stereotypes, and what these changes mean for women, it is essential to look closely at different stereotypical dimensions and at how they relate to the various roles that women may endorse. Cikara and Fiske suggest that it makes little sense to talk about one general stereotype of women today. As women become more heterogeneous in their life choices, stereotypes of women do not weaken—they multiply. Working women, for example, are seen as competent but cold (except if, or when, they become mothers, in which case they lose competence and gain warmth, a pattern that is not revealed among working men who become fathers). The stereotypes associated with women in different roles in turn elicit different types of prejudice and discriminatory behavior that together promote power differences at work. The question each woman faces today is thus not whether she can escape stereotyping or prejudice, but on which side of the competence–warmth trade-off she will be.

Taken together, the chapters in this part acknowledge the progress in the representation of women in the workplace. However, the empirical data reviewed in these chapters also suggest that the increased but modest representation of women in the workforce does not come without costs—both for individually successful women (who trade perceived competence for perceived warmth; see chap. 4, this volume) and for women as a group (as it obscures gender inequality; see chap. 3, this volume). These costs are, however, a great deal more subtle than they used to be. Although working women may no longer simply be seen to be less competent than men, it would be a mistake to conclude that women no longer face barriers to entry in high positions within organizations. These chapters indicate that although women no longer face a glass ceiling in the narrowest sense of complete lack of access to leadership positions, it is clear that they still face important barriers to entry into these positions, which underlines the relevance of this metaphor in current times.

In the second part of this volume the chapter authors take the perspective of women themselves and examine how they experience subtle barriers within the workplace. They examine how beliefs about women and the way they are treated affect women's well-being, their behavior, and the choices they make. Moreover, the authors look at the barriers that have been designated as internal (e.g., resulting from women's own attitudes and behaviors) and as external (e.g., resulting from attitudes and behaviors of others), and in doing so demonstrate that this distinction is not necessarily clear-cut and that such barriers interact and affect one another. The chapter by Manuela Barreto, Naomi Ellemers, Sezgin Cihangir, and Katherine Stroebe demonstrates that subtle sexist beliefs held by others can lead the targets of those beliefs to behave in ways that unwittingly confirm them and thereby legitimize the targets' disadvantage. In their chapter, titled "The Self-Fulfilling Effects of Contemporary Sexism: How It Affects Well-Being and Behavior," the authors show that despite the assumption that women are motivated to exaggerate the extent to which they are targets of sexism, they often fail to detect when they are targets of sexism. Barreto and colleagues further demonstrate that this unawareness of prejudice, when it occurs in performance contexts or contexts dominated by individualistic or meritocratic beliefs, often elicits negative self-directed emotions in women and leads them to behave in ways that confirm the negative beliefs. These emotions and behaviors constitute clear barriers to women's advancement, barriers that may appear purely internal to the particular individual (e.g., poor ability), but that are best viewed as emerging from societal ideologies, such as sexism and meritocratic beliefs. The authors show that this cycle can be broken both by factors that help targets cope with the negative consequences of subtle discrimination (e.g., high personal self-esteem) and by factors that help targets recognize the discrimination they face (e.g., increased awareness of the subtle forms discrimination can take). In fact, when targets are able to detect prejudice, they choose to confront these negative beliefs, such as by protesting against them.

The interconnection between internal and external barriers is also examined in the chapter by Shen Zhang, Toni Schmader, and Chad Forbes, titled "The Effects of Gender Stereotypes on Women's Career Choice: Opening the Glass Door." In this chapter Zhang and colleagues consider the social psychological effects of the mere suggestion that there are gender differences in ability and outline two ways in which gender stereotypes shape men's and women's career paths. The first path is a process of socialization, of continuous and chronic exposure to gender stereotypes that strongly influence interest in (and perception of) different activities, starting in early childhood. Here the external becomes internal as people develop their sense of self in relation to others and learn to differentiate between who they are and who they are not. The second path is encountered by women who have surpassed the initial career hurdles and have opted to enter male-dominated fields of employment. Here, the authors describe how cultural stereotypes affect the performance and motivations of women, creating gender differences in career aspirations and performance. Zhang and colleagues demonstrate how several individual and situational factors can alter this pattern and help women resist the powerful limits that gender stereotypes impose on who they are and who they can become.

Taken together, the chapters in this part demonstrate that although the barriers that women face may at first glance appear to be internal to the particular women themselves, these barriers can, in fact, be traced to existing stereotypes about women and their abilities. In turn, women's choices and behavior (influenced by stereotypical expectations) can feed existing stereotypes and thereby place further obstacles to their career development. Although focusing on different settings and outcome variables, both chapters in this part highlight the importance of moderating factors, at the individual level as well as at the situational level, that may help to break the cycle of disadvantage in which women often find themselves.

The third part of this volume considers how—once women have shattered the glass ceiling and entered high positions in organizations—gendered experiences in the workplace persist. The aim is not only to illustrate the ways in which women and men experience the workplace differently but also to demonstrate how beliefs and attitudes about gender characterize much of people's daily experiences. Michelle K. Ryan, S. Alexander Haslam, Mette D. Hersby, Clara Kulich, and M. Dana Wilson-Kovacs, authors of the chapter titled "The Stress of Working on the Edge: Implications of Glass Cliffs for Both Women and Organizations," consider the consequences of a new and subtle form of discrimination—the glass cliff—which results in women being more likely than men to be recruited for leadership positions that are associated with high risk of criticism and failure. Because of the precariousness of these positions, women tend to be exposed to more job stress than are their male counterparts, leading women to disidentify with and opt out of organizations. Arguing against the view that women leave organizations more often than do men because work is not a priority for women, Ryan and colleagues show that women who leave organizations tend to do so because their work conditions are uniquely stressful, relative to those of men, leading them to disidentify with the organization. The authors present evidence from both qualitative and quantitative studies in support of their gender–stress–disidentification model and in this way demonstrate how men and women often have fundamentally different experiences in the workplace.

The chapter authored by Margaret S. Stockdale and Gargi Bhattacharya, titled "Sexual Harassment and the Glass Ceiling," addresses another factor that contributes to gendered experiences in the workplace: sexual harassment. The authors describe legal and psychological definitions of sexual harassment and argue that because legal definitions require targets to label harassing behaviors as such, they leave a range of harassing behaviors undetected. After examining existing data on sexual harassment in organizations, Stockdale and Bhattacharya conclude that sexual harassment is still "disturbingly prevalent" (p. 178). Although sexual harassment can also target men, it particularly targets young women who attempt to achieve in traditionally male-dominated domains, that is, women who try to break the glass ceiling and in doing so threaten men's power position within organizations. The authors provide a thorough overview of recent insights into the consequences of sexual harassment, for both the individual and the organization. This review shows that sexual harassment leads to detrimental psychological and job-related outcomes, irrespective of whether the harassing behavior falls within legal definitions of sexual harassment, and of whether it is labeled as such by the target. Stockdale and Bhattacharya propose a range of measures that organizations can take to reduce or eliminate sexual harassment.

The final chapter in this part, authored by Laura Sabattini and Faye J. Crosby, focuses on the challenges people face when trying to combine work with care responsibilities outside work. Both men and women experience these challenges, but to different degrees and in different ways, as the workplace and family are still gendered contexts. The need to develop work–life balance programs stems in part from the raised awareness that what has long been regarded as women's choice not to participate in the workforce can best be seen as a forced choice, constrained by structural conditions, stereotyping, and gender discrimination (see also chaps. 6 and 7, this volume). Motivated by the goal of guaranteeing greater participation by women in the workforce, several work–life policies and programs have been developed in the past decades, but although they appear promising in their goals, they have been largely ineffective. Important reasons for this limited success are the existence of gender inequalities outside work, the stigmatizing effects of using these programs, and the suboptimal implementation of these programs by organizations. Sabattini and Crosby suggest that work–life policies that are aimed at both men and women have the best chance of reducing gender inequality because they have the potential of contributing to a more equal division of labor outside work. In addition, organizations must develop better implementation plans, which may include steps toward reducing the stigma associated with using these policies. However, the authors warn that changes are needed both with regard to work arrangements and with regard to the division of labor within the family, as changes in one without changes in the other are likely to meet only limited and short-term success.

Taken together, the chapters included in this part demonstrate that men and women have quite drastically different daily experiences at work. Women's work experiences are stained by factors such as precariousness, greater vulnerability to sexual harassment, and unsatisfactory or unusable work–life policies. All of these factors have been shown to be associated with negative outcomes, both for individual women and for the organizations in which they work. The chapters in this part point to several factors that must be taken into account in developing solutions to the problems that women still face in organizations.

The chapters in the final part of the book focus on solutions more directly. These chapters examine possible solutions at the individual and interpersonal level, as well as the team and organizational level. The first chapter in this part is authored by Laurie Hunt, Gina LaRoche, Stacy Blake-Beard, Eleanor Chin, Marisol Arroyave, and Maureen Scully and is titled "Cross-Cultural Connections: Leveraging Social Networks for Women's Advancement." This chapter provides an analysis of how cross-cultural networking and mentoring can serve women's advancement. Social and professional networks have been suggested as a key strategy to help women redress the disadvantages they face in the workplace. Social networks provide social capital, which has been identified as one of the resources that typically help men advance within organizations (i.e., the old boys' networks or the glass escalator) and that tend to be less available to women. This chapter examines the barriers women face in establishing networks, paying special attention to the situation of women who are also members of ethnic minority groups (i.e., double minorities). Hunt and colleagues consider how women can use social networking and mentoring, particularly if they cross cultural boundaries, as strategies to overcome discrimination. Rather than simply reviewing existing research on the topic, the authors provide an unorthodox and highly personal analysis of their own experiences to reflect on how cross-cultural networking and mentoring have benefited their own careers. An important observation made by the authors is that social networking requires individual effort and intentionality, which can partly explain why many social networks are relatively unproductive.

However, the authors stress that the personal and professional benefits of this strategy are likely to outweigh the costs.

In the next chapter, titled "Increasing the Representation and Status of Women in Employment: The Effectiveness of Affirmative Action," Aarti Iyer examines the effectiveness of affirmative action and looks at its implications both for women and for organizations. The author observes that affirmative action has had clearly positive effects with regard to increasing the representation of women in organizations while maintaining or even increasing organizational productivity and effectiveness. Although affirmative action is a procedure based on an analysis of objective factors, such as the numerical representation of women in organizations, more recently attention has turned to the more subjective implications of this procedure. This relatively new perspective has unveiled that a responsible use of this strategy needs to recognize that affirmative action can have both negative and positive effects that need to be anticipated and addressed. For example, recipients of affirmative action programs can feel stigmatized by their participation and express negative self-views, and those who are not direct beneficiaries of affirmative action can develop negative perceptions of beneficiaries. However, adequate implementation plans are also key in this context, as they can combat the potential negative effects of this strategy. The author argues for the need to take various levels of analysis into account (i.e., the individual, teams, and organizations) when examining the effectiveness of this strategy or planning its implementation.

In the final chapter, titled "Managing Diversity in Work Groups: How Identity Processes Affect Diverse Work Groups," Floor Rink and Naomi Ellemers examine barriers to diversity from yet another perspective by focusing on the factors that can either make diversity work or thwart its potential benefits. The importance of this perspective lies in the fact that a key barrier to diversity is often the very belief that diversity hinders group functioning and makes working in teams generally more effortful. If one is able to identify the conditions under which the benefits of diversity can be revealed in the absence of its costs, then one is better equipped to argue in favor of the inclusion of women and other minority group members in the workplace. In this chapter, Rink and Ellemers do not merely review existing literature in this area but offer an in-depth analysis of this literature and their own integrative perspective on the issue. In doing so, Rink and Ellemers propose that social identity processes can at times hinder, but at other times promote, the functioning of diverse work groups. Rink and Ellemers posit that when diversity is in line with group norms and this is clearly communicated to group members, it can come to define the group and form the basis of a common group identity, resulting in positive outcomes for group functioning. As such, this chapter outlines an important path toward reducing barriers to diversity: by communicating a culture of diversity to all group members that can lead them to evaluate and use their differences in a positive and effective way.

INTEGRATION: WHAT HAS CHANGED?

Although each chapter in this volume offers a detailed analysis of a particular problem or process, each reflects different methodologies and perspectives. Some of the work examines how women are viewed by others, whereas other chapters focus more on women's own experiences. Moreover, the chapters include experimental research, correlational and archival data, and personal insights about authors' own experiences. This variety of material creates a complex and nuanced picture of women in the workplace, with each approach expanding and complementing the other. Despite these differences, the chapters in this volume address some common themes. They all describe some of the changes that have taken place surrounding women's position in the workplace. Noticeable advances are the development of supportive legislation (e.g., see chaps. 8, 9, and 11, this volume), the increased numerical representation of women in the workforce as well as in leadership positions (e.g., see chaps. 2 and 7, this volume), and the reduction of overt forms of gender-based prejudice and discrimination (e.g., see chap. 5, this volume). Relative to the past, it is also possible to observe today a greater awareness of the importance of diversity (e.g., see chap. 12, this volume), and more deliberate attempts to increase diversity and its benefits through strategies such as affirmative action (see chap. 11, this volume) and work–life policies (see chap. 9, this volume).

On a less positive note, the work presented in this volume calls attention to the dangers of considering women's progress in the absence of a clear description of the inequalities that remain to be addressed (e.g., see chap. 3, this volume). Moreover, the research reviewed in this book demonstrates that, despite the positive trends observed, stereotyping of women is still prevalent, although it tends to take more subtle forms (e.g., see chaps. 4, 5, and 7, this volume). The consequences of subtle stereotypes and discrimination are not just that they can directly lead to the preference for men over women, but also that they may lead women to make choices and display behaviors that increase and justify their exclusion (e.g., see chaps. 5, 6, and 7, this volume). It is, however, important to note that clear forms of exclusion such as sexual harassment can still be observed, especially toward competent women (e.g., see chap. 8, this volume), and exclusion from old boys' networks and mentoring can be exacerbated for double minorities (e.g., see chap. 10, this volume), both of which place women in a position of disadvantage compared with men.

The chapters included in this volume also clarify that the progress made is accompanied by new challenges. At the individual level, women whose competence is recognized trade their reputation for being warm for being seen as competent but cold (e.g., see chap. 4, this volume). Although warmth is being increasingly recognized as an important managerial characteristic (e.g., see chap. 2, this volume), the finding that competent women are seen as cold raises some doubts that an increase in perceived competence will suffice to increase the extent to which women are perceived as good leaders. How to reduce the perceived trade-off between competence and warmth is a challenge for the future, and an advancement that would likely ease the acceptance and efficacy of women leaders. In addition, women may have gained greater access to higher positions, but this is more evident in domains that are traditionally associated with women, and less so in traditionally male-dominated domains. The increased representation of women in higher positions has led several authors in this volume to suggest that current barriers may no longer be vertical, as they were before, but that new barriers have emerged that can best be characterized as lateral (*glass walls* in chap. 4, this volume, and *glass doors* in chap. 6, this volume). At the group level, the cost of women's modest advancement is the suggestion that the glass ceiling has been shattered, even though this is the case for only a limited number of women. Indeed, although progress is modest, its effect on women as a group appears to be mainly negative, as it serves to obscure existing gender inequalities (e.g., see chap. 3, this volume).

Taken together, these observations clarify that to understand the progress made in resolving gender inequalities, as well as the challenges that lay ahead, one needs to examine the situation at different levels of analysis, as well as on various dimensions, and from different perspectives. It is important not only to examine statistical data or legal advances but also to study how individuals and organizations are affected by policies, particular characteristics of the social structure, and changes in any of these factors. Moreover, it is necessary to understand the day-to-day experiences of women in the workplace, their behaviors, their motivations, and their attitudes. Thus, a social psychological perspective appears particularly appropriate for examining this issue. An analysis that does not make such an effort is necessarily incomplete and will result either in an overly optimistic or in an overly pessimistic view of the existing barriers to women's advancement within organizations.

CONCLUSION: NUMBERS ARE NOT ENOUGH

The overall take-home message of this volume is that when one is examining the situation of women in organizations, numbers are simply not enough. This is true for various reasons. First, macrolevel statistics collected through large polls are often undifferentiated and open to interpretation. In addition, these statistics say little about the underlying processes driving stability or change, and therefore provide little information that can be of use to understand the real situation, let alone to change it.

Indeed, increasing the numerical representation of women in organizations, or in leadership positions, is not enough to reduce gender inequality. First, if this increase is modest, then its effect on women themselves, as individuals and as a group, can be more negative than positive. Although rising slopes do provide a catchy and appealing image of the situation, they run the risk of obscuring existing, ever more subtle barriers and leave those women who wish to enter these contexts unprepared for what they might encounter. Such a picture may also send the message to senior women who are in a position to mentor and otherwise support a younger generation that the battle has already been won and their support is no longer necessary. At the same time, focusing on numbers alone, especially if they are not differentiated and appropriately interpreted, presents a picture that is too rosy for those who make the decisions and form policy that can contribute to the improvement of women's position in the workplace.

Promoting gender equality cannot be only about numbers also because increasing the representation of women in the workplace without providing them with conditions that enable them to succeed only contributes to further inequality. For example, in Scandinavian countries women constitute 40% of board managers, but evidence shows that they are still exposed to a number of the obstacles outlined in this volume, such as glass-cliff positions and sexual harassment. Women who achieve leadership positions but are placed in a glass-cliff situation are likely to fail, as are women who are systematically confronted with subtle stereotyping and discrimination once they have entered traditionally male-dominated domains or positions. If all one cares about is numbers then one may fail to understand why women opt out of many organizations and leadership positions; one may not notice that they are given particularly stressful tasks to perform, or that their reputation as being competent has made them especially vulnerable to sexual harassment. If the focus is on numbers alone one may fail to realize that affirmative action is not without costs and that it can be seen as a sustainable strategy to promote gender equality only if it is implemented with great sensitivity to the negative side effects it can entail. Finally, if the primary goal is to ensure a numerically diverse workforce that includes both men and women, then one fails to realize that diversity is not without problems, and that its benefits can be revealed only under particular conditions, such as when its value is ingrained and communicated through the team or through organizational culture.

The way forward is to focus on numbers only insofar as one can ensure that women are in positions in which they can be successful, in addition to clearly identifying the dangers and costs associated with this advancement as well as deliberately trying to manage and minimize these costs. This diversity management must include a regular analysis of the obstacles that persist and sensitivity to the new and subtle barriers that appear once women move from one position to another.

Because this volume is about the barriers women face at work, it necessarily focuses on the experiences of only a cross-section of women. Women as a group experience discrimination across a wide range of domains, and particular groups of women—such as women from ethnic minorities and women in developing countries—face particular barriers that can be distinct from those outlined in this volume. However, it is not within the scope of this volume to address discrimination across all life domains, or for all groups of women. We feel that a careful analysis of the subtle barriers women face as they climb the career ladder, and an understanding of the psychological processes involved in creating and maintaining gender inequalities within the workplace, can improve our understanding of gender inequality more broadly.

Taken together, the chapters in this volume make clear that particular aspects of the metaphor of the glass ceiling are still relevant. For the most part, it is no longer the case that organizations and leadership positions are completely closed to all women, although it is clear that the ceiling is still a real barrier to career advancement for many women. It is therefore clear that women still face important obstacles to their career advancement and that—like glass—many of these are difficult to see. Thus, the main aim of this volume is to clarify to the reader how women experience the workplace and, in doing so, make visible the barriers that they face.

REFERENCES

Adams, R. (2002, October 5). Women struggle to shatter the glass ceiling. *The Guardian*. Retrieved November 21, 2007, from http://www.guardian.co.uk/business/2002/oct/05/executivepay.genderissues

BBC. (2004, December 30). *Women still face glass ceiling*. Retrieved November 21, 2007, from http://news.bbc.co.uk/1/hi/business/4133669.stm

Catalyst. (2007). *2006 Catalyst census of women in Fortune 500 corporate officer and board positions*. Retrieved April 4, 2007, from http://www.catalystwomen.org/knowledge/wbd.shtml

Equal Opportunities Commission. (2006). *Facts about women and men in Great Britain*. Manchester, England: Author.

European Commission. (2005). *Social values, science and technology*. Retrieved November 21, 2007, from http://ec.europa.eu/public_opinion/archives/ebs/ebs_225_report_en.pdf

Ferris, N. (2005, April 14). Women atop IT ladder say glass ceiling not apparent. *USA Today*. Retrieved November 21, 2007, from http://www.usatoday.com/tech/news/techpolicy/2005-04-12-glass-ceiling_x.htm

Frenkiel, N. (1984, March). The up-and-comers: Bryant takes aim at the settlers-in. *Adweek*. Special Report: Magazine World.

Holstein, W. J. (2006, June 18). Glass ceiling? Get a hammer. *New York Times*. Retrieved November 21, 2007, from http://www.nytimes.com/2006/06/18/business/yourmoney/18advi.html

Hymowitz, C., & Schellhardt, T. D. (1986, March 24). The corporate woman (a special report): The glass ceiling: Why women can't seem to break the invisible barrier that blocks them from the top jobs. *The Wall Street Journal*, pp. 1D, 4D, 5D.

Kanter, R. M. (1977). *Men and women of the corporation*. New York: Basic Books.

Macalister, T. (2002, September 30). Britain leads glass ceiling breakers. *The Guardian*. Retrieved November 21, 2007, from http://www.guardian.co.uk/business/2002/sep/30/genderissues.uknews

Miller, W., Kerr, B., & Reid, M. (1999). A national study of gender-based occupational segregation in municipal bureaucracies: Persistence of glass walls? *Public Administration Review, 59*, 218–229.

Parker, S. (2002, September 25). The glass ceiling. *The Guardian*. Retrieved November 21, 2007, from http://www.guardian.co.uk/society/2002/sep/25/guardiansocietysupplement2

Rudman, L. A., & Heppen, J. (2003). Implicit romantic fantasies and women's interest in personal power: A glass slipper effect? *Personality and Social Psychology Bulletin, 29*, 1357–1370.

Ryan, M. K., & Haslam, S. A. (2005). The glass cliff: Evidence that women are over-represented in precarious leadership positions. *British Journal of Management, 16*, 81–90.

U.S. Bureau of Labor Statistics. (2005). *Women in the labor force: A databook*. Washington, DC: U.S. Department of Labor.

U.S. Bureau of Labor Statistics. (2006). *Women in the labor force: A databook*. Report 996. Retrieved November 21, 2007, from http://www.bls.gov/cps/wlf-databook2006.htm

U.S. Census Bureau. (2007). *Statistical abstract of the United States: 2007*. Retrieved November 21, 2007, from http://www.census.gov/prod/www/statistical-abstract.html

U.S. Department of Labor. (1991). *A report on the glass ceiling initiative*. Washington, DC: U.S. Government Printing Office.

U.S. Glass Ceiling Commission. (1995). *Good for business: Making full use of the nation's human capital. Executive summary*. Washington, DC: U.S. Government Printing Office.

Williams, C. L. (1992). The glass escalator: Hidden advantages for men in the "female" professions. *Social Problems, 39*, 41–57.

Williams, K. Y., & O'Reilly, C. A. (1998). Demography and diversity in organizations: A review of 40 years of research. In B. Staw & R. Sutton (Eds.), *Research in organizational behavior* (Vol. 20, pp. 77–140). Greenwich, CT: JAI Press.

Women and Work Commission. (2005). *A fair deal for women in the workplace*. London: Department of Trade and Industry.

I

DEVELOPMENTS IN WORKPLACE GENDER EQUALITY

2

STEREOTYPES ABOUT WOMEN, MEN, AND LEADERS: HAVE TIMES CHANGED?

ALICE H. EAGLY AND SABINE SCZESNY

One important indicator that a society has achieved gender equality would be the presence of approximately equal numbers of women and men in leadership positions. Although in Western nations women have far more access to leadership than at any other period in history, 50–50 representation is surely not present. Nevertheless, there has been an impressive increase of women in leadership roles as managers, legislators, and officials (United Nations Development Programme, 2008; see Figure 2.1). However, these women are concentrated at lower levels of management. Across all economic sectors, men, more often than women, occupy positions conferring major decision-making authority and the ability to influence others' pay or promotions (Smith, 2002).

Women's power deficit is especially evident in their meager representation as executives in the most valuable corporations in the business sector. For example, in the largest publicly quoted companies in each of the 27 nations of the European Union, women average only 4% of the presidents and 10% of the members of the highest decision-making body (European Commission, 2007). In the Fortune 500 of the United States, women account for 16% of corporate officers and 15% of members of boards of directors (Catalyst, 2006). There are several intertwined causes of this disparity in power between women and men, as this volume documents.

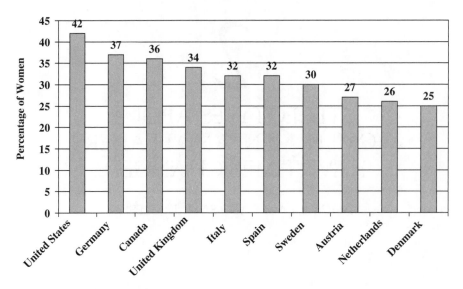

Figure 2.1. Percentage of women among managers, legislators, and senior officials in selected North American and European nations. Source data from United Nations Development Programme (2008).

In this chapter, we consider a social psychological cause of women's lesser representation in leadership roles in society: specifically, the construal of three social groups—women, men, and leaders. We argue that the disadvantages that women face as leaders are reflected in the similarity and dissimilarity between the cultural stereotypes of these three groups. In implicating stereotypes, our analysis validates the views of many women who have substantial experience as leaders. For example, a survey of 705 women at the vice president level and above in Fortune 1000 corporations found that 72% agreed or strongly agreed that "stereotypes about women's roles and abilities" are a barrier to women's advancement to the highest levels (Wellington, Kropf, & Gerkovich, 2003). Social science research confirms that attitudes toward social groups and the stereotypes that underlie them are a fundamental cause of discrimination in general and sex discrimination in particular (e.g., S. T. Fiske, 1998; Glick & Fiske, 2007).

The beliefs that individuals hold about women, men, and leaders tend to be consensual and therefore are part of the culture. Stereotypes about men and women are major components of gender—that is, of the cultural meanings associated with the differentiation of humans into two sexes. These cultural stereotypes, which are part of a society's shared knowledge, encompass two types of beliefs: expectations about what members of these groups are actually like and what they should be like (S. T. Fiske & Stevens, 1993; Heilman, 2001). Expectations about the actual characteristics of group members are known as *descriptive beliefs*; an example is the belief that leaders behave in an active, assertive manner. Expectations about what group members should be like are known as *prescriptive beliefs*; an example is the belief that leaders should behave in an active, assertive manner. Although descriptive and prescriptive beliefs generally encompass the same qualities, they diverge in some respects. For example, descriptive beliefs that men are overbearing and insensitive and women are whiny and complaining are not accompanied by prescriptive beliefs that they should behave in these ways.

When people hold descriptive stereotypes about a group of people, they expect that members of that group possess traits and exhibit behaviors consistent with those stereotypes. Encoding processes usually favor information that is consistent with these expectations (e.g., von Hippel, Sekaquaptewa, & Vargas, 1995), and perceivers spontaneously fill in unknown details of people's behavior to be consistent with stereotypical expectations (Dunning & Sherman, 1997). But what happens when individuals are perceived in terms of both a leader stereotype and the stereotype associated with their gender? As we show, this situation is often problematic for women because of the usual inconsistency between stereotypes about women and stereotypes about leaders. First we consider gender stereotypes, then stereotypes about leaders and their similarity to stereotypes of men, and next the prejudices that can result from the conjunction of leader and gender stereotypes. Finally, we turn to the important question of whether these stereotypes are changing.

GENDER STEREOTYPES

Whether a person is male or female is the first thing that people notice about others, who are instantly and automatically categorized by sex (e.g., A. P. Fiske, Haslam, & Fiske, 1991). Categorization by sex evokes mental associations, or expectations, about men and women. Two sets of beliefs predominate in these associations: the *communal* and the *agentic* (e.g., Deaux & Lewis, 1984; see also chap. 4, this volume). Communal beliefs pertain to a concern with the compassionate treatment of others. Primary in the concept of *women* are communal qualities such as affectionate, helpful, friendly, kind, and sympathetic as well as interpersonally sensitive, gentle, and soft-spoken. In contrast, agentic beliefs pertain to assertion and control. Primary in the concept of *men* are qualities such as aggressive, ambitious, dominant, self-confident, and forceful as well as self-reliant, self-sufficient, and individualistic.

These beliefs about agency and communion form the main basis of gender stereotypes. In national polls and surveys of university students conducted in many nations, people consistently describe women in terms of communion and men in terms of agency (Newport, 2001; Survey Research Consultants International, 1998; J. E. Williams & Best, 1990). In addition, gender stereotypes encompass additional themes having to do with, for example, cognitive abilities and physical characteristics (Cejka & Eagly, 1999; Deaux & Lewis, 1984). Moreover, any observed difference between a man and woman is likely to be incorporated, at least temporarily, into beliefs about men and women in general (Prentice & Miller, 2006). Nonetheless, communion and agency predominate in gender stereotypes. These two basic themes appear to emerge in virtually all cultures, despite some cross-cultural variation in how the themes are shaped (J. E. Williams & Best, 1990).

These ideas about communion and agency are prescriptive as well as descriptive. People generally think that it is a good thing for women to be nice, nurturing, and kind and for men to be strong, assertive, and ambitious. Yet, the qualities that are prescribed for one sex are not necessarily forbidden to the other sex (Prentice & Carranza, 2002). Feminine communal qualities such as sensitivity and cooperativeness are not regarded as bad in men, nor are masculine agentic qualities such as ambition and willingness to take risks regarded as bad in women. However, these qualities are experienced as more desirable in one sex than the other. Therefore, men are not especially encouraged to be sensitive and cooperative, and women are not especially encouraged to be ambitious or take risks. In addition, people often adopt the prescribed aspects of gender stereotypes as personal ideals for themselves and therefore allow these ideals to guide their behavior (e.g., Wood, Christensen, Hebl, & Rothgerber, 1997).

The more dangerous, forbidden realm of behavior for each sex pertains to the negative qualities that are ascribed to the other sex (Prentice & Carranza, 2002). People generally find that undesirable feminine qualities such as being weak, gullible, or melodramatic are unacceptable in men but regard them as more tolerable in women. And they find that undesirable masculine qualities such as being controlling, promiscuous, or stubborn are unacceptable in women but regard them as more tolerable in men.

The power of gender stereotypes derives from their pervasiveness. In fact, sex provides the strongest basis of classifying people; it exceeds race, age, and occupation in the speed and ubiquity with which people categorize others (A. P. Fiske et al., 1991; Stangor, Lynch, Duan, & Glass, 1992; van Knippenberg, van Twuyver, & Pepels, 1994). Merely classifying a person as male or female automatically evokes masculine and feminine qualities (e.g., Banaji & Hardin, 1996; Blair & Banaji, 1996; Ito & Urland, 2003). These mental associations, or stereotypes, are influential even when people are unaware of their presence (e.g., Sczesny & Kühnen, 2004). These associations color perceptions of individuals because perceivers ordinarily assimilate others to stereotypes—that is, they tend to perceive individual men and women as more similar to their respective societal stereotypes than they actually are.

Stereotypes about men and women are not arbitrary but are rooted in a society's division of labor between the sexes (Eagly, Wood, & Diekman,

2000; Koenig & Eagly, 2008). Because social perceivers cannot directly observe people's traits, they form impressions of these traits by observing how people behave and usually assuming that their behaviors reflect their personality. This psychological process of inferring traits from observations, known as *correspondent inference*, is ubiquitous (Gawronski, 2003; Ross, Amabile, & Steinmetz, 1977; Schaller & O'Brien, 1992) and spontaneous (Uleman, Newman, & Moskowitz, 1996). Caring behavior implies a nice, caring person; and aggressive behavior implies a dominant, aggressive person, and so on. Merely because women and men typically engage in different behaviors in the family and workplace, the two sexes are perceived as having somewhat different personality traits. These stereotypical beliefs thus reflect sex-typical social roles—especially men's more common occupancy of breadwinner and high-status roles and women's more common occupancy of homemaker and lower-status roles (e.g., Conway, Pizzamiglio, & Mount, 1996; Eagly & Steffen, 1984).

STEREOTYPES OF LEADERS: THEIR SIMILARITY TO STEREOTYPES OF MEN

Traditional stereotypes about leaders are predominantly masculine in their emphasis on agentic qualities. This emphasis is not surprising, given that the majority of people occupying leadership roles have been men. For example, a well-known portrayal of managers in business organizations blends descriptive and prescriptive leader stereotypes by stating six activities presumed to be required of leaders (Miner, 1993): (a) engaging in competition with peers involving occupational or work-related activities, (b) telling others what to do and using sanctions in influencing others, (c) behaving in an active and assertive manner, (d) assuming a distinctive position of a unique and highly visible nature, (e) executing activities of a day-to-day administrative nature, and (f) developing positive relationships with superiors. This description emphasizes competition and hierarchy: Managers are expected to rise above their coworkers, to tell them what to do, and to compete with other managers.

Portrayals of managers in contemporary research have somewhat more emphasis on feminine qualities such as being helpful and supportive as well as on gender-neutral qualities such as being smart and dedicated. Still, culturally masculine qualities have continued to be well represented. For instance, in one study (Atwater, Brett, Waldman, DiMare, & Hayden, 2004), business students identified many managerial behaviors, including delegating, disciplining, strategic decision making, problem solving, and punishing, as masculine. Yet, they identified some other managerial behaviors, including recognizing and rewarding, communicating and informing, and supporting, as feminine.

Despite this inclusion of some communal qualities in leader stereotypes, people generally view leaders as more similar to men than to women. Schein demonstrated this phenomenon in relation to organizational managers and labeled it the "think manager–think male" effect (see review by Schein, 2001). In Schein's studies, respondents rated women, men, or successful middle managers on traits that are stereotypical of women or men. The results showed that managers were perceived as similar to men on a large number of agentic characteristics, such as being competitive, self-confident, objective, aggressive, and ambitious and having leadership ability. Managers were perceived as similar to women on a few communal qualities, such as being intuitive and helpful. Schein and other researchers have replicated these findings in the United States and other nations. Also, studies of the content of stereotypes of managers and leaders have shown that they are perceived as more agentic, or masculine, than communal, or feminine (e.g., Powell, Butterfield, & Parent, 2002; Sczesny, 2005).

This dissimilarity, or incongruity, of people's beliefs about leaders and women would not be important if gender stereotypes merely faded away in employment contexts. However, even though these stereotypes do become less important in the presence of the other information that is salient in workplaces (Bosak, Sczesny, & Eagly, 2007), gender stereotypes continue to be influential (e.g., Ridgeway, 2001). Because these stereotypes are highly accessible in people's minds, their effect does not disappear in group and organizational settings. Therefore, in thinking about women as leaders, people would combine two somewhat divergent sets of expectations—those about leaders and those about women. In contrast, in thinking about men as leaders, people would combine largely redundant expectations. Consistent with these assumptions about stereotyping, Heilman and her associates (Heilman, Block, & Martell, 1995; Heilman, Block, Martell, & Simon, 1989) found that "men managers" were perceived as more similar to "successful middle managers" than were "women managers." Moreover, "women managers" were perceived as more agentic and less communal than women in general, which suggests that perceivers average the woman and manager stereotypes in thinking about female managers.

CONSEQUENCES OF STEREOTYPE INCONGRUITY: FEMALE LEADERS AT A DISADVANTAGE

Prejudice against women leaders would follow from the usual incongruity between people's beliefs about women and leaders. In leadership roles, especially if they are male-dominated, women generally do not seem as "natural" or appropriate as do men because these roles prime masculine associations (Lemm, Dabady, & Banaji, 2005). These often automatic associations then constrain the downstream cognitive processes of decision making and choice that determine, for example, whether female or male candidates are selected for jobs.

In general, prejudice against members of certain groups results from the mismatch between the attributes that people ascribe to a group and the attributes that they believe would produce success in a valued social role, as several theorists have argued (Burgess & Borgida, 1999; Eagly & Diekman, 2005; Eagly & Karau, 2002; Heilman, 2001). It follows that people are often prejudiced against men as child-care providers and secretaries as well as against women as leaders, regardless of an individual's real qualities. Such prejudice is not necessarily explicit and overt but often implicit and covert. As we subsequently show, what can result is an attitudinal penalty on, or lower evaluation of, people who are stereotypically mismatched to a role. Because of descriptive stereotypes, they are viewed as not having the "right stuff" for the role and thus have less access to the role than do people who are stereotypically matched to a role. Because of prescriptive stereotypes, people who actually occupy a role to which they are stereotypically mismatched are likely to have their role performance less favorably evaluated than are those who are stereotypically matched.

The mismatch between beliefs about women and leaders underlies the double bind that female leaders often face (Carli & Eagly, 2007; Eagly & Carli, 2004, 2007). People expect and prefer such women to be communal because of their beliefs about women and to be agentic because of their beliefs about leaders. Complying with pressures to be both agentic and communal can entail a difficult balancing act. Women leaders who manifest considerable communion can be rejected for seeming to be insufficiently masculine (not tough, decisive, or competent enough) and too feminine (weak, uncertain, or ineffectual). Women leaders who manifest considerable agency can be rejected for seeming to be too masculine (dominant, very competent, or self-promoting) and insufficiently feminine (not warm, selfless, or supportive enough). It is ironic that women leaders are often criticized as lacking the stereotypically directive and assertive qualities of good leaders—that is, disparaged as "not tough enough"—but often disliked when they display these very directive and assertive qualities—that is, denigrated as being "just like a man." Women leaders thus face cross-pressures as they try to avoid seeming too masculine or too feminine. Negotiating this dilemma can be difficult, as Carly Fiorina, former CEO of Hewlett-Packard, complained: "In the chat rooms around Silicon Valley . . . I was routinely referred to as either a 'bimbo' or a 'bitch'—too soft or too hard, and presumptuous, besides" (Fiorina, 2006, p. 173).

Research on attitudes toward female and male leaders provides evidence of prejudice toward female leaders—that is, of the evaluative penalty that follows from the incongruity between stereotypes of women and leaders.

National polls have asked representative samples of respondents for their attitudes toward men and women as leaders. For example, a 2005 poll of citizens of the European Union indicated that approximately 27% agreed that on the whole men make better political leaders than do women (European Commission, 2005, p. 30; see Figure 2.2). In addition, there were substantial differences between European nations in respondents' endorsement of male

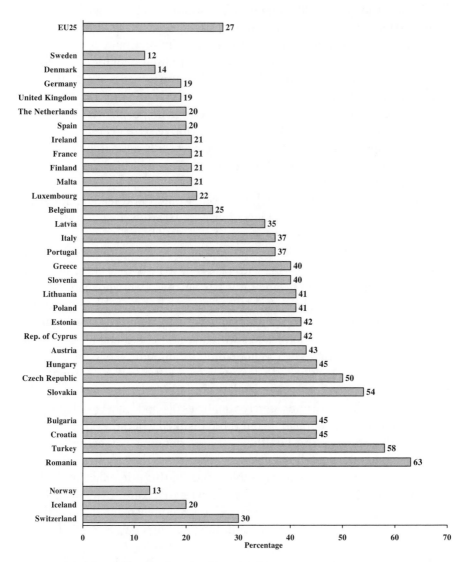

Figure 2.2. Percentage of respondents agreeing with the statement "On the whole, men make better political leaders than women." Source data from European Commission (2005). EU25 = Members of the European Union.

superiority, ranging from more than 50% of respondents in some nations (e.g., Romania, 63%; Turkey, 58%) to less than 15% in some Nordic countries (Sweden, 12%; Norway, 13%; Denmark, 14%). Also, a 2004 poll of citizens of the United States indicated that approximately 25% agreed that "Most men are better suited emotionally for politics than are most women" (Davis, Smith, & Marsden, 2005). Even though only a minority of respondents endorsed these traditional, evaluative beliefs that men are more qualified than women for political leadership, the existence of these significant minorities creates serious barriers to gender equality.

Because the prejudice that follows from the disjunction between stereotypes of women and leaders tends to produce discriminatory behavior, such attitudes reduce women's access to leadership roles and foster discriminatory reactions to women who occupy such roles. To test for the presence of discrimination, economists and sociologists have evaluated the access of women and men to leadership roles through a large number of studies that have implemented regression methods. To explain gender gaps in wages and rank in organizational hierarchies, researchers have assessed whether variables that may differ between the sexes, such as hours worked per year, type of occupation, years of education, and work experience, account for gender gaps in wages or promotions (e.g., Blau & Kahn, 2006; Maume, 2004; U.S. Government Accountability Office, 2003). Researchers determined whether sex still predicts wages or promotions even after the effects of the other variables are controlled for, thus making men and women statistically as equivalent as possible except for their sex. The gender gap that remains after such adjustments is generally interpreted to be due, at least in part, to sex discrimination. These techniques have almost always obtained a gender gap consistent with the claim that women, compared with men, suffer from a discriminatory disadvantage in wages and promotions (see Bergmann, 2007; Eagly & Carli, 2007).

To examine the prejudice and discrimination that limit women's access to many roles, other investigators, mainly researchers in psychology and organizational behavior, have used experimental methods. The most popular type of design has participants evaluate a hypothetical male or female job candidate or manager, although a small number of field experiments have presented equivalent male and female job candidates to organizational evaluators who do not realize that they are part of a research study (i.e., audit studies; see Riach & Rich, 2002). This method allows researchers to hold constant all features of this individual except for sex. Participants evaluate how suitable male or female candidates are for hiring or promotion or how competent and effective managers are in their jobs.

In one rendition of such experiments, participants evaluate application materials such as resumes with either a male name or a female name attached to the materials. Different participants receive the otherwise identical male and female versions of the materials. This research shows the power of descriptive stereotypes: Gender stereotypes constrain the types of job-relevant competencies that individual men and women are thought to possess. Specifically, the most recent meta-analytic review of these experiments, integrating the findings of 49 reports (Davison & Burke, 2000), found that men were preferred over women for masculine jobs such as auto salesperson and sales manager for heavy industry (mean $d = 0.34$), and women over men for feminine jobs such as secretary and home economics teacher (mean $d = -0.26$). For integrated jobs such as psychologist and motel desk clerk, which are occupied more equally by women and men, men were also preferred over women, but to a somewhat lesser extent than for masculine jobs (mean $d = 0.24$; H. K. Davison, personal communication, April 5, 2005). These findings thus show men's advantage over equivalent women, except in culturally feminine settings. These biases are substantial. For example, the bias against women in masculine jobs roughly corresponds to rates of positive evaluation, such as a favorable recommendation for a job, of 59% for men and 42% for women.

These biases affect women's access to leadership because most leader roles would fall in the masculine or integrated groups in Davison and Burke's (2000) classification of jobs. Because women were preferred over men in feminine domains, it might seem that women would have an advantage over men for advancement to higher positions in female-dominated fields such as nursing and social work. However, this is not the case because leadership is characterized as masculine even in feminine fields. In fact, even in such fields, men generally ascend faster than do women, despite their rarity. Christine Williams (1992, 1995) dubbed this effect the *glass escalator*—that is, the tendency for men to ascend career ladders faster than do women even in female-dominated fields. Because men also ascend faster than do women in male-dominated fields, it appears that a consistent bias favors men as leaders—regardless of whether a field is traditionally masculine or feminine.

Other experiments have examined evaluations of people who already occupy leadership roles. In these experiments participants usually receive written descriptions of managerial behavior that differ only in the sex of the leader. Some experiments instead obtain subordinates' evaluations of male and female confederates who act as leaders in the same leadership style. This research shows the power of prescriptive stereotypes: Gender stereotypes constrain the types of job-relevant behaviors that are perceived as desirable in individual men and women. A meta-analysis of 61 of these experiments assessing evaluations of equivalent male and female leaders found that these women's small overall disadvantage became more consequential for male-dominated leadership roles and especially for leaders with more autocratic and directive styles (mean $d = 0.05$ for overall bias, 0.09 for male-dominated roles, 0.30 in autocratic style; Eagly, Makhijani, & Klonsky, 1992). Dominant, autocratic leader behaviors are proscribed for women and more tolerable in men.

In summary, both correlational and experimental studies demonstrate discriminatory disadvantage for women as leaders. This bias in favor of men extends even to more feminine settings such as nursing and social work, in which men also advance more quickly than do women.

SEX STEREOTYPING OF LEADERSHIP: IS IT DISAPPEARING?

It might seem that the sex stereotyping of leadership as more masculine than feminine should have been stamped out by the phenomenon that we noted at the beginning of this chapter—namely, the presence of many more women in leadership roles. As we have argued, stereotypes derive from observations of the representation of group members in roles. Therefore, the influx of women into leadership roles may change stereotypes of women and of leaders, bringing them closer together. However, although the data demonstrating the traditional stereotyping of leadership as masculine extend back to the 1970s (e.g., Schein, 1973, 1975), there are more recent demonstrations as well (Powell, Butterfield, & Parent, 2002; Schein, 2001). The continuation of these phenomena could nonetheless be consistent with some weakening of this stereotyping. In fact, some researchers have reported hints of change. In particular, Schein (2001) reported data suggesting that women in the United States no longer engaged in think manager–think male stereotyping and instead viewed leaders as equally similar to men and women. In research in other countries (China, Germany, Japan, United Kingdom), Schein (1973, 1975) found that both women and men still endorsed traditional stereotypes according to which managers are perceived as more similar to men than to women.

Our own more recent findings present a mixed picture. They do give additional evidence of the lingering presence of the stereotyping of leadership as masculine (Sczesny, 2005). In particular, German business students (Sczesny, 2003a) and German managers (Sczesny, 2003b) ascribed agentic traits less often to women than to leaders in general. Similar findings have emerged among U.S. managers and students (Duehr & Bono, 2006). Such results suggest that a perceived deficit of agentic traits in women can still hinder their access to leadership roles. Nevertheless, conventional tests of the think manager–think male effect in the U.S. study found that the effect was intact only among the student participants, and stronger among the male than the female students (Duehr & Bono, 2006). The traditionally greater similarity of managers to men than to women was not present among the male or female managerial respondents, in large part because of an apparent shift in beliefs about "successful middle managers" toward less agency and more communion than in the past.

Despite the still-present tendency for women in general to be perceived as less agentic than are leaders, female leaders may now be perceived quite similarly to male leaders. In research by Sczesny and her colleagues (Sczesny, 2003a, 2003b; Sczesny, Bosak, Neff, & Schyns, 2004), business students and managers of both sexes in Australia, Germany, and India indicated their descriptive beliefs about leaders in general, male leaders, or female leaders by indicating the percentage who possessed agentic and communal traits. They also indicated their prescriptive beliefs by rating the importance of these traits for each group. On agentic traits, the traditional perception of male leaders as more similar than female leaders to leaders in general emerged in only one sample (German business students; Sczesny, 2003a). In contrast, a perception of male and female leaders as equally similar to leaders in general emerged in samples of German managers (Sczesny, 2003b) and Australian, German, and Indian business students (Sczesny et al., 2004). The participants in these samples also judged agentic traits as equally important for the three groups of leaders. However, on communal traits, the participants indicated that female leaders exceed male leaders and leaders in general. U.S. samples yielded similar findings except for male students' tendency to give female managers low ratings on agency (Duehr & Bono, 2006). Such results suggest change in beliefs about female and male leaders such that in leadership roles women have become indistinguishable from men on agentic qualities but exceed men on communal qualities.

All in all, the think manager–think male stereotype appears to be changing, at least in some cultures and samples of respondents. This phenomenon raises the question of exactly what is changing—stereotypes about women, men, or leaders? A decrease in the perceived incongruity of the female and leader stereotype could follow from change in gender stereotypes, change in leader stereotypes, or change in both stereotypes (Eagly & Karau, 2002). We now evaluate these possibilities.

Changes in Social Roles and Gender Stereotypes

There are good reasons to think that gender stereotypes should have changed. Such changes would follow from shifts in the distribution of men and women into social roles (Eagly et al., 2000). Evidence indicates that observations of women in nontraditional roles can change stereotypes about women, at least temporarily. In an excellent demonstration of such changes (Dasgupta & Asgari, 2004), female students were exposed to photos and brief biographies of famous women such as Toni Morrison, Meg Whitman, and Marian Wright Edelman. These exposures reduced students' gender stereotyping on an implicit measure that assessed how quickly they associated male names with agentic qualities and female names with communal qualities. A related field study conducted by these researchers compared the gender stereotypes of students at a women's college with those of students at a coeducational college. By the students' second year, gender stereotypes had weakened at the women's college but not at the coeducational college. The magnitude of the reduction of gender stereotyping at the women's college was correlated with the amount of experience that these students had with female faculty in the classroom. In general, when people repeatedly and consistently observe women fulfilling nontraditional roles, their stereotypes about them change to reflect the qualities demanded by these roles.

Have women's roles changed sufficiently to change consensual stereotypes of women? It is abundantly clear that women's roles have changed in many nations as they have entered the paid labor force in large numbers (see chap. 3, this volume). For example, in the United States, women's labor force participation rose from 20% in 1900 to 59% in 2005 (U.S. Census Bureau, 1975, 2007). During this period, the percentage of men in the labor force fell from 88% to 73%. Still, in the United States, as in other nations, women's rate of employment remains somewhat lower than men's (United Nations Development Programme, 2008).

When women enter the paid labor force, they do not necessarily enter occupations that are dominated by men (see chap. 6, this volume). In fact, the entry of women into male-dominated occupations proceeded only gradually after the entry of large numbers of women into the labor force in the 20th century (Inglehart & Norris, 2003). Women's inroads into such occupations are especially apparent in management. In the United States, the proportional increase of women in the occupational category of management exceeds women's increase in any other grouping (Wootton, 1997). For instance, the percentage of women in management, business, and financial occupations has risen from only 18% in 1972 to 43% in 2007, and the narrower occupational category of management occupations is 38% women (U.S. Bureau of Labor Statistics, 2008). European nations now have substantial, although somewhat smaller, representations of women in managerial roles (see Figure 2.1). Yet, this entry of women into manager roles has not for the most part displaced men because these occupational categories have expanded, thus accommodating larger numbers of women (Wootton, 1997).

Despite this evidence of what might be considered enormous change in women's roles, some researchers have argued that there is little evidence of change in gender stereotypes. For example, Lueptow, Garovich-Szabo, and Lueptow (2001; see also Lueptow, 2005) found little change when comparing assessments of stereotypes among students at a particular college, except for some increase in the perceived communion of women. However, other researchers have found some evidence of change, especially an increase in the perceived agency of women (Duehr & Bono, 2006). Valid assessments of changes in gender stereotypes await more systematic analysis of trends over time. Still, there is little evidence of large changes in gender stereotypes.

Why have the changes that have occurred in women's roles not revolutionized the cultural stereotype of women? One reason is that the changes in women's roles are not as profound as they may seem from inspecting data on labor force participation and women in management. In particular, on average, employed women have shorter hours than do employed men, with more women than men holding part-time jobs. Averaged over the European nations, 29% of women and only 7% of men are employed part time. In the United States, the comparable figures are 18% of women and 8% of men (Organisation for Economic Co-operation and Development, 2007). Women's fewer hours of paid employment, combined with their greater responsibility for domestic work (Bianchi, Robinson, & Milkie, 2006), produces a modified form of the traditional division of labor that still favors ascribing somewhat greater agency to men and greater communion to women.

It is also true that women and men tend to be employed in different occupations. Despite a decline in the sex segregation of occupations, at least in the United States, occupations have remained quite segregated (e.g., Bridges, 2003; Tomaskovic-Devey et al., 2006). In fact, more than half of all workers in the United States would have to switch jobs to produce an equal distribution of men and women in all jobs (Tomaskovic-Devey et al., 2006). In addition, most European nations have greater occupational sex segregation than does the United States (Bridges, 2003).

Considerable segregation exists even within the occupational category of "manager." Women managers are concentrated in the service sector, with its culturally "softer" images. For example, in the United States, women are especially concentrated in medical and health services (70%), human resources (70%), social and community services (66%), and education (64%; U.S. Bureau of Labor Statistics, 2008). To the extent that gender stereotypes follow from groups' typical roles (Eagly et al., 2000), more substantial change in gender stereotypes would flow from women entering the managerial occupations that have remained male-dominated, such as industrial production managers (16% women), engineering managers (7% women), and construction managers (8% women).

In many nations, women have remained concentrated primarily in traditionally female-dominated occupations. In fact, the most numerous occupational categories for U.S. women are (in descending order) secretaries and administrative assistants; registered nurses; cashiers; elementary and middle school teachers; retail salespersons; and nursing, psychiatric, and home health aides (U.S. Department of Labor, Women's Bureau, 2007). In general, most women have remained in occupations perceived to reward communion more than agency (Cejka & Eagly, 1999), thus perpetuating traditional gender stereotypes.

In addition, psychological processes restrain the changes in groups' stereotypes that might otherwise follow from changes in their roles, with the consequence that stereotype change lags behind actual role change. In particular, social perceivers tend to subtype individuals who strongly disconfirm their group's stereotype—that is, they regard them merely as exceptions and thereby leave the overall group stereotype intact (e.g., Brewer, Dull, & Lui, 1981; Richards & Hewstone, 2001). For example, the emergence of Angela Merkel as chancellor of Germany or Hillary Clinton as a U.S. presidential candidate might not change perceptions of women in these countries very much because these women are extremely unusual in occupying such prominent roles. In addition to subtyping, an even more subtle psychological process that retards stereotype change is that perceivers have difficulty encoding counterstereotypical behavior, as shown by Scott and Brown (2006) in relation to women enacting agentic leadership behavior. To the extent that women's agentic behaviors are not seen as reflecting agentic traits, even their more masculine behaviors may have a limited impact on the stereotype of women.

In summary, changes in the social roles of men and women are not as massive as often assumed, making it understandable that changes in gender stereotypes may be relatively small. Despite only limited evidence of actual change in gender stereotypes as shown by comparing data from stereotype studies conducted in differing years (e.g., Lueptow et al., 2001), research by Diekman and her colleagues has shown that people believe that today's women are different from women of the past and that women of the future will be different from women of the present (Diekman & Eagly, 2000; Wilde & Diekman, 2005). People view women as acquiring a greater measure of masculine personality traits, masculine cognitive skills, and even masculine physical strength as they increasingly occupy roles outside of the home. For the most part, people do not think that women have lost culturally feminine qualities such as warmth and sensitivity, and they generally find it acceptable that women have added relatively masculine qualities (Diekman & Goodfriend, 2006). In contrast to this perception of change in women, people regard men as changing very little. It thus appears that people's ideas about what women were like in the past produced an exaggerated picture of stereotype change, compared with respondents' stereotypes at different time periods.

Changes in the Definition of Good Leadership

The traits of women and leaders might also become more similar because of a change in the definition of leadership roles over time. To the extent that managerial roles require more of the communal characteristics typically ascribed to women and fewer of the agentic characteristics typically ascribed to men, these roles would be more congruent with the stereotype of women (Eagly & Karau, 2002). In fact, some evidence indicates that such changes have occurred. In comparisons of 1984 and 1999 data from samples of business students, the concept of "good manager" became somewhat less agentic over time (Powell et al., 2002). Furthermore, Duehr and Bono (2006) found that male and female managers and students perceived managers as more communal and less agentic than did the male managers in Heilman et al.'s (1989) study.

Other evidence about changes in managerial roles consists of trends in management theory and practice. Although leadership was traditionally associated with predominantly masculine sex-typed skills and abilities, experts on management now emphasize a wider range of qualities that includes more communal characteristics. In fact, beginning in the last decades of the 20th century, descriptions of good leadership increasingly encompassed democratic relationships, participatory decision making, delegation, and team-based skills that are more congruent with the communal characteristics ascribed to women than were earlier descriptions of leadership (e.g., Garvin, 1993; Juran, 1988; Rastetter, 1997; Senge, 1990). For example, feminine sex-typed communal qualities such as empowering and communicating effectively are prevalent in the advice of managerial experts (see Fondas, 1997).

These changes in expectations about leaders probably reflect changing organizational environments, marked by rapid shifts in technology, increasing workforce diversity, less hierarchical organizational structures, and the growing interdependence of organizations through the weakening geopolitical boundaries. These changed circumstances call for new modes of managing suited to contemporary organizational environments (Kanter, 1997; Lipman-Blumen, 1996). In contemporary organizations, many managers no longer focus primarily on traditional managerial functions of planning, organizing, directing, and controlling. Instead, they support teams of employees who execute tasks. "Command and control" has become less useful, and instead managers communicate, listen, mentor, teach, and encourage.

In many organizations, good leadership is increasingly defined in terms of qualities of a good coach or teacher rather than a highly authoritative person who directs others in a commanding manner. Illustrating this shift in the United States, Mike Krzyzewski, the coach of the highly successful Duke University men's basketball team, who is known for his mentoring and interpersonally sensitive leadership style, has become a leadership guru who is in demand for giving lectures and workshops to business executives (Sokolove, 2006). Krzyzewski's prominence as a model of good leadership is a sign of this shift toward a coach or teacher model of leadership.

Leadership researchers responded to these changing ideas about leadership by defining good leadership as fostering followers' commitment and ability to contribute creatively to organizations. Political scientist James McGregor Burns (1978) provided an early statement of these themes by delineating a type of leadership that he named *transformational*. As this concept was developed by leadership researchers (e.g., Avolio, 1999; Bass, 1998), transformational leadership became a composite style that emphasizes establishing oneself as a role model by gaining followers' trust and confidence. Such leaders define organizations' goals, develop plans to achieve those goals, and innovate creatively, even when their organizations are already successful. Transformational leaders also mentor and empower their subordinates so that they contribute effectively to their organization.

The changes in valued forms of leadership illustrated by transformational leadership suggest that many leader roles are becoming more androgynous, incorporating culturally feminine qualities along with culturally masculine ones. Indeed, transformational leadership appears to be somewhat more aligned with communal than agentic qualities (e.g., Duehr & Bono, 2006), especially its Individualized Consideration subscale, which emphasizes mentoring and encouraging subordinates (Hackman, Furniss, Hills, & Paterson, 1992). To the extent that norms about effective management encompass communal qualities, the perceived incongruity between women and leaders should lessen.

How widely people endorse this contemporary view of leadership as collaborative, mentoring, and generally transformational is not fully understood. Yet, research on contemporary definitions of management has shown a blending of culturally masculine and feminine qualities among U.S. business school students (Atwater et al., 2004). Moreover, a study conducted in the Netherlands and the United States with largely managerial respondents revealed beliefs that promotions are enhanced by the "good practices" qualities of transformational leadership and the reward rather than punishment (Vinkenburg, van Engen, Eagly, & Johannesen-Schmidt, 2008).

An important caveat about a communal shift in definitions of leadership roles is that they can differ greatly in their demands (Eagly & Karau, 2002). Expectations for a role such as school principal or nursing supervisor are quite different from those for a role such as military officer or CEO of an industrial corporation. Middle manager roles may especially incorporate communal behavior because of the socially complex elements of the required activities. When asked to rate the importance of various abilities for their jobs, managers at the middle level emphasized social relations skills that involve cooperative effort and motivating and developing subordinates. In contrast, managers at the top level indicated that their positions require activities such as monitoring information, manifesting entrepreneurial ability, and engaging in long-range planning (Gomez-Mejia, McCann, & Page, 1985; Paolillo, 1981; Pavett & Lau, 1983). Even though executive roles appear to have a strong emphasis on agency (e.g., Martell, Parker, Emrich, & Crawford, 1998), these roles are changing to some extent because executives have to function in a landscape of increasing complexity and interdependence inherent in many organizations' multiple stakeholders and multifaceted agendas. Therefore, many executive roles appear to have changed to demand a repertoire of competencies that includes a good measure of "soft skills." For example, one business journalist noted, "Boards are increasingly looking for CEOs who can demonstrate superb people skills in dealing with employees or other stakeholders while delivering consistent results" (Tischler, 2005).

FUTURE PROSPECTS FOR WOMEN IN LEADERSHIP ROLES

At the beginning of this chapter, we stated that the equal representation of women and men in leadership roles would be one indication that a society has attained gender equality. What are the chances that the post-industrial nations of North America and Europe will achieve such representation and develop substantially greater gender equality in the coming years? The answer is not obvious. Multiple barriers to gender equality still remain, and in this chapter we have analyzed one barrier: the importance of cultural stereotypes about women, men, and leaders. On the basis of research on these stereotypes, we have argued that definitions of leadership roles have shifted somewhat in a culturally feminine direction. We also found that changes in the stereotype of women are less well established empirically. Given these findings, we ask whether we can expect a lessening of prejudice toward women as leaders and a higher representation of women in influential leadership positions in the near future.

The changes that we observed in stereotypes about leaders should help to reduce prejudice toward female leaders and therefore should increase the numbers of women in leader roles. There is in fact some evidence that prejudice has lessened. For example, especially dramatic evidence of lessening in prejudice toward female leaders over time emerged from a Gallup poll question asking U.S. respondents, "If you were taking a new job and had your choice of a boss, would you prefer to work for a man or woman?" Figure 2.3 presents the responses obtained from representative samples of Americans from 1953 to 2006. These data show a clear preference for male bosses over female bosses but a considerable lessening of this preference over the years

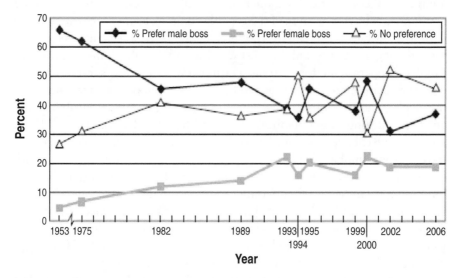

Figure 2.3. Percentage of respondents preferring a man or woman as boss in Gallup polls from 1953 through 2006. Source data from Carroll (2006).

(Carroll, 2006). Despite the erosion of the huge approval advantage that male bosses once enjoyed, men retained some advantage in 2006, with these preferences registering at 37% for a male boss, compared with 19% for a female boss. Although the poll did not assess respondents' rationale for their choices, the most remarkable aspect of these findings is that 43% of the respondents in 2006 indicated no preference for one sex over the other. This egalitarian, politically correct response emerged even though respondents had to break away from the man versus woman response options given by the poll question.

Such changes in attitudes toward female leaders are consistent with more general changes in attitudes pertaining to gender in Western nations. People who support women's opportunities to be leaders also endorse less traditional gender roles and approve of women's participation in the paid labor force (Inglehart & Norris, 2003). For example, Figure 2.4 presents European citizens' agreement with the statement "If jobs are scarce, women have as much right to a job as men" (see European Commission, 2005, p. 29). Averaged across the European Community, 86% of respondents endorsed equal job opportunity for women. Such attitudes have changed very substantially, often with very pronounced movement toward greater endorsement of equality in the 1970s and 1980s, generally with some leveling off or even small reversals in quite recent years. For instance, a small reversal between 2002 and 2006 can be detected in the attitudes toward female and male bosses displayed in Figure 2.3. Whether such data merely represent a pause in progress toward gender equality or a more profound reversal or backlash is unknown. Social scientists have just begun to debate this issue (Blau, Briton, & Grisly, 2006).

Change in gender stereotypes should also be fueled by men entering traditionally female-dominated occupations and sharing domestic work more equally with women. Yet, men's roles have changed far less than women's roles have. Although men have not entered female-dominated occupations in large numbers (e.g., Hartmann, Rose, & Lovell, 2006), the household division of labor has changed somewhat. At least in the United States, men perform substantially more housework and child care than they did in the past (Bianchi et al., 2006). However, despite men's greater participation, women continue to do much more domestic work than do men, thus contributing to the maintenance of traditional gender stereotypes. International comparisons indicate that men's contributions to domestic work are variable and responsive, not only to the status of women and women's employment, but also to national social policies such as the length of available parental leave and men's eligibility to take parental leave (Hook, 2006). Social provision directed specifically to women in the labor force (e.g., long maternity leaves, part-time employment) perpetuates traditional inequality in domestic obligations and maintains traditional gender stereotypes. The maintenance of these stereotypes in turn contributes to the lesser representation of women in influential leadership positions.

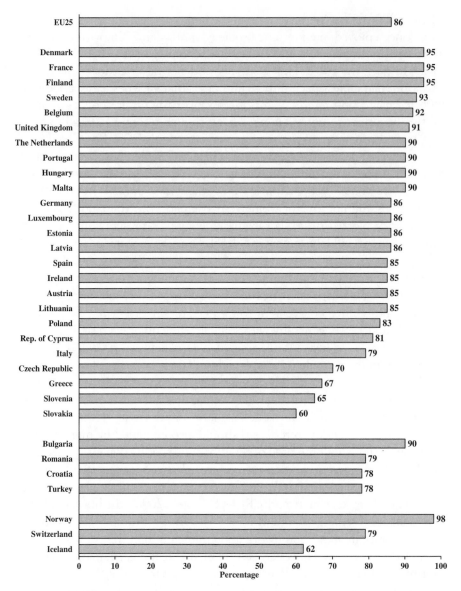

Figure 2.4. Percentage of respondents agreeing with the statement "If jobs are scarce, women have as much right to a job as men." Source data from European Commission (2005). EU25 = Members of the European Union.

It is clear that stereotypes about women, men, and leaders continue to function as impediments to women's advancement into leadership roles even though the perceived incongruity of women and leadership has lessened. As we have shown, there is evidence of change in ideas about leadership, but it is doubtful that this change is great enough to entirely remove the incongruity problem, especially for leadership roles that are male dominated and highly influential. In addition, gender stereotypes appear to change only slowly with observations of women and men in nontraditional roles, and these changes likely proceed with some lag in relation to actual social change. Despite a considerable shift in role distributions in the past decades, a moderated male–female division of labor prevails, perpetuating somewhat weakened stereotypes about women, men, and leaders. The remaining incongruity between women and leadership is still problematic for women who aspire to power and authority in society.

REFERENCES

Atwater, L. E., Brett, J. F., Waldman, D., DiMare, L., & Hayden, M. V. (2004). Men's and women's perceptions of the gender typing of management subroles. *Sex Roles, 50*, 191–199.

Avolio, B. J. (1999). *Full leadership development: Building the vital forces in organizations*. Thousand Oaks, CA: Sage.

Banaji, M. R., & Hardin, C. D. (1996). Automatic stereotyping. *Psychological Science, 7*, 136–141.

Bass, B. M. (1998). *Transformational leadership: Industrial, military, and educational impact*. Mahwah, NJ: Erlbaum.

Bergmann, B. R. (2007). Discrimination through the economist's eye. In F. J. Crosby, M. S. Stockdale, & S. A. Ropp (Eds.), *Sex discrimination in the workplace: Multidisciplinary perspectives* (pp. 213–234). Malden, MA: Blackwell.

Bianchi, S. M., Robinson, J. P., & Milkie, M. A. (2006). *Changing rhythms of American family life*. New York: Russell Sage Foundation.

Blair, I. V., & Banaji, M. R. (1996). Automatic and controlled processes in stereotype priming. *Journal of Personality and Social Psychology, 70*, 1142–1163.

Blau, F. D., Briton, M. C., & Grisly, D. B. (Eds.) (2006). *The declining significance of gender?* New York: Russell Sage Foundation.

Blau, F. D., & Kahn, L. M. (2006). The gender pay gap: Going, going . . . but not gone. In F. D. Blau, M. C. Briton, & D. B. Grisly (Eds.), *The declining significance of gender?* (pp. 37–66). New York: Russell Sage Foundation.

Bosak, J., Sczesny, S., & Eagly, A. H. (2007). Die Bedeutung von Informationen zur sozialen Rolle für die Reduktion geschlechtsstereotypen Urteilens: Ein methodisches Artefakt? [The meaning of information about social roles for the reduction of gender-stereotypical judgments: A methodological artifact?] *Zeitschrift für Sozialpsychologie, 38*, 277–284.

Brewer, M. B., Dull, V., & Lui, L. (1981). Perceptions of the elderly: Stereotypes as prototypes. *Journal of Personality and Social Psychology, 41*, 656–670.

Bridges, W. P. (2003). Rethinking gender segregation and gender inequality: Measures and meanings. *Demography, 40*, 543–568.

Burgess, D., & Borgida, E. (1999). Who women are, who women should be: Descriptive and prescriptive gender stereotyping in sex discrimination. *Psychology, Public Policy, and Law, 5,* 665–692.

Burns, J. M. (1978). *Leadership.* New York: Harper & Row.

Carli, L. L., & Eagly, A. H. (2007). Overcoming resistance to women leaders: The importance of leadership style. In B. Kellerman & D. L. Rhode (Eds.), *Women and leadership: The state of play and strategies for change* (pp. 127–148). San Francisco: Jossey-Bass.

Carroll, J. (2006, September 1). *Americans prefer male boss to a female boss.* Retrieved September 10, 2006, from http://www.gallup.com/poll/24346/Americans-Prefer-Male-Boss-Female-Boss.aspx

Catalyst. (2006). *2005 Catalyst census of women corporate officers and top earners of the Fortune 500.* Retrieved September 2, 2006, from http://www.catalystwomen.org/files/full/2005%20COTE.pdf

Cejka, M. A., & Eagly, A. H. (1999). Gender-stereotypic images of occupations correspond to the sex segregation of employment. *Personality and Social Psychology Bulletin, 25,* 413–423.

Conway, M., Pizzamiglio, M. T., & Mount, L. (1996). Status, communality, and agency: Implications for stereotypes of gender and other groups. *Journal of Personality and Social Psychology, 71,* 25–38.

Dasgupta, N., & Asgari, S. (2004). Seeing is believing: Exposure to counterstereotypical women leaders and its effect on the malleability of automatic gender stereotyping. *Journal of Experimental Social Psychology, 40,* 642–658.

Davis, J. A., Smith, T. W., & Marsden, P. V. (2005). *General social surveys, 1972–2004.* [Cumulative data file]. 2nd ICPSR version. Chicago: National Opinion Research Center [Producer]; Storrs, CT: Roper Center for Public Opinion Research, University of Connecticut; Ann Arbor, MI: Inter-university Consortium for Political and Social Research; Berkeley, CA: Computer-assisted Survey Methods Program (http://sda.berkeley.edu), University of California [Distributors].

Davison, H. K., & Burke, M. J. (2000). Sex discrimination in simulated employment contexts: A meta-analytic investigation. *Journal of Vocational Behavior, 56,* 225–248.

Deaux, K., & Lewis, L. L. (1984). Structure of gender stereotypes: Interrelationships among components and gender label. *Journal of Personality and Social Psychology, 46,* 991–1004.

Diekman, A. B., & Eagly, A. H. (2000). Stereotypes as dynamic constructs: Women and men of the past, present, and future. *Personality and Social Psychology Bulletin, 26,* 1171–1188.

Diekman, A. B., & Goodfriend, W. (2006). Rolling with the changes: A role congruity perspective on gender norms. *Psychology of Women Quarterly, 30,* 369–383.

Duehr, E. E., & Bono, J. E. (2006). Men, women, and managers: Are stereotypes finally changing? *Personnel Psychology, 59,* 815–846.

Dunning, D., & Sherman, D. A. (1997). Stereotypes and tacit inference. *Journal of Personality and Social Psychology, 73,* 459–471.

Eagly, A. H., & Carli, L. L. (2004). Women and men as leaders. In J. Antonakis, A. T. Cianciolo, & R. J. Sternberg (Eds.), *The nature of leadership* (pp. 279–301). Thousand Oaks, CA: Sage.

Eagly, A. H., & Carli, L. L. (2007). *Through the labyrinth: The truth about how women become leaders.* Boston: Harvard Business School Press.

Eagly, A. H., & Diekman, A. B. (2005). What is the problem? Prejudice as an attitude-in-context. In J. F. Dovidio, P. Glick, & L. Rudman (Eds.), *On the nature of prejudice: Fifty years after Allport* (pp. 19–35). Malden, MA: Blackwell.

Eagly, A. H., & Karau, S. J. (2002). Role congruity theory of prejudice toward female leaders. *Psychological Review, 109,* 573–598.

Eagly, A. H., Makhijani, M. G., & Klonsky, B. G. (1992). Gender and the evaluation of leaders: A meta-analysis. *Psychological Bulletin, 111,* 3–22.

Eagly, A. H., & Steffen, V. J. (1984). Gender stereotypes stem from the distribution of women and men into social roles. *Journal of Personality and Social Psychology, 46,* 735–754.

Eagly, A. H., Wood, W., & Diekman, A. B. (2000). Social role theory of sex differences and similarities: A current appraisal. In T. Eckes & H. M. Trautner (Eds.), *The developmental social psychology of gender* (pp. 123–174). Mahwah, NJ: Erlbaum.

European Commission. (2005). Special Eurobarometer 225: Social values, science and technology. *Wave 63.1.* Retrieved January 2, 2007, from http://ec.europa.eu/public_opinion/archives/ebs/ebs_225_report_en.pdf

European Commission. (2007). *Decision-making in the largest publicly quoted companies.* Retrieved June 13, 2008, from http://europa.eu.int/comm/employment_social/women_men_stats/out/measures_out438_en.htm

Fiorina, C. (2006). *Tough choices: A memoir.* New York: Penguin.

Fiske, A. P., Haslam, N., & Fiske, S. T. (1991). Confusing one person with another: What errors reveal about the elementary forms of social relations. *Journal of Personality and Social Psychology, 60,* 656–674.

Fiske, S. T. (1998). Stereotyping, prejudice, and discrimination. In D. T. Gilbert, S. T. Fiske, & G. Lindzey (Eds.), *The handbook of social psychology* (4th ed., Vol. 2, pp. 357–411). Boston: McGraw-Hill.

Fiske, S. T., & Stevens, L. E. (1993). What's so special about sex? Gender stereotyping and discrimination. In S. Oskamp & M. Costanzo (Eds.), *Claremont Symposium on Applied Social Psychology: Vol. 6. Gender issues in contemporary society* (pp. 173–196). Newbury Park, CA: Sage.

Fondas, N. (1997). Feminization unveiled: Management qualities in contemporary writings. *Academy of Management Review, 22,* 257–282.

Garvin, D. A. (1993). Building a learning organization. *Harvard Business Review, 71*(4), 78–91.

Gawronski, B. (2003). On difficult questions and evident answers: Dispositional inference from role-constrained behavior. *Personality and Social Psychology Bulletin, 29,* 1459–1475.

Glick, P., & Fiske, S. T. (2007). Sex discrimination: The psychological approach. In F. J. Crosby, M. S. Stockdale, & S. A. Ropp (Eds.), *Sex discrimination in the workplace: Multidisciplinary perspectives* (pp. 155–187). Malden, MA: Blackwell.

Gomez-Mejia, L. R., McCann, J. E., & Page, R. C. (1985). The structure of managerial behaviors and rewards. *Industrial Relations, 24,* 147–154.

Hackman, M. Z., Furniss, A. H., Hills, M. J., & Paterson, T. J. (1992). Perceptions of gender-role characteristics and transformational and transactional leadership behaviours. *Perceptual and Motor Skills, 75,* 311–319.

Hartmann, H., Rose, S. J., & Lovell, V. (2006). How much progress in closing the long-term earnings gap? In F. D. Blau, M. C. Briton, & D. B. Grisly (Eds.), *The declining significance of gender?* (pp. 125–155). New York: Russell Sage Foundation.

Heilman, M. E. (2001). Description and prescription: How gender stereotypes prevent women's ascent up the organizational ladder. *Journal of Social Issues, 57,* 657–674.

Heilman, M. E., Block, C. J., & Martell, R. F. (1995). Sex stereotypes: Do they influence perceptions of managers? *Journal of Social Behavior and Personality, 10,* 237–252.

Heilman, M. E., Block, C. J., Martell, R. F., & Simon, M. C. (1989). Has anything changed? Current characterizations of men, women, and managers. *Journal of Applied Psychology, 74,* 935–942.

Hook, J. L. (2006). Care in context: Men's unpaid work in 20 countries, 1965–2003. *American Sociological Review, 71,* 639–660.

Inglehart, R., & Norris, P. (2003). *Rising tide: Gender equality and cultural change around the world.* New York: Cambridge University Press.

Ito, T. A., & Urland, G. R. (2003). Race and gender on the brain: Electrocortical measures of attention to the race and gender of multiply categorizable individuals. *Journal of Personality and Social Psychology, 85,* 616–626.

Juran, J. M. (1988). *Juran on planning for quality.* New York: Free Press.

Kanter, R. M. (1997). *Rosabeth Moss Kanter on the frontiers of management.* Boston: Harvard Business School Press.

Koenig, A., & Eagly, A. H. (2008). *The sources of stereotypes: How observations of groups' social roles shape stereotype content.* Unpublished manuscript.

Lemm, K. M., Dabady, M., & Banaji, M. R. (2005). Gender picture priming: It works with denotative and connotative primes. *Social Cognition, 23,* 218–241.

Lipman-Blumen, J. (1996). *The connective edge: Leading in an interdependent world.* San Francisco: Jossey-Bass.

Lueptow, L. B. (2005). Increasing differentiation of women and men: Gender trait analysis 1974–1997. *Psychological Reports, 97,* 277–287.

Lueptow, L. B., Garovich-Szabo, L., & Lueptow, M. B. (2001). Social change and the persistence of sex typing: 1974–1997. *Social Forces, 80,* 1–36.

Martell, R. F., Parker, C., Emrich, C. G., & Crawford, M. S. (1998). Sex stereotyping in the executive suite: "Much ado about something." *Journal of Social Behavior and Personality, 13,* 127–138.

Maume, D. J., Jr. (2004). Is the glass ceiling a unique form of inequality? Evidence from a random-effects model of managerial attainment. *Work and Occupations, 31*, 250–274.

Miner, J. B. (1993). *Role motivation theories*. New York: Routledge.

Newport, F. (2001, February 21). *Americans see women as emotional and affectionate, men as more aggressive: Gender specific stereotypes persist in recent Gallup poll.* Retrieved January 25, 2004, from Gallup Brain, http://brain.gallup.com

Organisation for Economic Co-operation and Development. (2007). *OECD employment outlook 2007: Statistical annex.* Retrieved June 12, 2008, from http://www.oecd.org/dataoecd/29/27/38749309.pdf

Paolillo, J. G. (1981). Manager's self assessments of managerial roles: The influence of hierarchical level. *Journal of Management, 7*, 43–52.

Pavett, C. M., & Lau, A. W. (1983). Managerial work: The influence of hierarchical level and functional specialty. *Academy of Management Journal, 26*, 170–177.

Powell, G. N., Butterfield, D. A., & Parent, J. D. (2002). Gender and managerial stereotypes: Have the times changed? *Journal of Management, 28*, 177–193.

Prentice, D. A., & Carrranza, E. (2002). What women and men should be, shouldn't be, are allowed to be, and don't have to be: The contents of prescriptive gender stereotypes. *Psychology of Women Quarterly, 26*, 269–281.

Prentice, D. A., & Miller, D. T. (2006). Essentializing differences between women and men. *Psychological Science, 17*, 129–135.

Rastetter, D. (1997). Frauen, die besseren Führungskräfte? "Soft Skills" als neue Anforderungen im Management [Women who are better managers? "Soft Skills" as new demands in management]. *Journal für Psychologie, 5*, 43–56.

Riach, P. A., & Rich, J. (2002). Field experiments of discrimination in the market place. *Economic Journal, 112*, F480–F518.

Richards, A., & Hewstone, M. (2001). Subtyping and subgrouping: Processes for the prevention and promotion of stereotype change. *Personality and Social Psychology Review, 5*, 52–73.

Ridgeway, C. L. (2001). Gender, status, and leadership. *Journal of Social Issues, 57*, 637–655.

Ross, L., Amabile, T. M., & Steinmetz, J. L. (1977). Social roles, social control, and biases in social-perception processes. *Journal of Personality and Social Psychology, 35*, 485–494.

Schaller, M., & O'Brien, M. (1992). "Intuitive analysis of covariance" and group stereotype formation. *Personality and Social Psychology Bulletin, 18*, 776–785.

Schein, V. E. (1973). The relationship between sex-role stereotypes and requisite management characteristics. *Journal of Applied Psychology, 57*, 95–100.

Schein, V. E. (1975). Relations between sex-role stereotypes and requisite management characteristics among female managers. *Journal of Applied Psychology, 60*, 340–344.

Schein, V. E. (2001). A global look at psychological barriers to women's progress in management. *Journal of Social Issues, 57*, 675–688.

Scott, K. A., & Brown, D. J. (2006). Female first, leader second? Gender bias in the encoding of leadership behavior. *Organizational Behavior and Human Decision Processes, 101,* 230–242.

Sczesny, S. (2003a). A closer look beneath the surface: Various facets of the think-manager–think-male stereotype. *Sex Roles, 49,* 353–363.

Sczesny, S. (2003b). Führungskompetenz: Selbst- und Fremdwahrnehmung weiblicher und männlicher Führungskräfte. *Zeitschrift für Sozialpsychologie, 34,* 133–145.

Sczesny, S. (2005). Gender stereotypes and implicit leadership theories. In B. Schyns & J. R. Meindl (Eds.), *Implicit leadership theories: Essays and explorations* (pp. 159–172). Greenwich, CT: Information Age.

Sczesny, S., Bosak, J., Neff, D., & Schyns, B. (2004). Gender stereotypes and the attribution of leadership traits. A cross-cultural comparison. *Sex Roles, 51,* 631–645.

Sczesny, S., & Kühnen, U. (2004). Meta-cognition about biological sex and gender-stereotypic physical appearance: Consequences for the assessment of leadership competence. *Personality and Social Psychology Bulletin, 30,* 13–21.

Senge, P. M. (1990). *The fifth discipline: The art and practice of the learning organization.* New York: Currency Doubleday.

Smith, R. A. (2002). Race, gender, and authority in the workplace: Theory and research. *Annual Review of Sociology, 28,* 509–542.

Sokolove, M. (2006, February). Follow me. *New York Times Sports Magazine,* 96–101, 116–117.

Stangor, C., Lynch, L., Duan, C., & Glass, B. (1992). Categorization of individuals on the basis of multiple social features. *Journal of Personality and Social Psychology, 62,* 207–218.

Survey Research Consultants International. (1998). *Index to international public opinion, 1996–1997.* Westport, CT: Greenwood Press.

Tischler, L. (2005, September). The CEO's new clothes. *Fast Company,* 27–28.

Tomaskovic-Devey, D., Zimmer, C., Stainback, K., Robinson, C., Taylor, T., & McTague, T. (2006). Documenting desegregation: Segregation in American workplaces by race, ethnicity, and sex, 1966–2003. *American Sociological Review, 71,* 565–588.

Uleman, J. S., Newman, L. S., & Moskowitz, G. B. (1996). People as flexible interpreters: Evidence and issues from spontaneous trait inference. In M. P. Zanna (Ed.), *Advances in experimental social psychology* (Vol. 28, pp. 211–279). San Diego, CA: Academic Press.

United Nations Development Programme. (2008). *Human development report 2007/2008.* New York: Oxford University Press. Retrieved June 12, 2006, from http://hdr.undp.org/en/media/hdr_20072008_en_indicator_tables.pdf

U.S. Bureau of Labor Statistics. (2008). *Household data, annual averages, table 11, employed persons by detailed occupation, sex, race, and Hispanic or Latino ethnicity.* Retrieved June 12, 2008, http://www.bls.gov/cps/cpsaat11.pdf

U.S. Census Bureau. (1975). *Bicentennial edition: Historical statistics of the United States, Colonial Times to 1970*. Retrieved December 15, 2006, from http://www2.census.gov/prod2/statcomp/documents/CT1970p1-01.pdf

U.S. Census Bureau. (2007). *Statistical abstract of the United States: 2007*. Retrieved December 18, 2006, from http://www.census.gov/prod/www/statistical-abstract.html

U.S. Department of Labor, Women's Bureau. (2007). *20 leading occupations of employed women; full-time wage and salary workers; 2006 annual averages*. Retrieved June 10, 2007, from http://www.dol.gov/wb/factsheets/20lead2006.htm

U.S. Government Accountability Office. (2003). *Women's earnings: Work patterns partially explain difference between men's and women's earnings* (GAO-04-35). Retrieved July 30, 2004, from http://www.gao.gov/new.items/d0435.pdf

van Knippenberg, A., van Twuyver, M., & Pepels, J. (1994). Factors affecting social categorization processes in memory. *British Journal of Social Psychology, 33*, 419–431.

Vinkenburg, C. J., van Engen, M. L., Eagly, A. H., & Johannesen-Schmidt, M. L. (2008). *Is transformational leadership a route to women's career advancement? An exploration of stereotypical beliefs about leadership styles*. Manuscript submitted for publication.

von Hippel, W., Sekaquaptewa, D., & Vargas, P. (1995). On the role of encoding processes in stereotype maintenance. In M. Zanna (Ed.), *Advances in experimental social psychology* (Vol. 27, pp. 177–254). San Diego, CA: Academic Press.

Wellington, S., Kropf, M. B., & Gerkovich, P. R. (2003, June). What's holding women back? *Harvard Business Review, 81*(6), 18–19.

Wilde, A., & Diekman, A. B. (2005). Cross-cultural similarities and differences in dynamic stereotypes: A comparison between Germany and the United States. *Psychology of Women Quarterly, 29*, 188–196.

Williams, C. L. (1992). The glass escalator: Hidden advantages for men in the "female" professions. *Social Problems, 39*, 41–57.

Williams, C. L. (1995). *Still a man's world: Men who do women's work*. Berkeley: University of California Press.

Williams, J. E., & Best, D. L. (1990). *Measuring sex stereotypes: A multination study*. Newbury Park, CA: Sage.

Wood, W., Christensen, P. N., Hebl, M. R., & Rothgerber, H. (1997). Conformity to sex-typed norms, affect, and the self-concept. *Journal of Personality and Social Psychology, 73*, 523–535.

Wootton, B. H. (1997). Gender differences in occupational employment. *Monthly Labor Review, 120*(4), 14–24.

3

ROSE-COLORED GLASSES: HOW TOKENISM AND COMPARISONS WITH THE PAST REDUCE THE VISIBILITY OF GENDER INEQUALITY

MICHAEL T. SCHMITT, JENNIFER R. SPOOR, KELLY DANAHER, AND NYLA R. BRANSCOMBE

In the 1980s the metaphor of the glass ceiling emerged to describe the experience of women in organizations, and in society more generally, who faced invisible or difficult-to-recognize barriers that prevented them from reaching the highest ranks in organizations (see chap. 1, this volume). Despite some improvements in the status of women, such barriers still exist. Women are highly underrepresented in high-status, powerful positions, and they continue to face a number of disadvantages relative to men.

The glass-ceiling metaphor remains relevant not only because barriers to women's advancement remain but also because such barriers remain difficult for people to see. To the extent that women fail to perceive the barriers that prevent their advancement, they will find it difficult to seek to eliminate or overcome them. Yet, despite clear evidence of continuing gender inequality, references to the glass ceiling imply that women are breaking through and shattering the glass ceiling. Consider how Nancy Pelosi expanded on the metaphor in her opening speech as the first female leader of the U.S. House of Representatives:

> It is a moment for which we have waited for over 200 years. Never losing faith, we waited through the many years of struggle to achieve our rights. But women were not just waiting; women were working. Never losing

faith, we worked to redeem the promise of America that all men and women are created equal. For our daughters and our granddaughters, today we have broken the marble ceiling. For our daughters and our granddaughters, the sky is the limit. Anything is possible for them. (Pelosi, 2007)

Although we can only speculate as to what the future will hold, the current reality is not one of shattered barriers and equal opportunity. Indeed, women as a group are severely underrepresented in the U.S. House of Representatives, accounting for only 16% of all representatives. In this context dominated by men, how is Pelosi able to articulate such a rosy portrait of equality of opportunity for women and men? In more general terms, how are people able to make persuasive claims of the existence of equality when it does not exist? In this chapter we consider two factors that can create the appearance of gender egalitarianism even in contexts that otherwise might be judged as sexist. Both factors are illustrated in Pelosi's statements. The first is the interpretation of the advancement of a few token women as evidence of equality of opportunity. The second is the framing of contemporary gender inequality in comparison with the past. In considering these issues, we draw on social identity theory to consider the ways in which tokenism and comparisons with the past affect perceptions of, and responses to, gender inequality.

A SOCIAL IDENTITY APPROACH TO GENDER INEQUALITY

Social identity theory (Tajfel, 1978; Tajfel & Turner, 1979) attempts to explain how people respond to their group memberships in stratified societies, and thus provides an ideal perspective from which to explore how women and men respond to gender inequality in organizations (see Schmitt, Ellemers, & Branscombe, 2003). The theory assumes that a person's sense of self is not limited to individual traits and characteristics, but can include their social identities—subjectively meaningful social categories to which the person belongs, defining an in-group ("us") in relation to an out-group ("them"). Furthermore, the theory assumes that when people identify with an in-group they are motivated to protect its values and interests, even when doing so might incur personal costs.

One important contribution of the social identity approach is the attention given to how processes of social comparison shape social identity. Our group identities do not exist in isolation; they are defined, constructed, and evaluated through comparisons with other groups. For example, women's gender group identity is typically defined using comparisons with men. In terms of organizational outcomes and treatment, women, like other disadvantaged groups, face a threat to their group identity. Comparisons between women and men, particularly on status-related dimensions (compensation, position in organizational hierarchy), indicate that women as a group are doing less well than men are. From a social identity perspective, when such identity threats are understood as resulting from illegitimate discrimination, women will be more likely to identify with women as a group and act on its behalf (Schmitt, Branscombe, Kobrynowicz, & Owen, 2002; Tajfel, 1978). In other words, women and members of other disadvantaged groups are likely to act in the interests of their group identities the more that they perceive the social context as illegitimately organized along group lines. Under these conditions, the more that intergroup comparisons suggest that the outcomes are different for women and men, with women being at a disadvantage, the more that women are likely to act on behalf of women as a group. Conversely, if comparisons between women and men suggest that opportunities for upward mobility are afforded equally to women and men, women will be more likely to focus on their individual outcomes rather than on those of women as a whole.

Thus, the most basic requirement for a group-based response to disadvantage is the perception that status and resources are denied in-group members solely on the basis of group membership. Indeed, women who perceive that their opportunities for advancement are hindered by pervasive gender discrimination express stronger gender group identification than do women who perceive gender discrimination as an isolated occurrence (Gurin & Townsend, 1986; Schmitt et al., 2002). Furthermore, experimental research has confirmed that perceived discrimination has a causal effect on minority group identification (Jetten, Branscombe, Schmitt, & Spears, 2001).

Although intergroup comparisons of organizational outcomes can suggest lower status and a negative identity for women, they have different implications for men's gender identity. For men, intergroup comparisons tend to affirm their group identity, as men tend to be favored in terms of organizational outcomes. Conversely, men's gender group identity is threatened when women are gaining in status and entering traditionally masculine domains, thus directly challenging men's positive distinctiveness on dimensions highly relevant to dominant constructions of men's group identity (Schmitt, Ellemers, et al., 2003). From a social identity theory perspective, perceptions of shrinking status differences will encourage men to identify with their gender in-group and attempt to protect its status and identity (Turner & Brown, 1978). Indeed, in experimental contexts, members of high-status groups tend to report greater group identification when members of lower status groups have the opportunity to join the ranks of the high-status group (Ellemers, Doosje, van Knippenberg, & Wilke, 1992).

Thus, social identity theory suggests that comparisons of the status differences between women and men are important determinants of whether women and men will respond as individuals on the basis of their personal interests, or as group members acting on behalf of their gender in-group. We focus on two processes that can result in perceptions of relative gender egalitarianism with no meaningful changes to gender relations: the observation of token progress for women, and the framing of contemporary gender inequality in comparison with the past. We argue that both processes blur the status differences between women and men and make opportunities for upward mobility appear equally afforded to women and men. We first review recent evidence that tokenism and comparisons with the past do affect the outcome of intergroup comparisons, specifically by reducing perceptions of gender inequality. We then explore the consequences of tokenism and comparisons with the past on women's and men's emotional responses and psychological well-being, degree of gender group identification, and collective action.

TOKEN ADVANCES FOR WOMEN
AND PERCEPTIONS OF GENDER INEQUALITY

Some of the most visible advances and achievements by individual women reflect token progress that does little to affect the status of women as a group. A number of high-status positions, occupations, and stereotypically male-dominated areas are characterized by tokenism as only a small minority of women have actually advanced into these positions. The success of these token women is often touted as an indicator of women's progress. Although the number of women in the highest levels of management in U.S.-based companies has indeed increased, women occupy only about 15% of all corporate officer positions (Catalyst, 2006; see also chap. 2, this volume), and these positions are often limited to relatively small companies (Bertrand & Hallock, 2001). Women have also broken into many traditionally male-dominated occupations, but the representation of women in many of these fields remains low, ranging from only about 3% of firefighters to 25% of physicians in the United States (Caiazza, Shaw, & Werschkul, 2004). These small numbers do indicate an increase in representation compared with the past, allowing women to have some representation in positions of high status and power. Nonetheless, these changes directly affect only a minority of women, and progress toward increasing women's representation beyond tokenism has been slow. For example, a Catalyst (2006) report projected that at the current rate of change, it will take at least 70 years for men and women to reach equity in high-level positions in U.S. corporations.

Much of the existing research on tokenism concerns the social and psychological consequences of being a member of a highly underrepresented group. In her initial theorizing on tokenism, Kanter (1977) argued that the rarity of the minority group leads to increased performance pressures for and increased stereotyping of token individuals. Indeed, compared with women who are more equally represented, token women are more likely to experience gender discrimination (Redersdorff, Martinot, & Branscombe, 2004), receive lower evaluations from male subordinates (Eagly, Makhijani, & Klonsky,

1992; Lyness & Heilman, 2006), and generally experience less career success (Heilman & Okimoto, 2007; Stroh, Langlands, & Simpson, 2004). Token hires also tend to be perceived negatively by other members of the organization (Heilman, Block, & Lucas, 1992; Yoder & Berendsen, 2001). Persons explicitly hired as token representatives risk marginalization by coworkers (Fuegen & Biernat, 2002) that can undermine performance (Brown, Cervero, & Johnson-Bailey, 2000). More recent evidence suggests that the negative effects of tokenism emerge only when the token identity is a culturally low status group (Budig, 2002) entering a domain traditionally dominated by the high-status group (Barreto, Ellemers, & Palacios, 2004; McDonald, Toussaint, & Schweiger, 2004; Yoder, 1994). Indeed, although the effects of having a token identity are negative for women, male tokens in traditionally feminine occupations ride a "glass escalator" to the top—advancing more quickly than their female colleagues (Maume, 1999; Williams, 1992).

Tokenism by definition limits opportunities for women as a group, and simultaneously undermines the opportunities and performance of the few women who advance into token positions. Despite the clear negative implications for women in organizational contexts, tokenistic selection policies may nevertheless result in the perception that the organization is egalitarian—providing equal opportunities for advancement to women and men. Observing token successes may blur perceptions of current gender inequality and bolster beliefs concerning possibilities for individual advancement (see chap. 11, this volume; Wright, 1997). Thus, the advancement of a few token women into high-status positions may have important consequences for individuals' perceptions of gender inequality.

Although few researchers have examined how tokenism affects perceptions of intergroup inequality, a number of studies conducted by Wright and colleagues suggest that tokenism can undermine collective protest in response to discrimination (Wright, 1997; Wright & Taylor, 1998, 1999; Wright, Taylor, & Moghaddam, 1990)—what social identity theory would predict if tokenism does reduce the perception of gender inequality. To more directly investigate tokenism's effects on perceptions of gender inequality, Danaher and Branscombe (2008) examined whether tokenistic policies create a sense of egalitarianism and fairness. Women and men read about a fictitious company that was described as having a history of discrimination against women in hiring and promotion. Participants read about the company's new hiring policy and how this would affect the gender ratio within the company. Participants read that a new open policy would lead to an equal representation of women and men, that a closed policy would maintain the current ratio of 2% women, or that a tokenistic policy would lead to 10% women. As expected, the tokenistic policy did indeed lead to more optimistic assessments of gender equality than did the closed policy. Participants rated the company's hiring practices to be fair for women when it would lead to equal representation, and unfair when it would maintain the very low 2% representation of women. The tokenistic policy was rated as significantly more fair to women than was the closed policy, despite the fact that on the whole women would not be much better off under the tokenistic policy. Participants, regardless of gender, recognized the negative consequences of hiring practices for women under the closed policy, but the negative consequences were less obvious for participants considering a policy leading to only a token increase in women's representation.

The women in this study also perceived that their likelihood of promotion would vary with the company's hiring practices. Women believed that they would be more likely to be promoted under the open policy than under the tokenistic and closed policies. However, the tokenistic policy did boost women's expectations for promotion compared with the closed policy, even though such a restrictive policy would have only a small effect on women's overall advancement. It is interesting that men expressed equal optimism regarding their chances of promotion under the tokenistic and closed policies, but were more pessimistic under the open policy. These findings suggest that tokenism might make future success seem more plausible for women without threatening men's beliefs about their future success.

In a subsequent study (Danaher & Branscombe, 2008), female undergraduates read an information sheet about their university's Board of Regents stating that it was composed of an equal ratio of women to men (open), a 1:9 ratio of women to men (tokenistic), or no women (closed). This study examined whether women who were exposed to token representation would recognize the injustice experienced by their gender group and whether they would continue to believe in the idea that "hard work pays off." Female participants who had read about the gender composition of the Board of Regents as either open, closed, or tokenistic later reported their endorsement of meritocractic beliefs (e.g., "All people have equal opportunity to be financially successful," "Effort is the largest component of success"). When no women were represented on the Board, participants did express lower endorsement of meritocracy compared with when there was at least some representation of women. Also, participants facing tokenistic representation endorsed meritocracy to the same degree as did women with equal representation. Although disparities are inherent in tokenistic systems, those women who were exposed to tokenism continued to believe that hard work pays off.

In summary, despite offering limited opportunities for women's advancement, tokenism can make gender relations appear more egalitarian—sometimes as egalitarian as truly open systems are. From a social identity theory perspective, these perceptions of relative equality can have consequences for emotions, identity, and willingness to challenge gender inequality. Before exploring these consequences, however, we first address another set of rose-colored glasses that make gender inequality less visible: comparisons with the past.

COMPARISONS WITH THE PAST
AND PERCEPTIONS OF GENDER INEQUALITY

Although tokenism has benefited a fortunate few women, on some dimensions progress has affected women more generally (see chap. 2, this volume). In the United States, for example, women obtained voting rights in 1919, and women's voting rates typically outnumber men's (Center for American Women and Politics, 2005). Women have also gained broad protections of their civil liberties, such as the Civil Rights Act of 1964. Title IX, passed in 1975, guaranteed women and girls equal opportunity in education, including sports, and women's rates of participation in both higher education and athletic endeavors have steadily increased. Since the early 1980s, women have constituted the majority of undergraduates, and the percentage of women seeking post-baccalaureate degrees has also increased (Freeman, 2004). Women are working outside the home in higher rates, and women's compensation for their work has also increased such that there has been a steady, albeit slow, decline in the gender wage gap (Dey & Hill, 2007). In addition, antiharassment and antidiscrimination laws and policies have improved the quality of women's work environments (Equal Employment Opportunity Commission, 2007). Stereotypes of women have also changed, so that in addition to being seen as communal, women are seen as increasingly agentic (Diekman & Eagly, 2000), reflecting women's entrance into traditionally masculine roles requiring more stereotypically masculine traits.

Although there are numerous examples of women's progress as a group, women's status has certainly not improved uniformly across all contexts. Indeed, in several domains women have actually lost status in recent years. For example, recent court cases and legislation in the United States have limited women's reproductive rights (Stevens, 2007) and women's ability to file sex discrimination cases (Andronici, 2007; see chap. 8, this volume). Even with some improvements, such as the lessening wage gap, women continue to be at greater risk of becoming poor than are men (Agency for Healthcare Research and Quality, 2005) and receive less compensation for comparable paid work (Dey & Hill, 2007). Thus, other changes, such as cuts in welfare and government-sponsored health and retirement programs, disproportionately harm women. When thinking about what progress women have achieved, one must keep in mind that improvements in status have not been equally granted to different groups of women. Ethnic minority women and women of lower socioeconomic status continue to face discrimination and inadequate access to quality health care (Agency for Healthcare Research and Quality, 2005), access to quality education, and overall ability to accumulate wealth (Ohlemacher, 2006). Finally, women in developing countries often face the challenge of meeting basic needs, such as access to clean water and adequate shelter as well as protection from violence.

However, despite such evidence of stagnation and regression, media and cultural representations tend to focus on women's advances (e.g., Women's History Month), contributing to a widely shared belief that members of disadvantaged groups are doing better compared even with the recent past (Pew Research Center, 2005). Thus, when gender inequality is framed in comparison with the past, contemporary gender relations will appear relatively egalitarian, such that when women in the present are compared with their counterparts in the past they will appear to be doing fairly well. In this comparative context, women and men in the present appear quite similar to each other in status relative to the low status of women of the past (Turner, Hogg, Oakes, Reicher, & Wetherell, 1987). Similar effects of comparative context have been observed for judgments of racial inequality. Eibach and Ehrlinger (2006) found that both Black and White Americans perceived greater progress toward racial equality when progress was framed in comparison with the past compared with when progress was framed in comparison with an ideal standard of complete racial equality.

Although the implications of comparisons with the past have been considered infrequently, social identity theory does highlight other comparative processes that have similar implications (Tajfel & Turner, 1979). For example, women might shift from comparing themselves with men to comparing their position with that of a different out-group that is lower in status, such as women in countries characterized by more gender inequality than is one's own country (Major, 1993). Disadvantaged groups may also enhance their social identity by shifting the focus of comparison to dimensions on which the group is positively distinct. Women can respond to their lower status by emphasizing comparison dimensions on which gender stereotypes suggest women are positively distinct (e.g., nurturance). In a similar manner, focusing on even trivial advantages afforded to women (e.g., a man opening a door for a woman) can protect women's evaluation of their gender group (Branscombe, 1998). We suggest that comparisons with women's low status in the past might similarly protect women's gender group identity by obscuring discrimination in the present.

To explore these ideas, Spoor and Schmitt (2008) conducted three experiments to examine whether framing women's status in a comparative context that emphasized women's progress over time (i.e., a temporal comparison) would depress perceptions of contemporary gender inequality relative to framing women's status in comparison with that of contemporary men (i.e., an intergroup comparison). Participants in all studies were randomly assigned to either an intergroup or a temporal comparison condition. In the first two studies, participants in the intergroup condition read statements describing inequality between men and women today, such as women's underrepresentation in high-status jobs, overrepresentation in low-status jobs, and the current gender wage gap. In the temporal condition, participants read statements describing how women's status today is better than women's status in the past, such as women's increase in wages over time and increase in college attendance. In both conditions, participants read statements adapted from credible sources such as the U.S. Census Bureau and Department of Labor. The manipulation in the third study was similar except that participants were asked to generate their own examples of each comparative context (i.e., either women's treatment compared with men today or women's treatment today compared with women's treatment in the past).

Following the temporal or intergroup comparison manipulation, participants completed questionnaire measures assessing their perceptions of contemporary gender inequality. Participants in all studies completed items from the modern sexism scale (Swim, Aikin, Hall, & Hunter, 1995) focusing on whether women experience gender discrimination in the present. For this measure, a similar pattern emerged in all three studies, such that participants who made comparisons with the past perceived less discrimination against contemporary women than did participants who made intergroup comparisons, and there was no evidence that this effect was moderated by participant gender. In Study 1, Spoor and Schmitt (2008) asked participants to complete a measure of public collective self-esteem (Luhtanen & Crocker, 1992). Women who engaged in comparisons with the past indicated that women were more respected than women who had thought only of intergroup comparisons did. In contrast, men perceived that men as a group were less respected after engaging in comparisons with the past than in intergroup comparisons. Thus, when they focused their comparisons on women's progress over time, both men and women appeared to perceive that women face less gender discrimination.

Moreover, in the second study, participants provided estimates of the frequency with which they personally would experience gender discrimination during the next month (e.g., once per week, several times per day). As shown in Figure 3.1, women who made comparisons with the past estimated that they would experience little gender discrimination, especially when compared with women who made intergroup comparisons. In contrast, men who made temporal comparisons estimated that they would experience more gender discrimination than did men who made intergroup comparisons. Men typically report experiencing less discrimination than do women (e.g., Schmitt et al., 2002), but after making comparisons with the past, women and men report equal expectations for encountering discrimination.

Taken together, the results of these studies suggest that framing gender inequality in comparison with the past leads to the perception of less inequality in the present. Thus, like tokenism, comparisons with the past provide a set of rose-colored glasses that make the present social context appear relatively fair and open. In the remainder of the chapter, we consider the consequences of tokenism and comparisons with the past for emotions and well-being, identity, and collective action.

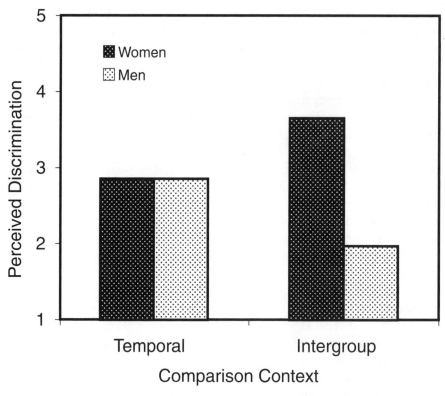

Figure 3.1. Women's and men's estimates of the frequency of experiencing gender discrimination after temporal and intergroup comparisons. Responses were given on 1 through 7 scales such that higher numbers correspond to higher estimated frequency of experiencing discrimination.

CONSEQUENCES FOR EMOTIONS AND WELL-BEING

Both tokenism and comparisons with the past make gender relations appear more egalitarian. From a social identity perspective, these perceptions have important consequences for the positive distinctiveness of women's and men's gender group identities. For women, increased perceptions of egalitarianism should be relatively affirming, whereas perceptions of lower status and limited opportunities for advancement should be experienced as threats. With respect to gender group inequality, prior research has demonstrated that women who perceive that gender discrimination is pervasive exhibit more negative emotional consequences than do those who perceive that discrimination is rare (Schmitt, Branscombe, & Postmes, 2003). Thus, women exposed to tokenism or comparisons with the past feel less threatened relative to contexts in which women's lower status is clearer (Ellemers, van Knippenberg, & Wilke, 1990; Schmitt, Branscombe, et al., 2003, Schmitt et al., 2002).

In contrast, perceptions of increasing gender egalitarianism threaten men's status and power. To the extent that men's gender group identity is based on having greater power and status than women (Kilmartin, 1994), the perception of decreased gender inequality and the entrance of women in greater numbers into traditionally male-dominated domains threaten the positive distinctiveness of their group. Indeed, Diekman and Goodfriend (2006) found that men tend to evaluate women's entry into traditionally masculine domains less favorably than do women, and Branscombe (1998) suggested that men's claims of reverse discrimination often derive from a sense of disadvantage relative to the privileged status position of men in the past.

In their study of open, tokenistic, and closed hiring policies in a historically sexist organization, Danaher and Branscombe (2008) also examined men and women's self-esteem (using the Single Item Self-Esteem Scale; Robins, Hendin, & Trzesniewski, 2001). As shown in Figure 3.2, women reported

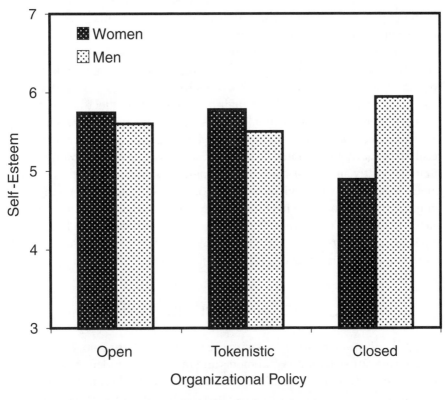

Figure 3.2. Women's and men's self-esteem after exposure to open, tokenistic, and closed organizations. Responses were given on 1 through 7 scales such that higher numbers correspond to higher self-esteem.

similar levels of self-esteem after reading about tokenistic or open policies, and significantly higher self-esteem compared with women who read about the closed policy. Men, however, reported similarly high levels of self-esteem regardless of the hiring policy. Thus, hiring policy had little effect on men's personal well-being. However, for women, the token policies did not threaten self-esteem in the same way a closed policy would, even though women's status would remain low.

In a similar manner, Spoor and Schmitt (2008, Study 2) found that framing gender inequality in comparison with the past led to different emotional responses in women and men. After reading the temporal or intergroup comparison facts, participants indicated the extent to which they experienced threat-related emotions (e.g., tense, worried) when thinking about themselves as a member of their gender group. In line with our reasoning that men's gender identity is threatened by considerations of women's advancement compared with the past, men tended to report more threat-related emotions after making comparisons with the past than after making intergroup comparisons. Women, as predicted, reported lower levels of threat-related emotions after comparisons with the past than after intergroup comparisons. This same pattern was replicated in Spoor and Schmitt's third study in which participants generated their own examples of either intergroup or temporal comparisons.

Focusing on token advances and broad advances for women compared with the past obscures perceptions of existing gender inequality, reflected in women's more positive affective reactions to such contexts. Organizations may have a particular interest in maintaining positive affect and reducing negative affect among employees (Fredrickson & Losada, 2005) because negative affective reactions are often associated with poor work outcomes. These results suggest that occasional promotions and advancements by women may improve positive affect, at least among women. Unfortunately, these effects might be obtained with policies that give only the appearance of change and progress, the net positive effect for women being negligible. Further complicating matters for organizations trying to keep their workforce happy, the appearance of progress has positive affective implications for women but may lead to more negative affective outcomes for men.

CONSEQUENCES FOR GROUP IDENTIFICATION

Tokenism and comparisons with the past have differing implications for the positive distinctiveness of women's and men's gender identities and, as a consequence, the extent to which women and men are likely to identify with their group. Prior research has demonstrated that threats to a group's status result in increased identification with the devalued group (Branscombe, Schmitt, & Harvey, 1999), particularly when the threats are perceived as illegitimate (e.g., Tajfel, 1978; Turner, Hogg, Turner, & Smith, 1984). Thus, factors that reduce perceptions of inequality, such as tokenism and comparisons with the past, undermine women's motivation to come together in support of the group. Indeed, in contexts in which individual social mobility appears possible, members of low-status groups tend to distance themselves from the in-group and select strategies aimed at individual mobility (Ellemers, 1993; Tajfel & Turner, 1979; Wright & Taylor, 1998). Although tokenism and comparisons with the past might undermine women's gender group identification, they may have the opposite effect on men's identities. Because men are likely to perceive reductions in status differences between women and men as threatening the positive distinctiveness of their in-group, they may feel a stronger connection to their gender in contexts that appear increasingly egalitarian.

In their research, Spoor and Schmitt (2008, Studies 2 and 3) tested whether comparisons with the past would have opposite implications for the strength of gender identification in women and men. After either making intergroup comparisons of contemporary gender inequality or comparing women's current status with that of women in the past, participants completed measures of gender identification (e.g., My gender group is an important reflection of who I am), adapted from existing measures of group identification (Cameron, 2004; Luhtanen & Crocker, 1992). In line with predictions, Spoor and Schmitt (2008) found that compared with participants making intergroup comparisons, women tended to report weaker gender identification after a temporal comparison, whereas men tended to report stronger gender identification after a temporal comparison. Thus, comparisons with the past seemed to depress gender group identification among women while encouraging stronger identification among men.

In addition to affecting gender group identification, perceived gender inequality might also affect women's identification with the organization or institution in which the relevant gender relations take place. In response to clear discrimination, women are likely to disidentify with the superordinate identity in which they are subordinated (see chap. 7, this volume). For example, women and minorities who perceive greater discrimination in the workplace typically report less job satisfaction and commitment to their organization (Ensher, Grant-Vallone, & Donaldson, 2001) as well as stronger intentions to leave the organization (Shaffer, Joplin, Bell, Lau, & Oguz, 2000). Thus, by decreasing perceptions of inequality, tokenism might encourage and maintain identification with the organization in which they are underrepresented. Evidence from research using laboratory-created groups supports these expectations. Reynolds, Oakes, Haslam, Nolan, and Dolnik (2000) asked participants to report their perceptions of both their low-status in-group and the high-status out-group. Members of the low-status in-group described the higher status out-group with negative traits when the high-status group denied entry to all of the lower status group, regardless of deservingness. However, when the high-status group adopted a policy of allowing a few tokens entrance into the high-status group, the low-status group endorsed positive stereotypes of the advantaged group.

In their study of gender-based tokenism within a historically male-dominated company, Danaher and Branscombe (2008) found that tokenistic policies protected positive impressions of the company in terms of the participants' ratings of the company's vice president (who was described as responsible for the new hiring policy). Women liked the vice president least when the hiring practices were described as closed. Women's liking of the vice president did not differ between the open and token policies. Men, however, rated the vice president as equally likable regardless of hiring policy. A semblance of progress for women in the form of tokenism led to relatively favorable evaluations of the organization's leadership, even though inequality still existed.

In their subsequent study of tokenism in university governance, Danaher and Branscombe (2008) found that when participants were asked to imagine being appointed to a vacant position on the board, tokenism influenced women's organizational identities, specifically their identification with their university's board of regents. Women presented with a closed system reported less identification with the board compared with women who were presented with open and tokenistic systems and who reported similar levels of identification. An apparent advancement for women, although hardly equal to the status of men, maintained women's identification with the discriminating organization. In sum, focusing on women's progress in the form of tokenism or broad advances may decrease women's identification with their own group (Spoor & Schmitt, 2008) while increasing identification with a group that may be discriminating against them (Danaher & Branscombe, 2008).

CONSEQUENCES FOR COLLECTIVE ACTION

By lowering perceptions of contemporary inequalities, observing women's progress in terms of token successes and comparisons with the past is likely to undermine attempts to further reduce inequality. Of course, people need to perceive inequality before they can begin to collectively act against it (see chap. 5, this volume). Indeed, for precisely this reason, managers of organizations might feel compelled to strategically engage in tokenism or frame the status of women in comparison with the past. From a social identity perspective (Tajfel & Turner, 1979), women are more likely to collectively challenge their low-status position the more that they see outcomes and treatment to be determined by gender group membership. As both tokenism and comparisons with the past can create the appearance of egalitarianism, they are likely to discourage collective responses by women.

In their studies of tokenism, Wright and colleagues (Wright, 1997; Wright et al., 1990; Wright & Taylor, 1998, 1999) examined the behavioral responses of disadvantaged groups. The experimental paradigm for these studies was such that members of a disadvantaged group believed that, depending on their performance and abilities, they would be able to join a higher status group (see Wright, 2001, for a review). Some participants were told that the high-status group subsequently imposed new and unfair standards that limited the disadvantaged group members' mobility, and participants believed that they personally would have to remain in the disadvantaged group. Participants then indicated their behavioral preferences in response to these organizational contexts. Consistent with social identity theory, participants who learned that no members of the lower status group would have an opportunity to advance into the higher status group were most likely to choose collective behaviors aimed at changing the intergroup context. In contrast, when just a few members of the low-status group would be given an opportunity to advance, participants preferred responses specific to improving one's individual position. The presence of token mobility undermined interest in collective action for members of the disadvantaged group.

From a social identity perspective, collective self-definition is a necessary precursor to collective action. Identification with the disadvantaged group is often a crucial link in increasing support for collective responses (Kelly & Breinlinger, 1996; Klandermans, 1997). For example, Duncan (1999) demonstrated that feminist consciousness mediated the relationship between personal experiences with discrimination and participation in feminist activism. In the previous section, we discussed evidence that observing progress depresses group identification among women. By undermining women's identification with women as a group, observing women's progress is likely to reduce willingness to support collective action aimed at improving the group's position.

Just as observing token successes may undermine collective responses, focusing on progress in the form of comparisons with the past may similarly decrease women's interest in collective action. At this point the research literature has not directly addressed this issue. However, a study by Spoor (2008) examined the consequences of temporal and intergroup comparisons on a related outcome: women's support for feminist ideologies. As a social change ideology, feminism is closely related to interest in collective action. After reading temporal or intergroup comparison statements adapted from Spoor and Schmitt (2008), women indicated whether they labeled themselves a feminist as well as their support for liberal feminist ideologies more broadly (Morgan, 1996). As expected, women were less likely to label themselves a feminist after a temporal rather than an intergroup comparison. An interesting additional finding, however, was that this effect emerged only for women who scored relatively high in gender group identification (on a pretest measure completed several weeks before). In contrast, women who had initially reported relatively weak gender group identification reported similar levels of endorsement of the feminist label regardless of the kind of comparisons they made. Similar results were found on the measure of support for feminist ideologies. This study provides preliminary evidence that temporal comparisons may undermine support for collective forms of self-definition that precede collective action. Furthermore, the results suggest that gender group identification, in addition to functioning as a mediator between perceptions of gender inequality and responses to it (Duncan, 1999), can also moderate how women respond to inequality. The results suggest that comparisons with the past have the strongest effect on highly identified women—undermining interest in collective action among those women who would otherwise be supportive of it (Kelly & Breinlinger, 1996; Klandermans, 1997).

OBSERVING WOMEN'S PROGRESS
THROUGH DIFFERENT NARRATIVE LENSES

The research that we have reviewed suggests that observing women's progress (through token advancement or comparisons with the past) may undermine the potential for additional progress by reducing the likelihood that women will perceive inequality and threats to their gender group identity, identify with women as a group, and engage in collective protest on women's behalf. Organizational leaders may use tokenism and comparisons with the past to reduce political unrest and decrease the likelihood of collective action on the part of lower status groups (Jackman, 1994). Furthermore, men may be able to capitalize on the contentment of low-status groups as a way of protecting their own high status. Thus, managers of organizations marked by inequality in the present may prefer to focus on a worse past or an optimistic future because such comparative contexts may help to keep the lower status group content, reinforce a belief that the world is fair, and legitimize the group hierarchy. However, the consequences of perceiving progress are not inevitable, and likely depend on the narrative used to explain how progress came about and how it might continue.

For example, women's progress could be attributed to women's collective action, concessions by men, or the natural course of time. Spoor and Schmitt (2008) suggested that women who attribute reductions in gender inequality to women's collective action might be more likely to increase solidarity with their group. If women's progress is attributed to the natural course of time (i.e., a belief that progress and equality are inevitable), however, the implication is that status differences will continue to decrease without collective action, and low-status group members would have little reason to identify with and assist their group (see Ellemers, 1993). Reactions to progress may also be influenced by whether group members expect the current trajectory of progress to continue into the future. In terms of their individual histories, people have a tendency to view their own past in terms of a combination of positive and negative events (and correspondingly mixed emotions), whereas they tend to see their own future in optimistic terms (Ross & Newby-Clark, 1998). In the context of women's progress, there may be a tendency to perceive that progress will continue even without collective action. Thus, reminding women of the role of collective action in women's progress might allow for evidence of progress to be used as inspiration for further change rather than a reason for passive acceptance.

Furthermore, conditions may exist under which people can come to recognize tokenism, comparisons with the past, and other strategies that minimize perceptions of inequality as discursive and structural practices that undermine collective resistance to lower status. In experimental research, Wright (1997) demonstrated that disadvantaged group members showed an interest in collective resistance to tokenism only when other members of the disadvantaged group expressed anger toward the high-status group and labeled the tokenism as discrimination. In a similar manner, women might come to recognize the ways in which comparisons with the past can be used to undermine their collective interests, and thus be less susceptible to these consequences. Indeed, we hope that this chapter helps to uncover the ways in which such rose-colored glasses are used strategically to undermine the interests of women and other disadvantaged groups.

Although tokenism may have the consequence of masking gender inequalities, the existence of tokenism as a phenomenon does represent progress compared with times past when the presence of even one woman in traditionally male-dominated domains was unthinkable to many. Even in contexts that might eventually achieve gender equality, token representation may exist at some stage, as the context moves from no representation to equal representation of women. In a similar way, although comparisons with the past undermine perceptions of contemporary inequality, they do so because gender inequality has been reduced in a number of ways. Thus, comparisons with the past cannot be ignored or disregarded. However, those who wish to promote gender equality would be advised to respond to token representation and comparisons with the past with reminders of the ways in which gender inequality exists in the present. Indeed, Tougas, Beaton, and Veilleux (1991) found that women endorsed stricter affirmative action policies when it was made clear that the current policies failed to meet intended goals (see also chap. 11, this volume). In a similar way, an emphasis on higher order goals of equality may also serve as a reminder that inequality exists and sustain an interest in social change (Eibach & Ehrlinger, 2006).

Finally, we should also note that although low-status group members may be more accepting of current inequality if they foresee a favorable future (e.g., more equality and better outcomes), this rosy future may actually motivate high-status group members to engage in collective action to protect their position. Indeed, members of advantaged groups are much less likely to support social programs that work against their group's status, especially if they have direct experience with the program (Garcia, Desmarais, Branscombe, & Gee, 2005). Spoor and Schmitt (2008) similarly found that men expressed more anxiety and increased their gender group identification after temporal framing of gender inequality, suggesting that observing women's progress was threatening to men. Thus, those attempting to promote social change to improve women's status need to consider not only those factors that lead to collective mobilization among women, but also those factors that encourage men to concede their privileges (Schmitt, Ellemers, et al., 2003).

CONCLUSION

The glass-ceiling metaphor has helped women and men to recognize gender discrimination in organizations and society in general. This very recognition has led to advancements by specific women, as well as progress for women as a group, and thus there have been striking examples of victories for women and women breaking through the glass ceiling. However, the research that we have reviewed in this chapter suggests that these advancements may have the ironic effect of maintaining the glass ceiling and rendering the barriers even more invisible. Thus, a challenge for future research, and for anyone interested in achieving gender equality, is to improve our understanding of how movement toward gender inequality can occur with masking remaining inequalities and thus deterring further progress.

REFERENCES

Agency for Healthcare Research and Quality. (2005). *Women's health care in the United States: Selected findings from the 2004 National Healthcare Quality and Disparities Reports*. AHRQ Fact Sheet Publication No. 05-P021. Retrieved January 16, 2008, from http://www.ahrq.gov/qual/nhqrwomen/nhqrwomen.htm

Andronici, J. (2007). *Court gives OK to unequal pay*. Retrieved August 3, 2007, from http://www.msmagazine.com/summer2007/ledbetter.asp

Barreto, M., Ellemers, N., & Palacios, M. S. (2004). The backlash of token mobility: The impact of past group experiences on individual ambition and effort. *Personality and Social Psychology Bulletin, 30*, 1433–1445.

Bertrand, M., & Hallock, K. F. (2001). The gender gap in top corporate jobs. *Industrial and Labor Relations Review, 55*, 3–21.

Branscombe, N. R. (1998). Thinking about one's gender group's privileges or disadvantages: Consequences for well-being in women and men. *British Journal of Social Psychology, 37*, 167–184.

Branscombe, N. R., Schmitt, M. T., & Harvey, R. D. (1999). Perceiving pervasive discrimination among African-Americans: Implications for group identification and well-being. *Journal of Personality and Social Psychology, 77*, 135–149.

Brown, A. H., Cervero, R. M., & Johnson-Bailey, J. (2000). Making the invisible visible: Race, gender and teaching in adult education. *Adult Education Quarterly, 50*, 273–288.

Budig, M. J. (2002). Male advantage and the gender composition of jobs: Who rides the glass elevator? *Social Problems, 49*, 258–277.

Caiazza, A., Shaw, A., & Werschkul, M. (2004). *Women's economic disparity in the states: Wide disparities by race, ethnicity, and region.* Washington, DC: Institute for Women's Policy Research.

Cameron, J. E. (2004). A three-factor model of social identity. *Self and Identity, 3*, 239–262.

Catalyst. (2006). *2006 Catalyst census of women corporate officers, top earners, and directors of the Fortune 500.* Retrieved June 28, 2007, from http://www.catalyst.org/publication/18/2006-catalyst-census-of-women-corporate-officers-and-top-earners-of-the-fortune-500

Center for American Women and Politics. (2005, June). *Sex differences in voter turnout.* Retrieved June 28, 2007, from http://www.cawp.rutgers.edu/Facts/Elections/Womensvote2004.html

Danaher, K. A., & Branscombe, N. R. (2008). *Maintaining the system: Bolstering of advancement beliefs and positive perceptions of the discriminatory organization under token conditions.* Unpublished manuscript.

Dey, J. G., & Hill, C. (2007). *Behind the pay gap.* Washington, DC: American Association of University Women Educational Foundation.

Diekman, A. B., & Eagly, A. H. (2000). Stereotypes as dynamic constructs: Women and men of the past, present, and future. *Personality and Social Psychology Bulletin, 26*, 1171–1188.

Diekman, A. B., & Goodfriend, W. (2006). Rolling with the changes: A role congruity perspective on gender norms. *Psychology of Women Quarterly, 30*, 369–383.

Duncan, L. E. (1999). Motivation for collective action: Group consciousness as mediator of personality, life experiences, and women's rights activism. *Political Psychology, 20*, 611–635.

Eagly, A. H., Makhijani, M. G., & Klonsky, B. G. (1992). Gender and the evaluation of leaders: A meta-analysis. *Psychological Bulletin, 111*, 3–22.

Eibach, R. P., & Ehrlinger, J. (2006). "Keep your eyes on the prize": Reference points and racial differences in assessing progress toward equality. *Personality and Social Psychology Bulletin, 32*, 66–77.

Ellemers, N. (1993). The influence on socio-structural variables on identity management strategies. *European Review of Social Psychology, 4*, 27–58.

Ellemers, N., Doosje, B. J., van Knippenberg, A., & Wilke, H. A. (1992). Status protection in high status minority groups. *European Journal of Social Psychology, 22*, 123–140.

Ellemers, N., van Knippenberg, A., & Wilke, H. A. (1990). The influence of permeability of group boundaries and stability of group status on strategies of individual mobility and social change. *British Journal of Social Psychology, 29,* 233–246.

Ensher, E. A., Grant-Vallone, E. J., & Donaldson, S. I. (2001). Effects of perceived discrimination on job satisfaction, organizational commitment, organizational citizenship behavior, and grievances. *Human Resource Development Quarterly, 12,* 53–72.

Equal Employment Opportunity Commission. (2007). *Sex-based discrimination.* Retrieved January 16, 2008, from http://www.eeoc.gov/types/sex.html

Fredrickson, B. L., & Losada, M. F. (2005). Positive affect and the complex dynamics of human flourishing. *American Psychologist, 60,* 678–686.

Freeman, C. E. (2004). *Trends in educational equity of girls & women: 2004* (NCES 2005–016). U.S. Department of Education National Center for Education Statistics. Washington, DC: U.S. Government Printing Office.

Fuegen, K., & Biernat, M. (2002). Reexamining the effects of solo status for women and men. *Personality and Social Psychology Bulletin, 28,* 913–925.

Garcia, D. M., Desmarais, S., Branscombe, N. R., & Gee, S. S. (2005). Opposition to redistributive employment policies for women: Principled objection, contemporary sexism, or group interest? *British Journal of Social Psychology, 44,* 583–602.

Gurin, P., & Townsend, A. (1986). Properties of gender identity and their implications for gender consciousness. *British Journal of Social Psychology, 25,* 139–148.

Heilman, M. E., Block, C. J., & Lucas, J. A. (1992). Presumed incompetent? Stigmatization and affirmative action efforts. *Journal of Applied Psychology, 77,* 536–544.

Heilman, M. E., & Okimoto, T. G. (2007). Why are women penalized for success at male tasks? The implied communality deficit. *Journal of Applied Psychology, 92,* 81–92.

Jackman, M. R. (1994). *The velvet glove: Paternalism and conflict in gender, class, and race relations.* Berkeley: University of California Press.

Jetten, J., Branscombe, N. R., Schmitt, M. T., & Spears, R. (2001). Rebels with a cause: Group identification as a response to perceived discrimination from the mainstream. *Personality and Social Psychology Bulletin, 27,* 1204–1213.

Kanter, R. M. (1977). Some effects of proportions on group life: Skewed sex ratios and responses to token women. *American Journal of Sociology, 82,* 965–990.

Kelly, C., & Breinlinger, S. (1996). *The social psychology of collective action: Identity, injustice and gender.* Philadelphia: Taylor & Francis.

Kilmartin, C. T. (1994). *The masculine self.* New York: Macmillan.

Klandermans, B. (1997). *The social psychology of protest.* Oxford, England: Basil Blackwell.

Luhtanen, R., & Crocker, J. (1992). A collective self-esteem scale: Self-evaluation of one's social identity. *Personality and Social Psychology Bulletin, 18,* 302–318.

Lyness, K. S., & Heilman, M. E. (2006). When fit is fundamental: Performance evaluations and promotions of upper-level female and male managers. *Journal of Applied Psychology, 91*, 777–785.

Major, B. (1993). Gender, entitlement, and the distribution of family labor. *Journal of Social Issues, 49*, 141–159.

Maume, D. J. (1999). Glass ceilings and glass escalators: Occupational segregation and race and sex differences in managerial promotions. *Work and Occupations, 26*, 483–509.

McDonald, T. W., Toussaint, L. L., & Schweiger, J. A. (2004). The influence of social status on token women leaders' expectations about leading male-dominated groups. *Sex Roles, 50*, 401–409.

Morgan, B. L. (1996). Putting the feminism into feminism scales: Introduction of a Liberal Feminism Attitude and Ideology Scale (LFAIS). *Sex Roles, 34*, 359–390.

Ohlemacher, S. (2006, November 14). Persistent race disparities found: Minorities still lag in income, education, Census data show. *The Washington Post*. Retrieved January 16, 2008, from http://www.washingtonpost.com/wp-dyn/content/article/2006/11/13/AR2006111301114.html

Pelosi, N. (2007, January 4). *Pelosi calls for a new America built on the values that made our country great*. Retrieved August 3, 2007, from http://speaker.gov/newsroom/speeches?id=0006

Pew Research Center. (2005, January). *Politics and values in a 51%-48% nation: National security more linked with partisan affiliation*. Retrieved August 3, 2007, from http://people-press.org/reports/display.php3?ReportID=236

Redersdorff, S., Martinot, D., & Branscombe, N. R. (2004). The impact of thinking about group-based disadvantages or advantages on women's well-being: An experimental test of the rejection-identification model. *Cahiers de Psychologie Cognitive/Current Psychology of Cognition, 22*, 203–222.

Reynolds, K. J., Oakes, P. J., Haslam, S. A., Nolan, M. A., & Dolnik, L. (2000). Responses to powerlessness: Stereotyping as an instrument of social conflict. *Group Dynamics, 4*, 275–290.

Robins, R. W., Hendin, H. M., & Trzesniewski, K. H. (2001). Measuring global self-esteem: Construct validation of a single-item measure and the Rosenberg Self-Esteem Scale. *Personality and Social Psychology Bulletin, 27*, 151–161.

Ross, M., & Newby-Clark, I. R. (1998). Construing the past and future. *Social Cognition, 16*, 133–150.

Schmitt, M. T., Branscombe, N. R., Kobrynowicz, D., & Owen, S. (2002). Perceiving discrimination against one's gender group has different implications for well-being in women and men. *Personality and Social Psychology Bulletin, 28*, 197–210.

Schmitt, M. T., Branscombe, N. R., & Postmes, T. (2003). Women's emotional responses to the pervasiveness of gender discrimination. *European Journal of Social Psychology, 33*, 297–312.

Schmitt, M. T., Ellemers, N., & Branscombe, N. R. (2003). Perceiving and responding to gender discrimination in organizations. In S. A. Haslam, D. van Knippenberg, M. J. Platow, & N. Ellemers (Eds.), *Social identity at work: Developing theory for organizational practice* (pp. 277–292). Philadelphia: Psychology Press.

Shaffer, M. A., Joplin, J. R. W., Bell, M. P., Lau, T., & Oguz, C. (2000). Gender discrimination and job-related outcomes: A cross-cultural comparison of working women in the United States and China. *Journal of Vocational Behavior, 57,* 395–427.

Spoor, J. R. (2008). [Effects of temporal comparisons on women's interest in collective action]. Unpublished raw data.

Spoor, J. R., & Schmitt, M. T. (2008). *It's about time? Affective and identity consequences of temporal comparisons of gender inequality.* Manuscript submitted for publication.

Stevens, A. (2007). *A major blow to Roe.* Retrieved August 3, 2007, from http://www.msmagazine.com/summer2007/blowtoroe.asp

Stroh, L. K., Langlands, C. L., & Simpson, P. A. (2004). Shattering the glass ceiling in the new millennium. In M. S. Stockdale & F. J. Crosby (Eds.), *The psychology and management of workplace diversity* (pp. 147–167). Malden, MA: Blackwell.

Swim, J. K., Aikin, K. J., Hall, W. S., & Hunter, B. A. (1995). Sexism and racism: Old-fashioned and modern prejudices. *Journal of Personality and Social Psychology, 68,* 199–214.

Tajfel, H. (1978). *The social psychology of minorities.* London: Minority Rights Group.

Tajfel, H., & Turner, J. C. (1979). An integrative theory of intergroup conflict. In W. G. Austin & S. Worchel (Eds.), *Psychology of intergroup relations* (2nd ed., pp. 7–24). Chicago: Nelson-Hall.

Tougas, F., Beaton, A. M., & Veilleux, F. (1991). Why women approve of affirmative action: The study of a predictive model. *International Journal of Psychology, 26,* 761–776.

Turner, J. C., & Brown, R. J. (1978). Social status, cognitive alternatives and intergroup relations. In H. Tajfel (Ed.), *Differentiation between social groups: Studies in the social psychology of intergroup relations* (pp. 201–234). London: Academic Press.

Turner, J. C., Hogg, M. A., Oakes, P. J., Reicher, S. D., & Wetherell, M. S. (1987). *Rediscovering the social group: A self-categorization theory.* New York: Blackwell.

Turner, J. C., Hogg, M. A., Turner, P. J., & Smith, P. M. (1984). Failure and defeat as determinants of group cohesiveness. *British Journal of Social Psychology, 23,* 97–111.

Williams, C. L. (1992). The glass escalator: Hidden advantages for men in the 'female' professions. *Social Problems, 39,* 253–267.

Wright, S. C. (1997). Ambiguity, social influence and collective action: Generating collective protest in response to tokenism. *Personality and Social Psychology Bulletin, 23,* 1277–1290.

Wright, S. C. (2001). Restricted intergroup boundaries: Tokenism, ambiguity, and the tolerance of injustice. In J. T. Jost & B. Major (Eds.), *The psychology of legitimacy: Emerging perspectives on ideology, justice, and intergroup relations* (pp. 223–254). New York: Cambridge University Press.

Wright, S. C., & Taylor, D. M. (1998). Responding to tokenism: Individual action in the face of injustice. *European Journal of Social Psychology, 28*, 647–667.

Wright, S. C., & Taylor, D. M. (1999). Success under tokenism: Co-option of the newcomer and the prevention of collective protest. *British Journal of Social Psychology, 38*, 369–396.

Wright, S. C., Taylor, D. M., & Moghaddam, F. M. (1990). Responding to membership in a disadvantaged group: From acceptance to collective protest. *Journal of Personality and Social Psychology, 58*, 994–1003.

Yoder, J. D. (1994). Looking beyond the numbers: The effects of gender status, job prestige, and occupational gender-typing on tokenism processes. *Social Psychology Quarterly, 57*, 150–159.

Yoder, J. D., & Berendsen, L. L. (2001). 'Outsider within' the firehouse: African American and White women firefighters. *Psychology of Women Quarterly, 25*, 27–36.

4

WARMTH, COMPETENCE, AND AMBIVALENT SEXISM: VERTICAL ASSAULT AND COLLATERAL DAMAGE

MINA CIKARA AND SUSAN T. FISKE

[Hillary Rodham Clinton's] most serious deficits are more personal than political. . . . She is notoriously thin-skinned, and her stony aloofness makes Al Gore and Bill Bradley look like Cheech and Chong.
—Clarence Page, *Chicago Tribune* (July 28, 2004)

I'm surprised they did a portrait of Hillary. I thought maybe an ice sculpture would have been more appropriate.
—Jay Leno, *The Tonight Show* (April 26, 2006)

Debate over the possibility of a female U.S. presidential candidate has centered on criticizing her lack of warmth; Margaret Thatcher, Indira Gandhi, and Golda Meir had the same problem. In contrast, debate over Harriet Miers as a potential U.S. Supreme Court nominee targeted her lack of competence. Rare is the successful woman who is seen as both brilliant and kind; male leaders have more often received such credit.

The glass ceiling blocks women's vertical progress up the ranks of the workplace, but in the past 20 years a great deal has been learned about the lateral side effects of gains in status and perceived competence. In this chapter we examine the more subtle consequences of vertical and lateral shifts within hierarchical social systems, focusing on how hostile and benevolent sexist ideologies promote power differences at work.

First, we review how prejudice, stereotyping, and discrimination stem from status systems and intergroup competition, according to the *stereotype content model* (SCM; Cuddy, Fiske, & Glick, 2008; Fiske, Cuddy, & Glick, 2007; Fiske, Cuddy, Glick, & Xu, 2002; Fiske, Xu, Cuddy, & Glick, 1999). We also examine the changing problems that women face as they gain status. Next, we consider the unique circumstances of gender relations used to justify gender inequality according to *ambivalent sexism theory* (AST; Glick & Fiske, 1996, 1999, 2001a, 2001b). Last, we review evidence to support our argument that benevolent and hostile ideologies guide individuals' responses to women in the workplace.

STATUS OF WOMEN IN THE WORKPLACE

By some accounts, women have closed the gender gap in the professional realm. In the United States, women constitute 46% of the paid labor force (U.S. Bureau of Labor Statistics, 2006a) and 50% of paid managers (U.S. Bureau of Labor Statistics, 2006b). In 2004, 51% of the bachelor degrees awarded in the United States went to women, as did 52% of advanced degrees, 35% of professional degrees, and 33% of doctorate degrees (U.S. Bureau of the Census, 2004). By contrast, in Fortune 500 companies, women represent only 4% of top officers, 3% of most highly paid officers, and 0.4% of CEOs (Catalyst, 2000). In the U.S. Congress, only 14% of senators and 15% of congressional representatives are women (Center for the American Woman and Politics, 2006). It is clear that the ratio of women in powerful leadership positions falls disturbingly short of the U.S. population's ratio.

Some origins of these disparities lie in the failure to reconcile stereotypic beliefs about women and stereotypic beliefs about people who hold elite positions (see also chap. 2, this volume). Similar to stereotypes about social groups, occupation stereotypes are seen as having well-defined gender and status dimensions. Participants' images of job types load on two orthogonal factors: prestige and gender type (Glick, Wilk, & Perreault, 1995). Specific gender-related attributes, however, sometimes load on the perceived occupational prestige factor instead of the gender-type factor. Even though the prestige and gender-type factors are orthogonal, masculine personality traits loaded on the occupational prestige factor, indicating that these attributes are more closely related to prestige than to perceived gender type of the job. Indeed, these masculine traits predict the prestige and salary of jobs (Glick, 1991). Thus, in hiring for a prestigious position, employers are more likely to value masculine qualities and therefore more likely to look for a man as the appropriate candidate (Heilman, 2001).

Gender is inextricably linked to prestige because gender stereotypes explicitly describe men's and women's status: men are imputed more status than are women. Inasmuch as people think gender category distinctions are rooted in biological underpinnings, most individuals believe not only that these distinctions are invariant over time and universal across cultures but also that the boundary distinctions are sharp and impervious to sociocultural influences (Haslam, Rothschild, & Ernst, 2000). To the extent such beliefs are shared, they are powerful. Status beliefs are particularly potent when both the dominant and the subordinate groups endorse them. High-status groups, of course, have an investment in the status quo, but, as we shall see, even low-status groups can be motivated to justify their social systems (Jost & Banaji, 1994). Given shared expectations about their competence, the dominant group maintains social power and access to resources because they are allegedly better qualified to perform in instrumental capacities (Carli, 1991; Ridgeway, 2001).

Cementing the link between gender and status, shared status beliefs are most likely to develop among groups who must cooperate with one another to get what they want (Glick & Fiske, 1999). Thus, because women and men are interdependent, women are nearly as likely as men to hold these status beliefs, in spite of their lower status position. As a result, we argue, women often cooperate in the existing status relation, when their self-interest might seem to lie elsewhere. We elaborate on the effect of these status beliefs when we review how they promote power differences in the workplace.

ORGANIZING BELIEFS ABOUT WOMEN IN AND OUT OF THE WORKPLACE

People like to have distinctive and positive group memberships (Tajfel & Turner, 1986). When boundaries between groups are impermeable and secure (as they are typically perceived to be in the case of gender relations), group identity and its boundaries engender in-group favoritism, which in turn reinforces the social categories of female and male (Ellemers, 1993; Hewstone, Rubin, & Willis, 2002). Favoritism involves resources, such that groups reserve resources for those they favor and withhold resources from those they derogate. Although evidence for in-group favoritism outweighs that for out-group derogation, in-group favoritism can hurt the out-group by exclusion. In particular, control over group images favors the powerful.

Some groups' favoritism matters more than that of other groups. A group's power derives from the value of the resource that the group controls in a given context (Fiske & Berdahl, 2007). For example, one social resource includes the reputation of a group or its members. Groups in power control intergroup reputations, in that their images carry more impact because the powerful also control other resources (e.g., money, access). The stereotypes people hold about various cultural groups thus manifest social power. Consider, for example, the generally positive evaluations of culturally dominant groups (e.g., the middle class, Christians) and the overtly negative evaluations of less culturally valued groups (e.g., the lower class, drug addicts).

Vertical and Lateral Dimensions: Warmth and Competence

Although this analysis might explain why women are stereotypically viewed as incompetent, it does not explain the many positive images of women on some dimensions. Men and women differ in their stereotypic specialties, which helps explain how they resolve the tension between interdependence and status disparity. The SCM (Cuddy et al., 2008; Fiske et al., 1999, 2002, 2007) organizes beliefs about cultural groups (including gender groups) along two dimensions: competence and warmth. The SCM posits that the content of a stereotype and of its accompanying prejudice follows from a social group's perceived status and cooperation in society. That is, the way an in-group feels about an out-group will depend on the perceived intent and capability of the out-group to harm the in-group. This 2 (intent: low or high warmth) × 2 (capability: low or high competence) mapping of intergroup space yields four classes of stereotypes (see Figure 4.1). Groups high on both are the in-group

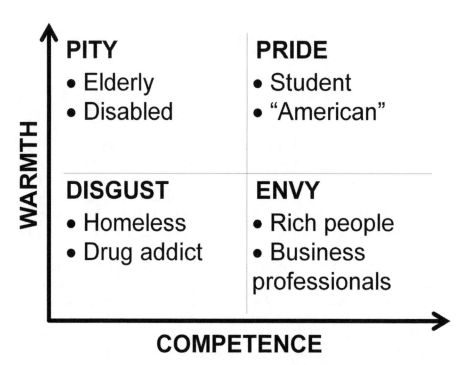

Figure 4.1. Stereotype content model warmth by competence space, stereotyped group exemplars, and associated emotions. Source data from Fiske et al. (2002).

and its allies (societal reference groups, e.g., the middle class or Christians); groups low on both are the worst off (people who are homeless, addicted, or poor).

The mixed case—groups high on one dimension but low on the other—are most relevant to gender relations. Paternalistic[1] pity targets allegedly warm but incompetent groups such as people who are older or disabled and (in some samples) housewives. Envious prejudice targets allegedly competent but cold groups such as Jewish or Asian people and female professionals (in U.S. samples).

According to the SCM, structural relations between groups (or relative levels of perceived status and competition) cause specific stereotypes regarding a group's competence and warmth, which in turn maintain the status quo. As we just noted, favorable stereotypes are reserved for the in-group, its allies, and culturally dominant groups. Because of in-group favoritism, these groups are perceived to be both warm and competent. They have no intention of competing with themselves and are therefore liked and respected. Liking and respect, in turn, legitimize the social power of the in-group.

Conversely, derogatory stereotypes describe out-groups that are seen as competitive or exploitative and having low status (e.g., people who are homeless). Because these groups are thought to usurp economic and political capital that would otherwise go to higher status groups in society, they are seen as competing in a zero-sum distribution of resources. These groups are seen as having low warmth and low competence, and they are disliked and disrespected as a result. Disliking and disrespect further undermine the social power of these groups.

In addition to uniform favoritism and derogation, the SCM allows for mixed-content stereotypes in which groups can be seen as having high warmth and low competence, or as having low warmth and high competence. Paternalistic stereotypes depict groups that are neither inclined nor capable of competing with the in-group, meaning they have low status and are not seen as competitive (e.g., people who are older and, in some samples, homemakers; e.g., Eckes, 2002; Fiske et al., 2002). These groups do not threaten the in-group and are therefore seen as incompetent but warm. This stereotype encourages paternalistic prejudice, which disrespects competence and rewards socially desirable but deferent qualities (e.g., compliant, subordinate; Glick & Fiske, 2001a, 2001b; Ridgeway, 2001). Paternalistic prejudice promotes compliance from subordinates with minimal conflict, allowing dominant groups to legitimate their higher status (Jackman, 1994).

In contrast, envious stereotypes are reserved for groups that have attained high status and are therefore seen as competitive (e.g., Asian people, career

---

[1]Although the word *paternalism* often refers to the hierarchical organization of a family in which the father, who is traditionally perceived to know best, makes decisions for the children, we use the word more broadly. In this chapter *paternalism* refers to belief systems that divest individuals of their rights and responsibilities, purportedly in their best interest, when in fact these belief systems better serve dominant groups' interest in maintaining the status quo.

women). Envious prejudice accepts the out-group's perceived competence because of their undeniable status or success but lowers their perceived warmth to justify their negative reactions toward the out-group. In short, these four classes of stereotypes stem from groups' status and perceived level of competition, but their function is the same in each case: The stereotypes legitimize the current social structure and, as long as they persist, continue to reinforce it.

Reinforcement takes concrete forms. Blocking or rejecting the power of disliked or disrespected groups maintains existing power hierarchies. As individuals' power increases, their evaluations of others become increasingly negative and their evaluations of self become increasingly positive (Georgesen & Harris, 1998, 2000); this potentially leads powerholders to believe they know what is best for everyone. Even disadvantaged groups may identify with certain aspects of the culturally dominant group and endorse its viewpoint. Not only can low-status groups explicitly (Haines & Jost, 2000) and implicitly (Jost, Pelham, Brett, & Carvallo, 2002) favor high-status groups, but the more disadvantaged a group is, the more likely that group is to defend the status quo (Jost, Pelham, Sheldon, & Sullivan, 2003), provided that intergroup relations appear to be stable and secure (Turner, 1999).

A great deal of prejudice is enacted by in-groups withholding resources and positive attributes from out-groups (Dovidio, Kawakami, & Gaertner, 2000; Mummendey, 1995). When the in-group is men and the context is a professional setting (a setting in which men are the culturally dominant group), different kinds of resources, when withheld, can undermine the social power of women. According to the SCM, liking and respect are two of the most important social resources in determining a group's place relative to other groups in society. Cooperation earns liking but not respect. Competition wins respect but not liking. We return to this later, but first we focus on some issues specific to working women: combining work with motherhood, and combining competence with warmth.

Businesswomen, Homemakers, and Mothers

In the case of gender, paternalistic prejudice rewards women who are in traditional roles by attributing more socially desirable traits (e.g., patience, warmth) to them. In essence, warmth is a consolation prize for renouncing competition with men for social power. When women transgress traditional gender norms of femininity by taking on a nontraditional role, one way to penalize their gain in status or their competition is to cast their behavior in a negative light. As predicted by the SCM, the negative reactions that arise as a result of competition posed by nontraditional women justify men's resentment of them, penalizing women's traditional advantage on the perceived warmth dimension.

Contemporary subtypes of women exemplify groups that would fall in the mixed (i.e., paternalistic or envious) stereotype categories. On average, women are thought to have less status than do men, but status can vary depending on the role of the woman in question. Once her status is assessed, that status influences the nature of her relationship with men (i.e., cooperative or competitive), ultimately determining whether she elicits paternalistic or envious prejudice. On the one hand, a female homemaker is seen as cooperative because she has taken on a traditionally female role, but she is also seen as low status because she is presumed to have little or no income and relatively less education than a typical man; she is perceived as warm but not competent outside the home. A female professional, on the other hand, contradicts stereotypes regarding women's normal status and, in light of the associations between status and power, can be seen as a formidable competitor. She is seen as having high status because she is presumed to have acquired considerable education and income and she is seen as competitive because she has managed to take on a traditionally male role. Thus, she is admittedly competent but not warm. Different subtypes of women include, but are not limited to, respected but disliked women (e.g. businesswomen, feminists) and disrespected but liked women (e.g., housewives, secretaries; Deaux, Winton, Crowley, & Lewis, 1985; Eckes, 1994, 2002; Noseworthy & Lott, 1984; Six & Eckes, 1991).

Working mothers pose a paradox all their own. How do people perceive mothers, normally targets of benevolence and paternalistic prejudice, when they operate in a setting in which women are more often the target of hostility and envious prejudice? Professional women exchange their perceived competence for perceived warmth when they become mothers (Cuddy, Fiske, & Glick, 2004). Working women with children are perceived not only as less competent than women without children, but also as less competent than they were before becoming mothers. Moreover, Cuddy et al. (2004) found that perceived competence predicted the likelihood that participants would hire, promote, or further train an employee, whereas warmth did not, indicating that the gain in warmth does not aid women but the loss in competence detracts from their appeal as employees. The underlying assumption is that working mothers are less dependable as employees (e.g., Halpert, Wilson, & Hickman, 1993) because they are perceived to be less committed to their job and that "taking on a primary caregiver role 'turns a person's brain to mush' " (Ridgeway & Correll, 2004, p. 692).

Obstacles to Progress: Confirming and Disconfirming Warmth Versus Competence

Women must walk a narrow path: Their competence may be doubted, as women, but their warmth may be doubted, as professional women. These two dimensions operate differently, making it difficult for professional women to gain both respect for their competence and liking for their warmth at the same time.

People tend to possess a negativity bias, a tendency to attend more to negative than to positive information (Baumeister, Bratslavsky, Finkenauer,

& Vohs, 2001). In fact, people are quicker to attribute negative traits but take longer to revise them once they have made a negative trait ascription (Rothbart & Park, 1986). For example, one need lie only once to be seen as untrustworthy, but one must be honest over a long period before observers will confidently ascribe trustworthiness. Conversely, people more easily revise positive trait ascriptions but more reluctantly confirm them. In other words, it is harder to shake a bad reputation than it is to get one, whereas the opposite is true for a good reputation.

Trait confirmability and disconfirmability are further moderated by trait content: a strong negativity effect occurs for traits related to warmth, but almost no negativity effect occurs for traits related to competence (Tausch, Kenworthy, & Hewstone, 2007). A person is expected to be nice by default, so one has to be rude only once to be seen as sporting a chip on one's shoulder, whereas an intelligent person may make an unintelligent comment without receiving the label "incompetent." Competence-related traits require many more instances to be disconfirmed than do warmth-related traits.

Consider how this bias handicaps women who are rising through the ranks of the workplace. The negative reactions that arise as a result of competition posed by nontraditional women justify the dominant group's resentment of them, resulting in the perception that successful women are competent but cold. Even if a woman is respected for her competence, she can be disliked and therefore denied access to promotions and raises. Thus, it seems incumbent on women to manage their images in a way that promotes warmth in addition to competence. However, given that people possess a negativity bias for warmth-related traits, one could imagine how a woman who has experienced a gain in status also has to fight an uphill battle. One inconsiderate remark and she is a bitch. Likewise, a woman who is trying to progress through the ranks of an organization is disadvantaged because stereotypes associated with her already cast her in a "cold" light.

The SCM says that the content of stereotypes and emotions elicited by different social groups can be predicted by how competitive or cooperative groups are (perceived warmth), in addition to how able they are to make good on any threat to the in-group (perceived competence). Although the relative status and interdependence of groups clearly shape male–female relations, several factors unique to gender further complicate the SCM prejudices. In the specific case of men and women, AST digs deeper to explicate the institutions and mechanisms by which gender inequality persists.

AMBIVALENT SEXISM THEORY: BENEVOLENT AND HOSTILE SEXISM

The extremity with which people generate and rate different subtypes of women provides some insight into the complexity of attitudes people have about them. AST (Glick & Fiske, 1996, 1999, 2001a, 2001b) contends that prejudice against women is not rooted in absolute antipathy. Rather, sexism combines complementary gender ideologies, held by both men and women worldwide (Glick et al., 2000), and these ideologies promote the persistence of gender inequality. Benevolent sexism is a paternalistic ideology that views women as subordinate, best suited for traditional, low-status roles; women need to be protected, cherished, and revered for their virtue. Hostile sexism, a closer relative of mere antipathy, is a combative ideology maintaining that women seek to control men and that they use sexuality or feminist ideology as a means to achieving status.

Hostile sexism and benevolent sexism follow predictably from the power differences and interdependence between men and women in all domains of everyday life. Specifically, patriarchy, gender differentiation, and heterosexual relations are variables somewhat unique to gender relations. More important, they predict specific behavioral outcomes for men and women in both the private and public domains. As AST describes, each of the three constructs has both a benevolent and a hostile component, giving way to complementary justifications for gender inequality. We review each variable in turn.

Patriarchy (male structural power) yields paternalism, the ideological justification of male dominance (i.e., the belief that, because men have more power in society, they should know what is best for women even if women do not necessarily agree). The hostile elements of patriarchy are based in *dominative paternalism*, which refers to the belief that men ought to have more power than do women and the concern that women might usurp men's power in the future. As a complement, the benevolent elements of patriarchy are based in *protective paternalism*, the belief that men need to protect and provide for women because they are weak.

Gender differentiation refers to the social distinctions all cultures make between men and women and the importance of gender identity in social hierarchy (Harris, 1991). Competitive (or hostile) gender differentiation is characterized by the idea that stereotypes associated with women inherently include inferiority and incompetence because of women's lower social status. However, complementary (or benevolent) gender differentiation stresses the usefulness of women in gender-conventional roles (e.g., mother) and accounts for the view that women are wonderful because they are nurturing and supportive or possess a moral purity (Eagly & Mladinic, 1994).[2]

Finally, the necessary condition of heterosexual relations and sexual reproduction highlights the interpersonal interdependence of men and women. The hostile interpretation of this interdependence is that women are purportedly able to use sex to control men, whereas the benevolent interpre-

---

[2]Note that the SCM warmth dimension links both friendly intent and trustworthiness, so it combines these ideas.

tation asserts that women are a valuable resource (e.g., essential for men's true happiness), even if they are inferior.

Both men and women report subscribing to these ideologies, albeit to varying degrees (Glick & Fiske, 1996; Kilianski & Rudman, 1998), and these ideologies perpetuate gender inequality. As noted, men are socially dominant by many accounts (e.g., higher status roles, greater income; United Nations Development Programme, 2005), and psychologists have proposed several mechanisms by which men are able to maintain their higher status. *System justification theory* argues that people are motivated to create beliefs that reinforce the status quo so that they can see the social system in which they live as fair and legitimate (Jost & Banaji, 1994); *social dominance theory* also posits that people create ideologies ("legitimizing myths") to support the hierarchy (Sidanius & Pratto, 1999). Therefore gender stereotypes that reinforce the current system emerge.

The dominant group also has incentive to reward subordinate group members, on whom they rely, for warmth and cooperation. Being hostile alone would never work to keep the subordinates in check (Glick & Fiske, 1999). Overt control leads powerholders and targets to attribute targets' behavior to force, which leads the powerholder to perceive the target as weak and the target to resent the powerholder (Kipnis, 1976, 1984). As soon as the powerholder is no longer present, the target will cease to enact the desired behavior. This kind of power maintenance is rare in the upper echelons of the workplace.

However, relational tactics (e.g., rewarding subordinates for compliance) lead both parties to perceive choice in the target's behavior, which allows the target to maintain self-respect and encourages self-sustaining behavior. Relational tactics suggest one way that men and women maintain the system, by some degree of perceived choice. This perception of perceived choice is essential, for the hierarchical gender system would never sustain itself for this long if it were maintained only by brute force.

Instead of using brute force, dominant groups endorse paternalistic ideologies that offer help and protection to subordinates to justify the hierarchy (Jackman, 1994). The system is arranged so that dominant groups confer benefits on the subordinate group members to keep them complacent. Subordinate group members, ever sensitive to their position and related stereotypes, are influenced by status beliefs in their own behavior, and cooperate to maintain amicable conditions (Seachrist & Stangor, 2001). In part, benevolent sexism stems from the perceived willing cooperation of the subordinates. In addition, seemingly "protective" gestures allow dominant group members to see subordinate group members as less competent while turning a blind eye to discriminatory acts (Glick & Fiske, 1996, 2001a, 2001b). In other words, dominant groups can deny subordinates education, organizational power, and economic participation under the guise of protection (Glick et al., 2000). If subordinate group members go along with the arrangement, dominant group members are free to assume that subordinate group members consent to the practice. If subordinate group members reject the "benefits," thereby refusing to cooperate, the dominant groups will react with hostility toward them, because they believe it is their right to maintain the system.

Some Consequences of Ambivalent Sexism

AST builds on the existing theories of gender inequality by demonstrating why it is that both hostile and benevolent ideologies contribute to persistent prejudice and discrimination against women. First, although benevolent sexism is seemingly innocuous and, in certain situations, is perceived as beneficial, it is problematic because it is yoked to hostile sexism; benevolent sexism does not exist without hostile sexism and the resulting prejudice and discrimination. Data from more than 15,000 participants in 19 countries illustrate that benevolent and hostile sexism are highly correlated with one another, and negatively correlated with other indicators of gender equality in economic and political life (Glick et al., 2000).

Second, benevolent sexism selectively favors only women who occupy traditional female roles. Ambivalent sexists reconcile their presumably conflicting ideologies about women by reserving benevolent beliefs for traditional women and hostile beliefs for nontraditional women (Glick, Diebold, Bailey Warner, & Zhu, 1997). Working women, especially aspirants for leadership, do not "benefit" from benevolent sexism.

Last, benevolent sexism reduces women's resistance to prejudice and discrimination because benevolence is often used to justify hostile acts. For example, women with higher benevolent sexism scores rated professional discrimination (e.g., boss promotes male employee instead of female employee, even though she is more qualified) as less serious when the perpetrator cited benevolent justifications (e.g., for women's protection). Similar effects occurred for interpersonal discrimination (e.g., husband forbids wife from going out at night), which might also predict husbands' resisting their wives' paid employment. Furthermore, higher benevolent sexism scores predicted women's greater tolerance for husbands' overtly hostile discrimination, although this last finding held only for women without paid employment (Moya, Exposito, & Casado, 1999). Benevolent sexism operates at the boundary between home and work.

Benevolent and hostile sexism both relate to several behaviors and individual differences that predict prejudice and discrimination against women in the workplace. Here are a few relevant examples: Hostile sexism predicts the likelihood of individuals passing on female- and male-disparaging jokes; hostile sexism also predicts how funny men think these jokes are (Thomas & Esses, 2004). Education negatively relates to benevolent and hostile sexism, and Catholicism predicts more benevolent but not hostile sexism (Glick,

Lameiras, & Castro, 2002). Most relevant to employment issues, the alleged protection promoted by benevolent sexism is contingent on wives occupying traditional roles and remaining subordinate to husbands' authority (Glick, Sakali-Urgulu, Ferreira, & deSouza, 2002). Finally, individuals who score high on hostile sexism are more likely to infrahumanize women (Viki & Abrams, 2003); that is, hostile sexists deem women as less than human because they tend to deny that women possess positive, uniquely human emotions (e.g., compassion, hopefulness). Once the effects of hostile sexism and benevolent sexism were controlled for, participant gender was not related to this effect. Considerable data, then, demonstrate the role of ambivalent sexism, with hostile sexism having a more direct role and benevolent sexism having an indirect role, through the home, in workplace issues. Ambivalent sexism contributes to social-status restrictions on women.

Related Analyses of Status Beliefs and Roles for Women

We have reviewed the pervasive benevolent and hostile ideologies that dictate social rewards and punishments. Gender relations also reflect a well-defined and deeply embedded hierarchy, which includes automatically accessed roles. As noted previously, gender is inextricably linked to social hierarchy because gender stereotypes explicitly describe men's and women's status, traits, and roles (Berger, Fisek, Norman, & Zelditch, 1977; Ridgeway, 2001; Webster & Foschi, 1988). Besides status, interdependence matters: Men and women have to work together to get what they need and want. Two significant trends emerge as a result of this gender-status link and cooperative interdependence: (a) the status-differentiating qualities of both groups are more likely to be highlighted than are other qualities and (b) men, when unchallenged, are likely to interpret cooperation of women as consent. So, on the surface, men and women contentedly continue the present arrangement, and both groups do the necessary cognitive gymnastics to make sense of the way things are (Jost & Banaji, 1994).

Furthermore, gender is a salient, and perhaps the most salient, social category (Fiske, 1998; Stroessner, 1996), and gender stereotyping is often automatic or unconscious (Dunning & Sherman, 1997). In other words, the mere sight of a woman can immediately elicit a specific set of associated traits and attributions, depending on the context (category-based perception; Fiske & Neuberg, 1990). As a result, the pressure on women to cooperate by enacting traditional gender roles is immediate.

Social-role theory (Eagly, 1987) suggests that gendered division of labor is the source of the stereotypes people hold about women and men to this day. Women are associated with domestic roles (e.g., mother), which require communal qualities (e.g., warmth, patience), whereas men are associated with high-status roles (e.g., professional), which require agentic traits (e.g., competence, independence). Thus, the "work" roles associated with each gender have shaped the content of the stereotypes people hold about men and women. Although the content of stereotypes for women may seem subjectively positive, public domains make it clear that these "favorable" attitudes are predicated on women occupying low-status roles.

The queen bee syndrome demonstrates yet another manner in which women may feel conflicted about rising through the ranks of the workplace. The term *queen bee syndrome* refers to the fact that women who have been individually successful in male-dominated environments are likely to oppose the women's movement and the promotion of female colleagues (Ellemers, van den Heuvel, de Gilder, Maass, & Bonvini, 2004; Staines, Tavris, & Jayaratne, 1974). One possible explanation for this finding comes from the social identity perspective: If women who have been successful in male-dominated domains see themselves as more masculine and thereby different from "regular women," it may be that they are motivated to emphasize intra-group differences in service of individual mobility goals (Ellemers et al., 2004; Tajfel, 1978). For women still advancing in the workplace the queen bee syndrome may have a two-fold effect: advancement may involve deemphasizing aspects that were previously central to the self (e.g., communality) as well as eliciting prejudice from those one expects to support them most (i.e., other, more senior female colleagues; Ellemers et al., 2004).

Given the features of gender relations—the clearly defined and deeply embedded hierarchy, the automatically accessed roles, and the pervasive benevolent and hostile ideologies that dictate social rewards and punishments—women in professional settings face a catch-22 every day. They have to choose between cooperating and competing, and they have to evaluate the possible outcomes of violating the status quo because, as the next section indicates, violations invite retaliation.

FALLOUT

In many domains men continue to surpass women in power and status (Pratto & Walker, 2001). Even when their objective behavior is equivalent, men and women are perceived as displaying divergent behaviors and possessing attributes indicative of differences in power, status, and dominance (Heilman, 2001). Moreover, particularly in masculine domains, women's relative power and status may be misperceived as being lower than objectively indicated. Women have to work harder than men do to be perceived as equally competent (Foschi, 2000).

Dominant groups endorse negative stereotypes that legitimize their privilege and withhold social power from subordinate groups. AST makes specific predictions about possible negative outcomes for women who operate in the public domain and have to navigate the fallout from benevolent and hostile ideologies. Some negative outcomes include patronizing discrimination, backlash, and sexual harassment.

Benevolence

Women are allegedly communal and men are allegedly agentic (Eagly, 1987), but employees seen as warm and incompetent may elicit patronizing discrimination (Glick & Fiske, 2007), which can have serious consequences for women in professional settings. Because stereotypes about women comprise status beliefs (i.e., women have less status than men), fewer agentic traits, and more communal traits, superiors tend to hold women to lower stereotyped-based standards in performance settings (Biernat & Kobrynowicz, 1997; Biernat & Manis, 1994; Biernat, Manis, & Nelson, 1991; Biernat, Vescio, & Manis, 1998). In masculine domains this activation of low or patronizing standards for women can lead evaluators to be more impressed with female candidates than male candidates because the female candidate readily surpasses minimum standards for a woman (a *wow effect*). A male candidate, however, is held to higher, male stereotype-based standards and therefore seems comparatively less impressive (Biernat & Kobrynowicz, 1997). Still, this "advantage" does not translate into getting the job because of an enormous behavioral gap between praising an applicant's qualities and actually putting applicants on the payroll (Biernat & Fuegen, 2001). These decisions distinguish between zero-sum and non-zero-sum behaviors (Biernat et al., 1998), such that zero-sum choices allocate limited but valuable resources (e.g., money, promotions), and non-zero-sum choices dole out unlimited but less-valued resources (e.g., verbal praise, positive nonverbal cues). Non-zero-sum decisions contrast with stereotypes, as a consequence of shifting standards (e.g., "She did a really great job giving that presentation, for a woman. We should definitely consider her for the job"). However, the really valuable, limited zero-sum choices assimilate to stereotypes (e.g., men are more competent than women, so hire the man; Biernat & Fuegen, 2001; Biernat & Vescio, 2002). In other words, although female applicants are likely to appear on the short list, they still lag in hiring, raises, and promotions (see also chap. 1, this volume, for an analysis of the glass cliff resulting from benevolent sexist beliefs).

More overt manifestations of patronizing discrimination include handicapping by overhelping, taking over, and limiting the responsibilities of targets (Rudman, Glick, & Phelan, 2008). In other words, people who are perceived as warm but incompetent will not be allowed to demonstrate their capabilities because the individuals who surround them will be reluctant to trust or burden them with the work that is required of others in comparable positions. Both women and men tend to respond with anger to patronizing behaviors of powerholders; but men subsequently perform better, whereas women perform worse as a consequence (Vescio, Gervais, Snyder, & Hoover, 2005).

Patronizing discrimination is embedded in benevolent sexism and maintains the dominant group's higher status. The double-edged nature of patronizing discrimination is precisely what makes benevolent sexism so insidious. It does not seem overtly sexist and in many cases is seemingly beneficial to the recipient. Furthermore, perpetrators may even think they are helping recipients. Women who accept paternalistic gestures do so either because they are not aware that they are reinforcing their own low-status role or because they understand they have to cooperate, and accepting benevolent gestures is a better alternative to enduring overt hostility (see chaps. 5 and 6, this volume, for other analyses of seeming prejudice acceptance).

Hostility

Given the pervasive and immediate nature of gender-status associations, women have to weigh the alternatives of cooperation versus perceived competition. Every day, women face a paradox in performance settings: They have to provide strong counterstereotypic information (e.g., that they are agentic and competent) to demonstrate that they are qualified for high-status professional roles (Glick, Zion, & Nelson, 1988), but this deviation from prescribed gender norms can elicit a backlash (Rudman, 1998).

Consider the consequences of refusing benevolent gestures or violating feminine norms. If a woman elects to reject patronizing assistance, she risks being seen as uncooperative. As a result, the benefits of paternalism, reserved for women who stick to traditional gendered behavior, are revoked and backlash rooted in hostile sexism can take its place. Manifestations of backlash include hiring discrimination (Heilman, Wallen, Fuchs, & Tamkins, 2004), harsher appraisals (Eagly, Makhijani, & Klonsky, 1992), sabotage (Rudman & Fairchild, 2004), social exclusion (Jackman, 1994), and sexual harassment (Fiske & Stevens, 1993; see also chap. 8, this volume). Indeed, high hostile sexism scores, but not benevolent sexism scores, are related to more negative evaluations and fewer management recommendations for female candidates and more management recommendations for male candidates (Masser & Abrams, 2004). Moreover, women are bound by workplace culture norms; the social costs of making attributions to discrimination prevent stigmatized individuals from dealing with the discrimination (Kaiser & Miller, 2001).

Hostile ideologies elicited by competitive or counternormative behaviors promote ideas that can be used to justify resentment. A hostile interpretation of heterosexual intimacy can motivate individuals to infer that female coworkers acquired their positions illegitimately (e.g., by sleeping with a superior), because sexuality is supposedly the domain in which women have the perceived ability to control men (Ely, 1994). As one might predict, men who are most concerned with protecting their status are also the most likely to harass (Maass, Cadinu, Guarnieri, & Grasselli, 2003). Individuals (men or women) who threaten men's status most often elicit harassment (Berdahl, 2004; Dall'Ara & Maass, 2000; Maass et al., 2003). Power is automatically linked to sex for some men: Those men who maintain strong sex-role stereotypes are more likely to harass and are prone to behave aggressively toward women (Bargh & Raymond, 1995; Bargh, Raymond, Pryor, & Strack, 1995; see also chap. 8, this volume). Furthermore, women who are perceived as "sexy" can elicit hostile reactions, from both men and women, and lead people to perceive sexual harassment as justified (Muehlenhard & MacNaughton, 1988). High-status women who dress in sexy ways are especially demeaned; for low-status women, sexy dress has no effect (Glick, Larsen, Johnson, & Branstiter, 2005). Thus, women at work pay a high price for a variety of counternormative behaviors.

Nonverbal norms complicate matters because women face an uphill battle to preserve their legitimacy once they are in positions of authority. Dominant nonverbal behavior is a major cue to power (Carli, LeFleur, & Loeber, 1995; Henley, 1995; LaFrance, Hecht, & Paluck, 2003). The trouble lies in the fact that many nonverbal behaviors function both as dominance cues and as cues of intimacy, depending on who is expressing them, when, and where. For example, individuals who touch are seen as more dominant than the target they are touching (Major, 1981), but physical touch between two people is also a clear signal of intimacy and closeness. Because dominant nonverbal behavior is a central avenue for control that also serves the dual function of communicating intimacy, women who enact these behaviors in an effort to communicate their authority run the risk of being misinterpreted. Indeed, research shows exactly this pattern: Not only are dominant behaviors seen as less dominant when displayed by women as compared with men, but dominant behaviors are also seen as more sexual when displayed by women as compared with men. These attribution patterns hold when women express dominant gestures in dyadic interactions (Henley & Harmon, 1985) as well as when they express dominant gestures in the absence of an interaction partner (e.g., sitting upright with arms resting away from the body, maintaining direct eye contact with the camera; Cikara & Morrow, 2004).

The misperception of women's dominance behaviors as sexual may be particularly pernicious and may disserve women in at least two ways. First, behavioral confirmation may work in concert with attributions to restrict women's ability to influence situations and other people. That is, misinterpreting dominance cues as gestures of intimacy may cause people to behave in ways that elicit stereotype-confirming behaviors from women, thereby promoting the erroneous notion that they acquired their status illegitimately. Perhaps rightly, women do not believe that they can be seen simultaneously as competent and sexual (Gutek, 1989). Second, women being seen as sexual rather than powerful leads male workers to objectify women, making the women more likely targets for harassment and unwanted sexual advances. As one might expect, flirtatiousness and harassment have negative consequences for women's self-confidence (Satterfield & Muehlenhard, 1997).

Although women generally tolerate harassment of others less than men do, ambivalent sexism is related to greater tolerance of harassment for both men and women, as measured by the Sexual Harassment Attitudes Scale (Russell & Trigg, 2004). Furthermore, behaving submissively in the face of harassment is not a solution. Submissive behavior undermines people's perception of social power and can also lead to exploitation (Richards, Rollerson, & Phillips, 1991). Attributing a woman's status to her sexuality, aggression, or coldness suggests she gained her power illegitimately. The more people endorse benevolent and hostile sexism, the greater the likelihood they will make these attributions. Thus, hostility toward women creates predictable forms of backlash against counternormative behavior by women.

CONCLUSION

Women face direct assault as they climb toward the glass ceiling, which casts doubt on their competence, but they also face lateral hostility as they bump up against glass walls that constrain their warmth to the straight and narrow confines dictated by gender roles. As women gain status and observers grudgingly admit their competence, women risk losing their perceived humanity, their warmth in particular. This is what happened to Hillary Clinton. But if women make sure to emphasize their warmth, loyalty, and sincerity, they may be discounted as less competent. Similar risks threaten men in positions of power, but they are exaggerated for women. Maybe these vertical assaults and collateral damages will attenuate if they are documented and they enter the popular mind. Particularly in the case of gender, people tend to neglect the importance of social structure. Thus, it is crucial that we highlight the structural conditions that give rise to gender inequity. It is not the case that disadvantage has to lead to system justification, and we would encourage resistance rather than denial or avoidance (e.g., see Reicher & Haslam, 2006; Schmitt, Branscombe, & Postmes, 2003). We hope the stereotypic competence-warmth trade-off will soon be seen for the outdated canard it is.

REFERENCES

Bargh, J. A., & Raymond, P. (1995). The naive misuse of power: Nonconscious sources of sexual harassment. *Journal of Social Issues, 51,* 283–298.

Bargh, J. A., Raymond, P., Pryor, J. B., & Strack, F. (1995). Attractiveness of the underling: An automatic power-sex association and its consequences for sexual harassment and aggression. *Journal of Personality and Social Psychology, 68,* 768–781.

Baumeister, R. F., Bratslavsky, E., Finkenauer, C., & Vohs, K. D. (2001). Bad is stronger than good. *Review of General Psychology, 5*, 323–370.

Berdahl, J. L. (2004). *The sexual harassment of "masculine" women.* Unpublished manuscript, University of Toronto.

Berger, J., Fisek, M. H., Norman, R. Z., & Zelditch, M., Jr. (1977). *Status characteristics and social interaction: An expectation states approach.* New York: Elsevier.

Biernat, M., & Fuegen, K. (2001). Shifting standards and the evaluation of competence: Complexity in gender-based judgments and decision making. *Journal of Social Issues, 57*, 707–724.

Biernat, M., & Kobrynowicz, D. (1997). Gender- and race-based standards of competence: Lower minimum standards but higher ability standards for devalued groups. *Journal of Personality and Social Psychology, 72*, 544–557.

Biernat, M., & Manis, M. (1994). Shifting standards and stereotype-based judgments. *Journal of Personality and Social Psychology, 66*, 5–20.

Biernat, M., Manis, M., & Nelson, T. F. (1991). Comparison and expectancy processes in human judgment. *Journal of Personality and Social Psychology, 61*, 203–211.

Biernat, M., & Vescio T. K. (2002). She swings, she hits, she's great, she's benched: Shifting judgment standards and behaviors. *Personality and Social Psychology Bulletin, 28*, 66–76.

Biernat, M., Vescio, T. K., & Manis, M. (1998). Judging and behaving toward members of stereotyped groups: A shifting standards perspective. In C. Sedikides, J. Schopler, & C. A. Insko (Eds.), *Intergroup cognition and intergroup behavior* (pp. 151–175). Mahwah, NJ: Erlbaum.

Carli, L. L. (1991). Gender, status, and influence. In E. J. Lawler, B. Markovsky, C. L. Ridgeway, & H. Walker (Eds.), *Advances in group processes* (Vol. 8, pp. 89–113). Greenwich, CT: JAI Press.

Carli, L. L., LaFleur, S. J., & Loeber, C. C. (1995). Nonverbal behavior, gender, and influence. *Journal of Personality and Social Psychology, 68*, 1030–1041.

Catalyst. (2000). *Census of women corporate officers and top earners.* New York: Author.

Center for the American Woman and Politics (2006). *Fact sheet.* Retrieved November 16, 2006, from http://www.cawp.rutgers.edu/Facts/Officeholders/cong–current.html

Cikara, M., & Morrow, J. (2004, May). *Effects of gender and dominance on perceptions of overt sexuality, sexual attractiveness, warmth, and competence.* Paper presented at the meeting of the American Psychological Society, Chicago, IL.

Cuddy, A. J. C., Fiske, S. T., & Glick, P. (2004). When professionals become mothers, warmth doesn't cut the ice. *Journal of Social Issues, 60*, 701–718.

Cuddy, A. J. C., Fiske, S. T., & Glick, P. (2008). Warmth and competence as universal dimensions of social perception: The Stereotype Content Model and the BIAS map. In M. P. Zanna (Ed.), *Advances in experimental social psychology* (Vol. 40, pp. 61–149). New York: Academic Press.

Dall'Ara, E., & Maass, A. (2000). Studying sexual harassment in the laboratory: Are egalitarian women at higher risk? *Sex Roles, 41*, 681–704.

Deaux, K., Winton, W., Crowley, M., & Lewis, L. (1985). Level of categorization and content of gender stereotypes. *Social Cognition, 3*, 145–167.

Dovidio, J. F., Kawakami, K., & Gaertner, S. L. (2000). Reducing contemporary prejudice: Combating explicit and implicit bias at the individual and intergroup level. In S. Oskamp (Ed.), *Reducing prejudice and discrimination* (pp. 137–163). Hillsdale, NJ: Erlbaum.

Dunning, D., & Sherman, D. A. (1997). Stereotypes and tacit inference. *Journal of Personality and Social Psychology, 73*, 459–471.

Eagly, A. H. (1987). *Sex differences in social behavior: A social-role interpretation.* Hillsdale, NJ: Erlbaum.

Eagly, A. H., Makhijani, M. G., & Klonsky, B. G. (1992). Gender and the evaluation of leaders: A meta-analysis. *Psychological Bulletin, 111*, 3–22.

Eagly, A. H., & Mladinic, A. (1994). Are people prejudiced against women? Some answers from research on attitudes, gender stereotypes, and judgments of competence. *European Review of Social Psychology, 5*, 1–35.

Eckes, T. (1994). Features of men, features of women: Assessing stereotypic beliefs about gender subtypes. *British Journal of Social Psychology, 33*, 107–123.

Eckes, T. (2002). Paternalistic and envious gender stereotypes: Testing predictions from the stereotype content model. *Sex Roles, 47*, 99–114.

Ellemers, N. (1993). The influence of socio-structural variables on identity management strategies. *European Review of Social Psychology, 4*, 27–57.

Ellemers, N., van den Heuvel, H., de Gilder, D., Maass, A., & Bonvini, A. (2004). The underrepresentation of women in science: Differential commitment or the queen bee syndrome? *British Journal of Social Psychology, 43*, 315–338.

Ely, R. J. (1994). The effects of organizational demographics and social identity on relationships among professional women. *Administrative Science Quarterly, 39*, 203–238.

Fiske, S. T. (1998). Prejudice, stereotyping, and discrimination. In D. T. Gilbert, S. T. Fiske, & G. Lindzey (Eds.), *The handbook of social psychology* (Vol. 2, 4th ed., pp. 357–411). New York: McGraw-Hill.

Fiske, S. T., & Berdahl, J. (2007). Social power. In A. W. Kruglanski & E. T. Higgins (Eds.), *Social psychology: Handbook of basic principles* (2nd ed., pp. 678–692). New York: Guilford Press.

Fiske, S. T., Cuddy, A. J. C., & Glick, P. (2007). Universal dimensions of social cognition: Warmth and competence. *Trends in Cognitive Sciences, 11*, 77–83.

Fiske, S. T., Cuddy, A. J. C., Glick, P., & Xu, J. (2002). A model of (often mixed) stereotype content: Competence and warmth respectively follow from perceived status and competition. *Journal of Personality and Social Psychology, 82*, 878–902.

Fiske, S. T., & Neuberg, S. L. (1990). A continuum of impression formation, from category-based to individuating processes: Influences of information and motivation on attention and interpretation. In M. Zanna (Ed.), *Advances in experimental social psychology* (Vol. 23, pp. 1–74). New York: Academic Press.

Fiske, S. T., & Stevens, L. E. (1993). What so special about sex? Gender stereotyping and discrimination. In S. Okamp & M. Costanzo (Eds.), *Gender issues in contemporary society* (pp. 173–196). Thousand Oaks, CA: Sage.

Fiske, S. T., Xu, J., Cuddy, A. C., & Glick, P. (1999). (Dis)respecting versus (dis)liking: Status and interdependence predict ambivalent stereotypes of competence and warmth. *Journal of Social Issues, 55,* 473–489.

Foschi, M. (2000). Double standards for competence: Theory and research. *Annual Review of Sociology, 26,* 21–42.

Georgesen, J. C., & Harris, M. J. (1998). Why's my boss always holding me down? A meta-analysis of power effects on performance evaluations. *Personality and Social Psychology Review, 2,* 184–195.

Georgesen, J. C., & Harris, M. J. (2000). The balance of power: Interpersonal consequences of differential power and expectation. *Personality and Social Psychology Bulletin, 26,* 1239–1257.

Glick, P. (1991). Trait-based and sex-based discrimination in occupational prestige, occupational salary, and hiring. *Sex Roles, 25,* 351–378.

Glick, P., Diebold, J., Bailey Werner, B., & Zhu, L. (1997). The two faces of Adam: Ambivalent sexism and polarized attitudes toward women. *Personality and Social Psychology Bulletin, 23,* 1323–1334.

Glick, P., & Fiske, S. T. (1996). The Ambivalent Sexism Inventory: Differentiating hostile and benevolent sexism. *Journal of Personality and Social Psychology, 70,* 491–512.

Glick, P., & Fiske, S. T. (1999). Sexism and other "isms": Interdependence, status, and the ambivalent content of stereotypes. In W. B. Swan, J. H. Langlois, & L. A. Gilbert (Eds.), *Sexism and stereotypes in modern society* (pp. 193–221). Washington, DC: American Psychological Association.

Glick, P., & Fiske, S. T. (2001a). An ambivalent alliance: Hostile and benevolent sexism as complementary justifications for gender inequality. *American Psychologist, 56,* 109–118.

Glick, P., & Fiske, S. T. (2001b). Ambivalent sexism. In M. P. Zanna (Ed.), *Advances in experimental social psychology* (Vol. 33, pp. 115–188). Thousand Oaks, CA: Academic Press.

Glick, P., & Fiske, S. T. (2007). Sex discrimination: The psychological approach. In F. J. Crosby, M. S. Stockdale, & S. A. Ropp (Eds.), *Sex discrimination in the workplace* (pp. 155–188). Malden, MA: Blackwell.

Glick, P., Fiske, S. T., Mladinic, A., Saiz, J., Abrams, D., Masser, B., et al. (2000). Beyond prejudice as simple antipathy: Hostile and benevolent sexism across cultures. *Journal of Personality and Social Psychology, 79,* 763–775.

Glick, P., Lameiras, M., & Castro, Y. R. (2002). Education and Catholic religiosity as predictors of hostile and benevolent sexism toward women and men. *Sex Roles, 47,* 433–441.

Glick, P., Larsen, S., Johnson, C., & Branstiter, H. (2005). Evaluations of sexy women in low- and high-status jobs. *Psychology of Women Quarterly, 29,* 389–395.

Glick, P., Sakali-Urgulu, N., Ferreira, M. C., & deSouza, M. A. (2002). Ambivalent sexism and attitudes toward wife abuse in Turkey and Brazil. *Psychology of Women Quarterly, 26,* 292–297.

Glick, P., Wilk, K., & Perreault, M. (1995). Images of occupations: Components of gender and status in occupational stereotypes. *Sex Roles, 32,* 564–582.

Glick, P., Zion, C., & Nelson, C. (1988). What mediates sex discrimination in hiring decisions? *Journal of Personality and Social Psychology, 55,* 178–186.

Gutek, B. A. (1989). Sexuality in the workplace: Key issues in social research and organizational practice. In J. Hearn, D. L. Sheppard, P. Tancred-Sheriff, & G. Burell (Eds.), *The sexuality of organization* (pp. 56–70). London: Sage.

Haines, E. L., & Jost, J. T. (2000). Placating the powerless: Effects of legitimate and illegitimate explanation on effect, memory, and stereotyping. *Social Justice Research, 13,* 219–236.

Halpert, J. A., Wilson, M. L., & Hickman, J. L. (1993). Pregnancy as a source of bias in performance appraisals. *Journal of Organizational Behavior, 14,* 649–663.

Harris, M. (1991). *Cultural anthropology* (3rd ed.). New York: HarperCollins.

Haslam, N., Rothschild, L., & Ernst, D. (2000). Essentialist beliefs about social categories. *British Journal of Social Psychology, 59,* 113–127.

Heilman, M. E. (2001). Description and prescription: How gender stereotypes prevent women's ascent up the organizational ladder. *Journal of Social Issues, 57,* 657–674.

Heilman, M. E., Wallen, A. S., Fuchs, D., & Tamkins, M. M. (2004). Penalties for success: Reactions to women who succeed at male gender-typed tasks. *Journal of Applied Psychology, 89,* 416–427.

Henley, N. M. (1995). Body politics revisited: What do we know today? In P. J. Kalbfleisch & M. J. Cody (Eds.), *Gender, power, and communications in human relationships* (pp. 27–61). Hillsdale, NJ: Erlbaum.

Henley, N. M., & Harmon, S. (1985). The nonverbal semantics of power and gender: A perceptual study. In S. L. Ellyson & J. F. Dovidio (Eds.), *Power, dominance, and nonverbal behavior* (pp. 151–164). New York: Springer-Verlag.

Hewstone, M., Rubin, M., & Willis, H. (2002). Intergroup bias. In S. T. Fiske, D. L. Schacter, & C. Zahn-Waxler (Eds.), *Annual Review of Psychology, 53,* 575–604.

Jackman, M. R. (1994). *The velvet glove: Paternalism and conflict in gender, class and race relations.* Berkeley: University of California Press.

Jost, J. T., & Banaji, M. R. (1994). The role of stereotyping in system-justification and the production of false consciousness. *British Journal of Social Psychology, 33,* 1–27.

Jost, J. T., Pelham, B. W., Brett, W., & Carvallo, M. R. (2002). Non-conscious forms of system justification: Implicit and behavioral preferences for higher status groups. *Journal of Experimental Social Psychology, 38,* 586–602.

Jost, J. T., Pelham, B. W., Sheldon, O., & Sullivan, B. N. (2003). Social inequality and the reduction of ideological dissonance on behalf of the system: Evidence of enhanced system justification among the disadvantaged. *European Journal of Social Psychology, 33,* 13–36.

Kaiser, C. R., & Miller, C. T. (2001). Stop complaining! The social costs of making attributions to discrimination. *Personality and Social Psychology Bulletin, 27*, 254–263.

Kilianski, S., & Rudman, L. A. (1998). Wanting it both ways: Do women approve of benevolent sexism? *Sex Roles, 39*, 333–352.

Kipnis, D. (1976). *The powerholders*. Chicago: University of Chicago Press.

Kipnis, D. (1984). The use of power in organizations and in interpersonal settings. *Applied Social Psychology Annual, 5*, 179–210.

LaFrance, M., Hecht, M. A., & Paluck, E. L. (2003). The contingent smile: A meta-analysis of sex differences in smiling. *Psychological Bulletin, 129*, 305–334.

Maass, A., Cadinu, M., Guarnieri, G., & Grasselli, A. (2003). Sexual harassment under social identity threat: The computer harassment paradigm. *Journal of Personality and Social Psychology, 85*, 853–870.

Major, B. (1981). Gender patterns in touching behavior. In C. Mayo & N. M. Henley (Eds.), *Gender and nonverbal behavior* (pp. 15–37). New York: Springer-Verlag.

Masser, B. M., & Abrams, D. (2004). Reinforcing the glass ceiling: The consequences of hostile sexism for female managerial candidates. *Sex Roles, 51*, 609–615.

Moya, M., Exposito, F., & Casado, P. (1999). *Women's reactions to hostile and benevolent sexist situations*. Oxford, England: European Association of Experimental Social Psychology.

Muehlenhard, C. L., & MacNaughton, J. S. (1988). Women's beliefs about women who "lead men on." *Journal of Clinical Psychology, 7*, 65–79.

Mummendey, A. (1995). Positive distinctiveness and social discrimination: An old couple living in divorce. *European Journal of Social Psychology, 25*, 657–670.

Noseworthy, C. M., & Lott, A. J. (1984). The cognitive organization of gender-stereotypic categories. *Personality and Social Psychology Bulletin, 10*, 474–481.

Pratto, F., & Walker, A. (2001). Dominance in disguise: Power, beneficence, and exploitation in personal relationships. In A. Lee-Chai & J. A. Bargh (Eds.), *The use and abuse of power* (pp. 93–114). Philadelphia: Taylor & Francis.

Reicher, S. D., & Haslam, S. A. (2006). Rethinking the psychology of tyranny: The BBC prison study. *British Journal of Social Psychology, 45*, 1–40.

Richards, L., Rollerson, B., & Phillips, J. (1991). Perceptions of submissiveness: Implications for victimization. *The Journal of Psychology, 125*, 407–411.

Ridgeway, C. (2001). Gender, status, and leadership. *Journal of Social Issues, 57*, 637–655.

Ridgeway, C., & Correll, S. J. (2004). Motherhood as a status characteristic. *Journal of Social Issues, 60*, 683–700.

Rothbart, M., & Park, B. (1986). On the confirmability and disconfirmability of trait concepts. *Journal of Personality and Social Psychology, 50*, 131–142.

Rudman, L. A. (1998). Self-promotion as a risk factor for women: The costs and benefits of counter-stereotypical impression management. *Journal of Personality and Social Psychology, 74*, 629–645.

Rudman, L. A., & Fairchild, K. (2004). Reactions to counterstereotypical behavior: The role of backlash in cultural stereotype maintenance. *Journal of Personality and Social Psychology, 87,* 157–176.

Rudman, L. A., Glick, P., & Phelan, J. E. (2008). From the laboratory to the bench: Gender stereotyping research in the courtroom. In E. Borgida & S. T. Fiske (Eds.), *Beyond common sense: Psychological science in the courtroom* (pp. 83–102). Malden, MA: Blackwell.

Russell, B. L., & Trigg, K. Y. (2004). Tolerance of sexual harassment: An examination of gender differences, ambivalent sexism, social dominance, and gender roles. *Sex Roles, 50,* 565–573.

Satterfield, A. T., & Muehlenhard, C. L. (1997). Shaken confidence: The effects of an authority figure's flirtatiousness on women's and men's self-rated creativity. *Psychology of Women Quarterly, 21,* 395–416.

Seachrist, G. B., & Stangor, C. (2001). Perceived consensus influences intergroup behavior and stereotype accessibility. *Journal of Personality and Social Psychology, 80,* 645–654.

Schmitt, M. T., Branscombe, N. R., & Postmes, T. (2003). Women's emotional responses to the pervasiveness of gender discrimination. *European Journal of Social Psychology, 33,* 297–312.

Sidanius, J., & Pratto, F. (1999). *Social dominance: An intergroup theory of social hierarchy and oppression.* New York: Cambridge University Press.

Six, B., & Eckes, T. (1991). A closer look at the complex structure of gender stereotypes. *Sex Roles, 24,* 57–71.

Staines, G., Tavris, C., & Jayaratne, T. E. (1974). The queen bee syndrome. *Psychology Today, 7*(8), 55–60.

Stroessner, S. J. (1996). Social categorization by race or sex: Effects of perceived non-normalcy on response times. *Social Cognition, 14,* 247–276.

Tajfel, H. (1978). *Differentiation between social groups: Studies in the social psychology of intergroup relations.* London: Academic Press.

Tajfel, H., & Turner, J. C. (1986). The social identity theory of intergroup behavior. In J. Worchel & W. G. Austin (Eds.), *Psychology of intergroup relations* (pp. 7–24). Chicago: Nelson-Hall.

Tausch, N., Kenworthy, J., & Hewstone, M. (2007). The confirmability and disconfirmability of trait concepts revisited: Does content matter? *Journal of Personality and Social Psychology, 92,* 554–556.

Thomas, C. A., & Esses, V. M. (2004). Individual differences in reaction to sexist humor. *Group Processes & Intergroup Relations, 7,* 89–100.

Turner, J. C. (1999). Some current issues in research on social identity and self categorization theories. In N. Ellemers, R. Spears, & B. Doosje (Eds.), *Social identity* (pp. 6–34). Oxford, England: Blackwell.

United Nations Development Programme. (2005). *Human development report 2005.* HDR Statistics. Retrieved November 16, 2006, from http://hdr.undp.org/en/statistics/indices/gdi_gem/

U.S. Bureau of the Census. (2004). Table 1: Educational Attainment of the Population 15 Years and Over, by Age, Sex, Race, and Hispanic Origin. *Current population reports: Educational attainment in the United States: 2004.* Retrieved November 16, 2006, from http://www.census.gov/population/www/socdemo/education/cps2004.html

U.S. Bureau of Labor Statistics. (2006a). Table A-19: Employed persons by occupation, sex, and age. *Annual average tables from the June 2006 issue of Employment and Earnings.* Retrieved November 16, 2006, from http://www.bls.gov/web/cpseea19.pdf

U.S. Bureau of Labor Statistics. (2006b). Table A-1: Employment status of the civilian population by sex and age. *News: The employment situation: June 2006.* Retrieved November 16, 2006, from http://www.bls.gov/news.release/empsit.t01.htm

Vescio, T. K., Gervais, S. J., Snyder, M., & Hoover, A. (2005). Power and the creation of patronizing environments: The stereotype-based behaviors of the powerful and their effects on female performance in masculine domains. *Journal of Personality and Social Psychology, 88,* 658–672.

Viki, G. T., & Abrams, D. (2003). Infra-humanization: Ambivalent sexism and the attribution of primary and secondary emotions to women. *Journal of Experimental Social Psychology, 39,* 492–499.

Webster, M., & Foschi, M. (1988). *Status generalization: New theory and research.* Stanford, CA: Stanford University Press.

II

RESPONSES TO SUBTLE
BARRIERS WOMEN FACE

5

THE SELF-FULFILLING EFFECTS OF CONTEMPORARY SEXISM: HOW IT AFFECTS WOMEN'S WELL-BEING AND BEHAVIOR

MANUELA BARRETO, NAOMI ELLEMERS, SEZGIN CIHANGIR, AND KATHERINE STROEBE

A careful examination of the available statistical evidence reveals that although women's social position has improved in the past 20 years, gender gaps persist. In fact, the position of women relative to men has not changed in recent years in important areas such as their employment rates, career success, or pay equality. For example, when one looks at statistics regarding the employment of men and women in the European Union, it is clear that employment rates have improved both for men and for women, but it is also clear that in 2005 the gender gap in employment remained considerable (16 percentage points; Eurostat, 2008). In addition, the gender pay gap has hardly changed in the past 10 years (see Blau & Kahn, 2007, for an analysis). In fact, in 1994 European women earned 17% less per hour than did their male counterparts, and in 2005 women still earned 15% less per hour than did men (Eurostat, 2008). Finally, the evidence also shows little change in

Manuela Barreto is now both at the University of Leiden and CIS–Lisbon University. We thank Michael T. Schmitt, Norann Richards, and Arnie Kahn for valuable comments on a prior version of this chapter. The research reviewed in this chapter was funded by a grant from the Dutch Science Foundation awarded to the first author (Vernieuwingsimpuls).
Address for correspondence Manuela Barreto, CIS, Av. das Forças Armadas–Ed. ISCTE, 1649-026, Lisbon, Portugal. E-mail: manuela.barreto@iscte.pt

the representation of women in managerial and decision-making positions. For example, in 1999 in Europe 30% of managers at all levels were women, and in 2004 this number was virtually the same, at 32% (Eurostat, n.d.). The differential career success of men and women is even more clearly visible when we examine higher levels of management (see also chaps. 2 and 7, this volume). For example, in 2005 women still occupied only 15% of full professor positions in the European Union. In sum, although the available evidence shows some improvement in women's position in the workplace, gender differences in employment, pay, and representation at the managerial level are still clearly visible.

What factors can be proposed to explain persisting differences in work-related outcomes? The available data show that these gender gaps cannot be explained by lack of education on the part of women. In fact, Eurostat (n.d.) data pertaining to 2005 show that fewer female (16%) than male (20%) students dropped out of secondary school, that women accounted for 58% of graduates, and that women held 41% of all PhDs. Gender gaps in educational attainment are thus negligible, and in some cases women even seem to achieve greater educational success than do men. Moreover, research in which differences in education level are parceled out still shows differences in the work-related outcomes of men and women (e.g., Roos & Gatta, 1999). Other research also indicates that women are disadvantaged relative to men, even if they have already established their competence and have been successful in their careers (Preston, 2004). The evidence also does not support the idea that women are simply less motivated or committed to work-related activities than are men. Employed men and women tend to express equal commitment to their career (e.g., Ellemers, van den Heuvel, de Gilder, Maass, & Bonvini, 2004). This finding held true even at a time when the gender gap in employment was wider, as demonstrated for example in Eurobarometer data from 1983 and 1996 (Eurostat, n.d.).

How can we explain these gender gaps? One possibility is that gender discrimination at various levels is responsible for much of the existing gender gaps in and around employment.[1] At the organizational level, sexist attitudes and beliefs are likely to be responsible for the endorsement of policies that impede (rather than facilitate) women's participation in the workforce (see, e.g., Benokraitis & Feagin, 1986; Maier, 1999). At a more micro level, research shows that endorsement of sexist beliefs (by male as well as female sources) is associated with the biased treatment of individual women, be it their selection for particular jobs, the evaluation of their performance, or promotion decisions (see, e.g., Bartol, 1999; Ellemers et al., 2004; Graves, 1999; Heilman, 2001).

---

[1]Throughout this chapter we use the term *gender discrimination* when referring specifically to behavior that discriminates between men and women. We use the term *sexism* when referring to a broader set of beliefs, as well as when we refer to the expression of sexist attitudes or opinions.

Moreover, sexist ideologies are often associated (among men as well as among women) with particular expectations regarding child-care responsibilities, such as the expectation that mothers—and not fathers—limit their work commitments when they have young children (see also chap. 9, this volume). These expectations directly affect women's (perceived) ability to invest in their career, and at the same time preclude the creation of family-friendly policies within organizations that would allow women to participate in the workforce on a basis equal to that of men (e.g., Crosby, Williams, & Biernat, 2004).

Despite this evidence, research also shows that people tend to believe that gender discrimination is no longer a problem in contemporary societies (Swim, Aikin, Hall, & Hunter, 1995; Tougas, Brown, Beaton, & Joly, 1995). How can this be? One answer to this question lies in the changed nature of sexist expressions that has made them more elusive and harder to recognize. The past decades may have seen some change in the pervasiveness of sexist ideologies, in the specific traits that tend to form the content of gender stereotypes, or even in the subtypes of men and women that can be distinguished in people's mental representations. However, to the extent that such sexist beliefs still exist, they are now expressed in different ways. This chapter focuses precisely on the implications of this change for how women perceive and experience the sexism they encounter.

OLD-FASHIONED SEXISM AND CONTEMPORARY SEXISM

We start our analysis by closely examining how expressions of sexism have changed, comparing contemporary forms of sexism with old-fashioned expressions of sexist beliefs. When we look at what people currently say about men and women, at first sight it may appear that people generally no longer endorse sexist beliefs. For example, a Eurobarometer opinion poll revealed that in 2005 only 19% of Europeans agreed that a university education is more important for a boy than for a girl (Eurostat, n.d.). In addition, although in 1983 only 60% of Europeans agreed that in times of job scarcity women have as much right to a job as do men, this percentage rose to 86% in 2005 (Eurostat, n.d.).

Although this evidence seems to reveal that sexism is not prevalent in contemporary societies, researchers have argued that this conclusion is not warranted because such data do not appropriately uncover people's sexist beliefs (Swim et al., 1995; Tougas et al., 1995). First, the particular beliefs that qualify as sexism in contemporary societies may be quite different from those that characterized older forms of sexism. For example, it is possible that the increased representation of women in leadership positions has over time also increased at least some people's confidence in women's leadership abilities. In addition, social norms have changed in such a way that even those who believe in older forms of sexism are less likely to express them. Indeed, as blatant expressions of sexism are less accepted, respondents are less likely to agree with statements that blatantly reflect a support for gender inequality. The statements used to assess public opinions as summarized earlier in fact tap blatant sexist beliefs. These statements are actually very similar to items that have been included in a scale designated as old-fashioned sexism, and that (precisely for the reasons outlined earlier) are nowadays considered nondiagnostic of people's actual beliefs regarding gender equality (Swim et al., 1995). In sum, although responses to opinion polls often appear to indicate that sexism is less of a problem than it used to be in many societies, it would be more correct to say that sexism continues to exist but has taken on new forms that are a great deal more subtle and more difficult to capture than are older forms of sexism (see also Benokraitis, 1997).

These developments in the expression of sexist beliefs parallel developments in the expression of other forms of prejudice, such as racism (Devine, Plant, & Blair, 2001; Dovidio, 2001; Kinder & Sears, 1981; McConahay, 1986; Pettigrew & Meertens, 1995). Although the precise changes that have taken place with regard to sexism and racism (or to other forms of prejudice) are not the same, they do share some basic developments. This is because the norms that govern these expressions tend to be quite general, prescribing the egalitarian treatment of all individuals (Katz & Hass, 1988; Kluegal & Smith, 1986). Some have internalized these norms, whereas others merely publicly comply with them, without a full endorsement of egalitarian beliefs (Plant & Devine, 1998). Those who do not fully endorse egalitarian beliefs tend to express prejudice in ways that are more ambiguous and thus less subject to social (or legal) sanctions, such as through nonverbal behavior (Crosby, Bromley, & Saxe, 1980). However, even those who have internalized egalitarian beliefs may hold them at the same time as they maintain subconscious prejudiced beliefs over which they have little or no control (Dovidio & Gaertner, 1986; Katz & Hass, 1988). This is what Dovidio and Gaertner (1986) designated as *aversive racism*: the coexistence of egalitarian beliefs with subconscious and subtle racism. The result is that prejudice is often expressed outside a person's awareness, even when people are subjectively convinced that they do not endorse prejudicial beliefs or are trying hard not to express them (Macrae, Bodenhausen, Milne, & Jetten, 1994). As a consequence, although people may be nonprejudiced with regard to behavior and verbal expressions that they can control (e.g., inviting women as well as men for job interviews), they may simultaneously express prejudiced attitudes in ways over which they have less control (e.g., showing less nonverbal enthusiasm toward a female rather than a male applicant). The result is that even though blatant prejudice still abounds, how prejudice is expressed in contemporary societies is often fundamentally different and a great deal more subtle than it was in the past.

THE SELF-FULFILLING NATURE OF SUBTLE SEXISM:
A THEORETICAL MODEL

To start examining the effects of these new forms of prejudice on their targets, we introduce a theoretical model that attempts to describe how subtle sexism can be involved in a self-fulfilling cycle that promotes stereotype confirmation and the maintenance of social inequalities (see Figure 5.1). As argued already, a fairly direct consequence of the fact that contemporary sexism is more subtle than old-fashioned sexism is that it is a great deal harder to detect, both by its targets as well as by external observers (e.g., Barreto & Ellemers, 2005).[2] One important consequence of this lack of detection is that other explanations for gender inequality in general, and individual outcomes in particular, become more plausible. For example, failure to recognize that rejection following a job interview was due to discrimination raises the likelihood that a person considers other causes such as bad luck or poor candidate performance. Among these alternative explanations, attributions to lack of ability or effort on the part of the candidate are particularly likely in contemporary societies. This is because contemporary societies are dominated by meritocratic ideologies and a strong individualistic focus. Meritocratic ideologies involve the belief that people generally deserve the outcomes they get, and generally get what they deserve (Bobo & Hutchings, 1996; Hafer & Olson, 1989; Kluegal & Smith, 1986; Lerner, 1977). Meritocratic beliefs are in themselves self-fulfilling because they tend to promote people's explanations of ambiguous events in terms of individual causes for success or failure (Jost & Banaji, 1994; Major et al., 2002). This self-fulfillment is even more likely to be the case in contexts such as job interviews, dating, or other seemingly interpersonal encounters in which the focus is on whether the individual has the qualities required to be accepted for a particular job or to be liked by a potential friend (see Crocker, Major, & Steele, 1998, for a review). Moreover, situations with such a focus on individual differences and personal identity make it harder to make inferences that may involve thinking of oneself as a member of a group (Tajfel, 1978; Tajfel & Turner, 1979) and that may be necessary to detect more systematic differences in group-based treatment (e.g., Operario & Fiske, 2001; Postmes, Branscombe, Spears, & Young, 1999).

It is important to stress that neither subtle discrimination nor meritocratic beliefs or individualistic settings are in themselves sufficient to promote attributions to lack of ability or effort. In fact, when subtle discrimination

---

[2]Although the statement that subtle prejudice often remains undetected may appear somewhat circular, it is worth noting that several individual and contextual factors can modify this relationship, making it easier or harder for targets to detect the same subtle prejudice treatment. We thus find it important to conceptually separate the idea of subtle prejudice, as the type of treatment engaged in by the perpetrator, and its detection on the part of the target. This is, however, not the focus of this chapter so we opted not to elaborate on this in the text.

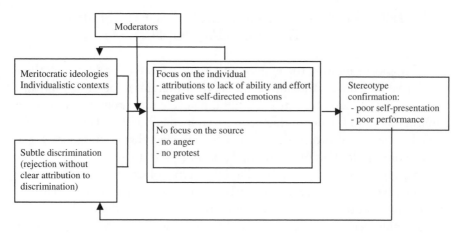

Figure 5.1. Theoretical model illustrating the self-fulfilling nature of subtle prejudice.

takes place, any causal explanation other than prejudice is likely to be seen as plausible (whereas blatant discrimination draws attention toward prejudice and away from other potential causes of the negative outcome). In turn, meritocratic beliefs are not necessarily associated with attributions to individual ability or effort. For example, when discrimination is clear, those who hold meritocratic beliefs are perfectly capable of recognizing discrimination and, as a result, of endorsing corrective measures (Son Hing, Bobocel, & Zanna, 2002). Rather, as we show in Figure 5.1, the combination of subtle discrimination and the individualistic focus of a particular context or (meritocratic) ideology is likely to promote the belief that failure is caused by lack of individual abilities or effort.

The self-fulfilling cycle continues when these contextual attributions made to explain particular outcomes feed back into more general beliefs about the legitimacy of outcome distributions in the broader social system. Thus, societal beliefs in meritocracy combined with subtle discrimination lead to patterns of attributions in specific contexts that feed back into more general societal beliefs. Because in this process these beliefs are in part determined by failure to detect discrimination that is in reality taking place, they can be more appropriately designated as illusions—illusions of meritocracy (see also Barreto, Ellemers, & Palacios, 2004; Ellemers & Barreto, in press).

Another feedback loop in this cycle occurs further in the process. We argue that the combination of these factors leads not only to attributions to poor performance but also to a more generalized focus on the individual that is associated with negative self-directed emotions (e.g., self-anger, disappointment with oneself), poor self-presentation, and poor performance. In turn, poor self-presentation and poor performance by targets of prejudice can confirm the negative stereotypes and group-based expectations that were at the basis of the discriminatory treatment received from the perpetrator at the start of this process. Moreover, poor performance and poor self-presentation provide clear justifications for rejection, a situation that is ideal for the operation of subtle biases. As repeatedly demonstrated by Dovidio and Gaertner (see Dovidio & Gaertner, 1986, for a review), it is exactly when alternative explanations are plausible that subtle biases operate at their best. If targets of subtle prejudice end up behaving in ways that provide those alternative explanations for rejection, then it can be said that targets of subtle prejudice unwittingly behave in ways that feed back into the prejudiced beliefs held by perpetrators.

Also included in this model is the fact that when discrimination is not detected, it is unlikely to elicit either anger toward the source of ill treatment or collective protest aimed toward addressing social inequalities. Simply said, if people do not clearly see what is wrong, they cannot try to fix it. This process is parallel to the enhanced individual focus that results from the combination of subtle discrimination and meritocratic ideologies, or individualistic contexts. Indeed, at the same time as individual focus is enhanced, attention is directed away from the source of prejudice, thereby reducing other-directed emotions and reactions, such as anger and protest.

A fundamental aspect of this model is the suggestion that several factors, such as perceived pervasiveness of discrimination, personal self-esteem, and social influence, are likely to determine the extent to which the combination of meritocratic or individualistic settings and subtle prejudice leads to an enhanced focus on the individual self and a reduced focus on the source of prejudice. We suggest that some of these factors will affect the emotions experienced by targets of prejudice, as well as the behavior they display, even when they do not alter the extent to which people realize that they have been targets of discrimination.

Now that we have described the general theoretical model that guided our research in this topic, in the remainder of this chapter we review work that examines some of the connections proposed and some of the factors that may moderate these connections. In doing so, we draw heavily on work from our own lab, but we also refer to a representative selection of relevant work in this area by other authors. In this research, we often chose to examine the effects of subtle discrimination by comparing it with the effects of blatant discrimination. This choice was guided by several criteria. First, although prejudice has become increasingly subtle, blatant prejudice still exists, especially with regard to particular social groups and in certain societies. Therefore, a more complete understanding of how prejudice affects its targets could be achieved by comparing the effects of these two forms of prejudice, rather than by focusing only on subtle forms. A second reason is that when examining the effects of subtle discrimination on its targets, we found it important to control for actual exposure to discrimination. Although prior research has most often compared reactions to subtle discrimination with reactions to rejection in the absence of discrimination (see Crocker et al., 1998, and Major, Kaiser, & McCoy, 2003, for reviews), our focus was on ascertaining how targets experience discrimination that can or cannot easily be recognized as such. A final reason was that we were interested in demonstrating that different factors moderate the effects of each type of discrimination on the variables included in the model. In the following sections we examine in more detail first how subtle prejudice leads to enhanced individual focus and stereotype confirmation, and second how it impairs collective protest.

HOW SUBTLE SEXISM LEADS TO STEREOTYPE CONFIRMATION

Subtle prejudice has concrete implications that can hinder members of minority groups in significant ways. First, although less obvious than blatant forms of discrimination, subtle discrimination still results in disadvantage for minority group members (e.g., Biernat & Fuegen, 2001; Ryan & Haslam, 2005). Second, subtle forms of prejudice influence how targets feel and act, even leading them to unwittingly behave in ways that contribute to justifying or perpetuating their own inferiority (Steele & Aronson, 1995; see also Ellemers & Barreto, 2008). In this section we focus on this second category of effects and first examine the effects of subtle prejudice on psychological well-being, and subsequently the effects of subtle discrimination on self-presentation and performance. The evidence presented in the two sections that follow stems partly from the same studies, but is discussed here separately so as to enable a more in-depth analysis of effects on well-being and effects on behavioral outcomes.

Effects of Subtle Sexism on Psychological Well-Being

On the basis of the results of prior research examining the effects of various forms of prejudice, it is fair to say that the effect of perceiving oneself as a victim of sexism on well-being is quite complex. On the one hand, it is no joy to be a victim of any form of discrimination. Thus, perceiving oneself or one's group as a target of discrimination has been associated with a number of psychological and physiological responses indicative of stress experiences (Clark, Anderson, Clark, & Williams, 1999), as well as with negative emotions, low self-esteem, and psychiatric symptoms (e.g., Barreto et al., 2004; Branscombe, Schmitt, & Harvey, 1999; Dion & Earn, 1975; Kobrynowicz & Branscombe, 1997; Landrine & Klonoff, 1997; Sellers & Shelton, 2003; see Schmitt & Branscombe, 2002a, for a review). One important reason why this may be the case is that perceiving oneself as a victim of discrimination implies a devaluation of an important part of oneself—one's social group membership—and communicates exclusion from society at large by virtue of this social identity (Branscombe et al., 1999; Schmitt & Branscombe, 2002b). A woman who thinks she is a target of gender discrimination not only has to deal with the negative outcome this implies but must also realize that something quite fundamental about her (her gender) is devalued by others. Consistent with this view, perceiving oneself as a target of prejudice or discrimination is associated with feelings of social exclusion (e.g., low collective self-esteem; Branscombe et al., 1999; Jetten, Branscombe, Schmitt, & Spears, 2001; Leonardelli & Tormala, 2003; Schmitt, Spears, & Branscombe, 2003). These feelings of exclusion and devaluation also imply negative expectations about future interactions, not only with the particular source of prejudice but also with the out-group as a whole (e.g., Tropp, 2003). At the same time, threats to feelings of inclusion enhance the need to see oneself as respected and accepted by others, which can elicit defensive responses that reduce the extent to which people are willing to see themselves as targets of discrimination (Carvallo & Pelham, 2006).

On the other hand, evidence seems to suggest that perceiving gender discrimination, or other forms of discrimination, can be positive for well-being. In particular, perceiving oneself as a victim of prejudice when the alternative is to fully accept personal responsibility for a negative outcome can protect well-being by shifting the blame for the negative outcome away from the self (e.g., Major, Kaiser, et al., 2003). Research has shown that individuals who receive a negative outcome and attribute this outcome to discrimination score better on measures of psychological well-being than do individuals who attribute this outcome to their own lack of personal deservingness.

Although these findings are at first sight contradictory, they can be reconciled. One crucial factor that moderates the effect of discrimination on well-being is whether discrimination is seen as an isolated event or an event that repeatedly permeates one's life experiences. Just as happens with other types of attributions, attributions to discrimination can vary in terms of their stability—the extent to which they apply across time and contexts or are tied to particular situations (Schmitt & Branscombe, 2002a). Attributing a negative outcome obtained in an isolated context to discrimination can be self-protective for individuals for whom this event is not pervasive—for example, for those who are not usually targets of discrimination, such as men or White Americans. By contrast, research shows that discrimination attributions are harmful for individuals for whom this event is pervasive, such as women or African Americans (Schmitt, Branscombe, Kobrynowicz, & Owen, 2002; see also Barreto et al., 2004; Eccleston & Major, 2006; Platow, Byrne, & Ryan, 2005). In a similar vein, discrimination that is portrayed or perceived as pervasive is more damaging for individual well-being than is discrimination that is portrayed as rare (Schmitt, Branscombe, & Postmes, 2003; see also Stroebe, Dovidio, Barreto, & Ellemers, 2007). This different impact of rare and pervasive discrimination may also partly explain why laboratory research often finds self-protective effects of discrimination, whereas research focusing on broader perceptions of discrimination across time and contexts tends to find that it is negatively associated with well-being. More generally, this research suggests that to understand the effects of discrimination on well-being, it is important not only to ascertain whether people perceive themselves as targets of discrimination, but also to inquire what exactly this perception means to them.

Although focusing on individual differences in optimism, Kaiser, Major, and McCoy (2004) also provided evidence in support of the idea that perceived pervasiveness of discrimination shapes its effects on well-being. It is presumed that those who have an optimistic outlook tend to believe that negative events, such as discrimination, happen less often to them, which can constitute an important source of resilience to the effects of discrimination. In three studies these authors showed that possessing an optimistic outlook on life can shield individuals from the negative effects of attributions to prejudice, whereas a pessimistic outlook constitutes a source of vulnerability among targets of prejudice. Indeed, women who were targets of gender discrimination reported feeling less stressed and evaluated their resources for coping with stress more positively when they had an optimistic rather than a pessimistic outlook on life.

Another important consideration to keep in mind when trying to reconcile the findings from past research is that past research examining effects of discrimination on well-being has focused on quite different comparisons. To start with, when the effects of subtle discrimination are compared with a control condition, the particular characteristics of the control condition are likely to make a difference. For example, subtle discrimination may offer some scope for the protection of the individual self in comparison with a control situation in which targets receive negative feedback that is attributed solely to internal causes. However, this self-protective effect is not likely when comparing the effects of exposure to a subtle sexist remark with a control condition in which there is no negative feedback that needs to be explained. That is, for subtle gender discrimination to afford some self-protection despite the costs it also implies, it needs to be compared with a situation that is even more costly. In addition, very different conclusions may be drawn concerning the effects of gender discrimination, depending on what is studied: how women experience subtle gender discrimination or how women experience blatant gender discrimination. Indeed, whereas some past research investigated the effect of perceptions of discrimination in ambiguous contexts, others examined the effects of perceiving discrimination that takes more blatant forms. Exposure to gender discrimination can have quite different effects depending on the type of gender discrimination encountered, highlighting the importance of comparing exposure to different types of discrimination within a single study.

Research has begun to uncover that these different forms of discrimination can indeed have quite different effects on particular indexes of well-being. For example, research by Major, Quinton, and Schmader (2003) demonstrated that self-esteem was lower when participants confronted subtle discrimination than when they encountered blatant discrimination. The authors reasoned that making attributions to discrimination can be self-protective when it is clear that these attributions are appropriate (as when discrimination is blatant), but that the same attribution would not be self-protective—and could in fact be hurtful—if it is made with a high degree of uncertainty, as happens when discrimination is subtle. The idea is that the uncertainty inherent in subtle discrimination erases the possible benefit that an attribution to discrimination may at times have, relative to an attribution to lack of individual merit.

Research from our own lab has also provided evidence that when sexism's effects on well-being are examined, it is important to take into account which type of sexism targets encounter. For example, in one study participants read the results of a (bogus) opinion poll about men and women in Dutch society and were asked to indicate how they felt as a consequence of what they read (Barreto & Ellemers, 2005). Half of the participants were told that a large proportion of men and women in this poll expressed agreement with blatantly sexist opinions (e.g., women are not as smart as men, I would rather have a man than a woman as a boss). The remaining participants were told that a large proportion of the respondents to the bogus opinion poll expressed agreement with sexist opinions that were more subtle (e.g., if women do not yet hold high-status positions in organizations, it is not because they are discriminated against; there no longer is gender discrimination in Dutch society). The items chosen to manipulate blatant versus subtle gender discrimination were taken from Swim et al.'s (1995) scale of old-fashioned and modern sexism. The results showed that, compared with blatant gender discrimination, subtle gender discrimination led to negative self-directed emotions, such as anxiety and self-directed anger (Barreto & Ellemers, 2005). In addition, this research demonstrated that negative affect is not unique to subtle discrimination. However the type of negative affect elicited by blatant discrimination is quite different. In fact, whereas subtle discrimination led to more anxiety than did blatant discrimination, participants confronted with blatant discrimination reported more anger and hostility directed at the source of sexism than did participants confronted with subtle discrimination (see also Vorauer & Kumhyr, 2001). In line with the theoretical model described in the previous section, we argue that these differential emotional responses happen because—in the individualistic contexts in which it was examined—subtle gender discrimination promotes a focus on the individual self and one's shortcomings, whereas blatant gender discrimination directs attention and emotional reactions toward the source of ill treatment.

A third point to consider when examining the effects of discrimination on well-being is that even when individuals report similar levels of perceived discrimination, individual and situational factors can alter the effect these perceptions have on their well-being. Results from prior research indeed demonstrate that similar perceptions of discrimination can be self-protective for some individuals even though they are mainly harmful for other individuals. For example, the research by Kaiser et al. (2004), which demonstrates that an optimistic outlook on life provides resources that offer important protection from the pernicious effects of discrimination, can also support the idea that individual difference variables can shape the effects of discrimination, even when they do not alter the degree to which it is recognized. In addition, research by Foster and Tsarfati (2005) shows that participants with similar perceptions of discrimination had different scores on measures of well-being depending on the extent to which they endorsed beliefs in meritocracy. In particular, whereas beliefs in meritocracy were positively associated with well-being under control conditions, they were negatively associated with well-being when participants were confronted with discrimination (see also Major, Kaiser, O'Brien, & McCoy, 2007). That is, only among people who believed in meritocracy did discrimination have hurtful effects. This finding also provides direct evidence for our suggestion that it is the combination of beliefs in meritocracy and subtle discrimination that induces negative affect, rather than any of these factors in and of itself (see Figure 5.1).

Our own lab examined the possibility that similar perceptions of discrimination would have different effects on well-being depending on individual differences in personal self-esteem (Cihangir, Barreto, & Ellemers, 2007a). We reasoned that situations that promote a focus on the individual self and individual inadequacies, such as subtle discrimination in a context with a strong focus on individual qualities (e.g., a job-interview context), should be particularly harmful for individuals for whom this self-focus is unpleasant, such as individuals with low self-esteem. As a result, by affording the opportunity to focus away from the self and on the source of ill treatment as a cause of the negative outcome, clearly discriminatory treatment would protect the well-being of individuals with low personal self-esteem. Because individuals with high personal self-esteem were not expected to be this vulnerable to a focus on the individual self, blatant discrimination was not expected to have this effect on them.

Participants in these studies underwent a computer-mediated job interview in which several gender-biased interview questions were used (e.g., "Are you often emotional at work because of something you did not manage to do?", "Do you think it will be hard to combine your family life with your career?"). In addition, in the subtle discrimination condition, participants were rejected and read that they had not been selected "because they had not answered the crucial questions properly." In the blatant gender discrimination condition, participants read the following:

> You are not selected, because you were not able to answer the crucial questions properly. By the way, women are generally not suitable candidates for these kinds of jobs. Since you are a woman, it would be very unlikely that you would be found to be a suitable candidate.

A pilot study established that the interview questions used were seen as gender biased, compared with a parallel set of questions used in a control condition that addressed the same issue but did not assume gender-stereotypical behavior on the part of female respondents (e.g., "Do you think you deal well with emotionally loaded situations?", "Do you find it important to make a career?"). Moreover, the results of the pilot study showed that participants in the subtle condition perceived the treatment they received as more discriminatory than did control participants, but as less discriminatory than did participants who had been targets of blatant discrimination.

In three subsequent studies, personal self-esteem was experimentally manipulated through performance on an easy (high personal self-esteem) versus a difficult (low personal self-esteem) IQ-type test. The manipulation of personal self-esteem was included after the job interview but before the rejection feedback was provided. This timing ensured that any effects of personal self-esteem on the dependent variables would be due to the possible effects of self-esteem not on how participants answered the interview questions, but on how they interpreted the feedback they received. This procedure also provided an examination of personal self-esteem as a resource to deal with threatening feedback, rather than as a determinant of performance that can in itself make negative feedback more or less appropriate. In line with our expectations, we found that although ratings of discriminatory treatment did not vary as a function of level of self-esteem, personal self-esteem did alter the effect of subtle discrimination on negative self-directed emotions (e.g., self-anger, disappointment with the self). Attributing a negative outcome to discrimination was beneficial for the well-being mainly of those individuals with low self-esteem, as compared with individuals with high self-esteem. Again, it is interesting to consider the possibility that individual levels of self-esteem may be intrinsically connected to perceptions regarding the (expected) pervasiveness of discrimination, or one's positive or pessimistic outlook on life.

In another set of studies, we examined how the identity of others who witnessed the event, and indicated that gender discrimination may have been the cause of a negative outcome received by the self, affected the well-being of targets of subtle gender discrimination (Cihangir, Barreto, & Ellemers, 2007b). We used a paradigm similar to that of Cihangir et al. (2007a), except that instead of manipulating personal self-esteem, we included an informal chat session after negative feedback was provided, in which either two male or two female participants gave their opinion about the interview procedure. In the first study, we varied whether these male or female witnesses indicated that they thought the procedure had been discriminatory of women or indicated approval of the selection procedure. In the second study, we varied whether the male or female witnesses indicated discriminatory treatment against women or indicated thinking that the procedure had not been discriminatory against women.

In these studies, women's attributions to discrimination were not affected by the gender of a bystander who suggested that discrimination was likely. However, participants' well-being was differentially affected by this manipulation. In particular, subtle gender discrimination resulted in more negative self-views among our female participants when other women indicated discriminatory treatment, than when men suggested that gender discrimination was the cause of their negative outcome. We propose that these results occurred because the motives of the other women who indicated discriminatory treatment were less clear than those of men. That is, women who indicate sexist treatment not only may offer support to the self, but also may be seen to avoid responsibility for their own negative outcome. In fact, prior research has shown that individuals who complain they have received discriminatory treatment are negatively evaluated (Kaiser & Miller, 2001), especially when the complainer is an in-group member (Garcia, Reser, Amo, Redersdorff, & Branscombe, 2005). Their (potentially supportive) behavior thus might be seen to reflect negatively on other in-group members, including the self (but cf. Wright, 1997). By contrast, men who suggest that a particular procedure may be discriminatory against women are seen to voice a legitimate opinion, void of self-interest, and thus provide a more valid explanation for the treatment received. The indication of discriminatory treatment by out-group members (who are usually expected to be the perpetrators of discrimination against the in-group) can also be seen to suggest hope for change. In this context, when men perceive and acknowledge discrimination, this might constitute a hopeful step toward future change rather than a mere description of a dismal present situation. In line with this idea, in our research it was also when men indicated discriminatory treatment (but not when this suggestion was made by other women) that participants were most inclined to engage in behavioral strategies directed at challenging the unjust situation (e.g., protest).

In sum, the evidence discussed in this section clarifies some of the circumstances under which recognizing discriminatory treatment tends to be harmful and explains when and why it can also be protective of individual well-being. Although the effects of subtle discrimination on well-being seem to be quite complex, we have identified several individual and situational factors that modify these effects. In the next section we go beyond effects on well-being and focus on the effect exposure to subtle gender discrimination has on the likelihood that individuals present themselves and behave in ways that confirm existing stereotypes.

Effects of Subtle Gender Discrimination on Individual Self-Presentation and Performance

Past research provided evidence that targets often confirm the stereotype-based expectations that their interaction partners have of them (for reviews see Klein & Snyder, 2003; Steele, Spencer, & Aronson, 2002; see also chap. 6, this volume). However, stereotype disconfirmation can also occur. Early research on behavioral confirmation demonstrated that targets of negative expectations can choose to react against others' negative expectations, instead of simply assimilating to them (e.g., Burgoon, Le Poire, & Rosenthal, 1995). Targets chose this strategy mainly when it was clear that their interaction violated the target's expectations or self-views, such as by explicitly disagreeing with them, and not when this violation was unclear (Swann & Ely, 1984). Although this phenomenon has been less researched with regard to behavioral confirmation of stereotype-based expectations, a similar process seems to hold in this case. For example, research by Kray, Thomson, and Galinsky (2001) examining stereotype confirmation in a negotiation setting showed that women tended to confirm stereotype-based expectations (by underperforming on a negotiation task) only when the gender stereotype was implicitly activated, not when it was explicitly activated. In fact, stereotype threat research most often uses such implicit activations of stereotypes, such as simply stating that a test is diagnostic of math abilities and leaving participants to make the connection between this dimension and the in-group stereotype, or by stating that the test usually shows differences between groups, leaving participants to wonder whether these differences are consistent with the stereotype. The research by Kray et al. (2001) shows that when the gender stereotype of women was made more explicit, by telling women that they were worse negotiators than were men, women were able to defend themselves and this actually led women to be more successful than men in their negotiation behavior.

We obtained a similar result in our own lab, with quite a different paradigm. We examined the effect of past in-group experiences on perceived feasibility of individual success and individual task performance at a current opportunity (Barreto et al., 2004). Men and women were told that a selection process would take place using the same procedure that had been used a few times in past years. Participants were shown the results of past selection procedures, making it clear that no women had been selected thus far, that only a few women had been selected in the past, or that a proportional amount of male and female candidates had been selected in the past. We showed that when the pattern of past group opportunities clearly indicated discriminatory treatment, this treatment had less deleterious effects on individual aspirations and actually boosted individual performance compared with when previous discrimination was ambiguous. Thus, suspecting that one is a target of stereo-typical expectations harms perceptions of future success and performance relative to actually knowing that this is the case. So, it is important to again note that even though being confronted with clear evidence of group-based discrimination can also have a negative effect on well-being, it provides targets with an important opportunity to redress unfair treatment.

We also examined the extent to which targets confirm stereotype-based expectations once they have been exposed to discriminatory treatment (Barreto et al., 2004; Cihangir et al., 2007a, 2007b). In line with the suggested importance of awareness of stereotype-based treatment in this process, we directly examined whether in this context failure to detect discriminatory treatment at an earlier time would be associated with more stereotype confirmation at a subsequent task. The procedures followed in these studies were already described in an earlier section. This second task used to assess performance was introduced as an opportunity given by the experimenters to ascertain the correctness of the (discriminatory) decision made earlier by the perpetrator. Our results indicate that, compared with women who had been targets of blatant discrimination, women who had been targets of more subtle discrimination—which was left undetected—tended to confirm stereotype-based expectations by endorsing more stereotypical self-descriptions. Moreover, women who had failed to detect discriminatory treatment (because they had been subject to subtle discrimination) also self-handicapped more and performed more poorly than did women who had been targets of blatant discrimination.

Our research also revealed that some factors are likely to modify this effect. In one set of studies we demonstrated that failing to detect discrimination led to stereotype confirmation only among women who were low in personal self-esteem and not among women who were high in self-esteem (Cihangir et al., 2007a). For stereotypical self-descriptions, this effect was mediated by an increased focus on the individual self and self-focused preoccupation that was elicited by the combination between subtle gender discrimination and low self-esteem. Individuals with low self-esteem who faced subtle gender discrimination felt worse about themselves and indicated being preoccupied with preventing future failure, which in turn led to poor self-presentation. By contrast, individuals with high self-esteem did not report negative self-directed emotions, nor preoccupation with preventing failure, and as a result presented themselves in less gender-stereotypic terms.

In addition, in another set of studies we found that women were more likely to disconfirm stereotypic expectations after having been a target of subtle gender discrimination when they were exposed to men who helped them attribute the negative outcome to prejudice, than when they were exposed to women who indicated discriminatory treatment (Cihangir et al., 2007b). For example, whereas exposure to other women who indicated discriminatory treatment led women who had been subjected to subtle discrimination to describe themselves in gender-stereotypic terms and made them perform suboptimally on an IQ-type task, exposure to the opinion of men who indicated that gender discrimination might be the cause of negative outcomes for women induced these women to self-stereotype less and led them to show a better task performance. Besides reflecting the possibility that a suggestion of discriminatory treatment stemming from a male source may be seen as more legitimate, these results may also be linked to a lower normative fit (and thus lower category salience and less stereotypical behavior) when men suggest discrimination than when women make this suggestion (Turner, Hogg, Oakes, Reicher, & Wetherell, 1987).

Taken together, these results suggest that targets of subtle gender discrimination are often likely to present themselves and behave in ways that confirm stereotypical expectations of themselves. However, a number of factors—such as personal self-esteem or the presence of out-group members who indicate discriminatory treatment—can turn this around and help targets of subtle discrimination behave in ways that disconfirm stereotypes about themselves and their group, thereby contributing to individual and collective position improvement.

HOW SUBTLE SEXISM IMPAIRS PROTEST

As mentioned earlier, targets of discrimination experience negative emotions, albeit different ones, irrespective of whether they are confronted with subtle or with blatant discrimination. However, contrary to what happens with subtle discrimination, perceiving oneself as a target of discrimination (as happens when it is blatant) can also encourage coping responses that protect well-being. For example, perceiving oneself as a target of prejudice is associated with an increase in group identification which in turn raises individual well-being (Branscombe et al., 1999; Jetten et al., 2001; Redersdorff, Martinot, & Branscombe, 2004; Schmitt, Spears, et al., 2003). In this way, although perceiving discrimination has a direct negative effect on well-being, it has an indirect positive effect on individual well-being by raising group identification (see also Schmitt & Branscombe, 2002a).

Exposure to blatant discrimination can elicit protest behaviors that might help redress systematic injustice, ultimately contributing to social change (see also Crosby, Pufall, Snyder, O'Connell, & Whalen, 1989; Major, 1994; Schmitt, Ellemers, & Branscombe, 2003; Wright, 2001). In the specific context of discriminatory treatment, evidence from our own laboratory also demonstrates that in contrast to subtle discrimination, blatant discrimination is clearly perceived as caused by prejudice from the source, which in turn leads to intentions to protest, objection to the behavior of the source, and even collective protest (Ellemers & Barreto, 2007). In a first study, participants were confronted with alleged results of opinion polls showing public endorsement of blatant or subtle sexist beliefs. Participants expressed more support for collective action in favor of women when confronted with blatant than with subtle sexism. In Studies 2 and 3 participants were confronted with a student supervisor who allegedly endorsed blatant or subtle sexist work-related beliefs. Participants expressed more objection to this supervisor (Study 2) and actually endorsed more protest behavior (Study 3) when the supervisor expressed blatant sexism than when the supervisor expressed subtle sexism. These results were mediated by the extent to which participants perceived the statements as sexist, which in turn predicted feelings of anger and, ultimately, protest behavior.

The fact that in contemporary societies blatant prejudice is likely to be perceived as relatively rare may also contribute toward the finding that it tends to be associated with responses directed at the source. Because blatant prejudice is relatively uncommon in contemporary societies, a source of blatant prejudice may appear somewhat odd, which is likely to direct attention toward the source as well as to elicit responses directed at confronting its behavior. In sum, in the theoretical model proposed here, a final path through which subtle discrimination contributes to the maintenance of social inequalities is by impairing collective protest, and thereby failing to contribute to social change (Tajfel, 1978; Tajfel & Turner, 1979).

Finally, the very negative emotions experienced as a result of blatant discrimination can function as a drive for these collective attempts to change the illegitimate system. In fact, prior research has shown that anger—an emotion that we have shown is more typical of responses to blatant than to subtle discrimination (Barreto & Ellemers, 2005; Ellemers & Barreto, 2007)—can function as an important precursor of collective action (e.g., van Zomeren, Spears, Fischer, & Leach, 2004). The negative emotions more typically elicited by subtle prejudice, such as anxiety, low self-esteem, or sadness, are less likely to lead to this type of response. Research by Gill and Matheson (2006) demonstrates how these differences in affect can determine how people cope with discrimination. In their studies, participants induced to feel sad were reliably less likely to endorse collective action as a response to discrimination than were participants made to feel angry.

CONCLUSION

In this chapter we argue that the way sexism is expressed has changed during the past decades; even though blatant sexism is still commonplace, especially in particular societies or with regard to specific domains, the most pervasive forms of sexism encountered in contemporary societies are not blatant, but subtle in nature. We have also argued that this change has fundamentally modified the way targets experience gender-based discrimination. The fact that expressions of sexism have shifted away from traditional images of what sexism is all about means that it has become harder to recognize sexist treatment. This difficulty, combined with dominant societal beliefs in meritocracy and with a contextual focus on the individual, leads to attributions of negative outcomes obtained by individuals in specific contexts to lack of ability or effort. These contextual attributions, in turn, feed back into beliefs about how outcomes are distributed in society as a whole, perpetuating an illusion of meritocracy.

This self-fulfilling cycle is worsened by another feedback loop that occurs when targets of subtle discrimination focus on their own individual inadequacies and fail to present themselves in ways that allow them to succeed. Individual and collective chances of self-improvement depend not only on fair treatment from others but also on individual group members' ability to present themselves and behave in ways that disconfirm existing stereotypes. Stereotype confirmation by individual group members undermines the interests of the group because it reproduces and legitimizes perceived intergroup distinctions and in this way constitutes an obstacle to social change. It also harms the individual directly because it confirms that stereotypic group expectations are appropriately applied to the individual in question. In this way, subtle prejudice contributes to the confirmation of social stereotypes, feeds prejudiced beliefs, and perpetuates social inequalities.

Making matters worse, subtle discrimination is also unlikely to be addressed—both because it does not appear illegitimate and because it does not elicit the type of emotion that leads to protest. At this stage it is worth noting that blatant discrimination can also be self-fulfilling. For example, by eliciting anger toward the perpetrator and collective protest from the group being discriminated against, blatant discrimination can worsen intergroup tensions and feed back into prejudiced beliefs. However, it is also important to note that not all forms of protest are equally hostile and thus likely to worsen such tensions, and they may in fact contribute to raising the awareness of members of the dominant group (as well as of those discriminated against), creating allies instead of enemies.

Taken together, the evidence reviewed here points to the need to address social inequalities by exposing the illusory nature of meritocratic beliefs and thereby limit the extent to which negative outcomes are attributed to characteristics internal to the individual or to disadvantaged groups. Another important step would be to increase the likelihood that subtle forms of sexism would be recognized as such by raising awareness of the different forms sexism can take. Finally, informing targets of prejudice about the self-fulfilling nature of meritocratic and sexist beliefs could help them break the cycle, as well as help others understand why particular individuals behave as they do.

All in all, the evidence discussed in this chapter shows that the greatest change regarding sexism during the past decades is not that women now experience less sexism but that women's experience of discrimination is now a great deal more complex than it used to be. This complexity arises mainly from the subtle character of contemporary sexism. However, a particular expression of sexism is not subtle in itself, but only until it is not publicly exposed and defined as antinormative. The concrete improvement of women's position thus appears to rely on the close and continuous monitoring of how men and women are treated, and the systematic identification and exposure of new and covert forms of sexist treatment.

REFERENCES

Barreto, M., & Ellemers, N. (2005). The perils of political correctness: Responses of men and women to old-fashioned and modern sexism. *Social Psychology Quarterly, 68*, 75–88.

Barreto, M., Ellemers, N., & Palacios, M. (2004). The backlash of token mobility: The impact of past group experiences on individual ambition and effort. *Personality and Social Psychology Bulletin, 30*, 1433–1445.

Bartol, K. M. (1999). Gender influences on performance evaluations. In G. M. Powell (Ed.), *Handbook of gender and work* (pp. 165–178). London: Sage.

Benokraitis, N. V. (1997). *Subtle sexism: Current practice and prospects for change*. Thousand Oaks, CA: Sage.

Benokraitis, N. V., & Feagin, J. R. (1986). *Modern sexism: Blatant, subtle, and covert discrimination*. Englewood Cliffs, NJ: Prentice-Hall.

Biernat, M., & Fuegen, K. (2001). Shifting standards and the evaluation of competence: Complexity in gender-based judgment and decision making. *Journal of Social Issues, 57*, 707–724.

Blau, F. D., & Kahn, L. M. (2007). The gender pay gap: Have women gone as far as they can? *Academy of Management Perspectives, 21*, 7–23.

Bobo, L., & Hutchings, V. L. (1996). Perceptions of racial group competition: Extending Blumer's theory of group composition to a multiracial social context. *American Sociological Review, 61*, 951–972.

Branscombe, N. R., Schmitt, M. T., & Harvey, R. D. (1999). Perceiving pervasive discrimination among African Americans: Implications for group identification and well-being. *Journal of Personality and Social Psychology, 77*, 135–149.

Burgoon, J. K., Le Poire, B. A., & Rosenthal, R. (1995). Effects of preinteraction expectancies and target communication on perceiver reciprocity and compensation in dyadic interaction. *Journal of Experimental Social Psychology, 31*, 287–321.

Carvallo, M., & Pelham, B. W. (2006). When fiends become friends: The need to belong and perceptions of personal and group discrimination. *Journal of Personality and Social Psychology, 90*, 94–108.

Cihangir, S., Barreto, M., & Ellemers, N. (2007a). *Dealing with discrimination: The moderating role of self-esteem in responses to subtle and blatant discrimination.* Manuscript submitted for publication.

Cihangir, S., Barreto, M., & Ellemers, N. (2007b). *When "they" help more than "us": The impact of ingroup and outgroup opinions on self-views, performance, and protest within a subtle discrimination context.* Manuscript submitted for publication.

Clark, R., Anderson, N. B., Clark, V. R., & Williams, D. R. (1999). Racism as a stressor for African Americans: A biopsychosocial model. *American Psychologist, 54,* 316–322.

Crocker, J., Major, B., & Steele, C. (1998). Social stigma. In D. T. Gilbert, S. T. Fiske, & G. Lindzey (Eds.), *The handbook of social psychology* (Vol. 2, 4th ed., pp. 504–553). Boston: McGraw-Hill.

Crosby, F., Bromley, S., & Saxe, L. (1980). Recent unobtrusive studies of Black and White discrimination and prejudice: A literature review. *Psychological Bulletin, 87,* 546–563.

Crosby, F., Pufall, A., Snyder, R. C., O'Connell, M., & Whalen, P. (1989). The denial of personal disadvantage among you, me, and all the other ostriches. In M. Crawford & M. Gentry (Eds.), *Gender and thought* (pp. 79–99). New York: Springer-Verlag.

Crosby, F. J., Williams, J. C., & Biernat, M. (2004). The maternal wall. *Journal of Social Issues, 60,* 675–682.

Devine, P. G., Plant, E. A., & Blair, I. V. (2001). Classic and contemporary analyses of racial prejudice. In R. Brown & S. Gaertner (Eds.), *Blackwell handbook of social psychology: Intergroup processes* (pp. 198–217). Oxford, England: Blackwell.

Dion, K. L., & Earn, B. M. (1975). The phenomenology of being a target of prejudice. *Journal of Personality and Social Psychology, 32,* 944–950.

Dovidio, J. F. (2001). On the nature of contemporary prejudice: The third wave. *Journal of Social Issues, 57,* 829–849.

Dovidio, J. F., & Gaertner, S. (1986). *Prejudice, discrimination, and racism.* San Diego, CA: Academic Press.

Eccleston, C. P., & Major, B. (2006). Attributions to discrimination and self-esteem: The role of group identification and appraisals. *Group Processes & Intergroup Relations, 9,* 147–162.

Ellemers, N., & Barreto, M. (2007). *Collective action in modern times: How modern expressions of prejudice prevent collective action.* Manuscript submitted for publication.

Ellemers, N., & Barreto, M. (2008). Putting your own down: How members of disadvantaged groups unwittingly perpetuate or exacerbate their disadvantage. In A. Brief (Ed.), *Diversity at work* (pp. 202–264). New York: Cambridge University Press.

Ellemers, N., & Barreto, M. (in press). Maintaining the illusion of meritocracy. In S. Demoulin, J. P. Leyens, & J. F. Dovidio (Eds.), *Intergroup misunderstandings: Impact of divergent social realities.* New York: Psychology Press.

Ellemers, N., van den Heuvel, H., de Gilder, D., Maass, A., & Bonvini, A. (2004). The underrepresentation of women in science: Differential commitment or the queen bee syndrome? *British Journal of Social Psychology, 43,* 315–338.

Eurostat. (n.d.). *European Commission, Eurostat home page, data navigation tree: Employment.* Retrieved July 16, 2008, from http://epp.eurostat.ec.europa.eu/portal/page?_pageid=1996,45323734&_dad=portal&_schema=PORTAL&screen=welcomeref&open=/&product=STRIND_EMPLOI&depth=2

Eurostat. (2008). *The life of women and men in Europe: A statistical portrait* (2008 ed.). Retrieved July 16, 2008, from http://epp.eurostat.ec.europa.eu/cache/ITY_OFFPUB/KS-80-07-135/EN/KS-80-07-135-EN.PDF

Foster, M. D., & Tsarfati, E. M. (2005). The effects of meritocracy beliefs on women's well-being after first-time gender discrimination. *Personality and Social Psychology Bulletin, 31,* 1730–1738.

Garcia, D. M., Reser, A. H., Amo, R. B., Redersdorff, S., & Branscombe, N. R. (2005). Perceivers' responses to in-group and out-group members who blame a negative outcome on discrimination. *Personality and Social Psychology Bulletin, 31,* 769–780.

Gill, R., & Matheson, K. (2006). Responses to discrimination: The role of emotion and expectations for emotional regulation. *Personality and Social Psychology Bulletin, 32,* 149–161.

Graves, L. M. (1999). Gender bias in interviewers' evaluations of applicants: When and how does it occur? In G. N. Powell (Ed.), *Handbook of gender and work* (pp. 145–164). Thousand Oaks, CA: Sage.

Hafer, C. L., & Olson, J. M. (1989). Beliefs in a just world and reactions to personal deprivation. *Journal of Personality, 57,* 799–823.

Heilman, M. E. (2001). Description and prescription: How gender stereotypes prevent women's ascent up the organizational ladder. *Journal of Social Issues, 57,* 657–674.

Jetten, J., Branscombe, N. R., Schmitt, M. T., & Spears, R. (2001). Rebels with a cause: Group identification as a response to perceived discrimination from the mainstream. *Personality and Social Psychology Bulletin, 27,* 1204–1213.

Jost, J. T., & Banaji, M. R. (1994). The role of stereotyping in system-justification and the production of false consciousness. *British Journal of Social Psychology, 33,* 1–27.

Kaiser, C. R., Major, B., & McCoy, S. K. (2004). Expectations about the future and the emotional consequences of perceiving prejudice. *Personality and Social Psychology Bulletin, 30,* 173–184.

Kaiser, C. R., & Miller, C. T. (2001). Stop complaining! The social costs of making attributions to discrimination. *Personality and Social Psychology Bulletin, 27,* 254–263.

Katz, I., & Hass, R. G. (1988). Racial ambivalence and American value conflict: Correlational and priming studies of dual cognitive structures. *Journal of Personality and Social Psychology, 55,* 893–905.

Kinder, D. R., & Sears, D. O. (1981). Prejudice and politics: Symbolic racism versus racial threats to the good life. *Journal of Personality and Social Psychology, 40,* 414–431.

Klein, O., & Snyder, M. (2003). Stereotypes and behavioral confirmation: From interpersonal to intergroup perspectives. In M. P. Zanna (Ed.), *Advances in experimental social psychology* (Vol. 35, pp. 153–234). New York: Guilford Press.

Kluegal, J. R., & Smith, E. R. (1986). *Beliefs about inequality: Americans' view of what is and what ought to be.* Hawthorne, NJ: Aldine de Gruyter.

Kobrynowicz, D., & Branscombe, N. R. (1997). Who considers themselves victims of discrimination? Individual difference predictors of perceived gender discrimination in women and men. *Psychology of Women Quarterly, 21,* 347–363.

Kray, L. J., Thompson, L., & Galinsky, A. (2001). Battle of the sexes: Gender stereotype confirmation and reactance in negotiations. *Journal of Experimental Social Psychology, 12,* 942–958.

Landrine, H., & Klonoff, E. A. (1997). *Discrimination against women: Prevalence, consequences, remedies.* Thousand Oaks, CA: Sage.

Leonardelli, G. J., & Tormala, Z. L. (2003). The negative impact of perceiving discrimination on collective well-being: The mediating role of perceived ingroup status. *European Journal of Social Psychology, 33,* 507–514.

Lerner, M. J. (1977). The justice motive: Some hypotheses as to its origins and forms. *Journal of Personality, 45,* 1–52.

Macrae, C. N., Bodenhausen, G. V., Milne, A. B., & Jetten, J. (1994). Out of mind but back in sight: Stereotypes on the rebound. *Journal of Personality and Social Psychology, 67,* 808–817.

Maier, M. (1999). On the gendered substructure of organization: Dimensions and dilemmas of corporate masculinity. In G. N. Powell (Ed.), *Handbook of gender and work* (pp. 69–94). Thousand Oaks, CA: Sage.

Major, B. (1994). From social inequality to personal entitlement: The role of social comparisons, legitimacy appraisals, and group membership. In M. P. Zanna (Ed.), *Advances in experimental social psychology* (Vol. 26, pp. 293–348). San Diego, CA: Academic Press.

Major, B., Gramzow, R. H., McCoy, S. K., Levin, S., Schmader, T., & Sidanius, J. (2002). Perceiving personal discrimination: The role of group status and legitimizing ideology. *Journal of Personality and Social Psychology, 82,* 269–282.

Major, B., Kaiser, C., & McCoy, S. K. (2003). It's not my fault: When and why attributions to discrimination protect self-esteem. *Personality and Social Psychology Bulletin, 29,* 772–781.

Major, B., Kaiser, C., O'Brien, L. T., & McCoy, S. K. (2007). Perceived discrimination as worldview threat or worldview confirmation: Implications for self-esteem. *Journal of Personality and Social Psychology, 92,* 1068–1086.

Major, B., Quinton, W. J., & Schmader, T. (2003). Attributions to discrimination and self-esteem: Impact of group identification and situational ambiguity. *Journal of Experimental Social Psychology, 39,* 220–231.

McConahay, J. B. (1986). Modern racism, ambivalence, and the modern racism scale. In J. F. Dovidio & S. L. Gaertner (Eds.), *Prejudice, discrimination, and racism* (pp. 91–125). San Diego: Academic Press.

Operario, D., & Fiske, S. T. (2001). Ethnic identity moderates perceptions of prejudice: Judgments of personal versus group discrimination and subtle versus blatant bias. *Personality and Social Psychology Bulletin, 27,* 550–561.

Pettigrew, T. F., & Meertens, R. W. (1995). Subtle and blatant prejudice in Western Europe. *European Journal of Social Psychology, 25,* 57–75.

Plant, E. A., & Devine, P. G. (1998). Internal and external motivation to respond without prejudice. *Journal of Personality and Social Psychology, 75,* 811–832.

Platow, M. J., Byrne, L., & Ryan, M. K. (2005). Experimentally manipulated high ingroup status can buffer self-esteem against discrimination. *European Journal of Social Psychology, 35,* 599–608.

Postmes, T., Branscombe, N. R., Spears, R., & Young, H. (1999). Comparative processes in personal and group judgments: Resolving the discrepancy. *Journal of Personality and Social Psychology, 76,* 320–338.

Preston, A. E. (2004). *Leaving science: Occupational exit from scientific careers.* New York: Russell Sage Foundation.

Redersdorff, S., Martinot, D., & Branscombe, N. R. (2004). The impact of thinking about group-based disadvantages or advantages on women's well-being: An experimental test of the rejection-identification model. *Current Psychology of Cognition, 22,* 203–222.

Roos, P. A., & Gatta, M. L. (1999). The gender gap in earnings: Trends, explanations, and prospects. In G. N. Powell (Ed.), *Handbook of gender and work* (pp. 95–124). Thousand Oaks, CA: Sage.

Ryan, M. K., & Haslam, A. S. (2005). The glass cliff: Evidence that women are overrepresented in precarious leadership positions. *British Journal of Management, 16,* 81–90.

Schmitt, M. T., & Branscombe, N. R. (2002a). The internal and external causal loci of attributions to prejudice. *Personality and Social Psychology Bulletin, 28,* 484–492.

Schmitt, M. T., & Branscombe, N. R. (2002b). The meaning and consequences of perceived discrimination in disadvantaged and privileged social groups. *European Review of Social Psychology, 12,* 167–199.

Schmitt, M. T., Branscombe, N. R., Kobrynowicz, D., & Owen, S. (2002). Perceiving discrimination against one's gender group has different implications for well-being in women and men. *Personality and Social Psychology Bulletin, 28,* 197–210.

Schmitt, M. T., Branscombe, N. R., & Postmes, T. (2003). Women's emotional responses to the pervasiveness of gender discrimination. *European Journal of Social Psychology, 33,* 297–312.

Schmitt, M. T., Ellemers, N., & Branscombe, N. R. (2003). Perceiving and responding to gender discrimination at work. In A. Haslam, D. van Knippenberg, M. Platow, & N. Ellemers (Eds.), *Social identity at work: Developing theory for organizational practice* (pp. 277–292). Philadelphia: Psychology Press.

Schmitt, M. T., Spears, R., & Branscombe, N. R. (2003). Constructing a minority group identity out of shared rejection: The case of international students. *European Journal of Social Psychology, 33,* 1–12.

Sellers, R. M., & Shelton, N. (2003). The role of racial identity in perceived racial discrimination. *Journal of Personality and Social Psychology, 84,* 1079–1092.

Son Hing, L. S., Bobocel, D. R., & Zanna, M. P. (2002). Meritocracy and opposition to affirmative action: Making concessions in the face of discrimination. *Journal of Personality and Social Psychology, 83,* 493–509.

Steele, C. M., & Aronson, J. (1995). Stereotype threat and the intellectual test performance of African Americans. *Journal of Personality and Social Psychology, 69,* 797–811.

Steele, C. M., Spencer, S. J., & Aronson, J. (2002). Contending with group image: The psychology of stereotype and social identity threat. In M. Zanna (Ed.), *Advances in experimental social psychology* (Vol. 34, pp. 379–440). San Diego, CA: Academic Press.

Stroebe, K., Dovidio, J. F., Barreto, M., & Ellemers, N. (2007). *Is the world a just place? Countering the negative consequences of pervasive discrimination by reaffirming a just world.* Manuscript submitted for publication.

Swann, W. B., Jr., & Ely, R. J. (1984). A battle of wills: Self-verification versus behavioral confirmation. *Journal of Personality and Social Psychology, 46,* 1287–1302.

Swim, J. K., Aikin, K. J., Hall, W. S., & Hunter, B. A. (1995). Sexism and racism: Old-fashioned and modern prejudices. *Journal of Personality and Social Psychology, 68,* 199–214.

Tajfel, H. (Ed.). (1978). *Differentiation between social groups: Studies in the social psychology of intergroup relations.* London: Academic Press.

Tajfel, H., & Turner, J. C. (1979). An integrative theory of intergroup conflict. In W. G. Austin & S. Worchel (Eds.), *The social psychology of intergroup relations* (pp. 33–47). Monterey, CA: Brooks/Cole.

Tougas, F., Brown, R., Beaton, A. M., & Joly, S. (1995). Neosexism: Plus ça change, plus c'est pareil. *Personality and Social Psychology Bulletin, 21,* 842–849.

Tropp, L. (2003). The psychological impact of prejudice: Implications for intergroup contact. *Group Processes & Intergroup Relations, 6,* 131–149.

Turner, J. C., Hogg, M. A., Oakes, P. J., Reicher, S., & Wetherell, M. S. (1987). *Rediscovering the social group: A self-categorisation theory.* Oxford, England: Blackwell.

van Zomeren, M., Spears, R., Fischer, A., & Leach, C. W. (2004). Put your money where your mouth is! Explaining collective action tendencies through group-based anger and collective efficacy. *Journal of Personality and Social Psychology, 87,* 649–664.

Vorauer, J., & Kumhyr, S. M. (2001). Is this about you or me? Self- versus other-directed judgments and feelings in response to intergroup interaction. *Personality and Social Psychology Bulletin, 27,* 706–719.

Wright, S. C. (1997). Ambiguity, shared consensus and collective action: Generating collective action in response to tokenism. *Personality and Social Psychology Bulletin, 23,* 1277–1290.

Wright, S. C. (2001). Restricted intergroup boundaries: Tokenism, ambiguity, and the tolerance of injustice. In J. T. Jost & B. Major (Eds.), *The psychology of legitimacy: Emerging perspectives on ideology, justice, and intergroup relations* (pp. 223–254). Cambridge, England: Cambridge University Press.

6

THE EFFECTS OF GENDER STEREOTYPES ON WOMEN'S CAREER CHOICE: OPENING THE GLASS DOOR

SHEN ZHANG, TONI SCHMADER, AND CHAD FORBES

In January 2005, the then president of Harvard University, Lawrence Summers, suggested that the underrepresentation of women in science and engineering might be due, at least in part, to inherent sex differences in cognitive abilities central to math and science. Dr. Summers's comments were viewed by many to reflect deep-seated stereotypes about men's and women's natural abilities. There has been much debate over different theories that might account for women's underinvolvement in math- and science-related careers (e.g., Bandura, Barbaranelli, Caprara, & Pastorelli, 2001; Benbow & Stanley, 1980). The focus of this chapter is not to directly consider the evidence to support or refute these stereotypic beliefs, but to consider instead the social psychological effect of the mere suggestion that there are underlying sex differences in ability. In other words, we address how cultural stereotypes help to diminish women's interest and performance in domains that have been traditionally dominated by men.

The belief that mathematics is a masculine domain dates back to Pythagoras, who in the 5th century BC founded a society in which abstract

Work on this manuscript was supported by a National Institute of Mental Health Grant #1R01MH071749 awarded to Toni Schmader.

thought and matters of the mind were seen as inherently male. Femaleness, in contrast, was associated with bodily matters and mundane aspects of earthly existence (Wertheim, 1995). Although we no longer live in a world in which women are deliberately or explicitly barred from pursuing careers related to math and science, math is still viewed as a domain better suited to men (Meece, Parsons, Kaczala, Golf, & Futterman, 1982). This view extends to fields that involve intensive mathematic components including physical science, computer science, and engineering (Nosek, Banaji, & Greenwald, 2002).

Moreover, evidence suggests that gender differences in attitudes and beliefs about various domains appear to develop in early adolescence. For example, girls often have low confidence for success in mathematics (e.g., Eccles, 1987), are more likely to experience math anxiety (Hyde, Fennema, Ryan, Frost, & Hopp, 1990), and are less likely to choose math-related academic programs compared with their male classmates (National Science Foundation, 2007). In one study of equally math-gifted college students, twice the number of men as women chose majors that involved a moderate level of mathematics such as architecture, business, and economics, and men were over four times more likely than women to pursue majors with high math content such as computer science, engineering, and mathematics (LeFevre, Kulak, & Heymans, 1992). At the same time, women receive lower scores on important standardized tests (Hyde et al., 1990), such as the SAT or Graduate Record Examinations (GRE), which constrain opportunities for them to receive advanced placements in math-intensive academic programs. As a result, fewer women complete advanced education in math-related fields, which often involve higher paid prestigious jobs that contribute to the gender gap in wages.

In this chapter, we acknowledge the negative consequences that stereotypes can have on women's professional aspirations and discuss two ways in which stereotypes affect women's eventual career decisions. One is a chronic process of socialization through which the accumulation of gender-stereotype knowledge influences women's interest in and perception of different activities. These pressures can shape at an early age what girls envision themselves doing. Unfortunately, even for those young women who have a supportive system of teachers, parents, and peers and are inclined to pursue male-dominated professions, they are likely to encounter repeated exposure to a second process by which stereotypes can have deleterious consequences on women's professional aspirations. This second process, known as *stereotype threat*, refers to the uncomfortable experience of being in a situation in which one faces possible stereotyped judgment associated with one's social group (Spencer, Steele, & Quinn, 1999). As we discuss, the desire to avoid anxiety and lower performance created in such situations can also lead many women to choose careers that do not involve the added burden of having to disprove a cultural stereotype.

With this framework in mind, we begin by reviewing the sociocultural literature on how women engage in different domains during their childhood and adolescent stages as a result of socialization and exposure to stereotypic information. Following this review, we address how cultural stereotypes affect the performance and motivations of women after they enter into masculine fields. Finally, we address what can be done to help women overcome the negative effects of gender stereotypes. Overall, this chapter aims to convey the idea that long-term forces from the sociocultural context interact with situational factors to affect women's academic performance and career paths. Our hope is that this review will provide inspiration for educators and policymakers to reduce the gender divide in career choice by addressing the pernicious effects of gender stereotypes.

STEREOTYPES SHAPE DOMAIN INVOLVEMENT FROM EARLY CHILDHOOD

From an early age, children are bombarded with implicit and explicit messages about what behaviors and activities are considered appropriate for their gender. Any toy store contains clear cues that advertise which toys are appropriate for boys and which are appropriate for girls. This gender division in the toy store not only reflects patterns of different styles of play but also forms a basis for communicating to children who they can become as adults. A quite telling example can be found in a television commercial for a line of Barbie products featuring a jingle that proclaims, "Be who you want to be!" while images on the screen portray the famed doll as an entertainer, a fashion model, a ballerina, and a food server. The message here is not even subtle: You can be anything you want, but it would be best for it to fit into stereotyped prescriptions. Targeting a slightly older generation of young adults and adolescents, the clothing company Abercrombie and Fitch introduced a women's T-shirt that read "Who needs brains when you have these?" The T-shirt was pulled from stores in November 2005, but again the implication was clear that intelligence might not be a woman's most notable endowment.

Cultural evidence of the existence of gender stereotypes in contemporary American society is easy to come by, and the earlier examples make it clear that these beliefs and biases are actively marketed to children and adolescents. In light of this exposure, it would not be surprising to learn that boys and girls begin forming different beliefs about their competencies at an early age—beliefs that shape their choices and behaviors regarding different careers. In fact, we might consider two ways in which these stereotypes might shape self-perceptions. One is through socialization processes whereby adults and peers directly or indirectly communicate expectations of what an individual can do, and the other is through exposure to information that shapes at an implicit level a person's very concept of self, gender, and domains of competence.

Socialization Discourages Women
From Pursuing Male-Dominated Careers

Perhaps the most well-known model of gender socialization processes is Eccles's expectancy-value model (Eccles, 1987). This model proposes that children's expectations for doing well in a particular domain and the value they place on that domain predict their choices to pursue activities in that arena. Past research has shown that both aspects of the model, expectancy and value, play critical roles in what activities children choose to pursue. For example, many studies have shown that gender socialization leads girls to devalue mathematical and scientific fields more so than it does boys (e.g., Crombie et al., 2005; Jacobs & Eccles, 1992; Meece, Wigfield, & Eccles, 1990). In a similar way, research has found that girls develop relatively low expectations for their own success in math in early elementary school and these beliefs reliably affect girls' subsequent math performance (e.g., Eccles, Wigfield, Harold, & Blumenfeld, 1993).

Eccles and others (Eccles et al., 1989; Meece et al., 1982) have posited that children's attitudes and beliefs about their competency toward a domain are shaped by parents and teachers. A substantial body of literature supports this assertion (e.g., Bandura, Barbaranelli, Caprara, & Pastorelli, 1996; Frome & Eccles, 1998). For example, during grade school and middle school, parents and teachers underestimate girls' math performance even in the absence of any actual gender difference in math grades; at the same time, they tend to make more favorable ratings of boys (Frome & Eccles, 1998; Jacobs & Eccles, 1992). It is not surprising that adults' beliefs are internalized by girls over time and can undermine their beliefs about their own abilities and their actual achievement (Jacobs & Eccles, 1992). In fact, these beliefs from significant others might have an even stronger effect on girls than would their actual grades in math and science classes (Frome & Eccles, 1998). As such, the perception that one's parents, teachers, or peers endorse gender stereotypes may bias girls' views about which areas they should invest their efforts in, which in turn influences their eventual career choices.

More recent evidence reveals that others' expectations can also influence self-evaluation on a moment-by-moment basis. Among other things, perceptions of how others see one's self can affect the way one sees one's self. For example, when individuals are subtly primed with negative evaluations (e.g., a frowning face), they rate themselves more negatively (e.g., Baldwin, Carrell, & Lopez, 1990). More specific to the topic of gender, women view themselves more stereotypically when they are primed with significant others who they think view them in a stereotypical way (Sinclair & Lun, 2006; see also chap. 5, this volume). This finding suggests that if women believe that important others in math-related domains (e.g., math teachers or mentors) perceive them in a stereotypical manner, these presumed expectations may then predict the likelihood that women will make more negative assessments of their own math ability. Thus, even when girls are not directly confronting negative expectations from parents and teachers, their internalized beliefs of what these important others think of them can also undermine the self-perceptions of their ability. This process suggests that the effects of social stereotypes in shaping career choice are not realized just in social contexts but are also part of women's concepts of themselves and their gender—an issue we next consider in more detail.

Unequal Distributions of Women in Certain Careers Shape Patterns of Implicit Association

Because girls may internalize stereotypic beliefs through gender socialization, part of the solution to facilitate women's involvement in male-dominant careers is to educate parents and teachers to communicate more positive expectations about girls' abilities to achieve success in domains that are traditionally masculine. But even if the parents and teachers with whom a child interacts reject prevailing gender stereotypes, children are still exposed to gendered conceptions of different occupations through broader cultural associations and mere observations of who is likely to be employed in what kinds of professions. There is reason to believe that this exposure is sufficient to shape attitudes and beliefs about one's abilities.

For example, Eagly's social role theory (Eagly & Steffen, 1984) suggests that stereotypes about women's and men's different competencies are the result of the mere fact that men and women are distributed unevenly in different social roles. Thus, children learn what occupations are supposedly suited to their nature through casual observation of the gender distributions in different jobs. Such exposure can lead to the formation of an implicit association between the domain and a given gender group. For example, both men and women generally hold an implicit association between their concept of "math" and their concept of "male" (Nosek et al., 2002). These implicit associations are not lost on children and can shape conceptions of what women can and cannot do. In a study by Hyde (1984), third and fifth graders heard a description of a novel occupation as a wudgemaker that used gendered (*he* or *she*) or neutral pronouns (*they* or *he or she*) to describe what a wudgemaker does. In their later responses, children assumed that a woman would be good as a wudgemaker only when neutral or female pronouns were used. They assumed a woman would not do well as a wudgemaker, however, when a male pronoun was used. However, the same manipulation had no effect on presumptions of men's abilities.

Furthermore, the cognitive associations that women have between *math* and *male* might also shape self-conceptions through subtle pressures to maintain cognitive consistency. Nosek et al. (2002) found that to the degree that women hold both a strong implicit masculine association with math and a strong implicit association between self and female, they exhibit a weaker cognitive link between their concepts of self and math. This pattern was seen even for those women who were in math-intensive majors. In other words, at a very cognitive level, a woman's sense of what it means to be female interferes with her personal association to a masculine domain. This finding might help to explain the basic process by which socialization efforts that increase the salience of young girls' gender identity can diminish their aspirations in a masculine domain (e.g., Abrams, Thomas, & Hogg, 1990). It also sheds light on why women who pursue math-related studies might feel the need to reject characteristics that they see as highly feminine (Pronin, Steele, & Ross, 2004).

In addition to the pressures to maintain cognitive consistency that might force women to choose between associating their self with either their gender or a masculine domain, other motivational processes help to explain why the implicit associations between a given gender and a given domain might be resistant to change. Namely, motivational pressures to justify existing systems of social hierarchy help to ensure that individuals, even women, endorse these gender stereotypes as a means of maintaining the status quo (Jost & Kay, 2005). For example, Schmader, Johns, and Barquissau (2004) found that women who endorse the legitimacy of status differences between men and women were also more likely to endorse gender stereotypes about women's math abilities. This stereotype endorsement in turn predicted more negative self-perceptions of math competence and less interest in continuing their education in math-related fields. Other research has shown that women who endorse gender stereotypes are more likely to compare their math performance only with that of other women, because men are less likely to be seen as appropriate sources of comparison (Blanton, Christie, & Dye, 2002). The possible consequence of this selective comparison is that gender disparities that are inherent in society might more readily go unnoticed and therefore uncorrected.

The research discussed thus far illustrates that in addition to gender biases that are communicated from close others, the mere distribution of men and women into certain social roles also helps to create and maintain a perception that certain occupations are better suited for men rather than women. On the positive side, such research suggests that simply seeing certain careers as something that women can do could play an important role in shaping children's beliefs about the suitability of those careers for themselves. In fact, research has confirmed that exposure to successful female scientists can change the implicit associations that women have between women and science (Dasgupta & Asgari, 2004). Fortunately, as social roles become less differentiated by gender, the stereotypic beliefs about men's and women's abilities may also diminish (Diekman & Eagly, 2000).

In the preceding section, we considered the ways in which the existence of gender stereotypes can influence girls' initial interest in pursuing math- and science-related activities. For those women who successfully run the gauntlet of cultural associations of math with maleness and negative expectancies that might be communicated from close others, unfortunately such stereotypes will throw another obstacle in their path: stereotype threat. In the next section we discuss the ways in which stereotype threat can have a subtle but negative effect on women's experience in male-dominated domains.

STEREOTYPE THREAT AND WOMEN'S PERFORMANCE IN MALE-DOMINATED FIELDS

For women in male-dominated domains, their performance and career decisions are inevitably affected by their knowledge of gender stereotypes. In addition to being stereotyped by teachers and supervisors, many women also suffer from a concern that they and their gender group will be viewed in stereotypic ways. Even for women who do not believe that gender stereotypes are true, the simple awareness that they might be judged in terms of negative stereotypes can elicit a disruptive mental state that can degrade their performance in stereotype-relevant domains. This predicament, termed *stereotype threat* (C. M. Steele & Aronson, 1995), creates a situational pressure that not only impairs performance but can directly affect the career aspirations of women. In this section, we review the evidence that stereotype threat can affect women's performance in male-dominated domains (particularly those that involve math) and discuss some situational factors and individual differences that can exacerbate or buffer the threat (see also chap. 5, this volume). We then consider how stereotype threat shapes women's motivation and career choices in the long run.

Stereotype Threat Impairs Women's Performance in Male-Dominated Domains

Research has clearly demonstrated that stereotype threat can affect women's performance on male-dominated tasks. Most of this research has examined the role of stereotype threat in creating a gender gap in performance on standardized math tests. For example, in a series of studies, Spencer et al. (1999) found that women's performance on a math test could be influenced by how the test is described. When it was described as showing gender differences in the past (thus making gender stereotypes relevant), women underperformed relative to their male counterparts; however, their performance was equivalent to men's when the test was described to them as being gender fair. Thus women's math performance varied dramatically depending on the testing situation, a finding that calls into question the assumption that gender differences in test performance necessarily indicate gender differences in math ability. This basic finding has now been replicated in dozens of experiments and has been shown for individuals targeted by other negative stereotypes based on race, ethnicity, and socioeconomic status (see C. M. Steele, Spencer, & Aronson, 2002, for a review).

Research suggests that the deleterious consequences of stereotype threat are actualized through a complex interplay of physiological, emotional, and cognitive processes (see Schmader, Johns, & Forbes, 2008, for a review). These include activation of negative stereotypes (C. M. Steele & Aronson, 1995), the elicitation of diffuse physiological arousal (Blascovich, Spencer, Quinn, & Steele, 2001), and an increased tendency to monitor situations for threat-related cues (Kaiser, Vick, & Major, 2006). Assuming that the activation of negative stereotypes promotes a tendency to interpret any number of ambiguous cues as a sign of failure, this biased interpretation can lead to an increase of negative thoughts and feelings (Cadinu, Maass, Rosabianca, & Kiesner, 2005; Keller & Dauenheimer, 2003) followed by active attempts to manage one's impression and suppress feelings of anxiety (Inzlicht, Aronson, Good, & McKay, 2006; Johns, Inzlicht, & Schmader, 2008).

These ongoing processes are resource-demanding in that they require a certain amount of focused attention and controlled processing. This demand creates few problems when tasks are sufficiently easy and well below one's maximum threshold. In fact, women reminded of gender stereotypes outperform men on easy math problems (O'Brien & Crandall, 2003). However, the added burden of stereotype threat reduces one's ability to perform well at tasks requiring active manipulation of complex information, particularly those that require high amounts of working memory capacity, that is, the ability to hold multiple pieces of information in one's short-term memory while tending to different tasks (Schmader & Johns, 2003). Such cognitive impairments mediate the effect of stereotype threat on women's performance on a GRE math test (Schmader & Johns, 2003).

Because entry into many male-dominated fields requires successful performance on these types of cognitively challenging standardized tests, the effect of stereotype threat on women's test scores undoubtedly contributes to the perception that women are less qualified to compete in these disciplines. Thus, women's underperformance on important standardized tests can place them at a disadvantage in their pursuit of advanced education and high-paying occupations typically done by men. A lower test score can also influence women's own beliefs that they have the ability to succeed in a given domain, a pattern that could lead many well-qualified women to self-select out of male-dominated fields. In addition, the challenge of having to engage in the kind of complex manipulation of information required for test performance while also evaluating and managing the impression of one's self in the context is likely to be ego-depleting (Inzlicht, McKay, & Aronson, 2006), adding to the sense that performance in stereotype-relevant domains is fatiguing and aversive.

Another interesting aspect of the stereotype threat phenomenon is that the very women who are most motivated to excel in male-dominated fields appear to be most at risk for experiencing a threat that their performance could confirm a negative stereotype about their group (C. M. Steele et al., 2002). In other words, stereotype threat is most likely to affect those women who have invested their self-concept in doing well in a male-dominated domain. Women who are highly math identified face a potentially vicious cycle; the added pressure caused by their motivation to succeed could aggravate the distracting thought processes that interfere with their performance. Their test scores might end up, on the surface, seeming to confirm the very stereotype they were trying so hard to refute. Although these processes have been examined most clearly in math-related domains, these same processes could affect women in any discipline (e.g., computer science; Smith, Sansone, & White, 2007), dimension (e.g., negotiation; Kray, Thompson, & Galinsky, 2001), or role (e.g., a leadership position; Davies, Spencer, & Steele, 2005) in which gender stereotypes exist. Furthermore, a variety of situational cues can trigger these stereotype threat processes, increasing the likelihood that women who pursue male-dominated careers will encounter stereotype threat. We next review some of these environmental triggers.

Situations That Trigger Stereotype Threat

The situational nature of stereotype threat implies that some contexts will be more likely than others to trigger the cascade of arousal and negative thoughts that limit attentional resources and lead to women's impaired performance on complex cognitive tasks. Although early research on women's experience of stereotype threat showed performance decrements resulting from very explicit reminders of gender differences in ability, more recent research has revealed that these same effects can be cued by more subtle features of a context. Any aspect of the situation that brings to mind gender-stereotypic assumptions about women's ability, highlights male dominance on the task or domain, or reminds women of their gender might be enough to create stereotype threat. Because understanding these triggers can help in identifying solutions, we next review each cue in more detail.

Cues to Assessing Inherent Ability

Particularly when people first enter a discipline, they frequently encounter situations in which they might feel that their natural talent for that field is being assessed. Entrance exams are the most straightforward examples of these kinds of assessments, but comments made in class, meetings with professors, or even casual shop-talk with new colleagues can all be framed as evaluative encounters. Even just knowing that one is performing a task meant to be a diagnostic measure of ability can raise evaluative concerns and cue the experience of stereotype threat (C. M. Steele & Aronson, 1995). Also, just being told that a task is math related is often enough to automatically activate deeply rooted stereotypes about the domain and induce a concern that one's performance might validate those stereotypes (Smith & White, 2002).

In addition to merely activating stereotypes, situations designed to diagnose abilities are also likely to prime in individuals an entity orientation toward skills in that domain. According to Dweck's work on lay theories of intelligence, entity theorists, in contrast to incremental theorists, tend to view ability as an unchangeable internal characteristic as opposed to something that can be increased through effort or experience (e.g., Dweck, Chiu, & Hong, 1995). An entity orientation tends to focus individuals more on the goal of demonstrating performance (and more specifically, avoiding any displays of failure), as opposed to achieving mastery of the material. If stereotype threat impairs performance in part by changing one's orientation toward performance, then situations that specifically cue the idea that one lacks inherent abilities are likely to be the most threatening to members of stigmatized groups. In support of this idea, Brown and Josephs (1999) demonstrated that gender differences on a math test were found only when the test was described as diagnostic of weak math abilities, as opposed to a test that would identify strengths.

The shift to an entity orientation under stereotype threat is also indicated by research suggesting that a standard stereotype threat prime impairs performance to the same degree as does learning about biological underpinnings of math performance. In this study, women underperformed men on a math test after reading about scientific evidence that gender differences in math performance are due to inherent ability, that is, biological factors such as genes (Dar-Nimrod & Heine, 2006). Women who read research suggesting that gender differences were the result of environmental factors such as socialization did not show lower math performance compared with men. To the degree that biological explanations imply a fixed ability as opposed to a malleable skill, this research provides some evidence that this shift to an entity orientation might underlie stereotype threat effects on performance. This finding suggests that women would face more of a challenge in male-dominated disciplines that emphasize a certain level of inherent ability as a necessary factor for success. Repeated exposure to situations of stereotype threat that cue women to see math ability as a fixed trait might increase their frustration with relatively minor setbacks and lead them to frame those setbacks as evidence that they do not belong in that domain.

Cues That Make Gender Salient

In addition to situations that cue a focus on inherent ability, stereotype threat can be elicited by exposure to explicit and implicit cues in one's environment that simply make gender salient. For example, when college students watch commercials that portray women in a stereotypically feminine way, women show lower performance on a subsequent math test compared with their male peers and with women who watch neutral commercials (Davies, Spencer, Quinn, & Gerhardstein, 2002). In addition, merely observing another woman perform poorly at math is enough to create a collective threat to one's sense of self (Cohen & Garcia, 2005). Aside from these relatively overt environmental cues, simply having females answer questions related to gender issues (Shih, Pittinsky, & Ambady, 1999) or color a picture of a girl (Ambady, Shih, Kim, & Pittinsky, 2001) has been found to engender stereotype threat and negatively affect women's and girls' attitudes and performance in math-related tasks. Even placing a cartoon depicting women being inferior in math in the periphery of an experimental setting might constrain women's attention to their gender identities and make them apprehensive about being the target of negative stereotypes (Oswald & Harvey, 2000).

Unfortunately, the simple fact that masculine domains are by definition composed mainly of men means that it is unlikely for women in these fields to be unaware of their minority status resulting from their gender. Research has clearly shown that when women represent the numeric minority in a situation, they perform more poorly than do those working in an all-women or sex-balanced group (Inzlicht & Ben-Zeev, 2000). This is partly because being outnumbered likely increases awareness of one's social identity (Abrams et al., 1990) and activates the relevant gender stereotypes. However, because an imbalanced gender composition of the classroom or the workplace can also reinforce stereotypic notions of what women can do (Eagly & Steffen, 1984), the underrepresentation of women in a domain can also validate the stereotype. Findings such as these argue for the importance of having a critical mass of women in male-dominated settings to help diffuse these effects (see also chap. 3, this volume).

In summary, even when women are strongly motivated to achieve success in male-dominated fields, and even when men in those professions have good intentions about facilitating women's advancement, situational cues that trigger stereotype threat can still create the appearance of a gender difference in ability. However, research also suggests that certain factors could make some women less susceptible to this threat. In the next section, we review some of the individual differences that could safeguard them from experiencing stereotype threat.

Individual Difference Factors That Moderate Stereotype Threat Effects

Although stereotype threat is defined as a situational pressure that can happen to any individual targeted by negative stereotypes, not all stigmatized individuals are equally debilitated by this psychological predicament. One obvious factor that moderates the experience of threat is *stigma consciousness* (Pinel, 1999)—the degree to which a person is chronically conscious of the possibility that she will be judged stereotypically by others. Individuals who rate low on this dimension are thought to be less vigilant in situations in which subtle threat-eliciting contextual cues are present and are less likely to perceive themselves as targets of discrimination. Consistent with this analysis, research has shown that women low in stigma consciousness are less likely to underperform on a math test under situations of stereotype threat (Brown & Pinel, 2003) presumably because these women do not anticipate being perceived stereotypically.

Whereas stigma consciousness might moderate stereotype threat effects by influencing the degree to which women worry about being stereotyped by others, women's own beliefs about the validity of gender stereotypes influence the degree to which they worry about confirming the stereotype for themselves (Shapiro & Neuberg, 2007). For example, although stereotype threat theory contends that one does not need to endorse the stereotype to experience its detrimental effects on performance, research does suggest that some women are buffered from threat effects on math performance by completely rejecting the idea that men are inherently better than women at math (Schmader et al., 2004). Because high stigma consciousness and stereotype endorsement are two variables that are likely to make gender stereotypes more chronically accessible, either of these factors might increase women's risk of stereotype threat by lowering the threshold for experiencing threat in ambiguous situations.

In addition, because stereotype threat stems from the fear that one's own actions could confirm a broader stereotype about one's group, any individual difference factor that raises the personal stake in defeating the stereotype could accentuate the experience of stereotype threat. This conjecture implies that threat would be greater for those women who are personally invested in succeeding in the domain and in maintaining a positive image of their gender group. For those who do not define themselves in terms of their gender, the cultural stereotypes about women should pose less of a threat to the self. Indeed, research has shown that these women do not show performance deficits when told that their score on a math test would be used to evaluate the abilities of women in general (Schmader, 2002). This result does not imply, however, that women must disavow their gender identity to succeed in a masculine domain. It is clear from other research that group identification confers psychological benefits (Schmitt, Branscombe, Kobrynowicz, & Owen, 2002), and women might be buffered from the negative experience of stereotype threat in contexts that highlight their gender's positive status on other dimensions (Derks, van Laar, & Ellemers, 2006). Thus, the important point might be to develop a more diffuse concept of the self that acknowledges the strengths of one's gender identity but that also recognizes gender as being but one aspect of self-definition. Research suggests that this multifaceted concept of the self can also serve as a buffer against stereotype threat. For instance, women who were able to list more identities for themselves were less likely to underperform on a math test than were those who could not (Gresky, Ten Eyck, Lord, & McIntyre, 2005).

Just as women are buffered from stereotype threat by investing less of their self-definition in their gender identity, they might also be buffered by investing less of their self-definition in the math domain. As mentioned previously, general research on stereotype threat suggests that the debilitating effects of threat cues on performance are largest among those who are most identified with the domain (Aronson, Lustina, & Good, 1999). The ironic nature of this finding is that those gifted female students who enter male-dominated domains despite social and stereotypic pressures to the contrary are mostly likely to be harmed by the negative stereotypes. Although some degree of domain identification is essential for motivation in the face of obstacles, we might wonder whether there is a way to retain a sense of value for the domain without necessarily defining one's self on the basis of one's performance in that domain. Evidence suggests that this indeed may be possible. For example, Nussbaum and Steele (2007) found that African American students who temporarily detached their sense of self-worth from the stigmatized domain persisted longer on a supposed diagnostic intelligence test compared with those taking a nondiagnostic task and did so while maintaining overall domain identification levels. Disengaging the self-concept from math performance might be similarly beneficial for women performing in male-dominated domains.

In fact, individual difference variables we have discussed thus far suggest that the women who are less likely to experience stereotype threat are those who do not frame a given performance situation as a self-defining moment. In support of this assessment, several general personality characteristics have been identified to moderate stereotype threat effects by leading women to appraise their performance in less self-oriented ways. For example, women with a high dispositional sense of humor were found to experience less performance impairment on math tests under conditions of stereotype threat, perhaps because they take the situation less seriously (Ford, Ferguson, & Brooks, 2004). More relevant is work examining stereotype threat among individuals with an external locus of control, who do not hold themselves responsible for their task performance but tend to make external attributions for their performance. In light of this tendency to discount their outcomes, it should come as little surprise that individuals with an external locus of control show weaker performance deficits in a situation of stereotype threat compared with those with internal locus-of-control beliefs (Cadinu, Maass, Lombardo, & Frigerio, 2006; see also chap. 5, this volume).

Another general personality variable that has been studied as a moderator of stereotype threat effects on women's math performance is self-monitoring, the tendency to adjust one's behavior in social contexts to conform to expectations held by others (Inzlicht et al., 2006). In light of our assertion that threat is exacerbated by focusing too much on the self, it seems counterintuitive that women high in self-monitoring are less likely to underperform on a math test when they are the only woman in a room of men (Inzlicht et al., 2006).

However, as Inzlicht et al. (2006) pointed out, these high self-monitors (i.e., those who are more sensitive to situational demands and particularly adept at conveying a desired public appearance to others) are actually buffered from stereotype threat because they are more adept at regulating their behavior to the demands of situations, and thus are less cognitively distracted by a situation that cues that type of vigilance.

Thus far, we have focused on the immediate consequence of experiencing stereotype threat on women's math-related task performance. We have described the various situational cues that can trigger stereotype threat as well as some of the individual difference variables that could buffer some women from these effects. However, even those women who are less susceptible to experiencing stereotype threat in a given situation could still experience the long-term effects of frequent exposure to the sorts of situational cues that trigger threat-based processes. In the next section, we address how stereotype threat may affect women's motivations and career decisions.

STEREOTYPE THREAT CAN DIRECTLY AFFECT CAREER CHOICE

Although some women might successfully buffer themselves from the experience of stereotype threat, the accumulated exposure to these pressures—pressures that are not experienced by men in the same domains—can undermine women's interest in remaining in these disciplines. Indeed, C. M. Steele et al. (2002) argued that many stigmatized individuals psychologically disidentify with stereotyped domains as a means to escape the constant rigors of trying to succeed in an area in which one's group is expected to fail. For example, one study showed that women majoring in math or science disciplines reported experiencing more stereotype threat and were more likely to contemplate changing their major than were women majoring in social sciences or the humanities (J. Steele, James, & Barnett, 2002).

Unfortunately, the tendency to disidentify from a domain in which one experiences stereotype threat might be preceded by being too personally invested in that domain. Individuals who excel in a domain in which their group is negatively stereotyped are more likely to become self-schematic for that domain (Von Hippel, Hawkins, & Schooler, 2001). This strong attachment of the self to the domain might make these high-performing members of stigmatized groups more finely attuned to interpreting their outcomes in very self-defining ways. For example, Crocker, Karpinski, Quinn, and Chase (2003) found that female engineering students were very reactive to bad grades they received in science courses such that they reported lower levels of self-esteem, affect, and identification with their major compared with male engineering students or female psychology students. Interpreting negative outcomes as threats to one's self-concept could become fatiguing and aversive and over time drive them away from those fields.

In addition to disidentification from male-dominated domains as a result of stereotype threat, other evidence suggests that even subtle reminders of gender stereotypes can lead women to steer clear of more masculine activities. In a series of experiments, Davies and colleagues showed that simply priming women with feminized examples of women (e.g., by showing them stereotypic television commercials) had a direct and significant effect on their behavioral choices (Davies et al., 2002, 2005). Women in this situation expressed significantly less interest in pursuing academic majors involving high levels of mathematics and, in another set of studies, avoided leadership roles in favor of subordinate roles. These findings suggest that continuous exposure to something as commonplace as stereotypic TV ads can have subtle influences that may ultimately push women to choose careers outside of math and science.

As can be seen, gender stereotypes not only affect how women perform in male-dominated domains but can also affect women's desire to take on roles or continue pursuing careers in which they are likely to face repeated exposure to stereotype threat. In light of the role of this phenomenon in helping to create the underrepresentation of women in these areas, it is critical to consider effective ways to combat the deleterious effects of stereotype threat.

CLOSING THE GAP: SUCCESSFUL STRATEGIES FOR DIFFUSING THE EFFECTS OF STEREOTYPES ON WOMEN'S CAREER CHOICE

As we reviewed in this chapter, stereotypes can influence women's choice of careers through socialization processes as well as the experience of acute stereotype threat. Although the effects of both processes can be quite profound, their focus on environmental forces offers some hope. Socialization cannot happen without appropriate social context, and stereotype threat by nature is a situational pressure. Because contexts can be altered, the negative effects of gender stereotypes can be circumvented by instituting policies and interventions designed to change the social environments to which young girls and women are exposed. Such change can happen through coordinating efforts to increase the representation of women in male-dominated domains, to create threat-free environments, and to educate the public about the role of social context in shaping performance. This last part of the chapter addresses approaches that aim to change the threatening context in hopes of superseding the negative influences of stereotypes on women (see also chaps. 9–12, this volume).

Increasing the Representation of Women in Male-Dominated Careers

In an ideal world, eliminating the negative effects of stereotypes would require a multifaceted effort to change the cultural representations to which people are exposed. However, stereotypes about women's lack of proclivity for certain fields, such as math and science, might be most likely to change when we see equal representation of women and men at the highest levels of achievement in male-dominated fields. Recall that just the observation of the unbalanced representation of women and men in a field can shape the views of who belongs in that domain (Eagly & Steffen, 1984). Therefore, direct efforts to change the gender representation in an organization or institution can be one way to avoid this biased sense of belonging. Because women's performance on math tests can be hampered by the simple fact that women are in the minority in that testing context (Inzlicht & Ben Zeev, 2000), changing the gender composition of a context can also help to directly close the performance gap. Meanwhile, when a critical mass of women is present in a masculine domain, women are also exposed to positive female role models who, as is discussed later, can inspire in them a greater sense of confidence and self-efficacy.

Of course, this first suggestion sets up a catch-22. A greater presence of women in masculine domains will no doubt change the socialized notion of what women can and cannot do, and will also alleviate the experience of stereotype threat on women's performance. However, the problem still remains of how to combat the influence of gender stereotypes at present so that more and more women are able to enter and excel in male-dominant arenas. One potential solution is to create what Davies et al. (2005) have called *identity safe* environments.

Creating an Identity Safe Environment

Earlier in this chapter we discussed how seemingly innocuous contextual cues, such as advertisements, can socialize young girls to shy away from masculine careers and can also elicit stereotype threat (Davies et al., 2005). Thus, combating the effects of gender stereotypes on women's career choices means minimizing these threatening cues. As mentioned earlier, one means of doing this is to provide women with positive female role models who alleviate stereotypic concerns (see also chap. 10, this volume). Because individuals derive a sense of identity from their group memberships, they can experience an increase in self-esteem when their fellow group members succeed. In line with this reasoning, research has demonstrated that women are less likely to underperform on a math test when in the presence of or after learning about a competent female researcher (Marx & Roman, 2002). In addition to alleviating stereotype threat effects on performance, exposure to female leaders can also reduce women's automatic stereotypic beliefs about their gender (Dasgupta & Asgari, 2004). In general, the presence of successful women in masculine domains sends an encouraging message to young people that women *are* capable of doing well there.

If one key to reducing the effects of stereotypes on women's self-concepts and career pursuits is to instill greater confidence in them about their math abilities, then success might be found with interventions designed to focus women on positive aspects of their individual character. For example, research has shown that people can maintain a certain level of self-esteem in the face of self-threats by affirming themselves as decent, moral, and competent (e.g., having a sense of humor, being creative, or having social skills; C. M. Steele, Spencer, & Lynch, 1993). Consistent with these findings, when women under stereotype threat affirmed a valued attribute, they performed at levels comparable to that of men (Martens, Johns, Greenberg, & Schimel, 2006). This effect can be achieved through group affirmation as well, such as by telling women before they take a diagnostic math test that they make better participants than do men (McIntyre, Paulson, & Lord, 2003). A more recent study shows how the positive effects of affirmation extend beyond a testing setting to have a reliable effect on academic performance and grades (Cohen, Garcia, Apfel, & Master, 2006). In this study, European and African American seventh graders wrote briefly about values most important to their self once during the beginning of the fall semester. Results showed across two separate samples that, compared with those who wrote about unimportant values, affirmed African American students demonstrated grades that were more comparable to those of European American students in a targeted course. In fact, interventions such as these might be most important when employed in middle school—a time when many girls begin to decide that they cannot excel in traditionally male classes such as math and science (Eccles et al., 1989).

Such research highlights the benefits of instilling in young girls a sense of confidence but other research suggests that simply focusing on one's self as an individual rather than as a stereotypic representative of one's group could also relieve stereotype threat effects on women's math performance (Ambady, Paik, Steele, Owen-Smith, & Mitchell, 2004). In this study, women who first listed their individual characteristics, even when this list included negative traits, did not show stereotype threat impairment on their math performance. Women were also buffered from stereotype threat effects on performance when prompted to think about characteristics shared between men and women (Rosenthal & Crisp, 2006). In both of these studies, efforts to reduce the degree to which gender stereotypes place women in a distinct and devalued social category were effective at combating stereotype threat. These findings highlight that one core problem with stereotypes is that they are categorical trait ascriptions that confer to an individual a social expectation about what she will be able to do. Thus, by definition, negative gender stereotypes constrain a woman's sense of what choices she has. Efforts to dismantle such categorical thinking can therefore be quite effective at opening up new possibilities.

In sum, an identity safe environment can be created by providing contexts that promote more positive and less stereotypical conceptions of women. For example, ensuring that campus math departments promote the appearance of successful female math figures (e.g., bringing female mathematicians in for colloquiums, hiring more female faculty, hiring female math tutors) and reducing the number of threatening subtle cues in the environment (e.g., having equal numbers of male and female restrooms, having posters that depict equal numbers of male and female students experiencing success) can all be means of engendering an identity safe environment. These strategies are likely to be effective across a variety of domains. But as reviewed earlier, much of the research on stereotype threat pertains to test performance. Because tests are so often interpreted, by both students and evaluators, as windows into one's ability, test scores are likely to play a unique role in women's choices to pursue certain careers. As such, we might consider remedies that specifically address the role that stereotypes play during a testing situation.

Reduce the Focus on Testing

Because of the debilitating effects that stereotype threat has on women's performance on standardized math tests, one must be cautious in assuming that test scores denote ability. However, universities and scholarship committees rely on the test scores of students to make decisions, and these decisions can have a profound influence on the career choices that are available to women. Although it might be impossible to do away with testing altogether, it would be helpful to be more mindful of how such assessments are framed and how much weight a student's math test scores are given in academic decisions.

One aspect of this increased mindfulness is to emphasize skill over ability by teaching students that learning is an incremental process, and that tests can be used to measure a step in the process toward mastery. In fact, the Educational Testing Service made a move in this direction when it changed the denotation of the A in SAT from *aptitude* to *assessment*. Research suggests that efforts to change people's lay theories about not just tests but intelligence itself can be effective. For example, Good, Aronson, and Inzlicht (2003) showed that when seventh-grade students were mentored by college students to think about intelligence as a malleable quality that increases with hard work, girls showed an increase in math performance by the end of the school year and the gender gap in test performance was eliminated.

In a similar vein, Walton and Cohen (2007) taught a sample of 1st-year college students to view the difficulties and challenges that they would face during their college career as a normal part of the learning process. The assumption is that individuals who are performing under a burden of negative stereotypes might be more likely to interpret any sign of difficulty as an indicator that they do not belong in college. Those who do not contend with these stereotypes are less likely to question whether they belong. By reminding students that struggle and self-doubt is a normal part of education and growth, students learned to reappraise their college experience and it showed in their performance. Minority students who received this intervention reported studying more for their classes and showed a significant increase in their grades measured 8 months later. We argue that these same interpretive processes affect women's experiences in traditional math domains such as science and math, in which even the former president of Harvard University believes that inherent abilities could be the root cause of women's low test scores.

Thus far we have described some of the policies and interventions that could help to combat the effects that stereotypes have on the underperformance and underrepresentation of women in male-dominated careers. Perhaps the most important first step to instituting these changes is to get the word out about the ways in which stereotypes affect women's attitudes, behavior, and performance. In fact, education is probably the approach that can be used most extensively to counteract not only stereotype threat but also negative stereotype influences in general.

Education

One notable aspect of the influence that stereotypes have on people is that their effects often go unnoticed or are misattributed. In fact, in much of the research on stereotype threat, manipulations that are shown to have an observable effect on women's test performance have little to no effect on women's conscious experience of the situation (e.g., Schmader, 2002). In a similar way, the strong implicit biases that women have between men and science are held even by female math majors who explicitly report strong identification with math (Nosek et al., 2002). Because the effects of stereotypes happen at an implicit level, it is all too easy to attribute group differences in behavior and performance as indicative, not of the stereotype, but of true underlying differences in ability. To counteract this fundamental attribution error, women and men alike need to be educated about the ways in which stereotypes exert their influence.

In fact, one way to alleviate the sting of stereotype threat is to teach women about its effects (Johns, Schmader, & Martens, 2005). At first glance, we might wonder whether publicizing stereotype threat would simply provide women with yet another hurdle that they need to overcome. However, research by Johns et al. (2005) suggests that knowing about stereotype threat provides women with an external explanation for their anxiety during a test, and being able to externalize anxious arousal might free up the cognitive resources needed for the task. Johns et al. (2005) showed that after learning about the deleterious consequences that negative stereotypes could have on their math performance, women performed similarly to men on a subsequent math test, and better than women who did not learn about stereotype threat (but who still took a test under threatening conditions). Furthermore, although both of these groups reported that gender stereotypes might have contributed to their anxiety during the test, only those women educated about stereotype threat performed better on the math test to the degree that they made this external attribution.

Among those women uneducated about stereotype threat, the tendency to focus on the role of gender stereotypes in creating their anxiety predicted lower performance. These results imply that teaching women to acknowledge stereotypes as an external source of anxious arousal during stereotype-relevant tasks might be an important way to deflect the threat that those stereotypes seem to pose to one's self and group identity.

Other research has shown similar effects based on the explanation that students are given for the gender gap in mathematical test performance (Dar-Nimrod & Heine, 2006). As mentioned previously, compared with men, women in this study underperformed on a math test after reading an essay summarizing evidence that the gender gap arises from genetic factors. However, women who read about the environmental causes of gender differences in math performance performed significantly better than did women given the genetic explanation and equal to men in the same condition. Because these effects of education could last beyond the immediate context, this type of intervention could be a powerful psychological tool to help stigmatized individuals cope with stereotype threat.

In addition to educating women, however, educators, administrators, policymakers, and parents must also be taught to understand the role that stereotypes could play in their own behavior toward young girls and interpretation of children's performance. To defeat the sort of direct socialization processes described earlier, mentors need to be aware of their own biased expectations as discussed in the beginning of this chapter, and take efforts to avoid them—but this does not mean being overwhelmingly positive. Research suggests that the best way to increase motivation among stigmatized students is through a combination of accurate criticism, emphasizing that standards are set high but also providing assurances that you believe that the student is up to the challenge of good performance (Cohen, Steele, & Ross, 1999). It is under these conditions of "wise mentoring" that students can be most intrinsically motivated to hone their skills and learn from their mistakes. We presume that these same mentoring tactics would be useful for women as well not only in the classroom but also in their career fields later on.

CONCLUSION

We have reviewed in this chapter studies showing the limiting effects that gender stereotypes continue to have for women. From a young age, gender stereotypes in culture socialize girls to shy away from careers in which women are the minority. But even for those women who buck these trends and enter male-dominated disciplines, the frequent exposure to situations of stereotype threat has the potential to turn them away. If the glass ceiling prevents women's advancement up a hierarchy to leadership positions

in almost any domain, the effects that stereotypes have o
choice might be more aptly characterized as a glass door—
entry to certain fields. In fact, the emphasis on career ch
title is a bit misleading, given that the research suggests
types limit the options that women have available to
more and more women enter into and are successful
careers, the stereotypes and their detrimental effects \
Whereas comments of the sort made by Lawrence Summers cou.
effect of closing the glass door more tightly, we counter that raising awareness of the influence that stereotypes can have might reveal that the door can
be opened.

REFERENCES

Abrams, D., Thomas, J., & Hogg, M. A. (1990). Numerical distinctiveness, social
   identity and gender salience. *British Journal of Social Psychology, 29*, 87–92.

Ambady, N., Paik, S. K., Steele, J., Owen-Smith, A., & Mitchell, J. P. (2004).
   Deflecting negative self-relevant stereotype activation: The effects of individuation.
   Journal of Experimental Social Psychology, 40, 401–408.

Ambady, N., Shih, M., Kim, A., & Pittinsky, T. L. (2001). Stereotype susceptibility in
   children: Effects of identity activation on quantitative performance. *Psychological
   Science, 12*, 385–390.

Aronson, J., Lustina, M. J., & Good, C. (1999). When White men can't do math:
   Necessary and sufficient factors in stereotype threat. *Journal of Experimental Social
   Psychology, 35*, 29–46.

Baldwin, M. W., Carrell, S. E., & Lopez, D. F. (1990). Priming relationship schemas:
   My advisor and the Pope are watching me from the back of my mind. *Journal of
   Experimental Social Psychology, 26*, 435–454.

Bandura, A., Barbaranelli, C., Caprara, G. V., & Pastorelli, C. (1996). Multifaceted
   impact of self-efficacy beliefs on academic functioning. *Child Development, 67*,
   1206–1222.

Bandura, A., Barbaranelli, C., Caprara, G. V., & Pastorelli, C. (2001). Self-efficacy
   beliefs as shapers of children's aspirations and career trajectories. *Child Development,
   72*, 187–206.

Benbow, C. P., & Stanley, J. C. (1980, December 12). Sex differences in mathematical
   ability: Fact or artifact? *Science, 210*, 1262–1264.

Blanton, H., Christie, C., & Dye, M. (2002). Social identity versus reference frame comparisons: The moderating role of stereotype endorsement. *Journal of Experimental
   Social Psychology, 38*, 253–267.

Blascovich, J., Spencer, S. J., Quinn, D., & Steele, C. (2001). African Americans
   and high blood pressure: The role of stereotype threat. *Psychological Science, 12*,
   225–229.

n, R. P., & Josephs, R. A. (1999). A burden of proof: Stereotype relevance and gender differences in math performance. *Journal of Personality and Social Psychology, 76*, 246–257.

Brown, R. P., & Pinel, E. C. (2003). Stigma on my mind: Individual differences in the experience of stereotype threat. *Journal of Experimental Social Psychology, 39*, 626–633.

Cadinu, M., Maass, A., Lombardo, M., & Frigerio, S. (2006). Stereotype threat: The moderating role of locus of control beliefs. *European Journal of Social Psychology, 36*, 183–197.

Cadinu, M., Maass, A., Rosabianca, A., & Kiesner, J. (2005). Why do women underperform under stereotype threat? Evidence for the role of negative thinking. *Psychological Science, 16*, 572–578.

Cohen, G. L., & Garcia, J. (2005). "I am us": Negative stereotypes as collective threats. *Journal of Personality and Social Psychology, 89*, 566–582.

Cohen, G. L., Garcia, J., Apfel, N., & Master, A. (2006, September 1). Reducing the racial achievement gap: A social psychological intervention. *Science, 313*, 1307–1310.

Cohen, G. L., Steele, C. M., & Ross, L. D. (1999). The mentor's dilemma: Providing critical feedback across the racial divide. *Personality and Social Psychology Bulletin, 25*, 1302–1318.

Crocker, J., Karpinski, A., Quinn, D. M., & Chase, S. K. (2003). When grades determine self-worth: Consequences of contingent self-worth for male and female engineering and psychology majors. *Journal of Personality and Social Psychology, 85*, 507–516.

Crombie, G., Sinclair, N., Silverthorn, N., Byrne, B. M., DuBois, D. L., & Trinneer, A. (2005). Predictors of young adolescents' math grades and course enrollment intentions: Gender similarities and differences. *Sex Roles, 52*, 351–367.

Dar-Nimrod, I., & Heine, S. J. (2006, October 20). Exposure to scientific theories affects women's math performance. *Science, 314*, 435.

Dasgupta, N., & Asgari, S. (2004). Seeing is believing: Exposure to counterstereotypic women leaders and its effect on the malleability of automatic gender stereotyping. *Journal of Experimental Social Psychology, 40*, 642–658.

Davies, P. G., Spencer, S. J., Quinn, D. M., & Gerhardstein, R. (2002). Consuming images: How television commercials that elicit stereotype threat can restrain women academically and professionally. *Personality and Social Psychology Bulletin, 28*, 1615–1628.

Davies, P. G., Spencer, S. J., & Steele, C. M. (2005). Clearing the air: Identity safety moderates the effects of stereotype threat on women's leadership aspirations. *Journal of Personality and Social Psychology, 88*, 276–287.

Derks, B., van Laar, C., & Ellemers, N. (2006). Striving for success in outgroup settings: Effects of contextually emphasizing ingroup dimensions on stigmatized group members' social identity and performance styles. *Personality and Social Psychology Bulletin, 32*, 576–588.

Diekman, A. B., & Eagly, A. H. (2000). Stereotypes as dynamic constructs: Women and men of the past, present, and future. *Personality and Social Psychology Bulletin, 26,* 1171–1188.

Dweck, C. S., Chiu, C., & Hong, Y. (1995). Implicit theories and their role in judgments and reactions: A word from two perspectives. *Psychological Inquiry, 6,* 267–285.

Eagly, A. H., & Steffen, V. J. (1984). Gender stereotypes stem from the distribution of women and men into social roles. *Journal of Personality and Social Psychology, 46,* 735–754.

Eccles, J. S. (1987). Gender roles and women's achievement-related decisions. *Psychology of Women Quarterly, 11,* 135–171.

Eccles, J. S., Wigfield, A., Flanagan, C., Miller, C., Reuman, D., & Yee, D. (1989). Self-concepts, domain values, and self-esteem: Relations and changes at early adolescence. *Journal of Personality, 57,* 283–310.

Eccles, J. S., Wigfield, A., Harold, R. D., & Blumenfeld, P. (1993). Age and gender differences in children's self- and task perceptions during elementary school. *Child Development, 64,* 830–847.

Ford, T. E., Ferguson, M. A., & Brooks, J. L. (2004). Coping sense of humor reduces effects of stereotype threat on women's math performance. *Personality and Social Psychology Bulletin, 30,* 643–653.

Frome, P. M., & Eccles, J. S. (1998). Parents' influence on children's achievement-related perceptions. *Journal of Personality and Social Psychology, 74,* 435–452.

Good, C., Aronson, J., & Inzlicht, M. (2003). Improving adolescents' standardized test performance: An intervention to reduce the effects of stereotype threat. *Journal of Applied Developmental Psychology, 24,* 645–662.

Gresky, D. M., Ten Eyck, L. L., Lord, C. G., & McIntyre, R. B. (2005). Effects of salient multiple identities on women's performance under mathematics stereotype threat. *Sex Roles, 53,* 703–716.

Hyde, J. S. (1984). Children's understanding of sexist language. *Developmental Psychology, 20,* 697–706.

Hyde, J. S., Fennema, E., Ryan, M., Frost, L. A., & Hopp, C. (1990). Gender comparisons of mathematics attitudes and affect: A meta-analysis. *Psychology of Women Quarterly, 14,* 299–324.

Inzlicht, M., Aronson, J., Good, C., & McKay, L. (2006). A particular resiliency to threatening environments. *Journal of Experimental Social Psychology, 42,* 323–336.

Inzlicht, M., & Ben-Zeev, T. (2000). A threatening intellectual environment: Why females are susceptible to experiencing problem-solving deficits in the presence of males. *Psychological Science, 11,* 365–371.

Inzlicht, M., McKay, L., & Aronson, J. (2006). Stigma as ego depletion: How being the target of prejudice affects self-control. *Psychological Science, 17,* 262–269.

Jacobs, J. E., & Eccles, J. S. (1992). The impact of mothers' gender-role stereotypic beliefs on mothers' and children's ability perceptions. *Journal of Personality and Social Psychology, 63,* 932–944.

Johns, M., Inzlicht, M., & Schmader, T. (2008). *Stereotype threat and executive resource depletion: The influence of emotion regulation.* Unpublished manuscript. Laramie: University of Wyoming.

Johns, M., Schmader, T., & Martens, A. (2005). Knowing is half the battle: Teaching stereotype threat as a means of improving women's math performance. *Psychological Science, 16,* 175–179.

Jost, J. T., & Kay, A. C. (2005). Exposure to benevolent sexism and complementary gender stereotypes: Consequences for specific and diffuse forms of system justification. *Journal of Personality and Social Psychology, 88,* 498–509.

Kaiser, C. R., Vick, S. B., & Major, B. (2006). Prejudice expectations moderate preconscious attention to cues that are threatening to social identity. *Psychological Science, 17,* 332–338.

Keller, J., & Dauenheimer, D. (2003). Stereotype threat in the classroom: Dejection mediates the disrupting threat effect on women's math performance. *Personality and Social Psychology Bulletin, 29,* 371–381.

Kray, L. J., Thompson, L., & Galinsky, A. (2001). Battle of the sexes: Gender stereotype confirmation and reactance in negotiations. *Journal of Personality and Social Psychology, 80,* 942–958.

LeFevre, J. A., Kulak, A. G., & Heymans, S. L. (1992). Factors influencing the selection of university majors varying in mathematical content. *Canadian Journal of Behavioral Science, 24,* 276–289.

Martens, A., Johns, M., Greenberg, J., & Schimel, J. (2006). Combating stereotype threat: The effect of self-affirmation on women's intellectual performance. *Journal of Experimental Social Psychology, 42,* 236–243.

Marx, D. M., & Roman, J. S. (2002). Female role models: Protecting women's math test performance. *Personality and Social Psychology Bulletin, 28,* 1183–1193.

McIntyre, R. B., Paulson, R. M., & Lord, C. G. (2003). Alleviating women's mathematics stereotype threat through salience of group achievements. *Journal of Experimental Social Psychology, 39,* 83–90.

Meece, J. L., Parsons, J. S., Kaczala, C., Golf, S. B., & Futterman, R. (1982). Sex differences in mathematics achievement: Toward a model of academic choice. *Psychological Bulletin, 9,* 324–348.

Meece, J. L., Wigfield, A., & Eccles, J. S. (1990). Predictors of math anxiety and its influence on young adolescents' course enrollment intentions and performance in mathematics. *Journal of Educational Psychology, 82,* 60–70.

National Science Foundation. (2007). *Women, minorities, and persons with disabilities in science and engineering.* Retrieved July 16, 2008, from http://www.nsf.gov/statistics/wmpd/

Nosek, B. A., Banaji, M. R., & Greenwald, A. G. (2002). Math = male, me = female, therefore math ≠ me. *Journal of Personality and Social Psychology, 83,* 44–59.

Nussbaum, A. D., & Steele, C. M. (2007). Situational disengagement and persistence in the face of adversity. *Journal of Experimental Social Psychology, 43,* 127–134.

O'Brien, L. T., & Crandall, C. S. (2003). Stereotype threat and arousal: Effects on women's math performance. *Personality and Social Psychology Bulletin, 29,* 782–789.

Oswald, D. L., & Harvey, R. D. (2000). Hostile environments, stereotype threat, and math performance among undergraduate women. *Current Psychology: Developmental, Learning, Personality, Social, 19,* 338–356.

Pinel, E. C. (1999). Stigma consciousness: The psychological legacy of social stereotypes. *Journal of Personality and Social Psychology, 76,* 114–128.

Pronin, E., Steele, C. M., & Ross, L. (2004). Identity bifurcation in response to stereotype threat: Women and mathematics. *Journal of Experimental Social Psychology, 40,* 152–168.

Rosenthal, H. E., & Crisp, R. J. (2006). Reducing stereotype threat by blurring intergroup boundaries. *Personality and Social Psychology Bulletin, 32,* 501–511.

Schmader, T. (2002). Gender identification moderates stereotype threat effects on women's math performance. *Journal of Experimental Social Psychology, 38,* 194–201.

Schmader, T., & Johns, M. (2003). Converging evidence that stereotype threat reduces working memory capacity. *Journal of Personality and Social Psychology, 85,* 440–452.

Schmader, T., Johns, M., & Barquissau, M. (2004). The costs of accepting gender differences: The role of stereotype endorsement in women's experience in the math domain. *Sex Roles, 50,* 835–850.

Schmader, T., Johns, M., & Forbes, C. (2008). An integrated process model of stereotype threat effects on performance. *Psychological Review, 115,* 336–356.

Schmitt, M. T., Branscombe, N. R., Kobrynowicz, D., & Owen, S. (2002). Perceiving discrimination against one's gender group has different implications for well-being in women and men. *Personality and Social Psychology Bulletin, 28,* 197–210.

Shapiro, J. R., & Neuberg, S. L. (2007). From stereotype threat to stereotype threats: Implications of a multi-threat framework for causes, moderators, mediators, consequences, and interventions. *Personality and Social Psychology Review, 11,* 107–130.

Shih, M., Pittinsky, T. L., & Ambady, N. (1999). Stereotype susceptibility: Identity salience and shifts in quantitative performance. *Psychological Science, 10,* 80–83.

Sinclair, S., & Lun, J. (2006). Significant other representations activate stereotypic self-views among women. *Self and Identity, 5,* 196–207.

Smith, J. L., Sansone, C., & White, P. H. (2007). The stereotyped task engagement process: The role of interest and achievement motivation. *Journal of Educational Psychology, 99,* 99–114.

Smith, J. L., & White, P. H. (2002). An examination of implicitly activated, explicitly activated, and nullified stereotypes on mathematical performance: It's not just a woman's issue. *Sex Roles, 47,* 179–191.

Spencer, S. J., Steele, C. M., & Quinn, D. M. (1999). Stereotype threat and women's math performance. *Journal of Experimental Social Psychology, 35,* 4–28.

Steele, C. M., & Aronson, J. (1995). Stereotype threat and the intellectual test performance of African Americans. *Journal of Personality and Social Psychology, 69*, 797–811.

Steele, C. M., Spencer, S. J., & Aronson, J. (2002). Contending with group image: The psychology of stereotype and social identity threat. In M. P. Zanna (Ed.), *Advances in experimental social psychology* (Vol. 34, pp. 379–440). San Diego, CA: Academic Press.

Steele, C. M., Spencer, S. J., & Lynch, M. (1993). Self-image resilience and dissonance: The role of affirmational resources. *Journal of Personality and Social Psychology, 64*, 885–896.

Steele, J., James, J. B., & Barnett, R. C. (2002). Learning in a man's world: Examining the perceptions of undergraduate women in male-dominated academic areas. *Psychology of Women Quarterly, 26*, 46–50.

Von Hippel, W., Hawkins, C., & Schooler, J. W. (2001). Stereotype distinctiveness: How counterstereotypic behavior shapes the self-concept. *Journal of Personality and Social Psychology, 81*, 193–205.

Walton, G. M., & Cohen, G. L. (2007). A question of belonging: Race, social fit, and achievement. *Journal of Personality and Social Psychology, 92*, 82–96.

Wertheim, M. (1995). *Pythagoras' trousers: God, physics, and the gender wars*. New York: Norton.

III

GENDERED EXPERIENCE IN THE WORKPLACE

7

THE STRESS OF WORKING ON THE EDGE: IMPLICATIONS OF GLASS CLIFFS FOR BOTH WOMEN AND ORGANIZATIONS

MICHELLE K. RYAN, S. ALEXANDER HASLAM, METTE D. HERSBY, CLARA KULICH, AND M. DANA WILSON-KOVACS

The most prestigious activities in our society expect of people who are going to rise to leadership positions . . . near total commitment to their work. They expect a large number of hours in the office, they expect a flexibility of schedules to respond to contingency, they expect a continuity of effort through the life cycle, and they expect . . . that the mind is always working on the problems that are in the job, even when the job is not taking place. And it is a fact about our society that this is a level of commitment that a much higher fraction of married men have been historically prepared to make than of married women.

—Larry Summers (2005)

There is no doubt that women continue to be underrepresented in the upper echelons of management. As is apparent from the other chapters in this volume, much research and media attention has concentrated on the barriers that women face as they climb the career ladder. However, more recently, the spotlight has focused on the large percentage of the women choosing to leave high-powered posts (e.g., Hewlett & Luce, 2005). As the preceding quote illustrates, Larry Summers, the then-president of Harvard University in the United States, (in)famously suggested that women were underrepresented at the top of

The authors thank Anne O'Brien, Shree Mishra, and Cate Atkins for their help with this research. This research was jointly funded by the European Social Fund (Project Reference 4130) and the ESRC (RES 062 23 0135).

science and engineering because such leadership positions required a level of commitment that they were not prepared to make. A 2005 survey of the U.K. retail industry published in *The Sunday Telegraph* similarly revealed that although its middle management is female dominated, women constitute fewer than 5% of its CEOs (Hall, 2005). In addition, the article noted that 40% of women on the boards of retail companies report consciously holding themselves back from seeking the top job, and that "women shy away from [these posts] because they are unwilling to sacrifice their family life, are less aggressive than their male counterparts, and less concerned about job status than men" (n.p.).

However, there are reasons for doubting whether such reports should be taken at face value. In particular, women's explanations of the glass ceiling in terms of their own voluntary decisions not to pursue leadership may be a strategic reaction to discrimination (e.g., Crosby, 1984; Schmitt, Branscombe, Kobrynowicz, & Owen, 2002) or an attempt to avoid the negative costs of challenging discrimination (e.g., Kaiser & Miller, 2001; Swim & Hyers, 1999). Moreover, reframing the failure to achieve leadership positions as a personal choice may be empowering because it gives women a sense of agency and control (e.g., Schmitt et al., 2002) and suggests that they need not fit into a "man's world" (Gerson, 1986). However, such an emphasis may downplay the importance of the social structural barriers that women face in the workplace. Indeed, as Larry Summers claimed that women were voluntarily choosing to opt out of demanding jobs, he simultaneously questioned the role of discrimination in sustaining the glass ceiling, suggesting that biological or natural differences may be to blame instead (for a discussion see Morton, Haslam, Postmes, & Ryan, 2006).

In contrast, this chapter presents research suggesting that women's decisions to leave organizations have little to do with any inability to cope with life at the top or any difference between women's priorities and men's. On the contrary, we argue that it is women's *differential experiences* in the workplace, such as their appointment to precarious glass-cliff leadership positions (Ryan & Haslam, 2005, 2007), that lead them to opt out of organizational life. In this context we propose a gender–stress–disidentification (GSD) model (Ryan, Haslam, Hersby, & Kulich, 2008), which provides an alternative account of women's underrepresentation in senior organizational positions. This model points to the importance of social structural barriers and the inherent stressfulness of women's positions above the glass ceiling as primary determinants of their decisions to exit organizations.

WOMEN LEAVING THE WORKPLACE

Evidence suggests that women are indeed opting out of jobs, particularly those at senior levels. In a survey of almost 2,500 professional women, Hewlett and Luce (2005) found that 37% had voluntarily taken time off from work, compared with only 24% of men. Moreover, of the women who had taken time off from work, 44% left for family reasons such as child care or needing to look after an elderly family member (see chap. 9, this volume). Although there is no doubt that many women choose family over work, the popularity of this explanation may, at least in part, be a result of society's stereotypical view of women as homemakers (Eagly, 1987; see also chaps. 4, 6, and 9, this volume). Indeed, women themselves may offer these "acceptable" explanations in their exit interviews rather than indicating more troublesome factors, to avoid confrontation (Gerson, 1986).

Other explanations of women's decisions to leave work focus on their differences from men on key dimensions such as ambition and drive. For example, whereas Fels (2004) acknowledged the detrimental pressures of family and social norms, she claimed it comes down to women's choices: "when the choice must be made, women choose to downsize their ambitions or abandon them altogether" (p. 60).

However, although women may be leaving particular organizations, evidence suggests that they do not necessarily opt out of work altogether (McDowell, 2006; Townsend, 1996). For example, a Catalyst study established that 90% of female professionals leaving the workplace (including those with young children) continued their career elsewhere, with over 70% remaining in full-time employment (Townsend, 1996). Taken with the evidence that an increasing number of women are becoming independent entrepreneurs— as demonstrated by a dramatic increase in female-owned firms (McDowell, 2006)—these data suggest that women may be motivated to leave their jobs for reasons other than a lack of ambition or a wish to stay at home with their children.

Along these lines, although Hewlett and Luce (2005) reported the influence of pull factors, that is, those family and lifestyle dynamics that influence women to voluntarily leave organizations, they also identify the importance of push factors, those features of the work environment that impel women to leave. Indeed, they reported that 17% of women leave work because their jobs are not satisfying or meaningful. Moreover, these researchers reported that in business sectors (as opposed to those such as teaching or medicine), feelings of being undervalued and a lack of opportunity outweigh family reasons as causes for women opting out.

Such findings are in line with research by Stroh, Brett, and Reilly (1996) that found that although more women left management positions than did men (26% vs. 14%, respectively), the primary reasons they gave for doing so were not related to family commitments but rather reflected disaffection with their organizations as a result of receiving suboptimal career opportunities. Taken together, these results suggest that women's experience in the workplace is very different from that of their male colleagues and that this differential experience may underpin the differential exit rates for men and women.

To examine the differential experience of men and women, we conducted a program of research looking at women's experience above the glass ceiling. This question is increasingly relevant because, although women are far from achieving equality in the workplace, growing numbers of them are obtaining senior positions (Bureau of Labor Statistics, 2005; Equal Opportunities Commission, 2006; Women and Equality Unit, 2004). In this research we have demonstrated that women who do pass through the glass ceiling are more likely than men to confront a glass cliff, such that their leadership positions are more precarious than are those of their male counterparts. These positions are consequently associated with greater risk of failure and criticism, as they are more likely to involve managing organizational units that are in crisis. Evidence pertaining to the glass cliff has been obtained using multiple methods, including archival, experimental, and qualitative research (see Ryan & Haslam, 2007, for a review).

In an initial examination of FTSE 100 companies (the 100 most highly capitalized companies listed on the London Stock Exchange), we investigated the share-price performance of companies both before and after the appointment of male and female board members (Ryan & Haslam, 2005). The results revealed that women were appointed to board positions under very different circumstances than were men. As can be seen in Figure 7.1, the appointment of men to the directorial boards of various FTSE 100 companies during a time of general financial downturn was preceded by a period of relatively stable

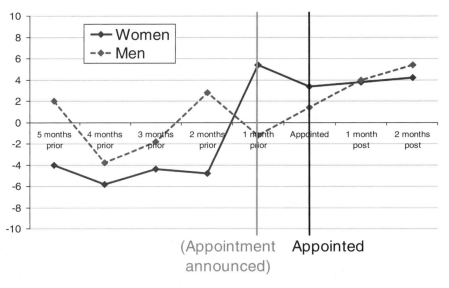

Figure 7.1. Company performance before and after the appointment of male and female board members.

company performance. In contrast, those companies that appointed a woman to their boards of directors had experienced consistently poor performance in the months prior to the appointment.

When we examined these data, it was apparent that female board members were entering very different situations than were their male counterparts. In fact, because of a continuing pattern of poor company performance, women's positions were associated with a high risk of failure and were therefore more precarious. Indeed, it follows from research on the romance of leadership (Meindl, Ehrlich, & Dukerich, 1985) that those who occupy glass-cliff leadership positions may take on a disproportionate share of the blame when things go wrong and are likely to be held accountable for events that were set in motion long before they took the helm (Ryan & Haslam, 2005).

This program of research has moved beyond the boardroom, finding evidence for glass cliffs across a diverse range of settings and sectors. One of the key questions the work has explored is whether women's overrepresentation in risky and precarious positions is a product of decision-making processes during leader selection. This idea has been tested using experimental scenario-based studies, which have examined people's preferences for male and female candidates under conditions of low and high risk (Haslam & Ryan, in press; see also Ashby, Ryan, & Haslam, 2007; Ryan, Haslam, & Kulich, 2008).

Across a range of scenarios, the results from these studies consistently show that when respondents are provided with the details of two equally qualified candidates for a leadership position—one of them a man and the other a woman—respondents overwhelmingly favor the female candidate over the male candidate when the position is in an organizational unit that is in crisis, and thus associated with an increased risk of failure. Moreover, respondents see the female candidate as significantly more suitable for a risky situation than for one in which the organization is running smoothly. Such a pattern of results has been demonstrated in studies in which participants selected (a) a financial director for a large multinational company (Haslam & Ryan, in press, Studies 1 and 3), (b) a lead lawyer for a legal case that was doomed to fail (Ashby et al., 2007), (c) a youth representative for a music festival experiencing declining popularity (Haslam & Ryan, in press, Study 2), and (d) a political candidate contesting an unwinnable by-election (Ryan, Haslam, & Kulich, 2008). Of equal significance, this pattern has been observed not only among undergraduates in relevant fields (e.g., law, politics) but also among senior business leaders (Haslam & Ryan, in press, Study 3). These experimental studies demonstrate that the glass cliff cannot be explained simply as a product of a tendency for women to prefer, and actively choose, leadership positions that are more risky (an explanation favored by some senior women themselves; see Ryan, Haslam, & Postmes, 2007; Woods, 2004). They also argue against the more drastic assertion that women leaders are actually the cause of organizational crisis (e.g., as argued by Judge, 2003).

As our research has progressed, it has become apparent that feelings of precariousness are not restricted to leadership positions with an inherent risk of failure. To provide in-depth analysis of the experiences of women in glass-cliff positions, we have conducted about 50 face-to-face interviews and a series of focus groups and online studies. The qualitative data obtained from these studies reveal that women are aware of a number of organizational factors that contribute to their leadership positions being more risky and precarious than those of men. One of the key factors identified is that they are often not included in the informal networks that exist within their workplace (see chap. 10, this volume). As one woman told us:

> I was placed on a project to manage that was the "project from hell." Was I set up for failure? I don't know. But I know it would have been different if I was male. I would have been part of the old schoolboy network that they had going.

One major consequence of women's exclusion from informal networks is that they often report not receiving the same amount of support as do men, making it more difficult for them to carry out their roles. In the words of one female professional: "I may be on [a glass cliff] right now. I often feel that there is not much support in regard to my situation, perhaps because I am not part of the still-present old-boy network." This support need not simply be emotional in nature, in the form of words of encouragement or a listening ear. Networks often function as an important source of practical information (House, 1981). Indeed, women commonly remark that they are asked to take on difficult jobs without being given enough information. As another respondent commented,

> I was asked to take on a role without the full background history. The vital information that was missing meant that the sensible approach to the problems would cause a serious backlash of unrest. Had I known (or asked) who had already refused it and why I would not have taken it on. I feel I was set up to fail.

A final factor that can add to the precariousness of a glass-cliff position is a lack of acknowledgment, both of the difficulties of a particular professional predicament and of achievements that are made despite these potential difficulties:

> I was promoted into a difficult management role (where the previous male manager had failed) with the hope that I would turn it around. When I did, the "reward" was to be moved to another turnaround role—without any additional financial reward or kudos. Meanwhile male peers appear to

work less hard and fewer hours—and with greater reward. I often wonder
if I'm just a fool to accept such challenges. I doubt that the men would.

This lack of support, information, and acknowledgment contributes to feelings
of precariousness and insecurity and makes leadership challenges harder to
tackle and overcome.

THE GLASS CLIFF AND STRESS

Although the phenomenon of the glass cliff is relatively well established,
more recent work has investigated the psychological processes that underlie
women's appointment to such positions (Ryan & Haslam, 2007; Ryan,
Haslam, et al., 2007). The results of this research suggest that the appointment
of women to risky and precarious positions is likely to arise from a myriad of
factors, including gender and managerial stereotypes (Ryan, Haslam, Hersby,
& Bongiorno, 2008; after Eagly & Karau, 2002; Schein, 1973), both hostile
and benevolent sexism (Ryan & Haslam, 2007; after Fiske, Cuddy, Glick,
& Xu, 2002), and the fact that women may not have access to other, less risky
opportunities (Haslam & Ryan, in press). However, one issue that is of particular relevance for this chapter is the role of stress in glass-cliff positions. Stress
is an important aspect of glass-cliff positions for two reasons. First, the perceived stressfulness of such positions has been shown to mediate the perceived
suitability of women for glass-cliff positions and, second, glass-cliff positions
have been shown to be inherently stressful.

Support for the first of these points emerges from a study in which
business leaders were (a) asked to evaluate a male or a female candidate for
a leadership position in a company that was performing either well or badly
and (b) asked to assess the perceived stressfulness of the work the candidate
would do (Haslam & Ryan, in press, Study 3). The results provided evidence
that the female candidate's suitability for the leadership position in a company whose performance was declining was fully mediated by beliefs that such
a position would be more stressful than a leadership position in a successful
organization would be. In other words, it appeared that women were selected
for the challenging position precisely because it was stressful. This result is
open to a number of interpretations. It can be seen as compatible with the view
that women leaders' traits and abilities render them particularly well-suited to
the management of crisis and the stress that this involves (e.g., Dunahoo,
Geller, & Hobfoll, 1996; Lindquist, Beilin, & Knuiman, 1997; Ryan, Haslam,
Hersby, & Bongiorno, 2008). Less positively, this pattern can be interpreted
as indicating that people place women in glass-cliff positions because they
want to expose them to stress (or to protect men from it).

In this regard, evidence suggests that glass-cliff positions are indeed
inherently stressful. As outlined earlier, such positions often involve (a) a
lack of support from colleagues and superiors, (b) inadequate information, or

(c) a lack of acknowledgment and respect. Each factor has been identified by the U.K. Health and Safety Executive as a significant workplace stressor (Health and Safety Executive, 2005; see also Cartwright & Cooper, 1997). In view of the fact that glass-cliff positions are also associated with the specter of organizational failure, it is therefore unsurprising that they are found to be highly stressful by those who hold them. This inherent stressfulness is made explicit in the following quote from a female manager:

> I am a management consultant. For my first ever project as "team manager" I was brought in halfway through a failing project to replace a more experienced male manager. I delivered successfully, but this was extremely stressful for me, as there was a great deal of pressure for me to succeed.

CONSEQUENCES OF THE GLASS CLIFF

Having made it to the top, many women feel battle-scarred by the experience, and in line with the preceding observations, many report high levels of burnout and withdrawal (e.g., Burke, 2004; Jick & Mitz, 1985; Nelson & Quick, 1985). Existing literature offers a number of explanations for women's burnout, including overrepresentation in vulnerable professions (e.g., Schaufeli & Greenglass, 2001), unbalanced work–life roles (Barnett & Baruch, 1985), and increased emotional labor (Pugliesi, 1999). However, consistent with the broad thrust of research into the glass cliff, this pattern may also reflect that as they advance up the corporate ladder, women are exposed to greater stress than are their male counterparts (Burke, 2004; Nelson, Hitt, & Quick, 1989).

Stress is increasingly associated with a range of negative workplace outcomes (Kompier, Cooper, & Geurts, 2000). Among other things, it has adverse effects on job performance (e.g., Motowidlo, Packard, & Manning, 1986), commitment (Cooper & Williams, 1994), and absenteeism (Spector, Dwyer, & Jex, 1988). In this way, glass-cliff positions may have negative consequences over and above an increased risk of failure. On the basis of this previous research, a particular possibility is that stressful glass-cliff positions lead to disillusionment, not just with one's job, but with the organization more generally. If this is the case, there is an increased likelihood that individuals facing glass cliffs will disidentify with their organizations and distance themselves from them (Haslam, 2004; Haslam, Jetten, O'Brien, & Jacobs, 2004; Reynolds & Platow, 2003). Indeed, such a response was expressed by one of our interviewees, a 28-year-old health and safety executive:

> There's a model where it's a balance between the employee and the organization, about give and take. And if it's gone too far one way, that you're doing all the giving and they're doing all the taking you become really disenchanted, and you lose faith, and you lose any kind of belief in the organization.

Research into the consequences of organizational identity (or lack of it) suggests that such disidentification is in turn likely to have significant negative implications (e.g., Haslam, 2004). Reduced organizational identification has been shown to engender (a) reduced workplace effort and motivation (e.g., van Knippenberg, 2000), (b) reduced cooperation (e.g., Tyler & Blader, 2001), (c) poor communication (e.g., Postmes, Tanis, & DeWit, 2001), (d) reduced leadership effectiveness (e.g., Fielding & Hogg, 1997; Turner, 1991), and (e) reduced commitment to decisions (e.g., Haslam, Ryan, Postmes, Jetten, & Webley, 2006) and to the organization itself (e.g., Ashforth & Mael, 1989).

This flagging commitment is revealed as the respondent mentioned previously went on to remark:

> I'm fed up now with fighting, and I just want something to work. And so I think it's good that I'm going overseas because if I wasn't, I would leave—it's very tiring to take that discrimination or Glass Cliff-iness on a daily basis for so long.

The constellation of factors here suggests that, ultimately, glass-cliff positions can be a source of demotivation and disenchantment that place a major brake on women's leadership aspirations and ambitions. This syndrome is articulated by a senior lawyer who commented:

> I just go to work at the moment really, I don't have any big career plans. I suppose when you feel you've been let down, like I felt I was, it takes something away from you with regards to ambition in your career.

THE GENDER–STRESS–DISIDENTIFICATION MODEL

The logic elaborated in the previous sections suggests that the appointment of women to glass-cliff positions can set in motion, or at least be a component of, a chain of events that are potentially damaging both for the women who hold them and the organizations that employ them. Our research also suggests that these distinctive facets of women's organizational experiences can be integrated into a coherent model that speaks to these various dimensions of their organizational lives: the GSD model, represented schematically in Figure 7.2.

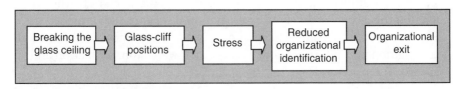

Figure 7.2. The gender–stress–disidentification model.

In summary, women are more likely than men to find themselves in risky and precarious leadership positions. The nature of these positions, including the uphill battle for success, together with the lack of support, resources, and information, renders these positions particularly stressful. In turn, the day-to-day experience of this stress can cause women to disidentify with organizations and to seek to distance themselves from them, a motivation most clearly realized in their decision to leave the organization altogether. It is significant, too, that this sequence of events can be seen, at least in part, to underlie the phenomenon addressed at the start of this chapter—whereby women come to display decreased levels of ambition and commitment.

EVIDENCE FOR THE
GENDER–STRESS–DISIDENTIFICATION MODEL

Although a large number of studies provide support for each element of the GSD model, it is crucial to test the model as a whole. In an initial attempt to provide such a test, we conducted an online survey with a large, multinational information technology company, with a sample of women from across Western and Eastern Europe, Africa, and the Middle East. As part of a larger questionnaire, we asked these women to respond to a series of questions about (a) their experiences of the glass cliff (including taking on risky positions and problematic tasks); (b) measures of key stressors (including feeling devalued at work, experiencing confusion about job requirements, and lacking support); (c) measures of organizational identification; and (d) job satisfaction and turnover intentions.

Correlational and multiple regression analyses revealed good support for the GSD model. Full analyses can be found in Ryan, Haslam, Hersby, and Kulich (2008), but the basic findings are summarized in Figure 7.3. For this sample of women, occupying a glass-cliff position was related to a number of negative workplace experiences. The results indicated that women who occupied glass-cliff positions were more likely to feel devalued, experience confusion about the requirements of their post, and report a lack of workplace support—all of which have been demonstrated to be key contributors to workplace stress (e.g., Cartwright & Cooper, 1997; Health and Safety Executive, 2005).

Furthermore, as hypothesized, experiencing these stressors was associated with a significant reduction in women's organizational identification, such that they were less likely to agree that their organization provided them with a sense of identity and belonging. Moreover, as hypothesized, this reduced identification was in turn related to reports of lowered job satisfaction and an increased intention to leave the organization.

Although this first study provides good evidence for the GSD model, it is limited in that it looks only at the experiences of women within a single

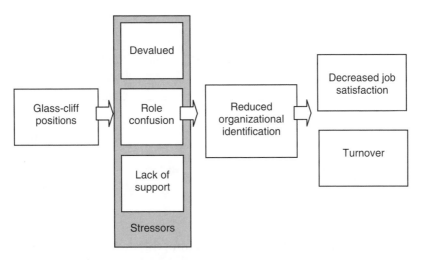

Figure 7.3. Model of the relationship between glass-cliff positions, stressors, identification, and motivation for women in information technology.

organization. To examine women's experiences in the workplace in comparison with their male counterparts, we conducted a second study with both men and women from across a number of organizations. As part of a larger questionnaire, measures included respondents' sense of (a) perceived gender inequality, (b) glass-cliff experiences, (c) stress and burnout, (d) organizational identification, (e) job satisfaction, and (f) turnover intentions.

Multiple regressions were conducted, providing further support for the GSD model. It is interesting that these analyses revealed differing patterns of results for men and women (see Ryan, Haslam, Mishra, & O'Brien, 2008, for full results). As shown in Figure 7.4, female participants' occupation of risky and precarious glass-cliff positions was associated with greater burnout, such that these women were more likely to report feelings of exhaustion, a lack of accomplishment, and callousness (e.g., Jackson, Schwab, & Schuler, 1986). These feelings of burnout, together with perceptions that women were discriminated against in their organization, were in turn associated with

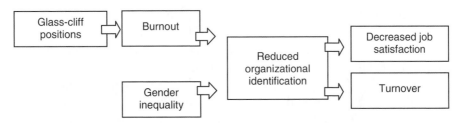

Figure 7.4. Model of the relationship between glass-cliff positions, burnout, perceived gender inequality, identification, and motivation for women.

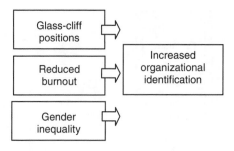

Figure 7.5. Model of the relationship between glass-cliff positions, burnout, and identification for men.

reduced organizational identification. In turn, this distancing from the organization was related to women reporting greater dissatisfaction with their jobs and increased intentions to leave.

In contrast, for men, glass-cliff positions did not appear to have the same negative consequences. As can be seen in Figure 7.5, for these male employees, occupying challenging glass-cliff leadership positions did not lead to burnout, but instead was associated with an increase in organizational identification. Moreover, organizational identification was also heightened when male employees perceived that their organization discriminated against women or, put another way, when they felt that it advantaged men.

Taken together, the results of these two studies assist in the comparison of experiences of men and women in the workplace and help shed light on why women appear to be more likely to choose to leave the organizations they work for. Overall, the studies are consistent with the idea that glass-cliff positions are inherently stressful for those women who hold them (but not necessarily for men) and that stress has a range of negative consequences. Appointing women to glass-cliff positions is likely to result in them distancing themselves from the stressfulness of their position through a reduction in organizational identification and commitment. The implication for organizations is that their female employees are less satisfied with their positions and, unsurprisingly, have stronger intentions to leave.

The second study also clearly demonstrates one way in which the experiences of men and women in the workplace differ. Although the experience of risky and challenging positions led women to question their organizational commitment, it actually led men to increase their organizational identification—perhaps a reflection of the greater support that men receive in these roles. Indeed, such results resonate with past research by Ohlott, Ruderman, and McCauley (1994) that suggests that although men's challenges are often experienced as positive and career enhancing, women's challenges are much more likely to be problematic and career limiting.

CONCLUSION

The GSD model has clear and tangible implications for organizations. Indeed, organizations that place women in risky and stressful positions have at least three reasons for wanting to address the issue. First, legislation in many countries mandates the protection of the health and safety of employees (e.g., Health and Safety Executive, 2006) with organizations liable to both civil and criminal charges if workplace stress is not addressed. Second, the economic cost of stress is well documented. Estimates suggest that stress-related absenteeism and sick leave can account for up to 10% of company profit (Hoel, Sparks, & Cooper, 2001; Martin, 1997). Finally, in light of the relationship between stress and increased turnover intentions, addressing the stress associated with women's positions is essential if organizations are to retain the talent of female employees.

The results presented in this chapter suggest that women's experiences in the workplace are very different from those of their male counterparts. Such findings provide an alternative to the claims of Larry Summers (and many others) that women lack the commitment to make it to the top, for they suggest that it is not necessarily an intrinsic lack of ambition or different priorities that lead women to opt out of organizations. Instead, lowered commitment may be a direct outcome of workplace practices that lead women to occupy inherently stressful positions. Thus, the blame for women's underrepresentation at the top should not be placed squarely on the shoulders of women themselves.

The program of research presented here suggests that equal opportunity is about the nature of leadership positions as well as their number. Thus, it is important to note not just that the quantity of women given senior positions is low but also that the quality of those positions is typically low too. Were these "facts about society" to change, it seems highly likely that women in turn would prove much more willing to make, and retain, their commitment to its leadership.

REFERENCES

Ashby, J., Ryan, M. K., & Haslam, S. A. (2007). Legal work and the glass cliff: Evidence that women are preferentially selected to lead problematic cases. *William and Mary Journal of Women and the Law, 13,* 775–794.

Ashforth, B. E., & Mael, F. (1989). Social identity theory and the organization. *Academy of Management Review, 14,* 20–39.

Barnett, R. C., & Baruch, G. K. (1985). Women's involvement in multiple roles and psychological distress. *Journal of Personality and Social Psychology, 49,* 135–145.

Bureau of Labor Statistics. (2005). *Women in the labor force: A databook.* Washington, DC: U.S. Department of Labor.

Burke, R. J. (2004). Work experiences, stress and health among managerial women: Research and practice. In M. J. Schabracq, J. A. M. Winnubst, & C. L. Cooper (Eds.), *The handbook of work and health psychology* (2nd ed., pp. 259–278). Chichester, England: Wiley.

Cartwright, S., & Cooper, C. L. (1997). *Managing workplace stress*. Thousand Oaks, CA: Sage.

Cooper, C. L., & Williams, S. (1994). *Creating healthy work organisations*. Chichester, England: Wiley.

Crosby, F. (1984). The denial of personal discrimination. *American Behavioral Scientist, 27*, 371–386.

Dunahoo, C. L., Geller, A., & Hobfoll, S. E. (1996). Woman's coping: Communal versus individualistic orientation. In M. J. Schabracq, J. A. M. Winnubst, & C. L. Cooper (Eds.), *Handbook of work and health psychology* (pp. 183–204). New York: Wiley.

Eagly, A. H. (1987). *Sex differences in social behavior: A social-role interpretation*. Hillsdale, NJ: Erlbaum.

Eagly, A. H., & Karau, S. J. (2002). Role congruity theory of prejudice toward female leaders. *Psychological Review, 109*, 573–598.

Equal Opportunities Commission. (2006). *Facts about women and men in Great Britain*. Manchester, England: Author.

Fels, A. (2004). Do women lack ambition? *Harvard Business Review, 82*(4), 50–60.

Fielding, K. S., & Hogg, M. A. (1997). Social identity, self categorization, and leadership: A field study of small interactive groups. *Group Dynamics: Theory, Research, and Practice, 1*, 39–51.

Fiske, S. T., Cuddy, A. J., Glick, P., & Xu, J. (2002). A model of (often mixed) stereotype content: Competence and warmth respectively follow from perceived status and competition. *Journal of Personality and Social Psychology, 82*, 878–902.

Gerson, K. (1986). *Hard choices: How women decide about work, career and motherhood*. Berkeley & Los Angeles: University of California Press.

Hall, J. (2005, June 19). We don't want to be the boss. *The Sunday Telegraph*. Retrieved July 16, 2005, from http://www.telegraph.co.uk/money/main.jhtml?xml=/money/2005/06/19/ccwomen19.xml

Haslam, S. A. (2004). *Psychology in organizations. The social identity approach* (2nd ed.). London: Sage.

Haslam, S. A., Jetten, J., O'Brien, A. T., & Jacobs, E. (2004). Social identity, social influence, and reactions to potentially stressful tasks: Support for the self-categorization model of stress. *Stress and Health, 20*, 3–9.

Haslam, S. A., & Ryan, M. K. (in press). The road to the glass cliff: Differences in the perceived suitability of men and women for leadership positions in succeeding and failing organizations. *Leadership Quarterly*.

Haslam, S. A., Ryan, M. K., Postmes, T., Jetten, J., & Webley, P. (2006). Sticking to our guns: Social identity as a basis for the maintenance of commitment to faltering organizational projects. *Journal of Organizational Behavior, 27*, 607–628.

Health and Safety Executive. (2005, March). *Tackling stress: The management standards approach*. London: Author.

Health and Safety Executive. (2006). *Work-related stress*. Retrieved July 20, 2007, from http://www.hse.gov.uk/stress/index.htm

Hewlett, S. A., & Luce, C. B. (2005, March). Off-ramps and on-ramps: Keeping talented women on the road to success. *Harvard Business Review, 83*(3), 43–54.

Hoel, H., Sparks, K., & Cooper, C. L. (2001). *The cost of violence/stress at work and the benefits of a violence/stress-free working environment*. Geneva, Switzerland: International Labour Organization.

House, J. S. (1981). *Work, stress and social support*. Reading, MA: Addison-Wesley.

Jackson, S. E., Schwab, R. L., & Schuler, R. S. (1986). Toward an understanding of the burnout phenomenon. *Journal of Applied Psychology, 71*, 630–640.

Jick, T. D., & Mitz, L. F. (1985). Sex differences in work stress. *Academy of Management Review, 10*, 408–420.

Judge, E. (2003, November 11). Women on board: Help or hindrance? *The Times*, p. 21.

Kaiser, C. R., & Miller, C. T. (2001). Stop complaining! The social costs of making attributions to discrimination. *Personality and Social Psychology Bulletin, 27*, 254–263.

Kompier, M. A. J., Cooper, C. L., & Geurts, S. A. E. (2000). A multiple-case study approach to work stress prevention in Europe. *European Journal of Work and Organizational Psychology, 9*, 371–400.

Lindquist, T. L., Beilin, L. J., & Knuiman, M. W. (1997). Influence of lifestyle, coping, and job stress on blood pressure in men and women. *Hypertension, 29*, 1–7.

Martin, P. (1997). *The sickening mind: Brain, behaviour, immunity and disease*. London: HarperCollins.

McDowell, J. (2006, August 17). *Women-owned firms increase nearly 20 percent* [News release]. Washington, DC: The Office of Advocacy of the U.S. Small Business Administration.

Meindl, J. R., Ehrlich, S. B., & Dukerich, J. M. (1985). The romance of leadership. *Administrative Science Quarterly, 30*, 78–102.

Morton, T., Haslam, S. A., Postmes, T., & Ryan, M. K. (2006). We value what values us: The appeal of identity-affirming science. *Political Psychology, 27*, 823–838.

Motowidlo, S. J., Packard, J. S., & Manning, M. R. (1986). Occupational stress: Its causes and consequences for job performance. *Journal of Applied Psychology, 71*, 616–629.

Nelson, D. L., Hitt, M. A., & Quick, J. C. (1989). Men and women of the personnel profession: Some differences and similarities in their stress. *Stress Medicine, 5*, 145–152.

Nelson, D. L., & Quick, J. C. (1985). Professional women: Are distress and disease inevitable? *Academy of Management Review, 10*, 206–218.

Ohlott, P. J., Ruderman, M. N., & McCauley, C. D. (1994). Gender differences in managers' developmental job experiences. *Academy of Management Journal, 37*, 46–67.

Postmes, T., Tanis, M., & DeWit, B. (2001). Communication and commitment in organizations: A social identity approach. *Group Processes & Intergroup Relations, 4,* 227–246.

Pugliesi, K. (1999). The consequences of emotional labor: Effects on work stress, job satisfaction, and well-being. *Motivation & Emotion, 23,* 125–154.

Reynolds, K. J., & Platow, M. J. (2003). On the social psychology of power and power-lessness: Social power as a symptom of organizational division. In S. A. Haslam, D. van Knippenberg, M. J. Platow, & N. Ellemers (Eds.), *Social identity at work: Developing theory for organizational practice* (pp. 173–188). New York: Psychology Press.

Ryan, M. K., & Haslam, S. A. (2005). The glass cliff: Evidence that women are over-represented in precarious leadership positions. *British Journal of Management, 16,* 81–90.

Ryan, M. K., & Haslam, S. A. (2007). The glass cliff: Exploring the dynamics surrounding women's appointment to precarious leadership positions. *Academy of Management Review, 32,* 549–572.

Ryan, M. K., Haslam, S. A., Hersby, M. D., & Bongiorno, R. (2008). *Think crisis–think female: Using the glass cliff to reconsider the think manager–think male stereotype.* Unpublished manuscript, University of Exeter, Exeter, England.

Ryan, M. K., Haslam, S. A., Hersby, M. D., & Kulich, C. (2008). *Teetering on the edge: The stressful consequences of the glass cliff.* Unpublished manuscript, University of Exeter, Exeter, England.

Ryan, M. K., Haslam, S. A., & Kulich, C. (2008). *Politics and the glass cliff: Evidence that women are preferentially selected to contest hard-to-win seats.* Unpublished manuscript, University of Exeter, Exeter, England.

Ryan, M. K., Haslam, S. A., Mishra, S., & O'Brien, A. T. (2008). *Challenge and stress: Men's and women's reactions to risky positions.* Unpublished manuscript, University of Exeter, Exeter, England.

Ryan, M. K., Haslam, S. A., & Postmes, T. (2007). Reactions to the glass cliff: Gender differences in the explanations for the precariousness of women's leadership positions. *Journal of Organizational Change Management, 20,* 182–197.

Schaufeli, W. B., & Greenglass, E. R. (2001). Introduction to special issue on burnout and health. *Psychology & Health, 16,* 501–510.

Schein, V. E. (1973). The relationship between sex role stereotypes and requisite management characteristics. *Journal of Applied Psychology, 57,* 95–105.

Schmitt, M. T., Branscombe, N. R., Kobrynowicz, D., & Owen, S. (2002). Perceiving discrimination against one's gender group has different implications for well-being in women and men. *Personality and Social Psychology Bulletin, 28,* 197–210.

Spector, P. E., Dwyer, D. J., & Jex, S. M. (1988). Relation of job stressors to affective, health, and performance outcomes: A comparison of multiple data sources. *Journal of Applied Psychology, 73,* 11–19.

Stroh, L. K., Brett, J. M., & Reilly, A. H. (1996). Family structure, glass ceiling, and traditional explanations for the differential rate of turnover of female and male managers. *Journal of Vocational Behavior, 49,* 99–118.

Summers, L. H. (2005, January 14). *Remarks at NBER conference on diversifying the science & engineering workforce*. Retrieved July 20, 2007, from http://www.president. harvard.edu/speeches/2005/nber.html

Swim, J. K., & Hyers, L. L. (1999). Excuse me—What did you just say? Women's public and private responses to sexist remarks. *Journal of Experimental Social Psychology*, 35, 68–88.

Townsend, B. (1996). Room at the top for women. *American Demographics, 18*(7), 28–37.

Turner, J. C. (1991). *Social influence*. Milton Keynes, England: Open University Press.

Tyler, T. R., & Blader, S. L. (2001). Identity and cooperative behavior in groups. *Group Processes & Intergroup Relations, 4*, 207–226.

van Knippenberg, D. (2000). Work motivation and performance: A social identity perspective. *Applied Psychology: An International Review, 49*, 357–371.

Women & Equality Unit. (2004). *Women & equality unit gender briefing*. Retrieved July 20, 2004, from http://www.womenandequalityunit.gov.uk/research/gender_ briefing_apr04.doc

Woods, J. (2004, September 9). Are female execs walking into trouble? *The Daily Telegraph*, p. 23.

8

SEXUAL HARASSMENT
AND THE GLASS CEILING

MARGARET S. STOCKDALE AND GARGI BHATTACHARYA

For a phenomenon whose legal roots are in the accidental genesis of *sex* as a prohibited classification for employment discrimination[1] and subsequently in judge-made law,[2] sexual harassment has garnered a significant amount of attention and concern around the globe. It is not accidental that sexual harassment concerns are concomitant with the glass ceiling. As we show in this chapter, women are particularly at risk for being sexually harassed when they encounter men who are threatened by their emerging power and status in spheres that have traditionally belonged to men. Other chapters in this volume address the important underlying causes and correlates of the glass ceiling such as gender stereotypes (see chap. 2, this volume), family-related barriers (see chap. 9, this volume), and other structural impediments that differentially affect women, such as women being assigned to particularly risky situations that set them up for failure (see chap. 7, this volume). We add sexual harassment to this list and build our argument by reviewing the general scholarship over the past decade and showing that sexual harassment of women by

---

[1]The classification of *sex* was added as a last-minute failed attempt at a poison pill to kill passage of the Civil Rights Act of 1964 (see Kanowitz, 1968).
[2]Sexual harassment was not statutorily defined as illegal in the Civil Rights Act, but was recognized in the U.S. Supreme Court as a claim of sex discrimination in *Meritor v. Vinson*, 1986.

men effectively shuts down women's career development in male-dominated occupations, such as top management.

With the growth of women in the paid labor force from 33% in the 1950s to 74% by the 1990s (Ridgeway & England, 2007), significant disparities remain in the representation of women at top levels of management. Only 8% of top leadership positions go to women, with only 2% as CEOs (Rhode & Williams, 2007). The presence of women on Fortune 500 boards of directors has increased from 9.6% in 1995 to only 14.7% in 2005 (Catalyst, 2006), and although sex segregation in occupations has been declining since the 1960s, the decline has slowed significantly since the 1990s (Ridgeway & England, 2007). Indeed, 18 million women and 18 million men in America would need to change jobs (from a job dominated by their gender to a job in which they are in the minority) to eliminate sex segregation (Bergmann, 2007). We show in this chapter that sexual harassment has a hand in shaping these statistics. Women in nontraditional, male-dominated occupations and work groups are disproportionately targeted for sexual harassment. This fact contributes to general occupational segregation, as well as the dearth of women in top management positions. We therefore argue that sexual harassment is a force that must be effectively eliminated if women are to achieve equality in the workplace.

In 1996, Stockdale commented on the state of sexual harassment scholarship in her introduction to the edited book *Sexual Harassment in the Workplace*. That review covered the first 15 years of empirical research in an effort to organize future efforts to understand the etiology and consequences of workplace sexual harassment for individuals and organizations. The purpose of this chapter is to provide an update on the sexual harassment scholarship with particular focus on the conceptualizations of sexual harassment, both legal and psychological, and the characteristics of situations, targets, and actors that are implicated in sexual harassment incidents. In so doing, we build our thesis that women who challenge men's power and privilege in the workplace are at risk for sexual harassment, and that experiences of sexual harassment drive women away from the rewarding spheres of work that have been historically dominated by men, such as top management and other "masculine" occupations. This review also reveals the "hot spots" that should be the focus of further research and intervention. Because this chapter is part of a broader volume on glass-ceiling issues, our focus is mostly on sexual harassment experiences of women, although reference to emerging scholarship on male sexual harassment is provided in various contexts.

The chapter develops in three sections. First, we review the legal and psychological developments in the definition and measurement of sexual harassment. Second, we summarize evidence on the scope of sexual harassment, and we document the effects and outcomes of sexual harassment, making the case that it is a significant workplace stressor, especially for women, affecting not only personal health and well-being but also work-adjustment factors such as job attitudes and work withdrawal. Moreover, we show that the effects of harassment extend beyond the individual target, with significant health and job-related decrements to coworkers and work teams whose members are sexually harassed. Third, we examine the characteristics of organizations, perpetrators, and targets that shape the context and explain the motivations behind sexual harassment experiences. In this section we show that although the etiology of harassment is by no means simple, it is by and large a social technology that enforces traditional gendered arrangement, perpetuates the glass ceiling, and reaffirms male dominance in the workplace.

THE NATURE OF SEXUAL HARASSMENT: LEGAL AND PSYCHOLOGICAL DEFINITIONS

Psychological and legal discourse on sexual harassment has focused extensively on definitional and perceptual issues. By necessity, no bright-line rule has been developed distinguishing harassing from nonharassing conduct; for the well-reasoned conclusion that as soon as such a line is drawn, clever perpetrators will invent new harassing conduct that circumvents the rule.

Most scholars and legal commentators agree that sexual harassment has both a legal definition and a psychological definition (see Fitzgerald, Swan, & Magley, 1997). For the most part, legal definitions derive from statutes, regulations, expert agency guidelines, and judicial interpretations of these statutes, regulations, and guidelines. Legal definitions provide an understanding of the nature of actions that courts will recognize as constituting a violation of the law, as well as the requirements for making a claim of sexual harassment. Judicial interpretations often provide more specific rules for deciding how issues in a case will be determined. For example, in *Burlington Industries v. Ellerth* (1998) the U.S. Supreme Court clarified under what conditions, and to what extent, an employer is liable for the harassing acts of its employees. Legal definitions, however, do not define how victims (targets) or bystanders perceive, interpret, or react to harassing behavior, nor should such definitions be the sole source of guidance for organizations in developing policies and actions to deal with harassment. Researchers have confirmed that harassing behaviors can have serious negative consequences regardless of whether the harassment rises to the legal definition of sexual harassment, that is, would likely be viewed by a court as constituting illegal sexual harassment (e.g., Rospenda, Richman, Ehmke, & Zlatoper, 2005; Schneider, Swan, & Fitzgerald, 1997). Nonetheless, the legal landscape provides an important context in which social science researchers frame their questions. In this section, we briefly review some of the advances in both the legal and psychological definitions of sexual harassment.

Advances in Legal Definitions Since 1996

The Equal Employment Opportunity Commission (EEOC) is the federal agency charged with enforcing Title VII of the Civil Rights Act and related laws. In guidelines published in the Code of Federal Regulations, the EEOC has defined sexual harassment as follows:

> unwanted sexual advances, requests for sexual favors, and other verbal or physical conduct of a sexual nature constitute sexual harassment when (1) submission to such conduct is made either explicitly or implicitly a term or condition of an individual's employment, (2) submission to or rejection of such conduct by an individual is used as the basis for employment decisions affecting such individual, or (3) such conduct has the purpose or effect of unreasonably interfering with an individual's work performance or creating an intimidating, hostile, or offensive working environment. (Equal Employment Opportunity Commission, 2006, n.p.)

Since 1996, four important U.S. Supreme Court decisions regarding sexual harassment have further shaped its legal definition. Prior to these cases, the U.S. Supreme Court recognized the emerging distinction between *quid pro quo* sexual harassment (employment consequences are conditioned on acceptance of the harassing conduct) and *hostile work environment* sexual harassment (conduct is sufficiently severe or pervasive but does not involve a tangible employment consequence; *Harris v. Forklift*, 1993; *Meritor v. Vinson*, 1986). U.S. Supreme Court cases since 1996 have addressed employer liability (*Burlington Industries v. Ellerth*, 1998; *Faragher v. City of Boca Raton*, 1998), same-sex sexual harassment (*Oncale v. Sundowner Offshore Serv., Inc.*, 1998), constructive discharge (*Pennsylvania State Police v. Suders*, 2004), and retaliation (*Burlington Northern v. White*, 2006[3]).

The employer liability cases (*Burlington Industries*, 1998; *Faragher*, 1998) reshaped the distinctions between quid pro quo and hostile work environment forms of sexual harassment. The court dismissed these terms in favor of categorizing whether the harassing conduct led to a tangible employment consequence, such as "hiring, firing, failing to promote, reassignment with significantly different responsibilities, or a decision causing a significant change in benefits" (*Burlington Industries*, 1998, p. 761). When the conduct has led to a tangible employment consequence, employers are held strictly liable. Otherwise, employers may raise an *affirmative defense*. If the employer can establish that

---

[3]*Burlington Northern* (*BNSF*) does not directly affect the definitional requirements of sexual harassment per se, so it is not thoroughly reviewed here. In essence, *BNSF* resolved which standard should be applied when deciding whether an employer's retaliatory behavior rises to an illegal level, as set forth by section 704(a) of Title VII. The Supreme Court held that any conduct that would dissuade a reasonable person from making or supporting a charge of discrimination is considered to be retaliation. This standard is considered to be more favorable to employees than are other standards that had been applied by courts prior to *BNSF*.

it took reasonable care to prevent and correct promptly any sexual harassment behavior, and if the plaintiff employee unreasonably failed to take advantage of the employer's corrective opportunities to avoid harm, then the damages the employer may have to pay would be substantially limited (*Burlington Industries*, 1998).

This affirmative defense was reiterated in *Pennsylvania State Police* (2004) with regard to constructive discharge, which involves working conditions that are so intolerable that a reasonable person in that situation would feel compelled to resign. The *Pennsylvania State Police* (2004) court held that unless a supervisor's actions within his or her official capacity as an agent of the employer led to the constructive discharge, the employer could raise an affirmative defense and, if successful, could avoid liability, if successful.

In *Oncale v. Sundowner* (1998), the U.S. Supreme Court recognized harassment initiated by persons of the same sex as the target of sexual harassment regardless of whether there was homosexual intent. Before hearing this case the circuits were split on whether nonhomosexual same-sex sexual harassment could legally constitute sexual harassment. Stockdale, Visio, and Batra (1999), among other commentators (DuBois, Knapp, Faley, & Kustis, 1998; Franke, 1997), theorized that such conduct needs to be viewed with the lens of gender socialization. Thus, men engage in sexually harassing behavior toward other men not necessarily to gain sexual access to their targets but to punish men who do not conform to traditional masculine gender-role expectations. Not addressing theory, Justice Scalia simply stated, "nothing in Title VII necessarily bars a claim of discrimination 'because of . . . sex' merely because the plaintiff and the defendant . . . are of the same sex" (*Oncale*, 1998, p. 79).

The current legal definition of sexual harassment, therefore, concerns severe or pervasive unwanted sexual behavior or sexually hostile work environments directed at male or female employees, regardless of the gender of the initiator. Employers will be held vicariously liable for harassment by their supervisors if the harassing conduct involves tangible employment consequences to an employee. Furthermore, if the supervisor abuses his or her authority to force a constructive discharge, the employer will be vicariously liable. Employers may not be liable for severe or pervasive harassing conduct by supervisors or other employees that did not culminate in a tangible employment consequence if they took reasonable care to prevent or promptly correct it and if the plaintiff employee failed to reasonably avoid harm by using the employer's complaint procedures.

The bar for a successful legal charge of sexual harassment against an employer is high, given these developments in the law. In various opinions, the U.S. Supreme Court has stated that Title VII is not intended to be a civility code. It does not "prohibit genuine or innocuous differences in the ways men and women routinely interact with members of the same sex and of the opposite sex" (*Oncale*, 1998, p. 81), and an objective assessment of the severity of the conduct should be judged from the perspective of a reasonable person in the plaintiff's position, considering "all the circumstances" (*Harris*, 1993, p. 23). Yet, social scientists and organizational leaders may be concerned about workplace conditions that have negative consequences for workers or organizational functioning regardless of whether the conduct meets or surpasses the legal bar. We turn next to recent developments in our understanding of the psychological definitions of and perspectives on sexual harassment.

Advances in Psychological Definitions and Measurement

Psychological definitions of sexual harassment involve the subjective interpretation of sexualized conduct in the workplace as unwelcome and harmful. Louise Fitzgerald and her colleagues have devoted considerable attention to understanding the nature and consequences of sexual harassment, within a larger, ecological model of workplace stress (Fitzgerald, Drasgow, Hulin, Gelfand, & Magley, 1997). Relying on a behaviorally based instrument, Fitzgerald, Swan, and Magley (1997) concluded that sexual harassment experiences fall into three overlapping (intercorrelated) categories. *Gender harassment* concerns "verbal behavior, physical acts, and symbolic gestures that are not aimed at sexual cooperation but that convey insulting, hostile, and degrading attitudes about women" (Fitzgerald, Swan, et al., p. 10). *Unwanted sexual attention* is, as the name implies, sexual behavior directed at the target that is unwanted. It includes "both verbal and nonverbal behavior that is unwelcome, offensive, and unreciprocated" (Fitzgerald, Swan, et al., p. 10), and *sexual coercion* "refers to the extortion of sexual cooperation in return for job-related considerations" (Fitzgerald, Swan, et al., p. 11).

The Sexual Experiences Questionnaires (SEQ), developed by Fitzgerald and her colleagues, generally measure these three categories of sexual harassment[4] and have been the dominant self-report instruments measuring behavioral incidents of unwanted sexual experiences (Gelfand, Fitzgerald, & Drasgow, 1995). The tripartite structure of the SEQ mapped onto the hostile work environment (gender harassment and unwanted sexual attention) and quid pro quo (sexual coercion) dimensions of the former legal definition of sexual harassment. Now that the legal definition has dropped these distinctions in favor of a "tangible job consequences" distinction, it is uncertain how well the SEQ can measure the legally relevant forms of sexual harassment.

---

[4]There are several versions of the SEQ, most of which conform to the three-factor model. However, the dimensions of the Sexual Harassment of Men Scale are gender harassment: lewd comments, gender harassment: negative remarks about men, gender harassment: enforcing the male gender role, gender harassment: unwanted sexual attention, and gender harassment: sexual coercion (Waldo, Berdahl, & Fitzgerald, 1998). In the SEQ-DoD (a version of the SEQ that was created to measure sexual harassment in the U.S. Department of Defense), the gender harassment subscale breaks down into gender harassment: sexist hostility and gender harassment: sexual hostility (Fitzgerald, Magley, Drasgow, & Waldo, 1999). Finally, Cortina's SEQ measure for Latinas includes a subscale that measures racial–sexual hostility (Cortina, 2001).

Although the SEQ and its variations have been extensively used in research and applied contexts, and have generally been touted as "the most theoretically and psychometrically sophisticated instrument available" (Fitzgerald, Gelfand, & Drasgow, 1995, p. 427), criticisms have been leveled against its validity for assessment of sexual harassment in a forensic context and for problems with its psychometric properties (Gutek, Murphy, & Douma, 2004). For example, a federal judge in the U.S. Court of Appeals for the 7th Circuit ruled that expert testimony that relies on SEQ-based assessment in a defendant organization is inadmissible (*EEOC v. Dial*, 2002) because the SEQ lacks validity. Of particular concern to the judge was the lack of comparability of SEQ scores. Gutek and her colleagues (Gutek et al., 2004) extensively reviewed the development of the SEQ and its various forms and found that the instruments vary in item length, item content, scale anchors, and instruction sets, making it impossible to establish any norms about the prevalence of sexual harassment. Norms are important in both applied and forensic contexts when organizations and litigants want to determine whether the frequency and severity of sexual harassment incidents are beyond normal standards. It can be argued that any amount of sexual harassment should not be tolerated, but the SEQ may measure low-frequency events that would not be regarded as harassing.

Despite these concerns, the SEQ surveys remain the most common set of instruments measuring the psychological definition of sexual harassment, although attempts have been made to develop a measure of sexual harassment experiences that follows the legal definition more closely (Gutek, Stockdale, Done, & Swindler, 2003). Fitzgerald and her colleagues have built a strong body of empirical evidence showing how various organizational conditions are associated with increases in harassing conduct, and how the experience of harassment—regardless of whether it is labeled by the target as sexual harassment, rises to a legal definition of sexual harassment, or even whether it is directly experienced by the target—is associated with negative job-related, psychological, and physical outcomes (Fitzgerald, Drasgow, et al., 1997; Glomb et al., 1997; Schneider et al., 1997). Our attention now turns to the broader understanding of the scope and consequences of sexual harassment.

SCOPE AND EFFECTS OF SEXUAL HARASSMENT

Since systematic surveys of sexual harassment have been conducted, the results have consistently shown that harassing activity is widespread and noxious. More recent research using strong instruments and comprehensive survey research designs confirmed what researchers suspected early on: Arguably half of all working women and a sizable number of men experience unwanted sexualized behavior on their jobs, and the more frequent the harassment the worse the outcomes for both the targeted individuals and their coworkers and work units.

Prevalence of Sexual Harassment in the United States

To shed light on the conditions that affect the occurrence of sexual harassment, let us first describe its prevalence. This task has proven to be fairly difficult because there has been no nationally representative survey of sexual harassment in the United States, although Gruber (1997) has reported on epidemiological studies in Canada. The federal government has surveyed its own employees three times (U.S. Merit Systems Protection Board, 1981, 1988, 1995), and the U.S. Department of Defense has conducted nationwide surveys of the armed services (Edwards, Elig, Edwards, & Riemer, 1997; Lipari & Lancaster, 2003). In addition, random surveys have been conducted of large metropolitan areas (Gutek, 1985), and many surveys have been conducted in universities and business organizations using convenience-sampling approaches.

Ilies, Hauserman, Schwochau, and Stibal (2003) meta-analyzed the extant empirical literature on the prevalence of sexual harassment in the United States. Distinguishing *direct query* approaches, in which survey participants are directly asked if they have been sexually harassed, from *behavioral experiences* approaches, in which participants indicate whether they have experienced any of a variety of potentially harassing experiences (e.g., as measured by the SEQ), Ilies et al. estimated that of almost 20,000 participants drawn from probability samples (26 samples), 24% responded in the affirmative to direct queries of sexual harassment. Among almost 70,000 participants in probability surveys using the behavioral experience approach, 58% reported at least one unwanted sexualized experience in the workplace. These prevalence figures are lower than those found in nonprobabilistic samples, in which the estimates are 35% for direct query surveys and 84% for behavioral experience surveys. Furthermore, among probability samples, reports of sexual harassment (direct or behavioral) were significantly higher in military samples than in private sector or academic samples (Ilies et al., 2003). Even if conservatively estimated by a direct experiences approach, the psychological experience of sexual harassment remains disturbingly prevalent.

Outcomes and Consequences of Sexual Harassment

Data have continued to accumulate over the past 10 years showing detrimental effects of sexual harassment on job-related and psychological outcomes. In correlational studies, sexual harassment, even at low frequencies, has been linked to job dissatisfaction, which in turn leads to work and job withdrawal, including turnover (Chan, Tang, & Chan, 1999; Fitzgerald, Drasgow, et al., 1997; Lim & Cortina, 2005; Schneider et al., 1997). Psychological dysfunction such as depression, somatic complaints, and posttraumatic stress disorder have also been correlated with sexual harassment experiences (Fitzgerald, Drasgow, et al., 1997; Lim & Cortina, 2005; Schneider et al.,

1997). A study of U.K. police found that these stress-related outcomes might be due to overperformance demands (Parker & Griffin, 2002). Female police officers who experienced gender harassment (a form of sexual harassment meant to demean and humiliate women) felt pressures to overperform to prove that they were worthy of being considered a legitimate police officer. These expectations in turn led to signs of psychological distress, such as loss of sleep and excessive worrying (Parker & Griffin, 2002).

More rigorous longitudinal data also support the causal links between sexual harassment and negative job-related and emotional outcomes. Controlling for other forms of stress, Rospenda, Richman, Ehmke, and Zlatoper (2005) found 1-year cross-lagged effects of sexual harassment (as well as nonsexualized generalized workplace harassment) on reports of illness, injury, or assault. Munson, Hulin, and Drasgow (2000) found 2-year cross-lagged effects of harassment on coworker and supervisor dissatisfaction. Their findings were also noteworthy because their pattern of results ruled out dispositional explanations for harassment effects. Thus, targets of harassment who report negative outcomes are not merely oversensitive "whiners."

Compelling data demonstrate that the negative effects of harassment reach beyond the direct targets. Stress arises when other employees witness or in other ways know that sexual harassment is occurring in their work environment. Glomb et al. (1997) labeled this phenomenon *ambient sexual harassment* (ASH) and reasoned that if it is pervasive in a work setting, women (in particular) may sense that others do not support them, or fear that they may be targeted next. Measuring ASH as the average of other employees' experiences of sexual harassment minus the focal employee (within a work unit), Glomb et al. found that ASH had stronger effects on job satisfaction and psychological functioning than did direct experiences of sexual harassment (see chap. 1, this volume). Job dissatisfaction, in turn, was significantly related to job withdrawal. Hitlan, Schneider, and Walsh (2006) similarly found that *bystander harassment,* a concept similar to ASH, predicted additional distress from one's own experiences of sexual harassment. Finally, Raver and Gelfand (2005) found that ASH had detrimental effects on team functioning, including relationship conflict, task conflict, and team cohesion, which, in turn, led to lower financial performance by the team. It is clear that sexual harassment directly and profoundly affects a large proportion of the population. In the next section we show that harassers tend to target women who challenge traditional gender roles, expressions, and careers—that is, those who aspire to transcend the glass ceiling.

RECENT ADVANCES IN SEXUAL HARASSMENT THEORY

Theories of sexual harassment have attempted to explain what types of individuals are likely to be harassers, what types of individuals are likely to be targets, and in what kinds of organizations or situations harassment is likely to occur. It was known fairly early in the history of systematic research on sexual harassment that these theoretical foci were entangled. Individuals with a propensity to harass targeted those individuals who threatened their perceived goals or privileges, and harassers engage in such activities under optimal conditions. More recent theoretical advances have clarified and expanded this basic understanding of harassing processes. The last major section of this chapter reviews these theoretical advances in more detail. We end with the presentation of a heuristic model that attempts to integrate and organize these theoretical precepts.

Perpetrators and Targets

As sexual harassment scholarship emerged, theories focused on broad explanations including men's so-called natural tendencies to sexually pursue women (Browne, 2002; Studd & Gattiker, 1991), the corrupting nature of organizational power, and the more ubiquitous influence of patriarchy (Tangri, Burt, & Johnson, 1982). These theories were refined by examining more specific conditions as well as personality and attitudinal correlates of potential harassers. For example, Gutek's sex-role spillover model (1985; Gutek & Morasch, 1982) predicted that women would be expected to embody traditionally female roles (e.g., sex object or nurturer–supporter; see chap. 2, this volume), and would thus be at risk for harassment under conditions that made gender salient in the workplace. These conditions included male- or female-dominated work environments and sexualized work environments (Gutek, 1985; Gutek & Morasch, 1982).

Another viable theory of sexual harassment that emerged in early days of sexual harassment scholarship and that remains supported is Pryor's person X situation model (Pryor, 1987; Pryor, LaVite, & Stoller, 1993). Pryor and others (e.g., Lee, Gizzarone, & Ashton, 2003) identified personality and attitudinal constellations that predispose individuals to sexually harass, but they also paid close attention to the situational contexts that may trigger these proclivities. In particular, when local norms, which include leader attitudes and behaviors as well as situational ambiguity, reduce moral pressure to behave responsibly, men with these personality and attitude structures may act out their proclivities to sexually harass (Pryor, Giedd, & Williams, 1995). Research on person X situation theory and its central construct, likelihood to sexually harass, is discussed later in this section.

Sex-role spillover theory and person X situation theory shed light on who will harass and when but do not fully explain why. Recent theoretical developments pinpoint more precisely men's motives for harassment. More and more, the story appears to support the patriarchal basis for harassment (originally labeled the *sociocultural model* by Tangri et al., 1982). Drawing on Franke's (1997) suggestion that sexual harassment is a "technology of sexism"

(p. 693), Stockdale, Visio, and Batra (1999) proposed that sexual harassment is used to police gender norms. Women and men who appear to violate traditional prescribed gendered expectations are harassed as a way to punish their deviant behavior and to reinforce the traditional structure of gender norms in which men dominate over women (see chaps. 2 and 4, this volume). Stockdale therefore argued that harassers are likely to be motivated by one of two overarching goals (Stockdale, 2005; Stockdale, Gandolfo, Schneider, & Cao, 2004). Approach goals represent a desire to gain greater sexual contact with the target and tend to involve behaviors that the target perceives as unwanted sexual attention. Rejection goals, on the other hand, represent a desire to drive the target away through debasement and humiliation. Rejection harassment serves the goal of policing traditional gender roles through attempts to remove gender deviants (Stockdale et al., 1999).

The distinction between approach and rejection motives is in line with other recent theoretical advances for understanding sexual harassment motives. Drawing on interpersonal aggression perspectives that emphasize the actors' (aggressors') goals, perceptions, and behaviors, O'Leary-Kelly, Paetzold, and Griffin (2000) developed a comprehensive theory of harassers' motives and behaviors. Defining sexual harassment as "sexual, work-related action taken with the expectation of imposing harm on another person or forcing his/her compliance in order to achieve some valued personal goal" (p. 373, italics omitted), the authors argued that harassment is intentional—that is, goal directed—although harm may be a by-product of another goal. Goals may be emotional (e.g., engaging in the harassing activity produces a desired emotional response for the harasser, e.g., a feeling of powerfulness; see Bargh, Raymond, Pryor, & Strack, 1995) or instrumental (e.g., leading to sexual favors, enacting retribution, contributing to a desirable presentation of the self). For example, harassing men may seek retribution against women who threaten their status in the workplace or who frustrate their goals. Or men may harass women (or weak men) to improve their status among other men in their social network (see, e.g., Quinn's [2002] discussion of "girl watching").

O'Leary-Kelly et al.'s (2000) theory also accounts for what types of harassing conduct perpetrators enact and what situational factors may intervene to increase or decrease the likelihood of harassing. Harassers may possess a variety of tactics to achieve their goal but tend to choose those that are perceived to be the most instrumental. Over time, these preferred actions become scripted, which means they may be enacted without deliberate conscious thought. Thus, some harassers may rely on sexist jokes, teasing, and taunting to achieve desired results, whereas others may tend to engage in sexual ogling, unwanted touching, and repeated requests for dates. Disengagement from moral control facilitates the enactment of harassing behaviors. This can occur when the target is dehumanized, such as by viewing women as sexual objects (e.g., by polluting the work environment with pornography) or by distorting the consequences of such illegal behavior. Organizations that do not have policies or that poorly enforce harassment policies contribute to such distortion.

Partial tests of O'Leary-Kelly et al.'s (2000) theory of harassment were conducted by Margaret Lucero and colleagues (Lucero, Allen, & Middleton, 2006; Lucero, Middleton, Finch, & Valentine, 2003). Using an innovative strategy for studying harasser behaviors, these researchers examined fact patterns in samples of published arbitration cases involving a sexual harassment dispute. The researchers reasoned that if harassers were goal oriented and had preferred ways of reaching their goals, they should engage in similar forms of behavior—in other words, "typologies" of harassers would emerge from examining these case facts. Indeed, Lucero et al. (2003) found that the majority of "repeat offender" harassers tended to engage in a similar pattern of behavior over time, such as sticking to gender harassment or unwanted sexual attention. The authors also found that harassers tended to fit into one of two categories: those who harassed relatively few individuals, albeit repeatedly; and those who were less discriminating, offending everyone or every woman in the work environment.

The idea that harassment motives can be categorized was also addressed by De Coster, Estes, and Mueller (1999), who evoked criminology's routine activities theory (Cohen & Felson, 1979) to explain sexual harassment activity. This theory posits that individuals whose routine activities (e.g., living, working) put them near motivated offenders are more likely than others to be victimized. With regard to sexual harassment, two theories potentially explain motivated offenders. Power-threat theory posits that men are motivated to engage in activities to harm others who threaten male power and privilege in the workplace (Brownmiller, 1975; De Coster et al., 1999). Sexual harassment is instrumental to achieving this goal. As such, likely targets are highly educated, work in traditional male occupations, occupy positions of authority, and have greater organizational tenure because such women threaten men's dominance in higher status positions in these occupations. In addition, young women are viewed as more threatening than older women because they are potentially more status seeking, and unmarried women are more threatening because they disturb the concept of traditional family structures. Victim-vulnerability theory posits that men prey on vulnerable women as a way of expressing their structural power over women (De Coster et al., 1999), and victims are thus likely to be young, unmarried, possibly minority women with low levels of education, holding nonauthority positions within female-dominated departments.

Routine activities theory also posits structural characteristics that make certain women more vulnerable to sexual harassment than others. For instance, women who are in close proximity to motivated offenders are at a higher risk. Thus, women in male-dominated work environments and in populated work environments are more likely to encounter motivated offenders (see also Berdahl, 2007; cf. Gutek, Cohen, & Konrad's contact hypothesis, 1990). Finally, vulnerability to victimization may be buffered by the presence of *capable guardians*—individuals or resources that can help prevent sexual harassment or help targets deal effectively with episodes of harassment (De Coster et al., 1999). The authors predicted that women with supportive supervisors, cohesive work groups, and supportive peers would experience less sexual harassment than would others.

De Coster et al. (1999) tested these hypotheses with the sample of nearly 6,500 male and female employees of a national telecommunications organization (sampled at over 200 locations). Significant predictors of sexual harassment included capable guardian variables, such as work-group solidarity, supportive work-group culture and supportive supervisors (negatively predicting sexual harassment), percentage of men in work environment, and population size of the location (both positive predictors). Furthermore, victimization was positively related to targets' education level, organizational tenure, and being single. Overall, the results tended to support routine activities theory of sexual harassment victimization and power-threat theory of motivated offenders.

Not all men sexually harass; indeed, most do not. Those who do harass tend to possess a personality or attitudes that make them particularly aware of their status and privilege. For example, men who tend to view women as adversaries, who automatically link sex cues with power, or whose personalities emphasize greed, deceit, and exploitation are more prone than others to engage in sexual harassment behaviors (Bargh et al., 1995; Pryor, 1987). Conducting research that aims to understand harassers or perpetrators is challenging for many reasons. First, work organizations rarely permit researchers to conduct naturalistic observations or other invasive studies in their settings for fear of potential legal ramifications if harassers are exposed. Second, because sexual harassment is generally perceived as socially undesirable, research participants may be hesitant to admit to such behavior. Third, it is arguably unethical to conduct laboratory research in which even an informed confederate may be exposed to sexual harassment. However, advances in understanding harasser attitudinal and personality constellations have been made through a variety of research methodologies that circumvent the difficulties of directly examining harasser conduct.

Rosen and Martin (1998) surveyed over 1,000 male soldiers in three Army posts in the United States. Tolerance of sexual harassment was positively associated with hostility toward women and negative masculinity (endorsing traits, e.g., arrogance, boastfulness), and was negatively associated with acceptance of women in the military. In addition, African American soldiers were less tolerant of sexual harassment than were Whites (Hispanics were not significantly different from African Americans or non-Hispanic Whites).

Although these data suggest that personality and attitudes may help explain what type of men may be more likely to sexual harass women, the dependent variable in the Rosen and Martin (1998) study (tolerance of sexual harassment) does not directly implicate harassing behavior per se. A more proximal self-report instrument is Pryor's (1987) Likelihood to Sexually Harass (LSH) scale, which asks men to read 10 scenarios of sexual coercion in work and academic settings and to rate the likelihood that they would engage in similar behavior if they were assured of not getting caught. A fairly extensive body of research has found LSH to be correlated with rape myth acceptance, likelihood to rape, attraction to sexual aggression, hypermasculine gender roles, dominance, and adversarial sexual beliefs (Pryor, 1987; Pryor et al., 1995). Lee et al. (2003) found a strong, negative correlation between LSH and an emerging personality dimension labeled *honesty–humility*, which the authors claim is distinct from the other major personality dimensions in the big five theory of personality. Lower scores on honesty–humility connote deceit, greed, and willingness to exploit, whereas high scores connote sincerity and trustworthiness.

Although studies of harassment pose ethical dilemmas, researchers have developed ingenious methods to investigate subtle harassing behaviors in the laboratory. Pryor (1987) first reported that men scoring high in LSH were more likely to touch a female confederate in a manner that she regarded as sexual when the participant was teaching her how to putt a golf ball (an activity in which the norms for touching are acceptable), but not when he was teaching her how to play poker (in which touching would appear abnormal). Pryor reasoned that high LSH men take advantage of situational ambiguity to enact their harassing tendencies. In a follow-up study, Pryor et al. (1993) found that high LSH men were more likely to mimic the harassing behaviors of a trained confederate who was acting as a supervisor for a research experiment, whereas low LSH men did not follow the lead of the harassing supervisor. Other research has found that naïve participants can identify high from low LSH men in sound-stripped video clips of men interviewing female subordinates (Driscoll, Kelly, & Henderson, 1998; Murphy, Driscoll, & Kelly, 1999).

Another innovative research design was created by Italian researchers Elena Dall'Ara and Anne Maass (1999), who developed a computer-based paradigm that led male participants to believe that they were interacting electronically with a female partner (the female partner did not exist). Under the impression that he was studying free associations, the participant was instructed to choose from a variety of images to send his or her partner to ostensibly determine her associations to the images. Of the two files of images to send, participants were asked not to send those in the second file because they were needed in another experiment. However, a set of images in the second file was labeled "porno." The question was whether participants would go against the wishes of the experimenter and send the pornographic pictures—a form of gender harassment. To complicate matters, a trained male confederate urged the participant to send the pornographic pictures. How much persuasion would be needed for the participant to send the pornographic pictures?

Dall'Ara and Maass (1999) measured various characteristics of the participants (e.g., personality, attitudes, LSH) and also manipulated characteristics of the fictitious female partner to investigate the parameters of this question. In one condition, she was characterized as having traditional gender roles (e.g., studying to be a teacher because the career allows time to balance work and family and does not want to compete with men), and in the other condition she was characterized as egalitarian (e.g., studying economics and wants a career in banking; wants to compete with men; involved in a union to defend equal rights). Finally, in one condition, male and female social identities were made salient, whereas in the other condition they were not. Dall'Ara and Maass found that men sent pornographic images to egalitarian women more often than to traditional women (58% vs. 38%, respectively) and required fewer persuasion attempts to do so. In addition, sexist attitudes, LSH, identification with the "male" category, and low self-monitoring (a personality variable related to accurately perceiving and responding to others' social behavior; Snyder, 1974) were negatively related to the number of persuasions attempts needed to harass the egalitarian (but not the traditional) female partner. In other words, men who tended to endorse these characteristics required fewer persuasion attempts. Finally, high LSH men required fewer persuasion attempts when the male and female social identities were salient. Relying on social identity theory (e.g., Tajfel & Turner, 1979), the authors reasoned that mistreatment of out-group members, such as women, is more likely when individuals strongly identify with the in-group or when they feel threatened by members of the out-group. Characterizing the female partner as "egalitarian" with a desire to compete against men and making the male and female categories salient in this study presumably increased feelings of animosity toward the out-group.

Dall'Ara and Maass's (1999) findings confirm that men with hostile attitudes toward women target status-seeking women, such as those aiming to break the glass ceiling. O'Connell and Korabik (2000) similarly found that young, highly educated women in male-dominated departments perceived that their organization had few sanctions against sexual harassment. These women reported higher rates of gender harassment than did others, and reported negative personal and work-related outcomes resulting from the harassment experience. In essence, young female faculty and administrative or managerial employees in male-dominated disciplines were the most vulnerable to sexual harassment by men who had greater organizational status than them. Such women were also vulnerable to gender harassment by their male peers. A second strand consisted of women in female-dominated work environments with low incomes and low educational attainment. These women, who were essentially clerical staff, reported higher rates of gender harassment by higher status men and unwanted sexual attention from their male peers.

In sum, harassers are individuals with particular attitudes and beliefs about gendered social structures. When they are embedded in cultures or situations that support or condone this structure, their harassing proclivities may be realized. Women endeavoring to advance in male-dominated occupations or into the upper echelons of management (also a male-dominated occupation) may be at particularly high risk for encountering such harassers for several reasons. First, the sheer number of men in such fields makes it likely that women will encounter potential harassers. Second, men with a propensity to harass may be threatened by the perceived encroachment of women into occupations they perceive to be their domain. Third, such women may be perceived as nontraditional or egalitarian, which evokes harassment proclivities. Finally, policies and practices against sexual harassment may be less standardized or formalized in upper management ranks.

Although this brief review has not covered harassment against men, nor has it adequately dealt with racial–ethnicity issues regarding sexual harassment (for research on these populations, see Berdahl, Magley, & Waldo, 1996; Bergman & Drasgow, 2003; Buchanan, 2005; Cortina, 2001, 2004; Kalof, Eby, Matheson & Kroska, 2001; Kennedy & Gorzalka, 2002; Matsui, Kakuyama, Onglatco, & Ogutu, 1995; Murrell, 1996; Pryor et al., 1997; Shupe, Cortina, Ramos, Fitzgerald, & Salisbury, 2002; Stockdale et al., 1999; Wyatt & Riederle, 1995), the picture of the prototypical target of sexual harassment is not one of an oversensitive, psychologically unstable woman who winces at the slightest off-color joke, but instead is one of a young, single, highly educated woman in a nontraditional, male-dominated work environment in which her supervisor and peers do not offer social support and cohesion. The most compelling reason for being a target of harassment is because she threatens harassing men's sense of power and privilege in the workplace (Berdahl, 2007). Thus, the nexus of sexual harassment and the glass ceiling threaten to be continuing challenges for women.

Groups, Context, and Organizations

Theories of sexual harassment that focus on characteristics of the offenders and targets—that is, individual-level variables—explain only a portion of the story. Theories focusing on group- and organizational-level influences on sexual harassment offer an enriched understanding in multiple ways. Higher level influences examine the context in which harassment is likely to occur. Indeed, theories discussed earlier, such as person X situation theory (Pryor et al., 1993), routine activities theory (De Coster et al., 1999), and O'Leary et al.'s (2000) actor-based perspective clearly argue that the situational or organizational context plays a critical role in predicting when individuals with a propensity to harass (e.g., high-LSH men, motivated offenders, goal-oriented aggressors) are likely to harass. These theorists view the context as either facilitating or detracting from would-be harassers' propensities or desires to harass. Contextual variables may be part of the causal chain of harassment (e.g., the climate of a work group itself may be a form of harassment or may cause harassment itself) or the sequelae of harassing activity (e.g., harassment causes detriment to others in the organization or to work-group functioning).

Researchers at the University of Illinois, led by Louise Fitzgerald, have advanced an integrated model of sexual harassment in organizations that situates sexual harassment at the level of group culture and organizational climate (Fitzgerald, Drasgow, et al., 1997). In other words, the Illinois model sees characteristics of the organization (and not of individuals per se) as the primary culprit of sexual harassment. This perspective is important for several reasons. First, it is consistent with legal doctrines that place liability on the organization (employers) and not individuals. Second, it sees sexual harassment as a systemwide issue needing organizational reform. Third, by extension, the model points to specific remedies for employers that could dramatically reduce the incidence of sexual harassment.

The past decade has seen a growth in the attention and sophistication paid to understanding organizational variables that shape sexual harassment experiences. A good deal of this attention has focused on understanding influences of organizational culture and climate on harassment; however, structural characteristics, such as the ratio of women to men in the work environment, continue to receive considerable research attention. In Fitzgerald, Drasgow, et al.'s (1997) integrated model of sexual harassment, organizational climate and job-gender context are the primary antecedents of harassment experiences. These authors rely on Naylor, Pritchard, and Ilgen's (1980) view of climate as "shared perceptions among members of a relevant group . . . of the contingencies between specific behaviors and their consequences" (Hulin, Fitzgerald, & Drasgow, 1996, p. 133). They thus define an organizational climate that is tolerant of sexual harassment as one in which it would be risky for a woman to complain about sexual harassment, unlikely that she would be taken seriously, and unlikely that the harasser would face serious consequences. In preliminary analyses of data from a large public utility, female employees, more than male employees, reported that their organizations were tolerant of sexual harassment, especially female employees with a male supervisor or who were one of the first female employees in their job category (Hulin et al., 1996). A later analysis found a strong correlation between SEQ scores assessed by self-report and climate for organizational tolerance of sexual harassment assessed by respondents' coworkers. That is, when work groups perceived that their organization was tolerant of sexual harassment, women within those work groups were likely to experience unwanted sexual behaviors (Fitzgerald, Drasgow, et al., 1997).

Hulin et al.'s (1996) conceptualization of organizational climate with regard to sexual harassment is an example of a perceptual approach to measuring climates conducive to harassment. Other scholars have examined the structural qualities of workplaces that affect the likelihood of harassing conduct. In addition to climate, Fitzgerald, Drasgow, et al. (1997) also emphasized the importance of job–gender context, defined as the gendered nature of the work context and operationalized as whether participants were one of the first of their sex to do their job, the gender of their immediate supervisors, and the ratio of women to men in their work groups. As a combined index of job–gender context, these factors were also significantly correlated with experiences of sexual harassment (as measured by the SEQ), such that women in traditionally male-dominated jobs reported greater experiences of unwanted social-sexual behavior than did others (Fitzgerald, Drasgow, et al., 1997).

Job–gender context plays a central role in other discussions of the organizational context for sexual harassment. Gruber (1998) provided an in-depth analysis of how occupational traditionalism shapes power dynamics in organizations to disadvantage women and make them vulnerable to sexual harassment. Occupations and job contexts that are essentially gender-segregated or male-dominated signify male power over women. Occupations that are traditionally male-dominated reproduce masculine cultures that emphasize "aggression, sexual bravado, embracing dangerous or risky situations, and bonding through rituals that celebrate male superiority" (Gruber, 1998, p. 303). Women in these environments are at risk for sexual harassment for at least three reasons: (a) Because of their numerical scarcity, the few women present in such environments are treated as tokens, which increases the salience of gender and expectations that they behave in stereotypically consistent ways. Tokenism also decreases women's access to informal networks (Kanter, 1977; Karakowsky & Siegel, 1999; Lyness & Thompson, 2000; Sackett, DuBois, & Noe, 1991; Spangler, Gordon, & Pipken, 1978; Yoder, 1994). (b) Such women are treated with hostility for violating male territory (Gruber, 1998). (c) Women in male-dominated work environments, by definition, have greater likelihood of contact with men, which increases their risk of experiencing unwanted social sexual behavior (Gutek et al., 1990).

Gruber (1998) found in his study of nearly 2,000 randomly sampled employed Canadian women that mere contact with men, more than the male traditionalism of the occupation per se, was the better predictor of harassment experiences. The presence of organizational policies and procedures to combat sexual harassment was associated with a decrease in sexual harassment experiences (Gruber, 1998). These findings suggest that the local conditions of work environment, as opposed to more distal sociological variables such as gender traditionalism, exert the strongest contextual influences on harassment experiences.

Other research also concludes that sound organizational practices have positive influences on reducing the incidence of sexual harassment. Mueller, De Coster, and Estes (2001) examined how systems of modern social control— that is, "modern organizational structures, which represent rational, employer-initiated control strategies designed to increase productivity and reduce turnover" (p. 413)—may affect sexual harassment and sexual harassment tolerance. They found in their study of nearly 6,500 telecommunications employees described in the De Coster et al. (1999) study discussed earlier that systems of modern social control that emphasize social integration, worker participation, structural differentiation, and decentralization were incrementally associated with decreased reports of sexual harassment. Perceptions of coworker and supervisory support, autonomy, promotional opportunities, and formalization of rules and procedures were associated with reduced incidence of sexual harassment above the effects of target characteristics (e.g., participants' age, marital status, education) and more proximal variables such as job–gender context and a climate tolerant of sexual harassment. The authors reasoned that these modern forms of social control that de-emphasize coercion and instead promote job satisfaction and commitment "cultivate a sense of community in the workplace" (Mueller et al., p. 417), which has an indirect yet positive effect on reducing sexual harassment. Timmerman and Bajema (2000) found similar effects of modern social control mechanisms (specifically, positive social climate and positive managerial attitudes toward work–family issues) on reduced incidence of sexual harassment in their study of a telecommunications company in The Netherlands.

Finally, a critical organizational feature that has important effects on the occurrence of sexual harassment is leadership. Many of the factors discussed earlier directly or indirectly implicate the role of leadership. Organizational climates tolerant of sexual harassment (Hulin et al., 1996), for example, indicate that leaders do not take complaints of sexual harassment seriously. Women are less likely to be sexually harassed when their leaders (supervisors) are women than when they are men (Fitzgerald, Drasgow, et al., 1997). Leaders develop and enact policies and practices that affect the social climate and sense of respect for employee empowerment (Mueller et al., 2001; Timmerman & Bajema, 2000). More directly, past research has also shown that leaders serve as catalysts for would-be harassers. Employees who have a propensity to sexually harass look for subtle clues from their leaders that their harassing activities may be tolerated or condoned (Pryor et al., 1993). It is not surprising, therefore, that Rosen and Martin (1997) found a strong negative group-level correlation between gender harassment and perceptions of leader–subordinate cohesion in their study of over 1,300 soldiers at three Army posts. Conversely, Offermann and Malamut (2002) found in their analysis of the Department of Defense Sexual Harassment Survey that honest and reasonable efforts by leaders at various organizational levels in the military to stop sexual harassment were associated with a sense of freedom to report sexual harassment, satisfaction with the complaint process, organizational commitment, and job satisfaction. In other words, true leader commitment to taking sexual harassment seriously helped targets to deal effectively with harassing conduct and to alleviate negative job-related consequences for them. Settles, Cortina, Malley, and Stewart (2006) similarly found that perceptions of effective leadership helped to counter the effects of sexual harassment and sex discrimination on female academic scientists' job satisfaction and perceptions of their influence and productivity within their departments.

The organizational context, therefore, affects the occurrence and severity of sexual harassment in complex ways. This brief review suggests that structural variables (e.g., job–gender context, mechanisms of modern social control) and social factors (e.g., shared perceptions of organizational climate, leadership behavior) may combine interactively to affect the likelihood of harassment occurring. This review also suggests a proximal rank-ordering of these variables in terms of their influence on sexual harassment occurrences, with work-unit climate for sexual harassment tolerance having the most proximal influence and broad sociological variables, such as masculine occupational characteristics, having a more distal influence.

Figure 8.1 suggests a possible model for considering these levels of influence. Those spheres closer to the core more strongly predict the occurrence of sexual harassment than do those at the periphery, yet those proximal influences may be part and parcel of the harassment phenomenon itself. An organization whose climate is tolerant of sexual harassment or whose leadership does not take sexual harassment seriously probably already has a sexual harassment problem. Those variables at the periphery, however, suggest possible indicators that can cue organizations to potential liabilities that they may wish to manage. Sexual harassment policies and leadership development activities should be given particular attention and close scrutiny when the occupation is traditionally masculine or when the immediate work environment is particularly male-dominated. Furthermore, organizations that continue to manage by controlling employee behavior through restrictive contingencies, instead of promoting autonomy and positive career growth, may find they have another problem on their hands in addition to dissatisfied and uncommitted workers. This model may serve as a guide to effective organizational development efforts to curb sexual harassment and workplace incivility as well as spur additional research on the interrelationships among organizational variables that affect sexual harassment occurrences and outcomes. Finally, the model is meant to be heuristic and not to suggest specific causal pathways or to rule out interactions and mediational relations between variables and concepts depicted in the model.

CONCLUSION

Although U.S. law recognizes a broad range of conduct that offends the nondiscrimination goal of Title VII, including hostile work environment, same-sex harassment, and retaliatory behaviors, it sets a high bar for individuals seeking a legal remedy for the damages resulting from sexual harassment. Were it up

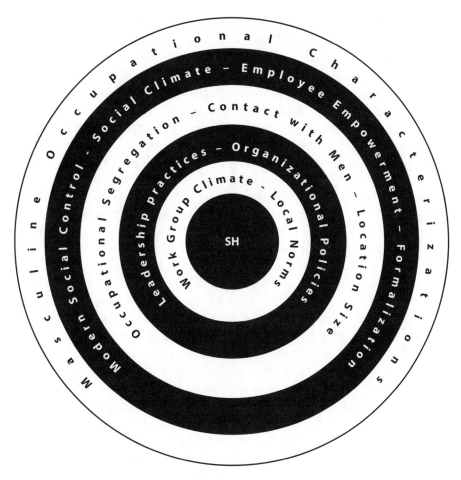

Figure 8.1. Organizational and occupational risk and protective factors for sexual harassment (SH).

to the law alone, low to moderate levels of sexual harassment would continue unabated. Moreover, as this chapter has shown, significant harm to individuals and work groups flows from even low frequencies of harassment—even to those who are not its direct targets. We implore organizational leaders, therefore, to actively monitor and correct conditions that foster a harassing environment.

Our review of the antecedents of sexual harassment points to several corrective steps managers can take—many of which will not only directly affect harassing conduct but may also eliminate other barriers to women's quest to break the glass ceiling. The first is to eliminate tokenism and work aggressively to balance the ratios of women and men in job contexts that are currently male-dominated. Affirmative action and other forms of active monitoring with concrete plans to increase women's representation across a broad spectrum of occupations and at all levels of the organizational hierarchy must be maintained (Crosby, 2004; Krieger, 2007; see also chap. 11, this volume). Although identity-conscious, affirmative action programs have been linked to increased representation of women in managerial positions (Kalev, Dobbin, & Kelly, 2006; Konrad & Linnehan, 1995), researchers may want to explore whether being perceived as an affirmative action beneficiary increases men's threat perceptions and harassing behaviors. Second, managers should scrutinize work-group climates for signs of sexual harassment tolerance. These might include perceptions that individuals who report harassment may not be taken seriously, or that offenders will not be appropriately punished (Hulin et al., 1996). Other conditions to watch include evidence that nonsexual yet offensive and demeaning conduct is occurring, because research indicates a strong link between generalized workplace harassment and sexual harassment (Glomb et al., 1997; Rospenda et al., 2005). At a broader level, managerial practices that promote social integration, worker participation, decentralization, and formalization of policies and practices set the background not only for worker satisfaction and commitment but also for healthy, productive, harassment-free environments (Mueller et al., 2001; see also chap. 12, this volume). Leaders at all levels of the organization need to take responsibility for fostering these healthy conditions (Offermann & Malamut, 2002).

Leaders and managers should also pay close attention to individuals in their organizations (or those seeking employment with their organizations) to identify those who may be at high risk for being sexually harassed as well as those who have high propensities to engage in harassing conduct. Although women (and men) can be targeted for harassment for several reasons, those who pose a threat to men's sense of power and privilege are the most vulnerable. These tend to be relatively young, egalitarian-minded women with aspirations to succeed in traditionally male occupations (Berdahl, 2007; Dall'Ara & Maass, 1999; De Coster et al., 1999; O'Connell & Korabik, 2000). In turn, individuals to monitor for their propensity to harass are those who express hostility toward women's advancement in the workplace, endorse traditional gender roles, and possess negative masculinity traits such as arrogance and boastfulness as well as deceitful, greedy, exploitative personalities (Lee et al., 2003; Pryor, 1987; Rosen & Martin, 1998). Putting such individuals in environments with lax policies or leadership practices undoubtedly spells trouble.

Although this review has tried to comprehensively cover the recent advances in defining and measuring sexual harassment and in understanding the conditions that foster or increase the risk of harassment, we should acknowledge those areas that are beyond the scope of this chapter. Such areas include coverage of ethnic and cultural issues both within the United States and abroad; a survey of sexual harassment scholarship beyond the borders of the United States; and issues surrounding *claiming, responding,* and *coping,* which is critically important because U.S. law now requires grievants to quickly exhaust all organizational remedies before bringing a claim to court (*Burlington*

Industries, 1998; *Faragher*, 1998). Moreover, we have not been able to articulate just what organizational remedies are effective, although our summary suggests several avenues for reform. At the risk of repeating ourselves, we suggest that effective solutions will require not only careful screening processes but also a careful audit of the environmental conditions that may be fostering a climate that is tolerant of harassment. This audit would include a close look at local norms, such as leaders and supervisors' attitudes and behaviors; perceptions of policy and training effectiveness; and scrutiny of more distal or macro-level factors such as the job–gender context, the masculinity of the work environment, and other indicators to determine the risk for women to be perceived as a threat to men's power and privilege. Coordinated efforts among managers, academic scholars, legal professionals, and advocacy groups are needed to help eliminate this important barrier to women's advancement in the workforce.

REFERENCES

Bargh, J. A., Raymond, P., Pryor, J. B., & Strack, F. (1995). Attractiveness of the underling: An automatic power → sex association and its consequences for sexual harassment and aggression. *Journal of Personality and Social Psychology*, 68, 768–781.

Berdahl, J. L. (2007). The sexual harassment of uppity women. *Journal of Applied Psychology*, 92, 425–437.

Berdahl, J. L., Magley, V. J., & Waldo, C. R. (1996). The sexual harassment of men: Exploring the concept with theory and data. *Psychology of Women Quarterly*, 20, 527–547.

Bergman, M. E., & Drasgow, F. (2003). Race as a moderator in a model of sexual harassment: An empirical test. *Journal of Occupational Health Psychology*, 8, 131–145.

Bergmann, B. R. (2007). Discrimination through the economist's eye. In F. J. Crosby, M. S. Stockdale, & S. A. Ropp (Eds.), *Sex discrimination in the workplace: Multidisciplinary perspectives* (pp. 213–234). Malden, MA: Blackwell.

Browne, K. R. (2002). *Biology at work: Rethinking sexual equity*. New Brunswick, NJ: Rutgers University Press.

Brownmiller, S. (1975). *Against our will: Men, women and rape*. New York: Simon & Schuster.

Buchanan, N. T. (2005). The nexus of race and gender domination: Racialized sexual harassment of African American women. In J. E. Gruber & P. Morgan (Eds.), *In the company of men: Male dominance and sexual harassment* (pp. 294–320). Boston: Northeastern University Press.

Burlington Industries, Inc. v. Ellerth, 524 U.S. 742 (1998).

Burlington Northern & Santa Fe Railway v. White, 126 S. Ct. 2405 (2006).

Catalyst. (2006). *2005 Catalyst census of women board directors of the Fortune 500*. New York: Author.

Chan, D. K. S., Tang, C. S., & Chan, W. (1999). Sexual harassment: A preliminary analysis of its effects on Hong Kong Chinese women in the workplace and academia. *Psychology of Women Quarterly, 23,* 661–672.

Cohen, L. E., & Felson, M. (1979). Social change and crime rate trends: A routine activity approach. *American Sociological Review, 44,* 588–608.

Cortina, L. M. (2001). Assessing sexual harassment among Latinas: Development of an instrument. *Cultural Diversity and Ethnic Racial Psychology, 7,* 164–181.

Cortina, L. M. (2004). Hispanic perspectives on sexual harassment and social support. *Personality and Social Psychology Bulletin, 30,* 570–584.

Crosby, F. J. (2004). *Affirmative action is dead: Long live affirmative action.* New Haven, CT: Yale University Press.

Dall'Ara, E., & Maass, A. (1999). Studying sexual harassment in the laboratory: Are egalitarian women at higher risk? *Sex Roles, 41,* 681–704.

De Coster, S., Estes, S. B., & Mueller, C. W. (1999). Routine activities and sexual harassment in the workplace. *Work and Occupations, 26,* 21–49.

Driscoll, D. M., Kelly, J. R., & Henderson, W. M. (1998). Can perceivers identify likelihood to sexually harass? *Sex Roles, 38,* 557–588.

DuBois, C. L. Z., Knapp, D. E., Faley, R. H., & Kustis, G. A. (1998). An empirical examination of same- and other-gender sexual harassment in the workplace. *Sex Roles, 39,* 731–749.

Edwards, J. E., Elig, T. W., Edwards, D. L., & Riemer, R. A. (1997). *The 1995 armed forces sexual harassment survey: Administration, datasets, and codebook* (Report No. 95-105, DTIC/NTIS No. AD A323 945). Arlington, VA: Defense Manpower Data Center.

EEOC v. Dial Corp., 2002 WL 31061088 (N.D. Ill. 2002).

Equal Employment Opportunity Commission. (2006). *Guidelines on discrimination because of sex, 29.* C.F.R. 1604.11.

Faragher v. City of Boca Raton, 524 U.S. 775 (1998).

Fitzgerald, L. F., Drasgow, F., Hulin, C. L., Gelfand, M. J., & Magley, V. J. (1997). Antecedents and consequences of sexual harassment in organizations: A test of an integrated model. *Journal of Applied Psychology, 82,* 578–589.

Fitzgerald, L. F., Gelfand, M. J., & Drasgow, F. (1995). Measuring sexual harassment: Theoretical and psychometric advances. *Basic and Applied Social Psychology, 17,* 425–445.

Fitzgerald, L. F., Magley, V. J., Drasgow, F., & Waldo, C. R. (1999). Measuring sexual harassment in the military: The SEQ-DoD. *Military Psychology, 11,* 243–263.

Fitzgerald, L. F., Swan, S., & Magley, V. J. (1997). But was it really sexual harassment? Legal, behavioral, and psychological definitions of the workplace victimization of women. In W. O'Donohue (Ed.), *Sexual harassment: Theory, research, and treatment* (pp. 5–28). Needham Heights, MA: Allyn & Bacon.

Franke, K. M. (1997). What's wrong with sexual harassment? *Stanford Law Review, 49,* 691–772.

Gelfand, M. J., Fitzgerald, L. F., & Drasgow, F. (1995). The structure of sexual harassment: A confirmatory analysis across cultures and settings. *Journal of Vocational Behavior, 47,* 164–177.

Glomb, T. M., Richman, W. L., Hulin, C. L., Drasgow, F., Schneider, K. T., & Fitzgerald, L. F. (1997). Ambient sexual harassment: An integrated model of antecedents and consequences. *Organizational Behavior and Human Decision Processes, 71,* 309–328.

Gruber, J. E. (1997). An epidemiology of sexual harassment: Evidence from North America and Europe. In W. O'Donohue (Ed.), *Sexual harassment: Theory, research, and treatment* (pp. 84–98). Needham Heights, MA: Allyn & Bacon.

Gruber, J. E. (1998). The impact of male work environments and organizational policies on women's experiences of sexual harassment. *Gender & Society, 12,* 301–320.

Guidelines on Discrimination Because of Sex, 29 C.F.R. Part 1609.11 (1997).

Gutek, B. A. (1985). *Sex and the workplace.* San Francisco: Jossey-Bass.

Gutek, B. A., Cohen, A., & Konrad, A. (1990). Predicting social-sexual behavior at work: A contact hypothesis. *Academy of Management Journal, 33,* 560–577.

Gutek, B. A., & Morasch, B. (1982). Sex-ratios, sex-role spillover, and sexual harassment of women at work. *Journal of Social Issues, 38,* 55–74.

Gutek, B. A., Murphy, R. O., & Douma, B. (2004). A review and critique of the sexual experiences questionnaire (SEQ). *Law and Human Behavior, 28,* 457–482.

Gutek, B. A., Stockdale, M. S., Done, R., & Swindler, S. (2003). *A short measure of sexual harassment.* Unpublished manuscript, University of Arizona, Tucson.

Harris v. Forklift Systems, Inc. 510 U.S. 17 (1993).

Hitlan, R. T., Schneider, K. T., & Walsh, B. M. (2006). Upsetting behavior: Reactions to personal and bystander sexual harassment experiences. *Sex Roles, 55,* 187–195.

Hulin, C. L., Fitzgerald, L. F., & Drasgow, F. (1996). Organizational influences on sexual harassment. In M. S. Stockdale (Ed.), *Sexual harassment in the workplace: Perspectives, frontiers, and response strategies* (pp. 127–150). Thousand Oaks, CA: Sage.

Ilies, R., Hauserman, N., Schwochau, S., & Stibal, J. (2003). Reported incidence rates of work-related sexual harassment in the United States: Using meta-analysis to explain reported rate disparities. *Personnel Psychology, 56,* 607–631.

Kalev, A., Dobbin, F., & Kelly, E. (2006). Best practices or best guesses? Assessing the efficacy of corporate affirmative action and diversity policies. *American Sociological Review, 71,* 589–617.

Kalof, L., Eby, K. K., Matheson, J. L., & Kroska, R. J. (2001). The influence of race and gender on student self-reports of sexual harassment by college professors. *Gender & Society, 15,* 282–302.

Kanowitz, L. (1968). Sex-based discrimination in American Law III: Title VII of the 1964 Civil Rights Act and the Equal Pay Act of 1963. *Hastings Law Review, 20,* 305–312.

Kanter, R. M. (1977). *Women and men of the corporation.* New York: Basic Books.

Karakowsky, L., & Siegel, J. P. (1999). The effects of proportional representation and gender orientation of the task on emergent leadership behavior in mixed-gender work groups. *Journal of Applied Psychology, 84,* 620–631.

Kennedy, M. A., & Gorzalka, B. B. (2002). Asian and non-Asian attitudes toward rape, sexual harassment, and sexuality. *Sex Roles, 46,* 227–238.

Konrad, A. M., & Linnehan, F. (1995). Formalized HRM structures: Coordinating equal employment opportunity or concealing organizational practices? *The Academy of Management Journal, 38,* 787–820.

Krieger, L. H. (2007). The watched variable improves: On eliminating sex discrimination in employment. In F. J. Crosby, M. S. Stockdale, & S. A. Ropp (Eds.), *Sex discrimination in the workplace: Multidisciplinary perspectives* (pp. 295–329). Malden, MA: Blackwell.

Lee, K., Gizzarone, M., & Ashton, M. C. (2003). Personality and the likelihood to sexually harass. *Sex Roles, 49,* 59–69.

Lim, S., & Cortina, L. M. (2005). Interpersonal mistreatment in the workplace: The interface and impact of general incivility and sexual harassment. *Journal of Applied Psychology, 90,* 483–496.

Lipari, R., & Lancaster, A. (2003). *Armed Forces 2002 sexual harassment survey* (No. 2003-026). Arlington, VA: Defense Manpower Data Center, Department of Defense.

Logan, T. K. (2006). *An examination of alcohol, violence, and health services in rural women: Final report.* Lexington: Department of Behavioral Sciences, University of Kentucky.

Lucero, M. A., Allen, R. E., & Middleton, K. (2006). Sexual harassers: Behaviors, motives, and change over time. *Sex Roles, 55,* 331–343.

Lucero, M. A., Middleton, K. L., Finch, W. A., & Valentine, S. R. (2003). An empirical investigation of sexual harassers: Toward a perpetrator typology. *Human Relations, 56,* 1461–1483.

Lyness, K. S., & Thompson, D. E. (2000). Climbing the corporate ladder: Do female and male executives follow the same route? *Journal of Applied Psychology, 85,* 86–101.

Matsui, T., Kakuyama, T., Onglatco, M., & Ogutu, M. (1995). Women's perceptions of social-sexual behavior: A cross-cultural replication. *Journal of Vocational Behavior, 46,* 203–215.

Meritor Savings Bank, FSB v. Vinson, 477 U.S. 57 (1986).

Mueller, C. W., De Coster, S., & Estes, S. B. (2001). Sexual harassment in the workplace: Unanticipated consequences of modern social control in organizations. *Work and Occupations, 28,* 411–446.

Munson, L. J., Hulin, C., & Drasgow, F. (2000). Longitudinal analysis of dispositional influences and sexual harassment: Effects on job and psychological outcomes. *Personnel Psychology, 53,* 21–46.

Murphy, J. D., Driscoll, D. M., & Kelly, J. R. (1999). Differences in nonverbal behavior of men who vary in the likelihood to sexually harass. *Journal of Social Behavior and Personality, 14,* 113–128.

Murrell, A. J. (1996). Sexual harassment and women of color: Issues, challenges, and future directions. In M. S. Stockdale (Ed.), *Sexual harassment in the workplace: Perspectives, frontiers, and response strategies* (pp. 51–66). Thousand Oaks, CA: Sage.

Naylor, J. C., Pritchard, R. D., & Ilgen, D. R. (1980). *A theory of behavior in organizations.* New York: Academic Press.

O'Connell, C. E., & Korabik, K. (2000). Sexual harassment: The relationship of personal vulnerability, work context, perpetrator status, and type of harassment to outcomes. *Journal of Vocational Behavior, 56,* 299–329.

Offermann, L. R., & Malamut, A. B. (2002). When leaders harass: The impact of target perceptions of organizational leadership and climate on harassment reporting and outcomes. *Journal of Applied Psychology, 87,* 885–893.

O'Leary-Kelly, A. M., Paetzold, R. L., & Griffin, R. W. (2000). Sexual harassment as aggressive behavior: An actor-based perspective. *Academy of Management Review, 25,* 372–388.

Oncale v. Sundowner Offshore Services, Inc., 523 U.S. 75 (1998).

Parker, S. K., & Griffin, M. A. (2002). What is so bad about a little name-calling? Negative consequences of gender harassment for overperformance demands and distress. *Journal of Occupational Health Psychology, 7,* 195–210.

Pennsylvania State Police v. Suders, 542 U.S. 129 (2004).

Pryor, J. B. (1987). Sexual harassment proclivities in men. *Sex Roles, 17,* 269–290.

Pryor, J. B., DeSouza, E. R., Fitness, J., Hutz, C., Kumpf, M., Lubbert, K., et al. (1997). Gender differences in the interpretation of social-sexual behavior: A cross-cultural perspective on sexual harassment. *Journal of Cross-Cultural Psychology, 28,* 509–534.

Pryor, J. B., Giedd, J. L., & Williams, K. B. (1995). A social psychological model for predicting sexual harassment. *Journal of Social Issues, 51,* 69–84.

Pryor, J. B., LaVite, C. M., & Stoller, L. M. (1993). A social-psychological analysis of sexual harassment: The person/situation interaction. *Journal of Vocational Behavior, 42,* 68–83.

Quinn, B. A. (2002). Sexual harassment and masculinity: The power and meaning of "girl watching." *Gender & Society, 16,* 386–402.

Raver, J. L., & Gelfand, M. J. (2005). Beyond the individual victim: Linking sexual harassment, team processes, and team performance. *Academy of Management Journal, 48,* 387–400.

Rhode, D. L., & Williams, J. C. (2007). Legal perspectives on employment discrimination. In F. J. Crosby, M. S. Stockdale, & S. A. Ropp (Eds.), *Sex discrimination in the workplace: Multidisciplinary perspectives* (pp. 235–270). Malden, MA: Blackwell.

Ridgeway, C. L., & England, P. (2007). Sociological approaches to sex discrimination in employment. In F. J. Crosby, M. S. Stockdale, & S. A. Ropp (Eds.), *Sex discrimination in the workplace: Multidisciplinary perspectives* (pp. 189–212). Malden, MA: Blackwell.

Rosen, L., & Martin, L. (1997). Sexual harassment, cohesion, and combat readiness in U.S. Army support units. *Armed Forces & Society, 24,* 221–244.

Rosen, L., & Martin, L. (1998). Childhood maltreatment history as a risk factor for sexual harassment among U.S. Army soldiers. *Violence and Victims, 13,* 269–286.

Rospenda, K. M., Richman, J. A., Ehmke, J. L. Z., & Zlatoper, K. W. (2005). Is workplace harassment hazardous to your health? *Journal of Business and Psychology, 20,* 95–110.

Sackett, P. R., DuBois, C. L. Z., & Noe, A. W. (1991). Tokenism in performance evaluation: The effects of work group representation on male-female and white-black difference in performance ratings. *Journal of Applied Psychology, 76,* 263–267.

Schneider, K. T., Swan, S., & Fitzgerald, L. F. (1997). Job-related and psychological effects of sexual harassment in the workplace: Empirical evidence from two organizations. *Journal of Applied Psychology, 82,* 401–415.

Settles, I. H., Cortina, L. M., Malley, J., & Stewart, A. J. (2006). The climate for women in academic science: The good, the bad, and the changeable. *Psychology of Women Quarterly, 30,* 47–58.

Shupe, E. I., Cortina, L. M., Ramos, A., Fitzgerald, L. F., & Salisbury, J. (2002). The incidence and outcomes of sexual harassment among Hispanic and non-Hispanic White women: A comparison across levels of cultural affiliation. *Psychology of Women Quarterly, 26,* 298–308.

Snyder, M. (1974). Self-monitoring of expressive behavior. *Journal of Personality and Social Psychology, 30,* 526–537.

Spangler, E., Gordon, M. A., & Pipkin, R. (1978). Token women: An empirical test of the Kanter hypothesis. *American Journal of Sociology, 84,* 160–170.

Stockdale, M. S. (1996). What we know and what we need to learn about sexual harassment. In M. S. Stockdale (Ed.), *Sexual harassment in the workplace: Perspectives, frontiers, and response strategies* (pp. 3–25). Thousand Oaks, CA: Sage.

Stockdale, M. S. (2005). The sexual harassment of men: Articulating the approach-rejection distinction in sexual harassment motives. In J. E. Gruber & P. Morgan (Eds.), *In the company of men: Re-discovering the links between sexual harassment and male domination* (pp. 117–142). Boston: Northeastern University Press.

Stockdale, M. S., Gandolfo, C., Schneider, R. W., & Cao, F. (2004). Perceptions of the sexual harassment of men. *Psychology of Men & Masculinity, 5,* 158–167.

Stockdale, M. S., Visio, M., & Batra, L. (1999). The sexual harassment of men: Evidence for a broader theory of sexual harassment and sex discrimination. *Psychology, Public Policy, and Law, 5,* 630–664.

Studd, M. V., & Gattiker, U. E. (1991). The evolutionary psychology of sexual harassment in organizations. *Ethology and Sociobiology, 12,* 249–290.

Tajfel, H., & Turner, J. C. (1979). An integrative theory of inter-group conflict. In W. Austin & S. Worchel (Eds.), *The social psychology of inter-group relations* (pp. 33–48). Pacific Grove, CA: Brooks/Cole.

Tangri, S., Burt, M., & Johnson, L. (1982). Sexual harassment at work: Three explanatory models. *Journal of Social Issues, 38,* 33–54.

Timmerman, G., & Bajema, C. (2000). The impact of organizational culture on perceptions and experiences of sexual harassment. *Journal of Vocational Behavior, 57,* 188–205.

U.S. Merit Systems Protection Board. (1981). *Sexual harassment in the federal workplace: Is it a problem?* Washington, DC: U.S. Government Printing Office.

U.S. Merit Systems Protection Board. (1988). *Sexual harassment in the federal workplace: An update.* Washington, DC: U.S. Government Printing Office.

U.S. Merit Systems Protection Board. (1995). *Sexual harassment in the federal workplace: Trends, progress, continuing challenges.* Washington, DC: U.S. Government Printing Office.

Waldo, C. R., Berdahl, J. L., & Fitzgerald, L. F. (1998). Are men sexually harassed? If so, by whom? *Law and Human Behavior, 22,* 59–79.

Wyatt, G. E., & Riederle, M. (1995). The prevalence and context of sexual harassment among African American and white American women. *Journal of Interpersonal Violence, 10,* 306–319.

Yoder, J. D. (1994). Looking beyond numbers: The effects of gender status, job prestige, and occupational gender typing on tokenism processes. *Social Psychology Quarterly, 57,* 150–159.

9

CEILINGS AND WALLS: WORK–LIFE AND "FAMILY-FRIENDLY" POLICIES

LAURA SABATTINI AND FAYE J. CROSBY

Although women have made considerable progress in the workplace, they remain largely underrepresented at the top management levels and across different occupations and industries (Goodman, Fields, & Blum, 2003; LaBeach Pollard, 2005; Lyness & Thompson, 1997). In 2005, women constituted almost half of the U.S. workforce and held more than 50% of all middle-management positions, but they made up only 2% of Fortune 500 and Fortune 1000 CEOs (Catalyst, 2006a). The European Commission similarly calculated that in 2006, averaged across 31 European nations, women represented 44% of the workforce, 30% of managerial positions, and only 3% of company CEOs (Catalyst, 2007; European Commission, 2006). The numbers are even smaller for women of color, who are less likely than White women to advance to top management positions (England, Garcia-Beaulieu, & Ross, 2004; Federal Glass Ceiling Commission, 1995; LaBeach Pollard, 2005). In 2005, African American women represented only 5% of all managers within Fortune 500 companies; Latinas constituted 3.3% and Asian women 2.6% (U.S. Bureau of Labor Statistics, 2006a). To understand these gaps, scholars and activists have intensified the search for the barriers that keep women and women of color from gaining parity with men at the top management positions, as well as the strategies that may facilitate their advancement.

An important set of barriers to women's professional advancement concerns work environments that make it particularly difficult for employees to manage the demands of jobs and careers, on the one hand, and family responsibilities, on the other hand. Because family and employment are gendered contexts, managing the demands of each domain can have different implications for women than it does for men (Acker, 1999; Ferree, 1990). The psychological and sociological literatures consistently show that women are still responsible for more hours of housework and child care than are men, regardless of their employment status and the financial contribution that they make to the household (Crosby & Sabattini, 2005; Hochschild & Machung, 1989; Steil, 2000, 2001). And although U.S. men in dual-earner families have recently increased their contribution to family labor (Coltrane, 2000, 2007), mothers are still more likely than fathers to reduce their work hours, change their work schedule, and report feeling distracted on the job because of child-care concerns (Catalyst, 2006b; Coltrane, 2007). To the extent that women (and especially women with children) are more likely than men to make several career changes so that they can manage family responsibilities, women's job experience, skills, opportunities, and earning capacity might decrease over time compared with men (and fathers in particular; Becker & Moen, 1999; Isaksson, Johansson, Lindroth, & Sverke, 2006; Williams, 2007).

Social scientists have observed that the unequal division of labor at home (i.e., unpaid domestic and relational labor) not only constitutes an obstacle to women's advancement but also affects their earnings. The pay gap between women and men is especially steep for women with dependent care and child-care responsibilities (Avellar & Smock, 2003; Budig & England, 2001). Some have referred to the high price of motherhood (Crittenden, 2002; Hewlett, 2002) and others have spoken of "the maternal wall" (Crosby, Biernat, & Williams, 2004) to describe this additional barrier that makes mothers particularly vulnerable to workplace bias and discrimination (Williams, 2007). Women's ability to manage work and family responsibilities becomes even more challenging in organizational contexts in which work norms and practices treat family and job commitments as incompatible with each other (Crosby & Sabattini, 2005; Rapoport et al., 1996; Williams, 2000).

To further explore these connections, in the rest of the chapter we examine the role of family-friendly policy in helping women break through professional ceilings and walls. We also discuss how work–life initiatives can help organizations create an inclusive workforce. Our starting observation is that to address the tensions between personal and work life, it is necessary to examine both domains; changing one (e.g., organizational norms) without any change in the other (e.g., gender roles and responsibilities within the family) is bound to be ephemeral. We also note that changes in organizational policies and practices are unlikely to increase gender equity in the workplace unless accompanied by changes in people's underlying assumptions about gender, work, and community (Lyness & Kropf, 2005; Sabattini & Crosby, 2008; Schmitt, Ellemers, & Branscombe, 2003). Although this chapter focuses on the U.S. context, it is important to note that beliefs about gender roles within the family and in the workplace vary cross-culturally, with important implications for the implementation and effectiveness of work–family initiatives (Isaksson et al., 2006; Lyness & Kropf, 2005).

The narrative advances in three parts. First, we outline the types of family-friendly workplace initiatives that have gained increased popularity in the United States.[1] Within this context, we situate the programs in a historical perspective, noting progress or lack thereof since the Glass Ceiling Commission issued its report in 1995. The chapter addresses mostly voluntary business initiatives, although we recognize that governmental policies can provide important guidelines and help companies set standards for working conditions (Levin-Epstein, 2007).

Second, we shift our attention to common challenges in the implementation and utilization of work–life programs. In the third and final section of our chapter, we reflect on ways to foster progress. We note that the barriers to effective implementation of work–life programs rest in the gendered nature of organizations. Therefore, to increase gender equity at work, work–family policy needs to move beyond isolated solutions (e.g., focusing solely on child care) and get to the core of the organizational culture. A comprehensive work–life strategy should include both women and men and take into consideration different aspects of their lives (see also Sabattini & Crosby, 2008).

ORGANIZATIONAL POLICIES AND PRACTICES

The institution of family-friendly supports in many larger organizations began during the 1960s and the 1970s, but it was not until the late 1980s and early 1990s that these programs began to show a notable increase, in both the number and types of initiatives (Gerkovich, 2006). Today, organizational policies and practices range from government-mandated policy, such as the Family and Medical Leave Act, to discretionary practices that address company-specific employee and business needs (Grandey & Cordeiro, 2002; Pitt-Catsouphes, 2002; Roehling, Roehling, & Moen, 2001). Work–life supports vary largely in objectives and focus. "Alternative" work arrangements, such as flextime, telecommuting, and part-time schedules, are generally intended to promote some level of time and place flexibility relative to traditional 8 a.m. to 5 p.m. office arrangements (Parker & Allen, 2001). Dependent-care supports (e.g.,

---

[1]In this chapter we use the terms *work–life* and *family-friendly* interchangeably to reflect the inconsistencies in the existing literature on the topic. Some experts, however, have noted that the label *work–life* is more inclusive of different policy, programs, initiatives, and beneficiaries (see Barnett, 1999; LaBeach Pollard, 2005; Pitt-Catsouphes, 2002).

information and referral, on-site child-care facilities, backup child care) can help decrease work and family conflict among employees with dependent-care responsibilities (Pitt-Catsouphes, 2002; Thompson, Beauvais, & Lyness, 1999). Family and personal leave of a temporary nature, such as sabbatical and parental leave, is designed to help employees in particular life or career stages (Pitt-Catsouphes, 2002). Finally, some employers offer resources designed to improve workers' quality of life, such as employee assistance programs, education and training (e.g., parenting classes, stress management), and conventional benefit packages (e.g., health insurance). In sum, many workplace initiatives have expanded from an initial focus on child-care supports to addressing a variety of life needs, many of which go beyond family responsibilities. The reasons for this development are both practical and ideological.

First, new technologies have made it more feasible and cost-efficient for organizations to implement alternative work arrangements (Valcour & Hunter, 2005). E-mail, voice mail, instant messaging, and other forms of communication, for example, make it possible for many employees to work remotely and for organizations to create "virtual teams" that can collaborate from different locations around the globe. New technologies also draw increased attention to the intersections of work and personal life, as they blur the boundaries between the two domains (e.g., working from home; Valcour & Hunter, 2005). Even workers employed in jobs that would typically not lend themselves to schedule flexibility, such as manufacturing and sales positions, can still benefit from initiatives that facilitate managing work and personal life; examples include shift-work options, child- and after-school-care resources, relocation programs that take into consideration employees' family needs, and other practices to help create supportive and inclusive work cultures (Catalyst, 2006b). The types of work–life programs available may also vary depending on the size of the company. In a Families and Work Institute's survey of U.S. employers, for example, small companies (50–99 employees) were more likely than large companies (more than 1,000 employees) to provide workplace flexibility, including flextime, gradual return to work after childbirth or adoption, and the ability to take time off for education and training. Large companies were more likely than small companies to offer direct cost benefits, such as retirement plans, on- or near-site and backup child care, and employee assistance programs (Families and Work Institute, 2005).

Second, there are strategic and ideological reasons why companies offer work–life supports. Research suggests that employees prefer to work in companies that provide some level of flexibility and that are sensitive to workers' personal needs (Catalyst, 2006b; Corporate Voices for Working Families, 2005; Thompson et al., 1999). Offering work–life programs can hence become a way for companies to attract and retain employees (see, e.g., Rapoport, Bailyn, Fletcher, & Pruitt, 2002). In the aforementioned 2005 Families and Work Institute study of employers, for example, companies cited recruiting and retaining talent, enhancing productivity, and increasing organizational commitment as the most important reasons for work–life initiatives (Families and Work Institute, 2005). Also, the demands of the global economy, including working across multiple time zones, can make it beneficial for organizations to promote less "traditional" schedules and allow employees to tailor their workday to both personal and business needs.

Workplace Flexibility and the Politics of Time

Most work–life initiatives include some elements of flexibility, although the specific (formal or informal) arrangements vary widely (Workplace Flexibility 2010, 2007). In general, flexible work arrangements concern the terms of when (e.g., flex-time and compressed work week) and where (flex-place may include working at home or other locations) work gets done (Valcour & Hunter, 2005), as well as the total amount of hours worked (e.g., part-time and job shares; Workplace Flexibility 2010, 2007).

Underlying the idea of workplace flexibility is the understanding that, to create a more inclusive work environment, there needs to be some level of discretion in the ways work gets done. Often, however, flexibility programs clash with ingrained cultural norms and behaviors that make flexible work arrangements particularly difficult to apply. Many workplaces, for example, still function under the assumption that the "ideal" employee always prioritizes work over family and personal commitments, and has the ability and resources to do so (DeGroot, 2005; Ferree, 1990; Williams, 2000; Williams Walsh, 2001). Another assumption concerns "face time" (i.e., time spent in the office) as the best indicator of job commitment and the only real evidence that workers are being productive (Thompson et al., 1999).

Both of these assumptions (prioritizing work over personal commitments and face time) constitute what some have called the *politics of time* (Allen, 2003; Rapoport, Bailyn, Fletcher, & Pruitt, 2002). Within this model, taking time off for child care, for example, becomes a sign of decreased organizational commitment, as does working on a part-time schedule or any other form of schedule flexibility that decreases work hours and time spent in the office (Williams, 2000, 2007). These beliefs, however, ignore the realities of today's workplace, in which the majority of families are dual-earner or single-parent households and have to manage work, personal life, child care, and sometimes elder care as part of one "balancing act" (Levin-Epstein, 2007). Furthermore, face time alone may fail to consider actual levels of productivity and results (Corporate Voices for Working Families, 2005).

Women are more likely than men to suffer from the negative economic and career consequences of the politics of time. In the United States and in Europe women are more likely than men to work part-time and to take career breaks (Francesconi & Gosling, 2005; Isaksson et al., 2006; U.S. Bureau of Labor

Statistics, 2006b). Williams (2007) observed that the economic penalty of working part-time is greater in the United States than in some European countries; in Sweden, for example, women who work part-time earn on average 3% less than those who work full-time, compared with a 21% decrease in the United States. Working on a part-time schedule can even affect women's long-term earning power. Francesconi and Gosling (2005) estimated that women in the United Kingdom who work part-time for only one year (and then switch to full-time work) will still be earning 10% less than women who work full-time 15 years later. All things considered, because women are more vulnerable to the negative effects of the politics of time, workplace flexibility is key to organizational change and can represent an important tool to increase gender equity at work.

Career Flexibility

In recent years, researchers and company leaders have been paying increased attention to career flexibility as a way to help employees manage career and personal goals over the life course and as different needs and situations unfold (Isaksson et al., 2006; Moss, Salzman, & Tilly, 2005; Shin-Kap & Moen, 1999). Similar to other types of workplace flexibility, the applicability of career flexibility programs may depend on a number of structural factors, including public policy, organizational characteristics, and job opportunities (Isaksson et al., 2006). In a study in which they interviewed human resource professionals from 36 different companies, Moss et al. (2005) found that although both schedule and career flexibility varied by type of industry, job level, corporate strategy, and managerial discretion, some level of flexibility was essential for good career progression among female employees.

Career flexibility is important because, although advancement is often discussed in gender-neutral terms, men's career options and opportunities are generally held as the norm, in terms of both rules (e.g., what it takes to advance) and progression (e.g., phases, number of career breaks, if any; Isaksson et al., 2006; Reskin, 2002). An example of how this assumption affects women's work experiences is the so-called "choice rhetoric" (Graf, 2007; Stone & Lovejoy, 2004; Williams, 2000). The choice rhetoric assumes that the gendered division of labor—both within the family and in employment—stems from personal (men's and women's) "preferences" for particular tasks and jobs. For example, *personal choice* is often used to explain women's decisions to cut back in hours worked, scale back their career (Becker & Moen, 1999; Singley & Hynes, 2005), or even stop working entirely (Stone & Lovejoy, 2004; Williams, 2007). As noted by Graf (2007), however, framing women's work–life choices as a personal rather than a public matter can be misleading. This perspective does not consider the systems of constraints around which women's career "choices" take place, including the gendered division of household labor, gender bias and discrimination, and work environments that are inhospitable to women (Crosby, Stockdale, & Ropp, 2007; Schmitt et al., 2003). Lack of workplace flexibility and of feasible career paths also contributes to women's limited work options and opportunities (Stone & Lovejoy, 2004). As noted by Williams (2007), systemic bias and poor alternatives tend to blur the boundaries between "choice" and "discrimination."

CHANGE AND STASIS

In the past decades, workplaces have experienced a number of transformations, including increasingly diverse workforces, new technologies, and globalization. In this section, we discuss some of these changes as well as what other changes are needed to increase gender equity at work.

Changes in Workplace Demographics

In the 1950s and early 1960s, only about a third of U.S. women were employed outside their homes (Crosby, 1982). Following the passage of the Civil Rights Act of 1964, the numbers of women employed for pay increased dramatically (Crosby, 1982). Throughout the 1980s and 1990s, U.S. workforce demographics continued to change, although at a slower rate than before (see chap. 2, this volume). Between 1989 and 1999, for example, the percentage of women holding jobs outside the home rose from 50% to 59% (U.S. Bureau of Labor Statistics, Women's Bureau, 2000).

Another important change occurred around age demographics in the workplace (Catalyst, 2001; Families and Work Institute, 2004). Whether as a result of changing population demographics (e.g., increasing life span and delayed retirement) or the flattening of organizations' hierarchies, different age groups and generations (the so-called Baby Boomers, Generation X, and Generation Y) are now working side by side, not only in the same companies, but often also on the same teams (see, e.g., Families and Work Institute, 2004). The increasing integration of different age groups and, hence, of individuals at different stages in their personal lives has important implications for the implementation of work–life initiatives. With demographic shifts come different attitudes and expectations about work, family, and personal life (Gerkovich, 2006), as well as the need to change organizations to reflect the new realities (Rapoport et al., 2002).

Attitudinal Changes

As the U.S. labor force became more diverse, some mores also began to change. In light of the finding that women are more likely to choose organizations that offer work–family supports, business started to pay increasing attention to work–life programs as a way to leverage this significant source of high-potential talent (Catalyst, 2000; Nord, Fox, Phoenix, & Viano, 2002). The increased level of attention directed at family-friendly organizations has also led to shifts in framework among researchers. Some have noted that to the extent that the word *family* remains gendered in Western societies, the terminology *family-friendly* and *work–family* might contribute to the perception that women remain the main beneficiaries of these programs (Barnett, 1999; LaBeach Pollard, 2005; Pitt-Catsouphes, 2002). Using the term *family* also seems to exclude those who are not currently managing family responsibilities but might still have other personal interests and concerns (Grandey & Cordeiro, 2002; Pitt-Catsouphes, 2002). To encourage thinking about work–life and work–family as issues that pertain to both women and men at different stages in their lives, some experts agree that it preferable to use the more inclusive term *work–life*. As we discuss later in this chapter, however, using what may seem to be gender-neutral terms will not promote gender-inclusive work environments unless accompanied by real changes in the underlying work norms and behaviors that are at the core of gendered inequality (Smithson & Stokoe, 2005).

To be sure, work–life is not only a woman's or a parent's issue. Flexible work arrangements and schedule flexibility, for example, represent one of the most effective ways to create an employee-supportive work environment for all (Allen, 2003; Thompson et al., 1999). Research suggests that, regardless of gender, flexible work arrangements actually increase workers' productivity, organizational commitment, and job satisfaction (Catalyst, 2006b; Corporate Voices for Working Families, 2005; Thompson et al., 1999). As added benefits, work scheduling control has been associated with increased quality of life (Thomas & Ganster, 1995), decreased work–family conflict (Thompson et al., 1999), and decreased parental concerns about child-care arrangements (among both fathers and mothers; see Catalyst, 2006b). Other investigations support the finding that both women and men prefer to work in companies that allow them to effectively manage work and personal commitments (Corporate Voices for Working Families, 2005; Rapoport et al., 1996, 2002).

The positive attitudes toward work environments that support employees' personal needs are especially notable among the newest generations entering the workforce (DeGroot, 2005). For example, in a survey study of 1,263 Generation X employees (born between 1961 and 1980), Catalyst found that over half (68%) of respondents reported the ability to manage work and personal life as an important factor in their decision to work for a company (Catalyst, 2001). Regardless of gender, when asked about their ideal work arrangements, Generation X respondents favored flexibility; 67% of respondents rated the compressed work week as a desirable arrangement, 59% telecommuting,

46% the ability to change their work schedule on an ad hoc basis, and 43% being able to take a leave or sabbatical. The same data also show that men and women expressed equal levels of dedication to their job and personal life. The Families and Work Institute (2004) similarly found that many women and men, including senior executives, cherished work and personal life to a similar extent (i.e., were "dual-centric").

Older generations and retiring workers are also engaging in conversations about the changing workplace (Sheaks, Pitt-Catsouphes, & Smyer, 2006), as suggested by increasing demands for different employment and retirement options. Survey data consistently find that many baby boomers (born between 1943 and 1960) plan to work past the traditional retirement age; the majority of those who want to continue to work, however, are not planning to do so full-time or on a regular, year-round schedule (Pitt-Catsouphes & Smyer, 2006). A new idea that specifically addresses retirement-age workers' demands for flexibility is phased or gradual retirement (Sheaks et al., 2006; Townsend, 2001). Phased retirement refers to any program or arrangement that enables retiring-age workers to gradually reduce their work hours and responsibilities as a transition to full retirement (Townsend, 2001). These arrangements require increasing flexibility on the part of employers, but organizations also benefit from a smoother transfer of knowledge and skills from the retiring to the new generations of employees.

Changes in Employee Programs

As noted earlier, family-friendly policies were originally conceived in response to the increasing numbers of women and mothers entering the paid labor force. Throughout the 1980s, programs were primarily geared toward meeting the needs of working mothers and were thought to facilitate their transition back to work. In 1985, for example, *Working Mother* magazine started publishing its list of the 100 best employers; at that time, a large majority of work–life programs focused specifically on child-care assistance and resources (Gerkovich, 2006). Programs such as schedule flexibility and part-time work were still seen as temporary arrangements for parents (and specifically mothers), rather than a permanent benefit for all employees (Catalyst, 2000). In the 1990s a shift in emphasis was detectable, and many organizations started to focus on work–life programs rather than exclusively on family-friendly programs (Rapoport et al., 1996, 2002); not only did the number of companies with solid programs increase, but so did the variety of policies and programs. The number of programs alone, however, is not always an indication of a family-supportive work culture (Lyness & Kropf, 2005; Thompson et al., 1999). To the extent that informal cultural norms are at odds with the formal policy, the latter is less likely to achieve its goals.

Given the obvious importance of family-friendly and work–life policies for gender equity, one may wonder why the proliferation of policies has not resulted in more rapid progress toward gender equity and why many of these programs are somewhat ineffective in achieving their goals. The answer to these questions entails a number of considerations.

First, inequities at work are only one aspect of gender inequality and are largely associated with gender inequities outside of work. As long as the division of unpaid household and child-care labor remains unequal, women's earnings and advancement opportunities will lag behind those of men (Lewis & Haas, 2005; Rapoport et al., 2002; Singley & Hynes, 2005). Lyness and Kropf (2005) underscored the importance of gender equality in understanding the effects of work–family supports, especially within different national contexts. In their study of European managers, they found a consistent positive relation between national gender equality (measured with the United Nations' gender-related development index), employees' perceptions of a supportive work–family culture, and availability of flexible work arrangements (Lyness & Kropf, 2005). The authors concluded that cultural contexts valuing women's talent are also more likely to lead to organizational efforts to address issues that are of concern to women, such as managing work and family.

Second, work–life programs are only part of the remedy for gender inequities. No policy or program will promote gender diversity at the top leadership levels if employees who use work–life programs remain disadvantaged compared with those who work in more "traditional" ways (Rapoport et al., 2002). It follows that, third, work–life policies are only as effective as their implementation. To fully apply work–life programs, companies ought to do so proactively. Unless organizations openly endorse and encourage the use of work–life programs, these benefits can do little to bring women to an equal par with men. Nor will they encourage more men and women to use these supports without fearing career repercussions.

One major consequence of ineffective implementation of work–life programs is underuse or uneven underuse by some groups of employees, generally women with family responsibilities (Gerkovich, 2006). Both underuse and uneven use of programs are linked partly to negative attitudes and beliefs about working flexibly, as well as to fears about the potential consequences of using flexible work arrangements. Although employees might find work–life programs useful, they often feel constrained in the extent to which they can use them without consequences (Schutte & Eaton, 2004).

Research shows that, despite a stated desire to work for companies that have work–life policies, both women and men tend to underuse the programs available to them (Nord et al., 2002; Singley & Hynes, 2005). Eaton (2003) labeled employees' perception that they can freely avail themselves of particular work–life supports as "perceived usability" (see also Schutte & Eaton, 2004). In a Catalyst survey of almost a thousand ($N = 948$) women and men executives, for example, respondents agreed that they would like to work flexible hours but their perceived usability was low. Among respondents who said they would want to work a compressed week (on average, 26% of both women and men), only 7% of women and 5% of men said that they have done so at some point in their career (Catalyst, 2004). Overall, less than 20% of these respondents agreed that they could use flexible work arrangements or even parental leave or sabbatical without jeopardizing their career (Catalyst, 2004). In a study of a large public sector organization in the United Kingdom, Bagilhole (2006) found that the majority of employees believed that using flexible work practices, such as reduced work hours, would limit their advancement opportunities. Eaton's (2003) respondents also noted that they did not feel free to use particular programs because doing so would hinder their career options.

When it comes to uneven use, work–life programs seem to reach men less often than they reach women. Bagilhole's (2006) study documented that men were more suspicious of programs than were women. Within this context, family circumstances and roles seem to play a role; a number of investigations have shown that employed women are more likely than men to use work–life programs or create more flexibility in their work arrangements after they have children (Becker & Moen, 1999; Shin-Kap & Moen, 1999). In addition, when comparing the use of women and men in dual-earner couples, Singley and Hynes (2005) found that women's usage of work–family programs was associated with a decreased likelihood that their husbands and male partners would use the family supports available at their own job.

Underuse of work–life programs can be problematic for both organizations and employees. Employers might conclude that their employees do not need these programs when in fact there are other reasons the programs are not being used. If underuse and uneven use of existing policies also lead to unequal access to advancement opportunities, how can use of available programs be increased? Several factors come into play. Once again, some factors concern practicalities and others ideologies. Devising practical solutions without addressing the underlying ideological resistance to change will have limited effect. Nor will progress come from the analysis of ideologies unaccompanied by practical solutions.

Organizational culture plays an important role in both dimensions of this problem (see chap. 12, this volume). Bagilhole (2006) identified different types of organizational responses to family-friendly and equal opportunity policies and defined these responses in terms of program implementation levels, from full implementation to lack thereof. The least effective type of organizational response is *passive toleration*; that is, the policies are in place but have not been implemented at all. An example of passive toleration is a company that puts a program in place but, in actuality, discourages employees from using it. *Reluctant opening* denotes more of a hesitant implementation.

The policies might have been instituted but barriers, such as lack of communication and knowledge about how to put the programs into practice, keep them from being effective. Catalyst and Brandeis University, for example, found that many working parents were not aware of which programs were actually available at their company (Catalyst, 2006b). Finally, *active formation* consists of the programs' full implementation and integration within the company's structure and culture. Cultural change remains an advanced step toward the integration of work–life policies; at this stage, the ability of employees to effectively manage work and personal life becomes an organizational goal in itself and is inherent in the organization's culture (Pitt-Catsouphes, 2002).

Support From the Top

Leadership support is an extremely important element to move an organization from passive toleration through reluctant opening to active formation. Clear messaging about work–life policies has been found to be especially effective when it comes from the top (Allen, 2003). No matter how useful to individual employees, organizational policies and programs will not be considered usable—that is, their perceived usability will remain low—unless fully endorsed by the company leadership (Eaton, 2003; Rapoport et al., 2002). Senior leaders ultimately have the power to bring about change (Bagilhole, 2006).

Support from first-line management is also necessary to promote work–family policies (Allen, 2003). Programs such as flexible scheduling and telecommuting, for example, are particularly difficult to implement without the commitment and understanding of direct managers, as these supports are based largely on supervisor approval. It is also helpful for managers and supervisors to model or encourage behaviors that promote work–life effectiveness and decrease the likelihood of burnout (Kossek, Barber, & Winters, 1999). In fact, Thompson et al. (1999) identified managerial support and sensitivity to employees' family responsibilities as a major component of a supportive work–family culture. And in a study by Catalyst and Brandeis University, supervisors' understanding of family and personal matters was linked to decreased after-school-care concerns (Catalyst, 2006b).

Kossek et al. (1999) noted the importance of leaders acting as role models when it comes to working flexibly and using work–life programs. Being a role model does not require supervisors to personally use the same programs as their staff. Rather, it may entail openly supporting the initiatives and those who do use them and, in general, communicating about the initiatives in positive terms (Catalyst, 2000, 2006b). Managers can also promote flexibility by rewarding results over face time, monitoring disparaging comments directed at those who use flexible work arrangements, and simply sharing some of their own personal challenges and strategies when it comes to work–life matters.

Conversely, inadequate communication from the top can lead to back-lash and misunderstandings about the programs' goals and beneficiaries, the so-called *policy underlife* (Bagilhole, 2006, p. 329). *Policy underlife* refers to the differential effect that many policies have on different groups of employees when the underlying assumptions are not openly addressed: To the extent that work–life programs are implemented within existing structures of inequality, their effects, uptake patterns, and outcomes will also be uneven. Unequal child-care responsibilities, for example, influence not only men's and women's decisions to use child-care-related programs, but also the extent to which having access to child-care supports will affect their work and advancement options (Williams, 2000).

Managerial and Employee Training

Research suggests that for effective implementation of work–life initiatives, it can be helpful to inform managers and employees about both the specific programs and big-picture goals of the initiatives, including the business case for effective implementation (Catalyst, 2006b). Nord et al. (2002) also recommended specific training for managers who are supervising remote workers, because "hard to supervise" is often cited as one of the major obstacles to implementing work–life policies (Families and Work Institute, 2005, p. 27). For example, supervisors could learn more about how new communication technologies can help them manage a virtual team. Because old managerial strategies might not work in new organizational contexts, managers' specialized training on work–life issues can hence become part of the larger change efforts within the organization (Catalyst, 2006b).

Integration

In the end, what does a family-friendly organization look like? A supportive organizational culture is one that seeks to address many of the issues discussed in this chapter. Thompson et al. (1999) identified three specific dimensions of work–family culture that facilitate employees' work–life effectiveness, encourage the use of work–family programs, and help decrease work–family conflict. These components include (a) time demands and expectations about how employees should allocate work and personal time, (b) possible career consequences associated with using work–life programs, and (c) managerial support. It is interesting that Thompson et al. (1999) found that employees' perception of a supportive work–family culture (as defined by these three components) was related to positive work attitudes and organizational commitment above and beyond the actual availability of benefits. In other words, benefits alone do not make an organization family-friendly.

It follows that, to be effective, work–life practices need to become part of a comprehensive diversity strategy (DeGroot, 2005; Moss et al., 2005; Sabattini & Crosby, 2008). As a way to promote diversity within their organization, companies can create programs that are more inclusive of employees' life situations and more sensitive to diverse sets of work–family challenges. Perhaps the most important step is making these programs more accessible to employees, regardless of their gender, marital status, and child-care responsibilities. Furthermore, integrating various diversity initiatives generally signals a progressive organizational culture by creating "shared assumptions, beliefs, and values regarding the extent to which an organization supports and values the integration of employees' work and family lives" (Thompson et al., 1999, p. 394).

As discussed earlier, framing work–family and work–life issues solely as women's issues may lead to additional challenges for women (Fletcher & Rapoport, 1996; Gerkovich, 2006). To the extent that work–life programs are viewed as an exception to the norm, and that family-friendly policy is an "accommodation" that the company has to make to benefit some employees, it becomes too easy to persist in the notion that women, and especially mothers, are not "ideal" employees (Williams, 2000). Normalizing the use of work–life programs does not mean ignoring gender or the unique challenges women face when it comes to managing work and family. Rather, it means trying to make alternative work arrangements more commonplace (i.e., normative), so that those who use them are not stigmatized or penalized. It also means encouraging organizations to integrate these programs within their culture. Likewise, if organizations were to look at work–life programs as talent management strategies that allow employees to work smart and effectively (Catalyst, 2006b), it is possible that the stigma and the negative career consequences associated with those who use these programs will vanish. Within this context, it is helpful to shift the attention from individual employees to organizations: The responsibility to promote workplace flexibility should rest on the organization and on work teams, rather than on individual employees.

Addressing Ideological Resistance

Just as organizations and researchers are making a conceptual transition from family-friendly to work–life policies, so must there be a change in the underlying assumptions about the reasons behind the efforts. Organizations can do so by noting that the establishment of good work–life policies is more than an ethical issue; it can also help organizations function well and stay profitable. As noted earlier, research strongly suggests that employees who can effectively manage different life demands are happier about—and more committed to—their company (e.g., Catalyst, 2006b; Corporate Voices for Working Families, 2005; Rapoport et al., 2002). A study conducted in a telecommunications company showed that employees who had been allowed to take personal time to deal with a divorce developed an intense loyalty to their employer and sought to "repay" the employer years later (Crosby, 1990). Allowing all employees to learn the business case for various programs may help reduce resistance to them (Sabattini & Crosby, 2008).

To the extent that resistance to work–life programs springs from unrecognized gender bias, educating people about their prejudices can be useful. Catalyst (2005) suggested that diversity training is a helpful strategy to address gender bias. Educating managers and employees about the origin and consequences of gender stereotypes, for example, can become a first step to addressing backlash. A comprehensive training program should include information about ways to recognize bias, possible inconsistencies between values (e.g., gender egalitarianism) and actual behavior, and information about causes and effects of gender inequality in the workplace (Catalyst, 2005).

In a similar way, when resistance to change results from biases and assumptions, it may also help to confront people's unquestioned beliefs of what constitutes "real" work (e.g., people who work from home are not really working) or commitment (e.g., employees who take career breaks are not really motivated). Also problematic is the complementary assumption that the "ideal" mother has no commitments outside her family (Ferree, 1990; Rapoport et al., 2002; Williams, 2000). Both types of assumptions lie in old beliefs about gender, work, and family (Crosby & Sabattini, 2005; Ferree, 1990). As noted by Rapoport et al. (2002), "relaxing the separation between the two spheres (paid work and private life) would mean that our ideal images in each domain would change, as well as our tacit definition of competence and commitment in each" (p. 37). If both organizations and individuals learn to openly acknowledge their tacit assumptions, work–life policies can help bring about change and improve gender equity at work.

Addressing Backlash

Another barrier to effective implementation of work–life programs is backlash, including negative attitudes and feelings of unfairness associated with particular programs and those who use them. Backlash generally occurs when organizations implement work–family programs that are perceived as benefiting particular groups of employees more than others (e.g., parents vs. nonparents, women vs. men; Grandey & Cordeiro, 2002; Lewis & Haas, 2005). Bagilhole (2006), for example, found that many employees held negative views of employed mothers who used work–family policies, as they believed it would result in additional work for themselves or limit their own time-off preferences. Employees might be reluctant to use flexible work arrangements for fear of being considered less reliable of a worker or of being stigmatized by others in their work group (Bagilhole, 2006; Halpern, 2005; Rapoport et al.,

2002; Rothausen-Vange, 2001); in addition, backlash can negatively affect the climate of the organization (Grandey & Cordeiro, 2002).

Because backlash is based partly on perceptions of fairness about the ways in which company resources are allocated, Grandey and Cordeiro (2002) recommended giving employees a voice about new programs, improving communication about why work–family programs are important, and being sensitive to both beneficiaries' and nonbeneficiaries' needs. Also, considering that these negative beliefs are related to the perception that work–life initiatives benefit some employees more than they benefit others, organizations can increase acceptance of the initiatives by transforming limited programs into more inclusive ones. For example, organizations can emphasize flexibility in scheduling for all employees and not just in particular circumstances, or focus on the work itself, rather than on the amount of time people work.

Many organizations allow their employees a certain number of paid "personal days" to be used as the employee sees fit and without explanation. If one person uses a day off to take the child to the doctor or attend the kids' play, and another uses the day to take care of a personal matter, so be it. In the end, both employees will be more committed to their job and less likely to burn out (Catalyst, 2006b; Corporate Voices for Working Families, 2005). A similar strategy for expanding work–life benefits is known as the "cafeteria approach to benefits," allowing employees to pick and choose which benefits they would like, so long as the total cost to the organization stays within certain bounds (Hills, 2005). A final strategy is to set up pretax accounts for employees for allowable health and child-care expenses. With careful planning (and minimal risk), each employee can save tax dollars for her- or himself at no cost to any other employee and at minimal cost to the organization.

Policy Implications

Although a discussion of governmental policy is beyond the scope of this chapter, public initiatives can play an important role in promoting family-friendly workplaces. At this time, the large majority of work–life programs in the United States are offered by companies on a voluntary basis (Pitt-Catsouphes & Smyer, 2006). In light of the challenges to effective implementation discussed here, some organizations could benefit from creating partnerships with local government and communities. Government guidelines, for example, can help normalize work–life benefits and equalize access and affordability for different groups of employees and organizations (Gornick, 2007; Levin-Epstein, 2007).

Governmental policies can also provide incentives to broaden the availability of programs (Pitt-Catsouphes & Smyer, 2006) and monitor the standards for particular supports, such as medical and parental leave (Gornick, 2007; Levin-Epstein, 2007). Both companies and local governments can invest in and use work–family programs and resources already available in their community. Companies can do so inexpensively through information and referral services or by providing transportation assistance for employees' children to get to community-based child care, for example (Catalyst, 2006b). Finally, organizations can demonstrate their commitment to their community by supporting national and regional policies that benefit working families (Isaksson et al., 2006; Pitt-Catsouphes & Smyer, 2006).

Within this context, having a limited number of progressive work–life initiatives can constitute a barrier to change, both at the organizational and at the larger societal level. Lack of specific governmental policy can reduce organizations' incentive to create change (Allen, 2003) and limit employed women's choices (Williams, 2007). When it comes to national and statewide regulations, the United States still lags behind other Western countries, especially in terms of family leave. Many European countries offer longer parental leave periods and their medical and parental leave policies apply to a wider range of companies and employees (for a detailed discussion of the U.S. Family and Parental Leave Act, see Nowicki, 2003). As noted by DeGroot (2005), "many existing policies only apply to *some* people *some* of the time. In the future, social policy that supports people to live integrated lives must affect *all* people *all* the time" (p. 8).

SUMMARY

There is no doubt that work–life policies and practices have contributed to increased gender equity at work. Less and less is it assumed that, on the one hand, demanding jobs belong only to men and, on the other hand, work–life effectiveness matters only to women. Nonetheless, progress is slow and incomplete, and challenges remain. Many work–life programs are limited in scope and do not reflect the complexity of today's workplace (Fletcher & Rapoport, 1996). Furthermore, organizations are not properly implementing work–life supports and, consequently, employees are not using them to the extent necessary for the programs to succeed.

Despite the challenges, work–life and family-friendly policies constitute an important tool to align workplaces and contemporary realities (Rapoport et al., 2002). Key to creating a truly employee-friendly workplace, one that promotes work–life effectiveness among all employees, is a shift in focus from accommodating an individual employee to facilitating organizational, cultural, and institutional change. A number of work–life researchers (Fletcher & Rapoport, 1996; Rapoport et al., 2002; Williams, 2000) have proposed an interactive, dual-agenda approach to guarantee these results. By promoting practices that enhance individual and business goals, the dual-agenda model highlights the synergy of the two domains (personal life and employment).

Furthermore, a dual agenda can facilitate a shift from an adversarial to a team perspective, not only between work and family but also between women and men, employers and employees, and organizations and communities.

Once outdated conceptions of how work and family should operate are proactively challenged, new possibilities will emerge. Should it become more feasible for both women and men to effectively integrate their work, personal, and family life without negative economic or career consequences, then, maybe, it will also become more feasible for men and women to be equally involved within their families and communities (outside of work) and overcome old gender-role constraints. As we discussed in this chapter, to make this possible, work–life leaders and activists must continue to address both the practical and the ideological reasons for resistance.

REFERENCES

Acker, J. (1999). Rewriting class, race, and gender: Problems in feminist rethinking. In M. M. Ferree, J. Lorber, & B. B. Hess (Eds.), *Revisioning gender* (pp. 44–69). Walnut Creek, CA: AltaMira Press.

Allen, T. (2003). Organizational barriers. *Sloan work and family encyclopedia.* Retrieved September 1, 2006, from http://wfnetwork.bc.edu/encyclopedia_template.php?id=247

Avellar, S., & Smock, P. J. (2003). Has the price of motherhood declined over time? A cross-cohort comparison of the motherhood wage penalty. *Journal of Marriage and Family, 65,* 597–607.

Bagilhole, B. (2006). Family-friendly policies and equal opportunities: A contradiction in terms? *British Journal of Guidance & Counselling, 34,* 327–343.

Barnett, R. (1999). A new work-life model for the twenty-first century. *Annals of the American Academy of Political and Social Science, 562,* 143–158.

Becker, P. E., & Moen, P. (1999). Scaling back: Dual earner couples' work-family strategies. *Journal of Marriage and Family, 61,* 995–1007.

Budig, M. J., & England, P. (2001). The wage penalty for motherhood. *American Sociological Review, 66,* 204–225.

Catalyst. (2000). *Flexible work arrangements III: Part-time arrangements for managers and professionals.* New York: Author.

Catalyst. (2001). *The next generation: Today's professionals, tomorrow's leaders.* New York: Author.

Catalyst. (2004). *Women and men in U.S. corporate leadership: Same workplace different realities?* New York: Author.

Catalyst. (2005). *Women "take care," men "take charge": Stereotyping of U.S. business leaders exposed.* New York: Author.

Catalyst. (2006a). *2005 Catalyst Census of women corporate officers and top earners of the Fortune 500.* New York: Author.

Catalyst. (2006b). *After-school worries: Tough on parents, bad for business.* New York: Author.

Catalyst. (2007). *The double-bind dilemma for people in leadership: Damned if you do, doomed if you don't.* New York: Author.

Coltrane, S. (2000). Research on household labor: Modeling and measuring the social embeddedness of routine family work. *Journal of Marriage and Family, 62,* 1208–1233.

Coltrane, S. (2007, March). What about fathers? Marriage, work, and family in men's lives. *The American Prospect Online: Special report.* Retrieved March 20, 2007, from http://www.prospect.org/cs/articles?articleId=12490

Corporate Voices for Working Families. (2005). *Business impacts of flexibility: An imperative for expansion.* Washington, DC: Author.

Crittenden, A. (2002). *The price of motherhood.* New York: Owl Books.

Crosby, F. J. (1982). *Relative deprivation and working women.* New York: Oxford University Press.

Crosby, F. J. (1990). Divorce and work life among women managers. In N. L. Chester & H. Grossman (Eds.), *The experience and meaning of work in women's lives* (pp. 121–142). Hillsdale, NJ: Erlbaum.

Crosby, F. J., Biernat, M., & Williams, J. (2004). The maternal wall: Introduction. *Journal of Social Issues, 60,* 675–682.

Crosby, F. J., & Sabattini, L. (2005). Family-work balance. In J. Worell & C. Goodheart (Eds.), *Handbook of girls' and women's psychological health: Gender and well-being across the life span* (pp. 350–358). New York: Oxford University Press.

Crosby, F. J., Stockdale, M. S., & Ropp, A. S. (Eds.). (2007). *Sex discrimination in the workplace.* Boston: Blackwell.

DeGroot, J. (2005). A historical perspective on social change. *Sloan work and family encyclopedia.* Retrieved September 20, 2006, from http://wfnetwork.bc.edu/encyclopedia_entry.php?id=1690

Eaton, S. C. (2003). If you can use them: Flexibility policies, organizational commitment and perceived performance. *Industrial Relations, 42,* 145–167.

England, P., Garcia-Beaulieu, C., & Ross, M. (2004). Women's employment among Black, White, and three groups of Latinas: Do more privileged women have higher employment? *Gender & Society, 18,* 494–509.

European Commission. (2006). *European Commission database: Social and economic domain decision-making in the top 50 publicly quoted companies.* Retrieved March 1, 2007, from http://europa.eu.int/comm/employment_social/women_men_stats/out/measures_out438_en.htm

Families and Work Institute. (2004). *Generations and gender in the workplace.* New York: Author.

Families and Work Institute. (2005). *2005 national study of employers.* New York: Author.

Federal Glass Ceiling Commission. (1995). *Good for business: Making full use of the nation's capital.* Washington, DC: Author.

Ferree, M. M. (1990). Beyond separate spheres: Feminism and family research. *Journal of Marriage and Family, 52,* 866–884.

Fletcher, J. K., & Rapoport, R. (1996). Work-family issues as a catalyst for organizational change. In S. Lewis & J. Lewis (Eds.), *The work-family challenge: Rethinking employment* (pp. 142–158). Thousand Oaks, CA: Sage.

Francesconi, M., & Gosling, A. (2005). *Career paths of part-time workers* (Working Paper Series No. 19). Manchester, England: Equal Opportunity Commission.

Gerkovich, P. R. (2006). Work/life policy and practice in the United States: Gendered premise. Radical potential? In F. Jones, R. J. Burke, & M. Westman (Eds.), *Work-life balance: A psychological perspective* (pp. 276–289). New York: Psychology Press.

Goodman, J. S., Fields, D. L., & Blum, T. C. (2003). Cracks in the glass ceiling: In what kind of organizations do women make it to the top? *Group & Organization Management, 28,* 475–501.

Gornick, J. C. (2007, March). Atlantic passages: How Europe supports working parents and their children. *The American Prospect Online, special report.* Retrieved March 20, 2007, from http://www.prospect.org/cs/articles?article=atlantic_passages

Graf, E. J. (2007, March/April). The opt-out myth. *Columbia Journalism Review.* Retrieved March 20, 2007, from http://www.cjr.org/essay/the_optout_myth.php

Grandey, A. A., & Cordeiro, B. L. (2002). Family-friendly policies and organizational justice. *Sloan work and family encyclopedia.* Retrieved September 1, 2006, from http://wfnetwork.bc.edu/encyclopedia_template.php?id=231

Halpern, D. F. (2005). Psychology at the intersection of work and family: Recommendations for employers, working families, and policymakers. *American Psychologist, 60,* 397–409.

Hewlett, S. A. (2002). *Creating a life: Professional women and the quest for children.* New York: Talk Miramax Books.

Hills, L. S. (2005). Developing a competitive benefits program. *Journal of Medical Practice Management, 20,* 195–198.

Hochschild, A. R., & Machung, A. (1989). *The second shift.* New York: Avon Books.

Isaksson, K., Johansson, G., Lindroth, S., & Sverke, M. (2006). Women's career patterns in Sweden: A life event approach. *Community, Work, & Family, 9,* 479–500.

Kossek, E. E., Barber, A. E., & Winters, D. (1999). Using flexible schedules in the managerial world: The power of peers. *Human Resource Management, 38,* 33–46.

LaBeach Pollard, P. (2005). A critical analysis of the glass ceiling phenomenon. *Sloan work and family encyclopedia.* Retrieved August 10, 2006, from http://wfnetwork. bc.edu/encyclopedia_entry.php?id=871

Levin-Epstein, J. (2007, March). Responsive workplaces: The business case for employment that values fairness and families. *The American Prospect,* A16–A18.

Lewis, S., & Haas, L. (2005). Work-life integration and social policy: A social justice theory and gender equity approach to work and family. In E. E. Kossek & S. J.

Lambert (Eds.), *Work and life integration: Organizational, cultural, and individual perspectives* (pp. 349–374). Mahwah, NJ: Erlbaum.

Lyness, K. S., & Kropf, M. B. (2005). The relationship of national gender equality and organizational support with work-family balance: A study of European managers. *Human Relations, 58,* 33–60.

Lyness, K. S., & Thompson, D. E. (1997). Above the glass ceiling? A comparison of matched samples of female and male executives. *Journal of Applied Psychology, 82,* 359–375.

Moss, P., Salzman, H., & Tilly, C. (2005). When firms restructure: Understanding work-life outcomes. In E. E. Kossek & S. J. Lambert (Eds.), *Work and life integration: Organizational, cultural, and individual perspectives* (pp. 127–150). Mahwah, NJ: Erlbaum.

Nord, W. R., Fox, S., Phoenix, A., & Viano, K. (2002). Real-world reactions to work-life balance programs: Lessons for effective implementation. *Organizational Dynamics, 30,* 223–238.

Nowicki, C. (2003). Family and Medical Leave Act. *Sloan work and family encyclopedia.* Retrieved March 20, 2007, from http://wfnetwork.bc.edu/encyclopedia_template.php?id=234

Parker, L., & Allen, T. D. (2001). Work/family benefits: Variables related to employees' fairness perceptions. *Journal of Vocational Behavior, 58,* 453–468.

Pitt-Catsouphes, M. (2002). Family-friendly workplace. *Sloan work and family encyclopedia.* Retrieved September 1, 2006, from http://wfnetwork.bc.edu/encyclopedia_template.php?id=232

Pitt-Catsouphes, M., & Smyer, M. A. (2006, March). *One size doesn't fit all: Workplace flexibility* (Issue Brief No. 5). Boston: The Center on Aging and Work at Boston College. Retrieved March 20, 2007, from http://agingandwork.bc.edu/documents/Center_on_Aging_and_Work_Brief_Five.pdf

Rapoport, R., Bailyn, L., Fletcher, J. K., & Pruitt, B. H. (2002). *Beyond family-work balance.* San Francisco: Jossey-Bass.

Rapoport, R., Bailyn, L., Kolb, D., Fletcher, J., Friedman, D. E., Eaton, S., et al. (1996). *Relinking life and work: Toward a better future.* Retrieved September 1, 2006, from http://www.cpn.org/topics/work/relink.html

Reskin, P. (2002). Career development of women. *Sloan work and family encyclopedia.* Retrieved September 30, 2006, from http://wfnetwork.bc.edu/encyclopedia_entry.php?id=221&area=business

Roehling, P. V., Roehling M. V., & Moen, P. (2001). The relationship between work-life policies and practices and employee loyalty: A life course perspective. *Journal of Family and Economic Issues, 22,* 141–170.

Rothausen-Vange, T. J. (2001). Work-family ideologies and roles. *Sloan work and family encyclopedia.* Retrieved September 20, 2006, from http://wfnetwork.bc.edu/encyclopedia_entry.php?id=241&area=business

Sabattini, L., & Crosby, F. (2008). Overcoming resistance: Structures and attitudes. In K. M. Thomas (Ed.), *Diversity resistance in organizations* (pp. 273–301). New York: Erlbaum.

Schmitt, M. T., Ellemers, N., & Branscombe, N. R. (2003). Perceiving and responding to gender discrimination in organizations. In A. Haslam, D. van Knippenberg, M. Platow, & N. Ellemers (Eds.), *Social identity at work: Developing theory for organizational practice* (pp. 277–292). New York: Psychology Press.

Schutte, K. J., & Eaton, S. C. (2004). Perceived usability of work/family policies. *Sloan work and family encyclopedia*. Retrieved September 30, 2006, from http://wfnetwork. bc.edu/encyclopedia_entry.php?id=248&area=business

Sheaks, C., Pitt-Catsouphes, M., & Smyer, M. A. (2006). Legal and research summary sheet: Phased retirement. *Age at Work: A Newsletter Focusing on the Aging Workforce, 1*, 1–9. Retrieved September 20, 2006, from http://agingandwork.bc.edu/ documents/Center_on_AgingandWork_Phased_Retirement.pdf

Shin-Kap, H., & Moen, P. (1999). Work and family over time: A life course approach. *Annals of the American Academy of Political and Social Science, 562*, 98–110.

Singley, S. G., & Hynes, K. (2005). Transitions to parenthood: Work-family policies, gender, and the couple context. *Gender & Society, 19*, 376–397.

Smithson, J., & Stokoe, E. H. (2005). Discourse of work-life balance: Negotiating 'genderblind' terms in organizations. *Gender, Work & Organization, 12*, 147–168.

Steil, J. M. (2000). Contemporary marriage: Still an unequal partnership. In C. Hendrick & S. S. Hendrick (Eds.), *Close relationships: A sourcebook* (pp. 125–152). Thousand Oaks, CA: Sage.

Steil, J. M. (2001). Family forms and member well-being: A research agenda for the decade of behavior. *Psychology of Women Quarterly, 25*, 344–363.

Stone, P., & Lovejoy, M. (2004). Fast-track women and the "choice" to stay home. *Annals of the American Academy of Political and Social Science, 596*, 62–83.

Thomas, L., & Ganster, D. C. (1995). Impact of family-supportive work variables on work-family conflict and strain: A control perspective. *Journal of Applied Psychology, 80*, 6–15.

Thompson, C. A., Beauvais, L. L., & Lyness, K. S. (1999). When work-family benefits are not enough: The influence of work-family culture on benefit utilization, organizational attachment, and work-family conflict. *Journal of Vocational Behavior, 54*, 392–415.

Townsend, B. (2001). *Phased retirement: From promise to practice* (Issue Brief No. 2). Ithaca, NY: Cornell Employment and Family Careers Institute.

U.S. Bureau of Labor Statistics. (2006a). *Current population survey: Employed and experienced unemployed persons by detailed occupation, sex, race, and Hispanic or Latino ethnicity, annual average 2005* [Data file].

U.S. Bureau of Labor Statistics. (2006b). *Current population survey: Persons at work by occupation, sex, and usual full- or part-time status* [Data file]. Washington, DC: Author.

U.S. Bureau of Labor Statistics, Women's Bureau. (2000). *Women at the millennium, accomplishments and challenges ahead (facts on working women)*. Retrieved September 20, 2006, from http://eric.ed.gov/ERICDocs/data/ericdocs2sql/content_ storage_01/0000019b/80/16/ba/24.pdf

Valcour, P. M., & Hunter, L. W. (2005). Technology, organizations, and work-life integration. In E. E. Kossek & S. J. Lambert (Eds.), *Work and life integration: Organizational, cultural, and individual perspectives* (pp. 61–84). Mahwah, NJ: Erlbaum.

Williams, J. (2000). *Unbending gender: Why family and work conflict and what to do about it*. New York: Oxford University Press.

Williams, J. (2007, March). The opt-out revolution revisited. *The American Prospect Online, special report*. Retrieved March 20, 2007, from http://www.prospect.org/cs/articles?articleID=12495

Williams Walsh, M. (2001, June 24). So where are the corporate husbands? For women at the top, something is missing: Social, wifely support. *The New York Times*. Retrieved June 25, 2001, from http://query.nytimes.com/gst/fullpage.html?res=9B0DE1DF1530F937A15755C0A9679C8B63

Workplace Flexibility 2010. (2007). *Flexible work arrangements: A definition and examples*. Retrieved March 20, 2007, from http://www.law.georgetown.edu/workplaceflexibility2010/definition/general/FWA_DefinitionsExamples.pdf

IV

SOLUTIONS: ADVANCING WOMEN'S EQUALITY IN THE WORKPLACE

10

CROSS-CULTURAL CONNECTIONS: LEVERAGING SOCIAL NETWORKS FOR WOMEN'S ADVANCEMENT

LAURIE HUNT, GINA LAROCHE, STACY BLAKE-BEARD, ELEANOR CHIN, MARISOL ARROYAVE, AND MAUREEN SCULLY

Social networks have long been touted as instrumental conduits for advancing one's career and gaining access to resources (Catalyst, 2004; Ibarra, 1995). Social networks are composed of connections with individuals that vary on a number of dimensions: formal vs. informal, strong vs. weak ties, homogeneity vs. heterogeneity, instrumental vs. psychosocial, and status, to name a few (Ibarra, 1993; Ibarra, Kilduff, & Tsai, 2005; Kram, 1985; Kristiansen, 2004; D. A. Thomas, 1990). The benefits that accrue from social network connections are considered social capital for individuals (Combs, 2003; Ibarra et al., 2005; Kristiansen, 2004; Murrell & Zagenczyk, 2006). From its origins social capital has morphed to become almost a kind of merit that those advancing toward the upper class seek to cultivate (Scully, 2000). It has become capital in the purse of individuals, rather than a tenor of social life collectively generated, as in its original sense. Most people are familiar with "the old boys' network" and the power and influence that it wields. How do women of color and White women create such value in their networks? Drawing on both the literature and the experiences of a diverse group of women, we explore women's cross-cultural connections. We examine the quality and diversity of one's social network in relation to the power structure, particularly in light of the increasing importance of cultural competence in the workplace.

Studies indicate that the quality of a person's social network can determine his or her social capital value and that a person's social capital can affect the quality of his or her social network (Ibarra et al., 2005; Kristiansen, 2004; Lin, 1999). This reciprocal relationship between social networks and social capital could be construed as a catch-22 for people of color and White women. Because senior positions in organizations are still held primarily by White men and their networks are made up predominantly of White men, it can be challenging for people of color and White women to get connected to this power structure. One of the reasons we were interested in exploring women's cross-cultural connections was to determine coping strategies that women of color and White women use to navigate the workplace. Also, given the international nature of business today, we wanted to explore how the ability to build and maintain relationships across cultures might contribute to women's social capital in their networks.

The increasingly global business environment as well as the ongoing shortage of talent is requiring organizations to reach beyond their typical closed circles. More and more people are required to interact and build relationships with people who are culturally different (Earley & Mosakowski, 2004; D. C. Thomas & Inkson, 2003). In recent years, a new measure for leadership competence has emerged. This ability to connect across cultures is referred to as cultural intelligence (CQ). D. C. Thomas and Inkson (2003) explained that

> cultural intelligence means being skilled and flexible about understanding a culture, learning more about it from your on-going interactions with it, and gradually reshaping your thinking to be more sympathetic to the culture and your behavior to be more skilled and appropriate when interacting with others from the culture. (p. 14)

Success in business and organizations means developing CQ to enhance relationships with customers and clients, industry experts, coworkers, and leaders. As the mix of people with whom one interacts diversifies, so must one's range of skills expand.

From this basis, we set out to explore women's cross-cultural connections and strategic mentoring relationships. Recognizing the importance of understanding different cultural perspectives in relation to our individual vantage points, we engaged in a dialogue to broaden our cultural lenses by learning from each other. We begin this chapter by providing a synopsis of our literature review on social identity, social networks, and social capital as they relate to the advancement of women. We include a snapshot of the status of women of color and White women in business today. We then describe our research approach of augmenting the existing literature through our conversations in which we shared and compared our individual professional and personal experiences. Synthesizing findings from our dialogue with the extant literature, we present our observations of the opportunities and challenges for women that result from developing cross-cultural connections. Last, we discuss the implications of these findings for research and practice with respect to social networks in an increasingly culturally diverse business environment.

BACKGROUND INFORMATION

We used a multidisciplinary and multicultural focus in our literature review to determine the current thinking about social networks and cross-cultural relationships. Social networks are considered an essential tactic to help women redress the disadvantages they face in the workplace that impede their advancement. Lack of access to powerful male-dominated networks is often cited as a top barrier to women's advancement (Catalyst, 2004; Combs, 2003; Ibarra, 1995; Ibarra et al., 2005; Pini, Brown, & Ryan, 2004). And for women of color, strategic attention to network development is especially vital (Blake-Beard, Murrell, & Thomas, 2006; Catalyst, 1999, 2004, 2006b; Combs, 2003; Hyun, 2005; Kanter, 1977).

The effect of the challenges faced by women in general and more significantly by women of color as a result of lack of access to influential social networks is clearly evident. When we look at corporate leadership in detail we see that women held 14.7% of Fortune 500 Board seats in 2005 and of those women-held seats, White women held 78.6% and women of color held the remaining 21.4%. Looking more closely at how board power is distributed among women of color, we find that in 2006 African American women held 67%, Hispanic women held 22%, and Asian American women held 11% of the Fortune 500 board seats attained by women (Catalyst, 2006a).

In a study by the American Bar Association (2006), 62% of women-of-color lawyers and 60% of White women lawyers working in a large law firm felt that they had been excluded from formal and informal networking opportunities, compared with 31% of men of color and 4% of White men (Women Lawyers of Color, 2006). Nearly half of women-of-color lawyers but only 3% of White men experienced demeaning comments or harassment. In Combs's (2003) analysis of the dual effects of race and gender on social network creation, she explored how African American women are more likely to experience covert discrimination and subtle prejudice and are often forced into out-group status, making it more difficult for them to establish connections and realize the associated social capital benefits. In addition, Browne and Askew's (2006) study of Latinas at work found that Latinas are also subject to negative stereotyping in which their abilities and competence are questioned by their coworkers. These findings point to the effect of social identity on social network access and social capital attainment.

Social identity is a critical aspect of accessing social networks and creating social capital. How we believe we are perceived, how we desire to be perceived, and how we perceive other people affects with whom we connect (Roberts, 2005). Tajfel (1972) defined *social identity* as "the individual's knowledge that [s/]he belongs to certain social groups together with some emotional and value significance to [her/him] of this group membership" (p. 292). Professionals seek to increase their social capital and improve their professional images through strategic social network connections. Roberts (2005) outlined a professional image strategy, which she named *social identity-based impression management*, by which individuals can influence how they are perceived to create a desired impression. "Social identity rests on intergroup social comparisons that seek to confirm or to establish ingroup status—favoring evaluative distinctiveness between ingroup and outgroup, motivated by an underlying need for self-esteem" (Hogg & Terry, 2000, p. 122). It is important to note how the characteristics of the organizational in-group become normative and anything different is seen as deviant (Coll, Cook-Nobles, & Surrey, 1997; Hill Collins, 1999; Martinez, 1998; D. C. Thomas & Inkson, 2003).

Contributing to the dominance of the majority group, much of the existing research either generalizes the experiences of all women from a White woman's perspective or puts women of color into one group and does not distinguish among their differing experiences. Betters-Reed and Moore (1995) named this tendency the "whitewash dilemma." Bell, Denton, and Nkomo (1993) suggested that to understand women's unique experiences, research approaches and theory development must be in line with how women see themselves. One objective in the research project described in this chapter is to provide the space for a diverse group of women's voices to be heard and for their experiences to be understood.

Although research has begun to differentiate women of color from White women and men (Burke, Rothstein, & Bristor, 1995; Ibarra, 1993, 1995; Pini et al., 2004), additional research is necessary to explore the richness of differing racial or ethnic backgrounds along with other factors such as class, age, nationality, and so on. Social network studies look at differences between men and women but few take into account gender and racial or ethnic differences simultaneously, although there is a promising move in that direction (Blake, 1999; Catalyst, 1999, 2003, 2006b; Combs, 2003; Kristiansen, 2004; Martinez, 1998; Sheridan, Holvino, & Debebe, 2004; Travers, Stevens, & Pemberton, 1997).

In this chapter, we probe several questions: What characteristics or aspects of our social identity will allow us to be connected to the organizational in-group and to each other? How do our networking strategies vary on the basis of our social identities and our perceived position with respect to the dominant group? Are we enhancing one another's social capital or steering around each other? What is it like to broach these questions openly across our racial and cultural identities? The next section describes our objectives for instigating the project and how we approached our research dialogues.

INSIDE THE LABORATORY: OUR PROCESS

We initiated a conversation among five women from diverse cultural backgrounds to share our experiences and perspectives for developing our social networks from a multicultural perspective. We wanted to find out how our approach to building our networks compared with the existing research. What strategies do we use? How intentional are we? How diverse are our networks? How do our cultural backgrounds influence the composition of our networks? What is the value each of us has realized from our network and what are the associated costs?

We were intentional in composing this group of women to represent a mix of backgrounds. Stacy and Gina are African American, Eleanor is Asian American, Marisol is Latina, and Laurie is Anglo Canadian (see Figure 10.1 for more information about the participants). The composition of our group influenced our dialogue and our findings. Our small exploratory sample means

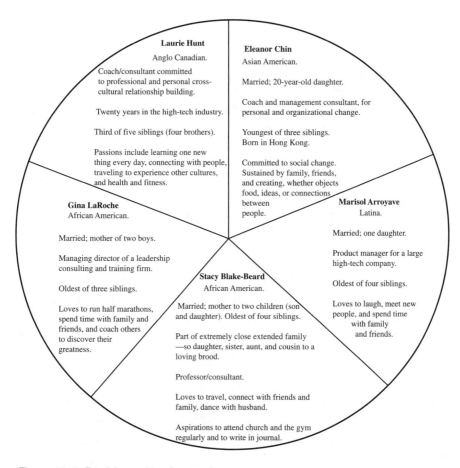

Figure 10.1. Participants' background.

findings are not necessarily representative of an entire cultural grouping or generalizable. Rather, our work together is meant to spark similar dialogues that both probe and represent cross-cultural connection.

For this study, we met face-to-face and over the phone as well as shared written responses to a series of questions about what our networks looked like and how we approached creating them (see Figure 10.2 for an outline of our process). We have noted the source of each author's comment at the end of each quote. Please refer to the process diagram to cross-reference the codes used.

As we neared the end of our analysis and writing, we invited Maureen to participate in this project because of her interest in both the topic and our approach. She is an Irish American woman who had worked with all five participants in a 2-day workshop on cross-cultural dilemmas. She connects to participants on other dimensions, as a professor and a mother. We do not have direct quotes from Maureen, but she engaged in the give and take of the editing process and her observations are incorporated throughout.

At the beginning of our process each of us mapped our network so we could see the mix of people and types of support we had in our networks (see Table 10.1 for a summary of our mapping observations and Appendix 10.1 for our template of the mapping exercise). We audiotaped and transcribed all our discussions. Our dialogues were primarily a reflection on the sharing of our written responses. We synthesized and analyzed the data from the writing and discussions to determine our findings. Although our intent from the onset was to study multicultural networks as a means for bringing about change, we were receptive to what we would discover as the process unfolded. We asked ourselves questions to find out what our experiences would teach us (see Figure 10.2 for a summary of the questions). This open-ended methodology allows researchers to acknowledge and include all the differences among people (Reinharz, 1992). Our multicultural ethnographic approach provided us with rich and varied data. We were living the experience that we were studying. Other similar studies served as a model for us as we developed our process. In their study of Black and White women and insider activism in the workplace, Bell, Meyerson, Nkomo, and Scully (2003) included their interactions as part of their research process. They drew on Hertz's model (1997) of "reflexive ethnography" as "an ongoing conversation about experience while simultaneously living in the moment" (p. 15).

Blake-Beard, Scully, et al. (2006) also used a similar process in their study of relationships between Black and White women. Their research team consisted of four Black women and four White women who, through a series of structured conversations, writing, and sharing, examined how Black and White women could work together. The information gathered is not simply reported but constructed through filters or interpretations from participants' own experiences. In the next section, we explore the insights gained from a synthesis of the literature and our findings.

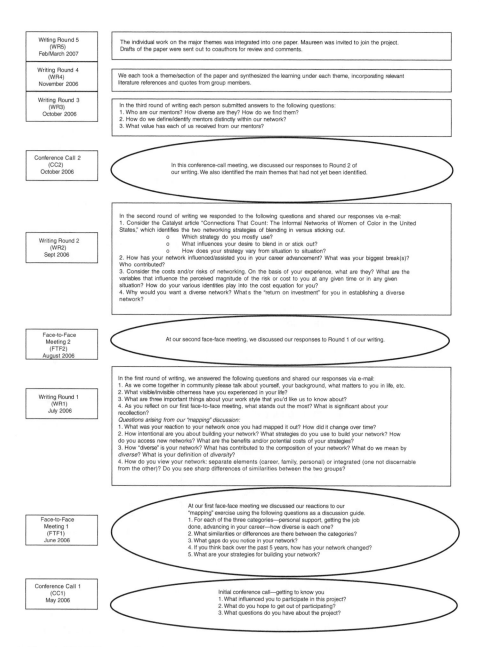

Writing Round 5 (WR5) Feb/March 2007	The individual work on the major themes was integrated into one paper. Maureen was invited to join the project. Drafts of the paper were sent out to coauthors for review and comments.
Writing Round 4 (WR4) November 2006	We each took a theme/section of the paper and synthesized the learning under each theme, incorporating relevant literature references and quotes from group members.
Writing Round 3 (WR3) October 2006	In the third round of writing each person submitted answers to the following questions: 1. Who are our mentors? How diverse are they? How do we find them? 2. How do we define/identify mentors distinctly within our network? 3. What value has each of us received from our mentors?
Conference Call 2 (CC2) October 2006	In this conference-call meeting, we discussed our responses to Round 2 of our writing. We also identified the main themes that had not yet been identified.
Writing Round 2 (WR2) Sept 2006	In the second round of writing we responded to the following questions and shared our responses via e-mail: 1. Consider the Catalyst article "Connections That Count: The Informal Networks of Women of Color in the United States," which identifies the two networking strategies of blending in versus sticking out. o Which strategy do you mostly use? o What influences your desire to blend in or stick out? o How does your strategy vary from situation to situation? 2. How has your network influenced/assisted you in your career advancement? What was your biggest break(s)? Who contributed? 3. Consider the costs and/or risks of networking. On the basis of your experience, what are they? What are the variables that influence the perceived magnitude of the risk or cost to you at any given time or in any given situation? How do your various identities play into the cost equation for you? 4. Why would you want a diverse network? What s the "return on investment" for you in establishing a diverse network?
Face-to-Face Meeting 2 (FTF2) August 2006	At our second face-face meeting, we discussed our responses to Round 1 of our writing.
Writing Round 1 (WR1) July 2006	In the first round of writing, we answered the following questions and shared our responses via e-mail: 1. As we come together in community please talk about yourself, your background, what matters to you in life, etc. 2. What visible/invisible otherness have you experienced in your life? 3. What are three important things about your work style that you'd like us to know about? 4. As you reflect on our first face-to-face meeting, what stands out the most? What is significant about your recollection? *Questions arising from our "mapping" discussion:* 1. What was your reaction to your network once you had mapped it out? How did it change over time? 2. How intentional are you about building your network? What strategies do you use to build your network? How do you access new networks? What are the benefits and/or potential costs of your strategies? 3. How "diverse" is your network? What has contributed to the composition of your network? What do we mean by *diverse*? What is your definition of *diversity*? 4. How do you view your network: separate elements (career, family, personal) or integrated (one not discernable from the other)? Do you see sharp differences of similarities between the two groups?
Face-to-Face Meeting 1 (FTF1) June 2006	At our first face-face meeting we discussed our reactions to our "mapping" exercise using the following questions as a discussion guide. 1. For each of the three categories—personal support, getting the job done, advancing in your career—how diverse is each one? 2. What similarities or differences are there between the categories? 3. What gaps do you notice in your network? 4. If you think back over the past 5 years, how has your network changed? 5. What are your strategies for building your network?
Conference Call 1 (CC1) May 2006	Initial conference call—getting to know you 1. What influenced you to participate in this project? 2. What do you hope to get out of participating? 3. What questions do you have about the project?

Figure 10.2. Research process.

INTEGRATING OUR INSIGHTS

Throughout this project we learned a great deal about one another and saw our experiences mirrored in the research on women and social networks. The issues of social identity, social networks, and social capital recurred in

TABLE 10.1

Mapping Observations

Author	Observations of her network
Laurie	I realize that my current network contains lots of women and few men. Since leaving the corporate life, I've focused on creating relationships with women really to the exclusion of men. As well, my network is much more multicultural. I also notice that I have a number of people who appear in all three segments: getting the job done, personal support, and advancing career.
Stacy	I think about my map all the time maybe because of the work that I do. I know that on my map, I need to have more women of color who are not African American. In terms of change, my network has shifted as I have grown in my career. As I move into the public, I have had to expand my network to include more people who help me move in those circles. While I have a strong network of women, I don't have many men in my network . . . and wonder what this means for what I may need to do to grow my network.
Gina	Before mapping my network for this group, I would have said that my network was integrated, diverse, and worked well for me. Now I see that my network is really two distinct groups: close and distant. I was actually disappointed during our meeting to see how small my network had become, how few close connections I have, and how I have let many of my loose ties go.
Eleanor	Mapping my network revealed how difficult it is to create a network that is intentionally diverse. Apart from family and family friends, I had always thought that I have very few Asian friends. I was pleasantly surprised that I know more Asians than I thought, although still, not many of them rise to the level of closeness that I would like. Comments from Stacy and Gina that they too lacked Asian or even Black friends helped me to validate how intentional and conscious we all have to be to bring those elements into our lives. Those opportunities to diversify our networks often don't appear naturally or effortlessly. We need to create them.
Marisol	I was very surprised to see that until recently I did not have many Latinos in my network! Since being the leader of the Latino employee circle where I work, this has changed! I can see that I am an international type of person because I have a lot of friends from all over the world! What had also changed over time is that my network used to be comprised mostly of men. Now I can see that I have a lot more women in my network, which makes me very happy!

our dialogues. Figure 10.3 depicts the reciprocal interactions between these three variables for connecting across cultures. Underpinning building relationships is trust, which is the ability to believe in and depend on another person (McKnight, Cummings, & Chervany, 1998). Many factors must be taken into consideration with respect to establishing trust as we illustrate in the examples from our conversations described later in this section.

Not only is one's social identity influenced and created by interactions with other people, (Hogg & Terry, 2000; Ibarra et al., 2005; Roberts, 2005) social networks are also altered as members' social identities change through connection with others. These relationships signal the possession of valued social capital.

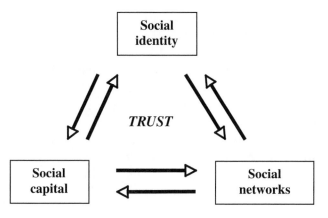

Figure 10.3. Tripartite model for connecting across cultures.

As reflections of social identity, networks also serve as signals to others about the current status or probable future of an individual. The ability to signal desirable traits such as competence and career advancement potential in turn affects an individual's ability to attract influential actors to his or her network circle. (Ibarra et al., 2005, p. 365)

As beneficial network connections accrue, so does social capital for individuals. When we take demographic characteristics such as gender and ethnicity into account, we see variations in how people approach building their networks and realize the diverging effects of their network connections. The following sections cover five predominant themes that emerged from our study: social identity awareness, sociohistorical perspective, network similarities and differences, mentoring, and costs and risks. These discussions provide a more detailed examination of the interrelation between social identity, social capital, social networks, and trust for building cross-cultural relationships.

Social Identity Awareness

The influence of our different social identities was evident throughout the data-gathering phase for this chapter. As our work continued we discovered that where each of us was on our own, respective social identity journey was a main determinant in how we had built our networks. Stacy raised this point with the following observation:

> Stacy: The thing that I was struck by was the identity work we have to do ourselves before we can connect with other people . . . who am I with Asian women, Latina women? Whenever I'm with Black women I immediately feel a "warm blanket." Immediate comfort. With the multicultural thing, there's a piece of individual social identity work that we need to do in

order to connect across. We need to do our own identity work and that's our life work (FTF2).[1]

Stacy's warm blanket represents the trust that is often automatically given to those whom we perceive to be most like us (McKnight et al., 1998). This selective perception perpetuates stereotyping because people tend to notice behavior that confirms their viewpoints and fail to notice the information that opposes the stereotype. People in a similar social category may miss important information and assume similar values that result in trusting behaviors (Jehn, Northcraft, & Neale, 1999; see also chap. 12, this volume). Gina and Stacy discussed this very point.

> Gina: Any time I see a Black person I will say hi to them. We also get burned because we grant too much trust and intimacy based on that surface similarity and then it comes out—then I feel even more betrayed. How could that sister do this to me? (FTF2)

> Stacy: It reminds me of experiences with Black women where they've thrown me under the bus—in the last 2 to 3 months where women of color behaved really inappropriately. What you talked about, Gina, reminds me of identity work we do with others—the trust we give away—we make assumptions about people based on surface similarities—we either overemphasize surface similarities or overexaggerate the surface differences and don't get to the real identity work—we have to dig down beyond the surface. (FTF2)

Harrison, Price, and Bell (1998) distinguished between surface-level and deep-level diversity. *Surface-level diversity* refers to overt biological characteristics including race, gender, and age. *Deep-level diversity* refers to less readily apparent differences such as attitudes, beliefs, and values. It is at this deeper level that people find points of connection that are especially important in forming cross-cultural relationships. What Gina and Stacy described earlier is the tendency to more readily grant trust to those whom we perceive to be more like us on the basis of the premise that their surface similarity means they share common goals and values with us (McKnight et al., 1998). Marisol found that although she values a diverse network, she gravitates toward others on the basis of perceived commonality as well.

> Marisol: If I see a Latina in the room then I go to them. I don't know much about Mexico, Chile, Colombia but we have Spanish in common. I now have this hunger for Latinas in similar professions, at my corporation, in board rooms. (FTF2)

---

[1]Please refer to Figure 10.2 to cross-reference the codes used.

Eleanor shared a different experience in the Asian community.

> *Eleanor:* In the Asian American community we can be very independent and not network with each other, missing opportunities to find strength with each other and aligning with the dominant culture as a way of succeeding. That's how I was socialized. . . . I had to do identity work on myself to get myself to the point where I reach out to other Asian Americans. You ladies [Gina and Stacy] had the opposite—you found a natural network among your sisters. (FTF2)

This comment could be seen as an example of how social group status overrides the race or ethnic similarity—Asians aligning themselves with the dominant group for greater social capital. Eleanor further clarified that "for many Asians, aligning with the dominant culture is about our value of respecting whoever is the authority figure" (WR4). By taking the time to understand different cultural experiences and perspectives, she realized that aspects of deep-level diversity are the important determinants of trustworthiness that can transcend race, ethnicity, gender, or other surface differences. As Marisol put it, "assumptions make barriers" (FTF1) and our awareness of them provided an opportunity to understand their effect and reach deeper to connect.

> *Eleanor:* It's about having similar core values and starting from there as a foundation. A person can be a male or female or another race or ethnicity but if you're connecting with them because they have similar values then [surface difference] really doesn't matter does it. (FTF2)

> *Marisol:* When we talk about what's important we're talking about our values. (FTF2)

> *Gina:* Any time I had a relationship—an intimate relationship or business relationship—"go south" it was because I assumed we had similar values. That goes back to granting trust to other Black women. Stacy, I suspect when you look at the Black women or women of color who have thrown you under the bus, when you peel those layers back you'll find you never did the values' piece. I think we skip over it because of the visible similarities. We then probably make the White women or White men or whoever is the most different from us jump over the most tremendous value hoops. (FTF2)

Our visible differences often serve as a cue that someone visibly similar to us shares deeper and harder-to-see identities, such as common heritage, standpoint, and values. We learned that this focus can lead to disappointment when the assumption of shared values is not fulfilled. It can also lead to missed opportunities when we fail to see past visible differences to find allies with shared values. Our individual histories complicate bridging our differences.

Sociohistorical Perspective

Compounding the effects of social identity on connecting cross-culturally, our historical past and race consciousness were also influential factors in our network relationships. As Hill Collins (1999) articulated, "African American women, Asian Indian women, Japanese American women, and White American women may all be considered 'outsiders within' in a given corporation, but quite different group histories got them there" (p. 86). As women, we may share the common experience of not belonging or feeling like an outsider; however, our differing cultural backgrounds and social identities influenced our experiences and how we established our networks and made use of our networks. Eleanor, born in Hong Kong, arrived in the United States as a toddler in the 1950s. Her mother "insisted on assimilation. We were raised to fit in with our new culture. I felt that in order to advance in this society I had no choice but to culturally blend in" (WR1). Marisol, arriving from the Dominican Republic as a student, came from a very different history.

> *Marisol:*   Coming from the Dominican Republic we have different issues than other countries. Our difficulty is around gender. Thank God for my dad pushing me ahead, he helped me define who I was so I didn't have to be cast in a traditional role of homemaker and mother. (FTF2)

As African Americans, Stacy and Gina have slavery and pervasive racial oppression as a part of their history that surfaced when examining multicultural networks. Gina stated, "I am not sure I can ever blend in even if I wanted to. Our society is so color conscious and I am so obviously Black that I really don't know what choice I have in the matter" (WR2). Laurie's mother's parents were immigrant farmers from Poland and had to assimilate into the dominant White culture upon arriving in Canada. Laurie explained how her mother's prejudices and stereotypes "arise from having to assimilate. My mother believes everyone has to do this because she had no choice" (FTF2). The challenge of assimilation in Laurie's past, however, is hidden behind the privilege associated with her social identity of being White, and being White means her past does not have a negative impact on her ability to make choices in her life. Coll (Coll et al., 1997) explained how:

> One of the things that impedes the process [of building relationships] is our collective histories; by that I mean the prior and current history of power differentials and conflicts between the groups that the individuals belong to . . . but in most instances it is more a part of the core experience of the oppressed than the oppressor. (p. 179)

Stacy shared how history as well as values plays an important role in establishing trust and connecting with people.

Stacy: Can you come into my world—do I always have to go to yours—every now and then so I don't have to go to yours—can you get it—you don't have to have my experience but can you get that there is an experience I'm having—listen and understand and not tell me I'm imagining things—can you be courageous? I can't be with you when I see that in the face of craziness you bow down. . . . If you'll do that then, when will you throw me under the bus? Speaks to the history of White women and women of color—women of color always waiting for White women to throw them under the bus. . . . We need to be willing to dig down to where are we similar—we do not have to be exactly alike but find some way to connect. And then not wash away or pretend that our differences don't exist on the surface. Don't always look at me and always see a Black woman and don't look at me and not see a Black woman. (FTF2)

There is a delicate balance of recognizing and acknowledging the effect of surface differences while at the same time looking for the deeper points of connection. Cook-Nobles (Coll et al., 1997) echoed Stacy's words when she referenced Black women's anger and asked "Can you hold my anger? Will you be with me in this process? Will you share this experience with me?" (p. 184). Because of the history of slavery and White women's role in it, much of Black women's anger is directed at White women. The task for White women of holding Black women's anger, as Cook-Nobles (Coll et al., 1997) explained, "involves being able to hear and to listen without being defensive" (p. 184). We saw how anger plays out as our discussion of the sociohistorical effect on relationships continued.

Gina: Could it be we make women of otherness jump through huge hoops to get to us? (FTF2)

Laurie: Seems more like something that Black women do in making themselves inaccessible more than other women of color. It's hardest for me to get to know Black women versus Asian women or Hispanic women or any other women. It feels like there is a test I have to pass and then once I pass it everything is fine but it feels like a test. (FTF2)

Stacy: I think that's tied to our social historic experiences here—tied back to slavery. And so not the same for Asians and Hispanics and versus how they came to this country and how we came to this country and our unique sociohistorical dance that we do with each other. I think that dance, that legacy haunts us every day. And either we figure out how to master it or we get shut down by it. (FTF2)

Laurie: For me from Canada—I wasn't part of the experience. (FTF2)

Eleanor:	It's not your history. (FTF2)
Laurie:	It's not, but it is. (FTF2)
Gina:	I wonder if there were other White women sitting here, if they'd feel that master/slave relationship was part of their history? I wonder if this is a historical cultural phenomenon for Black women and not for White women? (FTF2)

White women's lack of ownership of the history of slavery has been well documented (see Davis, 1981; Frankenberg, 1993; hooks 1981, 1984, 1994; Thompson, 2001). Of note in the preceding exchange is Laurie's struggle with her White identity and slavery as a Canadian. Laurie was admittedly not very knowledgeable about slavery until she moved to the United States and began studying in a gender and cultural studies program. Janet Surrey (as cited in Coll et al., 1997) pointed out the "difficulty [White women] have dealing with the complexity of [their] double identity as both victim and oppressor which is necessary for engaging in this dialog" (p. 193). We notice this duality expressed in Laurie's comment:

Laurie:	What I'm picking up in the conversation is that there's a big assumption about what life's like for White women. I grew up never fitting in anywhere. Just in the last twelve months I'm starting to find myself. I'm noticing in the conversation, the reference to women of color and with the assumption that it doesn't apply to White women. It strikes me that we all have pain. (FTF2)

However much truth there may be in her words, the fact of the matter is that for those who have been colonized or oppressed, there is a tendency to respond to the dominant group "not expecting mutuality and assuming a power differential between the two. . . . [I]t is a perceived power differential which might be real or not, but is as powerful as if it were real" (Coll et al., 1997, p. 180). Taking this analysis into account, we see how the complexity of social identity and the amount of identity work that we have done has an impact on how we establish our social networks and how we perceive the differences in social capital accrued to a person or group.

Network Similarities and Differences

In many dimensions our experience of our social networks was similar but in many places differences were vast. We noticed the gender imbalances in our networks immediately. When we examined the networks of the women who had worked for large for-profit corporations (Gina, Laurie, and Marisol), their networks were dominated by men. Gina wrote, "When I was in the corporate world my network was mostly male and White" (WR2). Laurie spoke of her network as being predominantly men while she was in the high-tech industry and Marisol also noticed, "I am in the IT [information technology] industry, which is dominated by men; so most of my professional interactions are with men" (WR1). Stacy commented that although on an academic career path, she had similar experiences at two universities in which her network was dominated by men.

The gaps we discovered around gender in our networks are not uncommon for women. Women tend to have separate networks of women for social support and networks with men for instrumental support and the two are generally not well integrated (Burke, Rothstein, & Bristor, 1995; Ibarra et al., 2005). Eleanor had a different experience than did the rest of the women, spending most of her career in nonprofit organizations led and managed by women. Those who now work outside of male-dominated organizations found their networks consist mostly of women and include more women of color than before.

> Gina: Now my network has more women and is now culturally diverse. I think as my work has become more personal—working as an entrepreneur, I seek people who are more like me—individuals who are not necessarily in a traditional career path. (WR2)

> Laurie: What's been interesting for me to observe is I went from a very White male world in the high tech environment and created a world of women around me and noticed mostly women of color. (FTF2)

> Stacy: I don't have many men in my network . . . and I wonder what this means for what I may need to do to grow my network. (FTF2)

We have gravitated toward working more with women, obtaining both instrumental and psychosocial support from those in our network and finding it easier to include more diversity outside corporate settings.

While working in male-dominated organizations, we relied on our external networks for support, connecting internally on an as-needed basis to get the job done. When Laurie and Gina were at large corporations they networked with people who were there to do the work and there was little thought behind their networking. Gina stated, "I worked with people internally because I had to; I gave no thought to a mentor or getting psychosocial support from them. I saved that for my friends and family, my life outside of the office" (WR2). The results of Burke et al.'s study (1995) of women's networks accord with our experience of relying more on outsiders for psychosocial support and missing out on internal career development support (e.g., mentoring). It is the social capital of internal networks that influence decisions regarding promotion and accept-ance and ultimate career success (Burke et al., 1995). In a study by Catalyst (2006b) in which they examined the networking strategies of women of color in organizations, they identified two strategies that are linked to promotion rates and organizational commitment. *Blending in* requires forming relation-ships with those who have power, who are typically White or male or both. *Sticking together* means creating informal networks made up of people who are racially or ethnically similar (Catalyst, 2006b, p. 7).

Using the concepts of blending in or sticking together as a guide, we shared how each of us developed our networks. We too found that our social identity along with the context or situation influenced our approach. Marisol realized the limits of any one strategy for her:

> *Marisol:* I don't think I have used the "blending in" strategy much. I have a very dynamic personality and mindset that makes it hard to blend in. I do, however, sometimes have to blend in for the sake of my team. (WR2)

She also realized how her unique social identity as a career woman affected her ability to connect within her own ethnic culture.

> *Marisol:* In my culture [it] is not "normal" for a woman to struggle for positions of power and leadership . . . especially if it means that you will not spend a lot of time at home. So it has been very hard for me to blend in with women of my own ethnic group or culture. I do, however, have a connection with a few Latina women and I love it! I can definitely stick together with them. (WR2)

In a different yet similar way, the intersection of race, gender, and class affects how Gina connects with people.

> *Gina:* I stick out by walking down the street because I look different from most other folks. When I am with other Blacks I feel like I stick out because I mainly grew up in White neighborhoods and lived an upper middle class life style. When I make a con-scious choice I look for women of color. I actively try to stick together with other Blacks when I walk into a networking event and in my personal network. We are in solidarity of not blending in. (WR2)

The effect of Gina's multiple identities occurring and interacting simul-taneously (Combahee River Collective, 1983; Holvino, 2001, 2006; Smith, 1998) is evident in her experience. In particular, Black women face a "gendered racism" (Blake, 1999, p. 85) as a result of the inability to separate the effects of race and gender. Crenshew (1989) explained how the effects of the intersectional experience for women of color are greater than racism and sexism added together. Stacy's observations further illustrate the complexity of social identity, social capital, and network connections for women of color.

> Stacy: At times, I prefer to stick out. On some occasions, I also need to blend in. And when I can, I find people with whom to stick together. When I read this question, it made me think about visibility and how "tokens" can get thrown into either hyper-visibility or invisibility. I think we need to be able to move between the options, to create our own form of tempered visibility. (WR2)

Tempered visibility is about being aware of our visibility and the impact we are having (Blake-Beard & Roberts, 2004). We are individually responsible for choosing how to present ourselves. However, for women of color, choices can be limited by needing to operate within contexts in which they are the racial minority, as Eleanor's situation illustrates.

> Eleanor: One might say that I chose to blend in with the dominant White culture. Almost all of my workplaces were predominantly women and much of the senior leadership was White women, with some White men in top leadership positions. So, in order to advance, I had no choice but to racially blend in. There were no other Asians to "stick" with. (WR2)

From the Catalyst (2006b) study we learned that because the representation of Latinas and Asian women in managerial ranks was so low, these two groups may not have any alternative but to blend in. Eleanor's and Marisol's experiences support this premise.

Getting beyond surface-level differences and making cross-cultural connections requires intentionality. Having moved from Toronto to Boston a few years ago, Laurie remarked on how she consciously created her network.

> Laurie: I was very intentional about building my network when I moved to Boston since I was transplanted out of my job, my friends, my network, my country—it's completely different. I have grown my network by consciously creating groups or mini networks. I've made a point of trying to have these groups be diverse. I also attend events that draw a more diverse group of attendees and so I naturally meet a wider variety of people. (WR1)

Blake-Beard, Murrell, et al. (2006) also found that intentionality was key to success in cross-cultural connecting and networking. Even when intentional, however, creating a diverse network can be challenging, as Eleanor observed:

> Eleanor: I was struck by how difficult it is to create a network that is intentionally diverse. Just as I was thinking that my own network is sorely lacking in Asian connections, comments from Stacy and Gina that they too lacked Asian or even Black friends helped me to validate how intentional and conscious we all have to be to bring those elements into our lives. Those opportunities to diversify our networks often don't appear naturally or effortlessly. We need to create them. (WR2)

Laurie's awareness of her network and the value of diverse relationships is a change from the past. Her increased social identity awareness has changed the way she makes connections.

> Laurie: What's really sticking in my mind right now is that what stage you are at in the identity process is very important. Sure I said I was intentional about my network, but ask me that five years ago and my focus was "who did I need to know in the company where I worked?" . . . I've gone through huge leaps and bounds in that identity process in recent years. (FTF2)

We observed from our experiences how our social identity is tied to our social capital and that how we approach establishing our network affects our success. The literature on developmental networks (Higgins & Kram, 2001; Higgins & Thomas, 2001) emphasizes the need for individuals to establish diverse networks or "relationship constellations" (Higgins & Kram, 2001, p. 264) to navigate one's career and be successful in the current changing global business environment. One important and valuable network connection is that of a mentor. Again, we appreciated the importance of intentionality in creating mentoring relationships.

Mentoring

Because lack of access to mentors is frequently cited as a key barrier to career success among women and especially for women of color (Blake-Beard, 2001; Blake-Beard, Murrell, et al., 2006; Catalyst, 1999, 2003, 2004, 2006b), the challenges of finding a mentor must then be addressed by intentionally forging relationships across race, gender, job level, job function, profession, or organizational culture (Blake-Beard, Murrell, et al., 2006). Ragins's (1997) study of diversified mentoring relationships confirms this point. Her findings showed that the social capital associated with a mentor's or protégé's social identity affected the outcomes that one could expect from the mentoring relationship. For example, a minority protégé with a minority mentor receives important psychosocial support; however, to gain significant instrumental outcomes such as career advancement, protégés fare better when connected to a majority mentor. Stacy summed up her perspective on diverse mentoring relationships this way:

> *Stacy:*   Given that there are all these different ways that we're doggy paddling—trying to survive—multicultural mentoring could be a lifeline. If we're in a world where we get reinforcement for not belonging—in a world where you are bossy because it is a survival mechanism, I'm going to control so I'm not controlled—mentoring becomes really important. I think the trouble we face as women of color is that we don't let people in. (FTF2)

Catalyst's (2006b) networking study supports Stacy's feelings about opening up to others. Building relationships involves sharing personal experiences and not doing so can be a barrier to fitting in. Personal disclosure was found to be an issue in particular for African American women likely because of the higher levels of workplace exclusion they perceived. Again we witness the sociohistorical effects combined with dual effects of race and gender on connecting and mentoring across cultures. As a way of navigating the emotional distance between people of color and White mentors, cross-race and -gender mentoring relationships often become more of an instrumental relationship (D. A. Thomas, 1989). Even though establishing cross-cultural mentoring relationships can be challenging, the efforts are worthwhile because they allow both the mentor and the protégé to test their preconceived notions and stereotypes and learn how to communicate across cultural differences (Bova, 1998). Hyun (2005) concurred as she elaborated on the importance of Asian women broadening their view of potential mentors:

> A sentiment shared by many Asian professionals . . . implies that Asian employees can benefit only from another Asian as their mentor. Nothing could be further from the truth. You may need to remove some cultural misperceptions of your own to get the coaching you need. (Hyun, 2005, p. 218)

In our group's conversations, Marisol, who works in a high-tech firm with predominantly White men, made a strong case for choosing mentoring across race and gender differences as a strategy for growth and learning:

> *Marisol:*   Mentors must be diverse in many ways. We should strategically choose our mentors with different levels of expertise, connection, and influence. I would add that our mentors should be from different backgrounds and across race. One of my mentors is from India. I have learned a lot from him. I have learned to respect and admire his culture and beliefs. (WR3)

According to D. C. Thomas and Inkson (2003), experiential learning is vital to the development of CQ. Cross-cultural mentoring provides the opportunity to learn while in the experience of the relationship. Mentoring can also lift a woman from the daily preoccupations of her job and give her a perch from which to view a larger landscape or a larger vision of her own abilities.

> Gina: I think the biggest value I received from my mentors was they saw me as bigger than I saw myself. They had a clear view of my future and the gaps I needed to fill and they went about filling those gaps in me through personal and professional development. (WR3)

We grow through our connection with people (Miller, 1976). Ragins and Verbos (2007) defined relational mentoring "as a developmental relationship that involves mutual growth, learning and development in personal, professional and career domains" (p. 91). A mentoring relationship is a unique type of network connection that creates the opportunity for mutual learning and increased outcomes for the mentor and protégé. A few of us remarked on our reciprocal approach to our mentoring relationships.

> Laurie: For me the key to building networks and developing mentoring relationships is to remember that it is a two-way street. I focus on what can I give and the result is often so much in return. (WR3)

> Eleanor: I can point to several peers and others who have provided critical support and connections. Some of these peers have even guided me to jobs. I would say that our relationships consist of mutual exchanges of being role models, supporters and mentors for each other. (WR3)

> Stacy: I can clearly say that I am where I am because others cared enough to hold my hand, to give me a little push in the back, to let me stand on their shoulders, to step aside to let me move ahead. I truly would never have been able to get to where I am now without my extraordinary network to support me. I have noticed as I look at this collection of people that I have reciprocal ties. I have given back to the people who have given to me, even with the power differentials that characterize our relationships. (WR3)

Mentoring relationships serve as crucial connections for accruing social capital through links to influential others. Along with our choices of how we network and who we connect to, we must also consider the costs and risks involved in those choices as we describe in the next section.

Costs and Risks

We were clear about the costs and risks of networking. We all discussed the cost of losing ourselves by assimilating and the risk of being left out for being different. We also noted that the work of building and maintaining networks can be time-consuming and it is not always easy to strike the right balance. Stacy summarized the costs and risks for her.

> Stacy: The costs and risks of networking are both numerous. Costs that come right to mind include time (to build the relationships) and sharing resources (so that the relationship is mutually beneficial). Risks that I can think of include someone could be exploitative; your intellectual property may be compromised, opening yourself up to a measure of vulnerability and you could run into people who use their networks to coast and have others do their work. It's called social loafing. (WR2)

Laurie looked at costs somewhat differently.

> Laurie: For me, there is a much greater cost of not "investing" in my network. I can hear myself saying, "What have I got to lose?" Being White certainly plays into my cost equation. It minimizes the costs. It allows me to take risks without being overly concerned with the outcome, assuming I'm taking smart risks. (WR2)

When we looked at our social identity inside the costs and risks discussion we saw that Gina's experience in the technology industry was confirmed by the experience of women of color at law firms. Gina told us, "It was the late 1980s and women acted like men to succeed. They wore ties and dressed as if they were men in skirts. It made me very uncomfortable to network with these women" (FTF2). The legal industry study revealed that

> Women of color in the survey and focus groups felt they could not "be themselves"; they downplayed and homogenized their gender and racial/ethnic identities. Some tried to act like the men in their firms, become "one of the boys"; others played down their femininity and tried to "mannify" themselves. The effort to minimize the impact of their physical differences was stressful to many women of color, an added burden to the long hours and hard work demanded by their firm. (American Bar Association, 2006, p. xii)

The costs were not being able to bring one's full self to work combined with the weight of trying to fit in and minimize differences. Eleanor expanded on the costs of trying to fit in:

Eleanor: For me and other Asian-Americans as well as other minorities, the cost of fitting into a dominant culture often are the same as the costs of assimilation—loss of some of my cultural identity. In some situations, by not blending in, a person of color may limit either her opportunities for organizational advancement or her connection to others of her race, and by extension her own racial identity. (WR2)

That cost can then extend to subsequent generations; as Eleanor noted, her own intentional assimilation was one of the reasons her daughter was not acculturated into her Chinese heritage. Marisol saw that her decision to pursue a career and her career choice isolated her from the gendered norms of her Dominican culture. Stacy pointed out that for all women the potential risk of networking is that "you could be trivialized or your work made invisible. It really does depend on the body you are in" (FTF1). The effect of social identity on networking strategies and social capital was interwoven through all aspects of our conversations. This research highlights the complexity and value of connecting across cultures and invites further investigation of multicultural networking on the advancement of women from their unique social identity perspectives.

CONCLUSION

Through our participation in this research project we learned about the interrelation between and significance of social identity, social capital, and social networks in connecting cross-culturally. Trust is necessary for building relationships; however, cultural differences and sociohistorical perspectives influence our willingness to grant trust. Choosing to trust requires a conscious decision based on identifiable factors (Hurley, 2006). Our conversations created opportunities for group trust and deeper exploration with each other and our own identities. "When people treat their cultural differences—and the conflicts and tensions that arise from them—as opportunities to seek a more accurate view of themselves, each other, and the situation, trust builds and relationships become stronger" (Ely, Meyerson, & Davidson, 2006, p. 87). Trusting is a choice that people intentionally make and "rather than being a self-protective wall, boundaries become the place of meeting and exchange" (Wheatley, 2005, p. 48).

Similarities and differences emerged as each woman shared her unique experience. We discovered and embraced the fact that each of us brought several different dimensions of our identities—our own complex intersections of race, class, nationality, gender, and familial patterns—into each conversation. Marisol described her learning from this experience:

Marisol: The learning from this group experience is that we have similar and different experiences, independent of us all being women and most being minority. Our cultural and ethnic experiences strongly influence how we see the world and behave with one another. The biggest learning is that while we may have similar limitations to advance in the business world as women, we have very different experiences and perspectives as a multicultural network. (WR3)

The following exchange exemplifies the learning and growth that can occur from open, trusting cross-cultural dialogue:

Gina: If I walked into a room with no Black women and saw Asian women and Latina women and White women I'd probably go toward the White woman. When I really think about it I proba- bly would. What really surprised me was . . . WOW . . . that Eleanor would talk to Black women. Because if I walk in, my ini- tial screen is not that this woman is a woman of color. If a Latina woman was dark, I'd talk to her thinking she was Black. But if she was light or looked White, then in my mind I'd be walking into a room with no women of color before this book chapter. (FTF2)

Laurie: So what prevents you from approaching the women of color if there are no Black women? (FTF2)

Gina: I wouldn't see them as women of color. I'd have walked into the room and I'd have said I'm in a room of White people. . . . I would- n't say that now but I would have a couple of months ago. (FTF2)

Working from Godamer's fusions of horizons theory, Neilsen (1990) described how "one's view is enlarged and broadened by the clashing of two cultures" (p. 29). Our "horizon" is limited on the basis of our personal experi- ences, and when we connect with people from cultures different than ours, that connection, or fusion, broadens our horizon. Ibarra et al. (2005) suggested that new knowledge emerges when "social equals" from different social circles connect. To network effectively across cultural boundaries we may need to adjust our expectations of a network when we move outside our own culture and acquire a broader range of networking skills (Travers et al., 1997). Cross- cultural knowledge and increased CQ will create valuable social capital for people in this ever-changing global world in which we live and work.

Networking is an active verb. For many people, it conjures images of walk- ing into a room and summoning the energy to introduce ourselves to people we do not know. In this moment, we may cling to visibly similar others in the hopes of gaining easy entry. This bias, of course, is at the root of the "homosocial repro- duction" of organizations (Kanter, 1977), whereby White men have selected other White men to be trusted colleagues in the highest positions in organiza- tions. Women have aspired to interrupt this process, in part by forging their own "old girls' networks." Our conversations show that even identifying and connect- ing to similar others has challenges in that we do not readily link to other women (as the often-used term *women in management* might suggest) nor do women from minority cultural groups connect seamlessly under the often-used term *women of color*. Connecting in ways that make our similarities (surface and deep) more accessible as well as connecting across differences is not an easy default course but an action that requires mindfulness (Langer, 1990). Coming home from a networking event with a briefcase full of business cards, we need to think consciously about which relationships to nurture. From our rolodex of existing connections, we need to think consciously about whom to call for plum assignments, job openings, or a friendly dinner. Our conversations have helped us to see both where we might subtly exclude other women and where we might find waiting allies in women (and men) whom we do not normally seek out. Through continued efforts to build relationships, women of color and White women are uniquely poised to capitalize on connecting cross-culturally and supporting their mutual advancement.

This chapter ends here, but the conversation does not. As we edited this chapter collaboratively, we sent e-mails with follow-up points, new thoughts, and clarifications. There were appreciative e-mails as well as some "flash points" that reminded us of our different vantage points. Knowing that the dialogues continue, we close with some reflections on two themes: what is unsaid and what is at stake.

Some things remained unsaid in our dialogues. Our process laid the groundwork for seeing and hearing each other. Learning about those outside our social identity group is a necessary building block for connection. Sometimes, the dialogue moved sequentially: "Oh, that's how it is for you? Here's how it is for me." But we know ourselves in relation to others, so there can be silent but noisy subtexts in even these simple accounts: "And it is harder for me. . . . And you could assimilate but I could not. . . . And my group knows a more enduring oppression. . . . And you are assuming I have it easier. . . ." These subtexts shift the dialogue from informative, sequential portraits to more interactive and potentially conflictual exchanges. The hard work of building trust requires both avoiding some conflicts and engaging others—and having the wisdom to know the difference. To be courageous and deeply engage in the uncertainty and complexity of human relationship means being able to dance with this ambiguity (Walker, 2007). Our next steps will come from listening both to what was said and to the silences.

Many things are at stake in our dialogues. The notion of social capital was introduced to help illustrate how inequality plays out with respect to social identity and social networks. Our dialogues probe how social capital can be generated on the basis of our awareness of our social identity and the connections that we have across race, gender, class, and other differences. Our dialogues also remind us that social capital is not an end unto itself, but something to nurture as we build our networks cross-culturally so that the work world becomes a place of learning, connection, and, dare we say it, sisterhood.

APPENDIX 10.1: MAPPING YOUR CAREER NETWORK

On the wheel below, identify the people in your career network. Indicate whether the relationship is close, moderate, or distant by how far from the center you place the person's name.

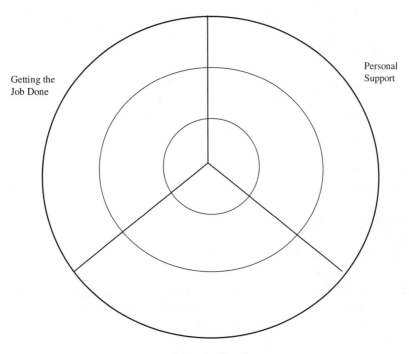

Advancing Your Career

REFLECTION QUESTIONS

1. What was your reaction to your network once you had mapped it out? How did it change over time?
2. How intentional are you about building your network? What strategies do you use to build your network? How do you access new networks? What are the benefits and/or potential costs of your strategies?
3. How "diverse" is your network? What has contributed to the composition of your network? What do we mean by diverse? What is your definition of diversity?
4. How do you view your network—as separate elements (career, family, personal) or integrated (one not discernable from the other)? Do you see sharp differences or similarities between the two groups?

REFERENCES

American Bar Association. (2006). Executive summary. In *Visible invisibility: Women of color in law firms*. Chicago: American Bar Association Commission on Women in the Profession. Retrieved November 10, 2006, from http://www.abanet.org/women/VisibleInvisibility-ExecSummary.pdf

Bell, E. L., Denton, T. C., & Nkomo, S. (1993). Women of color in management: Towards an inclusive analysis. In E. A. Fagenson (Ed.), *Women in management: Trends, issues, and challenges in managerial diversity* (pp. 105–130). Newbury Park, CA: Sage.

Bell, E. L., Meyerson, D., Nkomo, S., & Scully, M. (2003). Interpreting silence and voice in the workplace: A conversation about tempered radicalism among Black and White women researchers. *Journal of Applied Behavioral Science, 39,* 381–414.

Betters-Reed, B. L., & Moore, L. L. (1995). Shifting the management development paradigm for women. *Journal of Management Development, 14,* 24–38.

Blake, S. (1999). At the crossroads of race and gender: Lessons from the mentoring experiences of professional Black women. In A. J. Murrell, F. J. Crosby, & R. J. Ely (Eds.), *Mentoring dilemmas: Developmental relationships within multicultural organizations* (pp. 83–104). Mahwah, NJ: Erlbaum.

Blake-Beard, S. (2001). *Mentoring relationships through the lens of race and gender* (CGO Briefing Note No. 10). Boston: Center for Gender in Organizations, Simmons School of Management.

Blake-Beard, S., Murrell, A., & Thomas, D. (2006). *Unfinished business: The impact of race on understanding mentoring relationships* [Working paper]. Retrieved February 9, 2007, from http://hbswk.hbs.edu/item/5499.html

Blake-Beard, S., & Roberts, L. M. (2004). *Releasing the double bind of visibility for minorities in the workplace* (CGO Commentaries No. 4). Boston: Center for Gender in Organizations, Simmons School of Management.

Blake-Beard, S., Scully, M., Turnball, S., Hunt, L., Proudford, K., Porter, J., et al. (2006). The ties that bind and separate Black and White women. In M. F. Karsten (Ed.), *Gender, race and ethnicity in the workplace* (Vol. 1, pp. 177–204). Westport, CT: Praeger Publishers.

Bova, B. M. (1998). *Mentoring revisited: The African-American woman's experience.* Retrieved July 21, 2008, from http://www.edst.educ.ubc.ca/aerc/1998/98bova.htm

Browne, I., & Askew, R. (2006). Latinas at work: Issues of gender, ethnicity, and class. In M. F. Karsten (Ed.), *Gender, race and ethnicity in the workplace* (Vol. 1, pp. 223–251). Westport, CT: Praeger Publishers.

Burke, R. J., Rothstein, M. G, & Bristor, J. M. (1995). Interpersonal networks of managerial and professional women. *Women in Management Review, 10,* 21–28.

Catalyst. (1999). *Women of color in corporate management: Opportunities and barriers.* New York: Author.

Catalyst. (2003). *Women of color in corporate management: Three years later.* New York: Author.

Catalyst. (2004). *The bottom line: Connecting corporate performance and gender diversity*. New York: Author.

Catalyst. (2006a). *2005 Catalyst census of women board directors of the Fortune 500*. Retrieved November 10, 2006, from http://www.catalyst.org/files/full/2005%20WBD.pdf

Catalyst. (2006b). *Connections that count: The informal networks of women of color in the United States*. New York: Author.

Coll, C. G., Cook-Nobles, R., & Surrey, J. L. (1997). Building connection through diversity. In J. V. Jordan (Ed.), *Women's growth in diversity: More writings from the Stone Center* (pp. 176–198). New York: Guilford Press.

Combahee River Collective. (1983). The Combahee River Collective statement. In B. Smith (Ed.), *Home girls: A Black feminist anthology* (pp. 264–274). New Brunswick, NJ: Rutgers University Press.

Combs, G. M. (2003). The duality of race and gender for managerial African American women: Implications of informal social networks on career advancement. *Human Resource Development Review, 2*, 385–405.

Crenshew, K. (1989). Demarginalizing the intersection of race and sex: A Black feminist critique of antidiscrimination doctrine, feminist theory and antiracist politics. *University of Chicago Legal Forum*, 139–167.

Davis, A. Y. (1981). *Women, race & class*. New York: Vintage Books.

Earley, P. C., & Mosakowski, E. (2004, October). Cultural intelligence. *Harvard Business Review*, 139–146.

Ely, R., Meyerson, D. E., & Davidson, M. N. (2006). Rethinking political correctness. *Harvard Business Review, 84*, 78–87.

Frankenberg, R. (1993). *White women, race matters: The social construction of Whiteness*. Minneapolis: University of Minnesota Press.

Harrison, D. A., Price, K. A., & Bell, M. P. (1998). Beyond relational demography: Time and the effects of surface- and deep-level diversity on work group cohesion. *Academy of Management Journal, 41*, 96–107.

Hertz, R. (1997). *Reflexivity and voice*. Thousand Oaks, CA: Sage.

Higgins, M. C., & Kram, K. (2001). Reconceptualizing mentoring at work: A developmental network perspective. *Academy of Management Review, 26*, 264–288.

Higgins, M. C., & Thomas, D. A. (2001). Constellations and careers: Toward understanding the effects of multiple developmental relationships. *Journal of Organizational Behavior, 22*, 223–247.

Hill Collins, P. (1999). Reflections on the outsider within. *Journal of Career Development, 26*, 85–88.

Hogg, M. A., & Terry, D. J. (2000). Social identity and self-categorization processes in organizational contexts. *Academy of Management Review, 25*, 121–140.

Holvino, E. (2001). *Complicating gender: The simultaneity of race, gender, and class in organization change(ing)* (CGO Working Paper No. 14). Boston: Center for Gender in Organizations, Simmons School of Management.

Holvino, E. (2006). *"Tired of choosing:" Working with the simultaneity of race, gender, and class in organizations* (CGO Briefing Note No. 24). Boston: Center for Gender in Organizations, Simmons School of Management.

hooks, b. (1981). *Ain't I a woman: Black women and feminism*. Boston: South End Press.

hooks, b. (1984). *Feminist theory: From margin to center*. Boston: South End Press.

hooks, b. (1994). *Teaching to transgress: Education as the practice of freedom*. New York: Routledge.

Hurley, R. F. (2006). The decision to trust. *Harvard Business Review, 84*, 55–62.

Hyun, J. (2005). *Breaking the bamboo ceiling*. New York: HarperCollins.

Ibarra, H. (1993). Personal networks of women and minorities in management: A conceptual framework. *Academy of Management Review, 18*, 56–87.

Ibarra, H. (1995). Race, opportunity, and diversity of social circles in managerial networks. *Academy of Management Journal, 38*, 673–704.

Ibarra, H., Kilduff, M., & Tsai, W. (2005). Zooming in and out: Connecting individuals and collectivities at the frontiers of organizational network research. *Organizational Science, 16*, 359–371.

Jehn, K. A., Northcraft, G. B., & Neale, M. A. (1999). Why differences make a difference: A field study of diversity, conflict, and performance in workgroups. *Administrative Science Quarterly, 44*, 741–763.

Kanter, R. M. (1977). *Men and women of the corporation*. New York: Basic Books.

Kram, K. E. (1985). *Mentoring at work: Developmental relationships in organizational life*. Glenview, IL: Scott, Foresman.

Kristiansen, S. (2004). Social networks and business success. *American Journal of Economics and Sociology, 63*, 1149–1171.

Langer, E. J. (1990). *Mindfulness*. Reading, MA: Addison Wesley.

Lin, N. (1999). Building a theory of social capital. *Connection, 22*, 28–51.

Martinez, E. (1998). Seeing more than Black & White: Latino, racism and the cultural divides. In M. L. Andersen & P. Hill Collins (Eds.), *Race, class and gender: An anthology* (pp. 112–119). Belmont, CA: Wadsworth.

McKnight, D. H., Cummings, L. L., & Chervany, N. L. (1998). Initial trust formation in new organizational relationships. *Academy of Management Review, 23*, 473–490.

Miller, J. B. (1976). *Toward a new psychology of women*. Boston: Beacon Press.

Murrell, A. J., & Zagenczyk, T. J. (2006). Gender, race, and role model status: Exploring the impact of informal developmental relationships on management careers. In M. F. Karsten (Ed.), *Gender, race and ethnicity in the workplace* (Vol. 3, pp. 117–130). Westport, CT: Praeger Publishers.

Neilsen, J. M. (1990). *Feminist research methods: Exemplary readings in the social sciences*. San Francisco: Westview Press.

Pini, B., Brown, K., & Ryan, C. (2004). Women-only networks as a strategy for change? A case study from local government. *Women in Management Review, 19*, 286–292.

Ragins, B. R. (1997). Diversified mentoring relationships in organizations: A power perspective. *Academy of Management Review, 22*, 482–521.

Ragins, B. R., & Verbos, A. K. (2007). Positive relationships in action: Relational mentoring and mentoring schemas in the workplace. In J. E. Dutton & B. R. Ragins (Eds.), *Exploring positive relationships at work: Building a theoretical and research foundation* (pp. 91–116). Mahwah, NJ: Erlbaum.

Reinharz, S. (1992). *Feminist methods in social research*. New York: Oxford University Press.

Roberts, L. M. (2005). Changing faces: Professional image construction in diverse organizational settings. *Academy of Management Review, 30*, 685–711.

Scully, M. A. (2000). Manage your own employability: Meritocracy and the legitimation of inequality in internal labor markets and beyond. In C. Leana & D. Rousseau (Eds.), *Relational wealth: The advantages of stability in a changing economy* (pp. 199–216). New York: Oxford University Press.

Sheridan, B., Holvino, E., & Debebe, D. (2004). *Beyond diversity: Working across differences for organizational change*. Boston: Center for Gender in Organizations, Simmons School of Management.

Smith, B. (1998). *The truth that never hurts: Writings on race, gender and freedom*. New Brunswick, NJ: Rutgers University Press.

Tajfel, H. (1972). La catégorisation sociale. In S. Moscovici (Ed.), *Introduction a la psychologie sociale* (Vol. 1, pp. 272–302). Paris: Larousse.

Thomas, D. A. (1989). Mentoring and irrationality: The role of racial taboos. *Human Resource Management, 28*, 279–290.

Thomas, D. A. (1990). The impact of race on managers' experiences of developmental relationships (mentoring and sponsorship): An intra-organizational study. *Journal of Organization Behavior, 11*, 479–492.

Thomas, D. C., & Inkson, K. (2003). *Cultural intelligence: People skills for global business*. San Francisco: Berrett-Koehler.

Thompson, B. (2001). *A promise and a way of life: White antiracist activism*. Minneapolis: University of Minnesota Press.

Travers, C., Stevens, S., & Pemberton, C. (1997). Women's networking across boundaries: Recognizing different cultural agendas. *Women in Management Review, 12*, 61–67.

Walker, M. (2007). *What's so bad about being nice? . . . And other paradoxes in relational leadership*. Boston: Jean Baker Miller Spring Institute, Wellesley College.

Wheatley, M. J. (2005). *Finding our way: Leadership for an uncertain time*. San Francisco: Berrett-Koehler.

Women Lawyers of Color. (2006). New data show barriers to success. *Law Office Management & Administration Report, 10*, 8–9.

11

INCREASING THE REPRESENTATION AND STATUS OF WOMEN IN EMPLOYMENT: THE EFFECTIVENESS OF AFFIRMATIVE ACTION

AARTI IYER

Women around the world occupy a structurally disadvantaged position relative to men (Molyneux & Razavi, 2002). This systemic inequality is reflected—and perpetuated—in specific social contexts and institutions within society, including employment organizations. For instance, women are underrepresented in professional jobs (particularly at higher levels of management) in the United States (Agars, 2004), Great Britain (Equal Opportunities Commission, 2006a), Canada (Harvey & Blakely, 1993), and Australia (Office of the Status of Women, 2003). Although the gender wage gap has improved markedly over the past 20 years, women still earn between 65% and 75% of men's wages for equivalent work in the United States (Darity & Mason, 1998), Canada (Blau & Kahn, 1996), Great Britain and Europe (Blau & Kahn, 1996; Equal Opportunities Commission, 2006a), and Australia (French, 2001).

Empirical research suggests that gender inequality in the workplace can be (at least partly) explained by organizational policies and practices that discriminate against women (see also chaps. 1, 2, 7, and 9, this volume). For instance, negative stereotypes about female employees have been documented in the United States (DeArmond et al., 2006), Canada (Hadley, 2001), Great Britain and the European Union (Collins & Wickham, 2002), and Australia (Wallace, 2001). Also, research shows that female employees tend to be offered

257

fewer opportunities for training and advancement (compared with their male counterparts) in the United States (Blau & DeVaro, 2006), Canada (Hadley, 2001), Great Britain and Europe (Collins & Wickham, 2002), and Australia (Wallace, 2001).

Systemic efforts to reduce gender inequality in employment have sought to change organizational policies and practices that pose obstacles to the advancement of women. Such affirmative action (AA) programs have been implemented in various countries to increase the representation and status of female employees (see chap. 9, this volume, for another type of policy with a similar aim). AA is a controversial policy whose rationale and effectiveness have been called into question over the years (see Crosby & VanDeVeer, 2000). Social scientists (including economists, psychologists, and sociologists) have much to contribute to these debates, as they can offer theoretical frameworks and empirical data regarding the need for AA in employment (for a review, see Crosby, Iyer, Clayton, & Downing, 2003), the bases of individuals' support or opposition to the policy (for a review, see Harrison, Kravitz, Mayer, Leslie, & Lev-Arev, 2006), and the (positive and negative) consequences of AA.

The aim of this chapter is to evaluate the effectiveness of AA programs in moving organizations toward gender equality. In addressing this question, it is important to document whether AA has achieved its aims of increasing the representation and status of female employees. Other dimensions critical to this assessment include the costs that AA programs incur, and any additional social or psychological consequences of AA.

The chapter begins with an overview of AA programs and their implementation in various countries. In the second section I review evidence for four specific consequences of gender-based AA. In the final section I evaluate the overall effect of AA in the effort to achieve gender equality and offer recommendations for improving its effectiveness.

WHAT IS AFFIRMATIVE ACTION?

In this section I first outline the general goals of AA programs and the range of policies and practices they may include. I then review AA legislation in four countries: the United States, Canada, Australia, and Great Britain. Last, I describe voluntary AA that is undertaken by organizations.

Policies and Practices

AA programs in employment have two general aims. First, they seek to systematically combat past and present discrimination in an organization. Second, they implement strategies to improve the status of disadvantaged target groups, such as women (Kravitz et al., 1997). AA differs from the policy of (passive) equal opportunity, which seeks to achieve a system that gives each individual the same treatment as any other individual. Equal opportunity policies assume that fairness is achieved once intentional discrimination (e.g., on the basis of gender) is expressly prohibited. In contrast, AA assumes that good intentions on the part of employers and managers are not sufficient to ensure fair, nondiscriminatory treatment. Structural obstacles and subtle discrimination contribute to a system of inequality that is not easily recognized or changed (see Crosby et al., 2003). As such, AA implements concrete measures to actively monitor and change organizational policies and practices, both to ensure that bias is eliminated and to increase the representation and status of target groups.

Organizations with gender-based AA typically introduce a monitoring program to assess whether equal opportunity exists for qualified female workers. In the first step, the organization assesses the proportion of jobs and promotions granted to women. It then compares this number with the proportion of women in the workforce who have the requisite qualifications and experience for the position. If a discrepancy is found between these two proportions, the organization seeks to identify and eliminate policies and practices that discriminate against women (to ensure equal opportunity). It also introduces proactive strategies to increase the representation of women within its ranks.

One AA strategy focuses on increasing the number of women who apply for jobs and promotions. Organizations might formalize advertising procedures for every new hire and promotion, thus ensuring wider knowledge about available positions. Use of this strategy helps increase opportunities for women who might otherwise be shut out of the informal "old boys' networks" that typically distribute such information. In a similar way, organizations might expand recruitment efforts to reach beyond traditional sources of potential employees. For instance, they may attend job fairs at women's colleges as well as at coeducational institutions.

A second gender-based AA strategy offers female employees training programs to help develop the skills and knowledge to compete for jobs and promotions. Such programs are common in occupations and trades in which women are outnumbered by men (Reskin, 1998; Robinson, Seydel, & Douglass, 1998). A final AA strategy involves active adjustment of selection criteria for employment and promotion decisions. In such cases, a mix of demographic and merit factors is used to make selection decisions. However, as described in the following section, the use of hard quotas or reservations is prohibited in several countries that have implemented gender-based AA. In other words, it is often illegal for organizations to set aside a percentage of positions for female candidates, or to hire (or promote) employees solely on the basis of gender (Reskin, 1998).

Affirmative Action Legislation

United States

AA in the United States was established in 1965 with President Johnson's Executive Order (EO) 11246, which required federal contractors to ensure that hiring and promotion decisions were made without regard to applicants' race, creed, color, or national origin. In 1967, Johnson expanded the EO to include AA requirements to benefit women (Bruno, 1998). As presently administered by the Office of Federal Contract Compliance Programs, EO 11246 requires the federal government, as well as organizations with federal contracts (in excess of US$50,000) and 50 or more employees, to implement AA to prevent discrimination in their policies and practices (Dale, 2005).

As outlined in Table 11.1, firms that are federally mandated to implement AA must first conduct a self-audit to determine whether their employment of women is consistent with the availability of qualified women in the labor market. The organization must then develop an AA plan to eliminate any disparity found between these two proportions (Anderson, 1996). The AA plan should include hiring goals and timetables to which the contractor must commit its "good faith" efforts (Dale, 2005). However, the plans may not include strict quotas or strong preferential treatment (e.g., keeping separate lists of applicants based on group membership), which have been prohibited by various Supreme Court decisions (see Spann, 2000).

Enforcement of EO 11246 falls under the purview of the Equal Employment Opportunities Commission (EEOC), which was established by the Civil Rights Act of 1964 (although the EEOC did not gain enforcement of the gender discrimination provisions until 1973). Findings of noncompliance with federally mandated AA typically result in monetary fines. However, the emphasis placed on enforcement (e.g., by conducting periodic audits) has varied widely over the past 3 decades, on the basis of the contemporaneous political climate. For instance, enforcement of AA was truncated during the 1980s under Presidents Ronald Reagan and George H. W. Bush (Anderson, 1996). The inauguration of President Bill Clinton in 1993 saw increased resources in the EEOC devoted to enforcement of AA, but priorities have since shifted away from enforcement under President George W. Bush's administration (Dale, 2005).

Organizations not subject to EO 11246 may also be mandated to implement AA. The 1972 Equal Employment Opportunity Act (an amendment to the 1964 Civil Rights Act) empowered federal courts to require organizations to implement AA strategies when they are found guilty of discrimination. Such court-ordered programs constitute the exceptional cases in which quotas may be used to redress discrimination (Reskin, 1998).

TABLE 11.1

Summary of Federally Mandated Affirmative Action in the United States, Canada, Australia, and Great Britain

Country	Legislation	Program requirements	Prohibitions
United States	Executive Order 11246 (1965, amended in 1967)	(1) Calculate current workforce profile to determine whether qualified workers from target groups are adequately represented in organization. (2) If discrepancy exists between representation of target group in workforce and in applicant pool, take steps to eliminate discriminatory policies and develop proactive measures to increase representation.	(1) no quotas or set-asides
Canada	Employment Equity Act (1986, 1995)	(1) Develop organizational commitment and structure for program. (2) Consult and collaborate with employee representatives. (3) Conduct workforce survey to count the number of employees from designated target groups. (4) Undertake workforce analysis to compare the representation of designated group members with their representation in appropriate segments of Canadian workforce. (5) Examine all human resources policies and practices to determine if barriers to full employment of designated groups exist. (6) Develop and implement positive policies and practices to accelerate integration of designated group members and the elimination of employment barriers. (7) Monitor implementation of program.	(1) no quotas or set-asides (2) no requirement to hire unqualified individuals
Australia	Equal Opportunity for Women in the Workplace Act (1999)	(1) Complete workplace profile (employment patterns, salaries). (2) Analyze issues for women in the workplace. (3) Prioritize issues for action. (4) Implement program. (5) Evaluate effectiveness of program.	(1) no quotas or set-asides
Great Britain	Gender Equality Duty (2007)	(1) Gather information on the effect of policies and practices on men and women in employment. (2) Assess the impact of its current and future policies and practices on gender equality. (3) Consult relevant employees. (4) Take steps to implement scheme objectives. (5) Review and revise scheme at least every 3 years.	

Canada

The Canadian federal government's equal employment policy consists of two programs. Under the Federal Contractors Program (1986), organizations who have secured a federal goods or services contract of at least $200,000 and who employ at least 100 individuals are required to sign a certificate of commitment to implement employment equity in their workplace (Harvey & Blakely, 1993). The Employment Equity Act (1986; amended in 1995) directs employment organizations to (a) correct disadvantages in the workplace experienced by members of underrepresented target groups (e.g., women) and (b) implement special measures and accommodation of differences where needed. Organizations subject to the Act include all federally regulated employers with 100 or more employees; all private sector employers and Crown corporations; all federal departments; and other parts of the Public Service, such as the Royal Canadian Mounted Police (Department of Justice Canada, 2006).

As shown in Table 11.1, the Employment Equity Act requires employers to implement a monitoring program to identify underrepresentation of women in the organization (Steps 3–5) and to eliminate employment barriers and accelerate the integration of female employees by implementing positive policies and practices (Step 6). Organizations are required to provide a timetable for implementation, as well as short-term and longer term numerical goals. However, they are prohibited from imposing direct quotas (Human Resources Development Canada, 2006a).

The Canadian legislation also requires additional action to ensure the effective implementation of AA. Organizations are to make concerted efforts to develop an organizational commitment and structure for the AA program, and to consult with employee representatives about the program (Steps 1 and 2). In addition, organizations are required to monitor the implementation of their AA plan (Step 7) to ensure that sufficient progress is being made (Human Resources Development Canada, 2006a).

All federally regulated employers are required to report annually to the Labour Program of the Department of Human Resources and Skills Development Canada on their progress in achieving a representative workforce. In addition, the Canadian Human Rights Commission conducts periodic audits of both private and public sector employers to ensure compliance. Findings of noncompliance result in the Minister of Labour issuing a monetary penalty (Human Resources Development Canada, 2006b).

Australia

The Equal Opportunity for Women in the Workplace Act 1999 (which replaced the Affirmative Action [Equal Employment Opportunity for Women] Act 1986) requires all private sector companies, community organizations, nongovernmental schools, unions, and higher education institutions with 100 or more people to "establish a workplace program to remove the barriers to women entering and advancing in their organization" (Equal Opportunity for Women in the Workplace Agency, 2006). As shown in Table 11.1, organizations must develop a workplace profile that clearly shows where women are employed and what they earn. The next steps are to identify specific obstacles for women in the workplace and to prioritize them for action. The legislation encourages organizations to consult with employee representatives and other experts in this process. Finally, organizations are expected to implement the proposed plans and to conduct periodic evaluations to ensure continued success (Equal Opportunity for Women in the Workplace Agency, 2000).

Organizations subject to the Act are required to report annually to the Equal Opportunity for Women in the Workplace Agency on their equal opportunity program and its effectiveness (Equal Opportunity for Women in the Workplace Agency, 2000, 2006). The government announced in 2006 that reporting will become biennial for organizations who have complied with the Act for 3 consecutive years, although this change was not implemented for the 2007 reporting period (Equal Opportunity for Women in the Workplace Agency, 2006). If an organization fails to submit a report, it will be identified as noncompliant by the Agency (Office of Legislative Drafting, 2004).

Great Britain

Since the introduction of the Equal Pay Act (1970) and the Sex Discrimination Act (1975), federal legislation in Great Britain has concentrated primarily on outlawing gender discrimination (i.e., equal opportunity policies) rather than implementing AA as a proactive measure to increase the representation and status of female employees (Teles, 1998). The Equal Opportunities Commission (EOC) was originally charged with enforcing these Acts by identifying and correcting gender discrimination in British organizations (Equal Opportunities Commission, 2006b).

The EOC concluded that systemic discrimination against women is still rampant in the United Kingdom because there is no onus on organizations to change their culture and structures to actively promote gender equality (Equal Opportunities Commission, 2006a, 2006b). As such, the Equality Act 2006 seeks to "prohibit sex discrimination and harassment in the exercise of public functions" and to "create a duty . . . to promote equality of opportunity between women and men" (Great Britain, 2006a). The Act applies to all public authorities (e.g., government departments) and to any person or organization with functions of a public nature, such as a private security firm contracted to provide a public function (Great Britain, 2006b).

The Gender Equality Duty to promote equality of opportunity between women and men came into effect in April 2007. This program asks organizations subject to the Equality Act to prepare and publish a Gender Equality Scheme showing how they intend to fulfill the general and specific gender equality objectives (Equal Opportunities Commission, 2006b, 2006c). As shown in Table 11.1, organizations preparing the schemes are asked to assess the effects of their policies and practices on gender equality and to implement the scheme objectives (Equal Opportunities Commission, 2006c). As in Canada, organizations are also required to consult with employees and their representatives about the scheme (Step 3). The Duty is enforced by the Commission for Equality and Human Rights, which was established by the Equality Act 2006 (Great Britain 2006a, 2006b). The penalties for noncompliance had not been publicized at the time this chapter was written.

Voluntary Affirmative Action

Multinational companies such as Xerox, American Express, Pepsi-Cola International, and Lucent Technologies have recognized the positive contributions that diverse workforces make to their overall productivity and performance (Combs, Nadkarni, & Combs, 2005; Jackson, 1992). As a result, many employers around the world implement some form of AA even when they are not required to by legislation or court order. Such voluntary AA programs can include any of the legal strategies outlined in the previous section (Reskin, 1998).

THE EFFECTS OF AFFIRMATIVE ACTION

Empirical research on the consequences of AA in employment has been conducted in various social scientific disciplines and thus encompasses a range of empirical frameworks and methodologies. Some researchers test their hypotheses with data collected (in some form) from organizations. These studies include analyses of organizational reports and records, interviews or surveys of human resource personnel, and surveys of employees. Other researchers have taken an experimental approach, manipulating key variables to examine their effects on individuals' responses. For example, participants might be asked to evaluate an employee, whose group membership in the majority group (e.g., men) or the AA target group (e.g., women) is varied between conditions. Experimental studies are typically (although not always) conducted with university (undergraduate or postgraduate) student samples.

Social scientists have documented the consequences of gender-based AA in four specific dimensions of employment: (a) representation of women in organizations, (b) organizational productivity and efficiency, (c) self-views and self-confidence of (presumed) beneficiaries, and (d) perceptions of (presumed) beneficiaries.

Representation of Women in Organizations

The past 30 years have seen women take great strides toward equality in the workplace. The representation of women in the workforce has increased since the 1970s in the United States (Szafran, 2002), Canada (O'Donnell et al., 2006), Great Britain (Equal Opportunities Commission, 2006a), and Australia (Office of the Status of Women, 2003). Various factors have contributed to this increased employment opportunity. For one, increasingly liberal attitudes have resulted in greater expectations that women can be financially independent. Improved access to higher education has also increased the number of women qualified to hold professional jobs (see Molyneux & Razavi, 2002).

Systemic efforts to dismantle gender discrimination in the workplace have also played a key role in increasing the representation of women in employment. Organizations that implement AA (either voluntarily or by legal mandate) tend to have higher proportions of female employees relative to organizations without AA or with equal opportunity (antidiscrimination) programs. For instance, an analysis of employment records in 1,000 American organizations (between 1974 and 1980) showed that female employment increased at a faster rate at the organizations with AA, relative to comparable establishments without AA (Leonard, 1984a). Another study found that AA litigation significantly increased the proportion of female officers hired by municipal police departments between 1981 and 1991 in the United States (Sass & Troyer, 1999).

In a more recent study, Konrad and Linnehan (1995) surveyed 350 employers in a range of occupations (e.g., manufacturing, financial services, retail or wholesale trade) in the Philadelphia (U.S.) metropolitan area. Their analysis compared the proportion of female employees in organizations with identity-conscious (AA) human resource management (HRM) structures and organizations with identity-blind (equal opportunity) HRM structures. Results showed that identity-conscious HRM structures were associated with higher proportions of female employees in the organization as well as greater representation of women in management positions. Studies of 3,200 companies in four American metropolitan areas (Atlanta, Boston, Detroit, and Los Angeles) similarly found that organizations with AA hired more women than did organizations without AA (Holzer & Neumark, 1996, 2000a). Another study showed that organizations with AA used a greater variety of recruitment sources and scrutinized their applicants more closely than did employers without AA (Holzer & Neumark, 2000b).

The positive effect of AA has been demonstrated in other countries as well. Research in Canada has shown that organizations subject to the Employment Equity Act have hired greater proportions of female employees (Leck & Saunders, 1992) and have increased female employees' access to better-paying jobs, thus closing the wage gap more rapidly (Leck, St. Onge, & Lalancette, 1995). And in an analysis of employment reports from 1,976 Australian employers, French (2001) found that organizations with AA had a significantly higher number (and proportion) of female managers than did those with equal opportunity (antidiscrimination) programs.

The Importance of Enforcement

Although the finding that AA increases the representation of women in organizations is quite robust, it is important to note that AA programs work only to the extent that they are implemented comprehensively and effectively. Because AA is a controversial policy, it is likely that (at least some) employees will oppose their organization's efforts to introduce it. Such opposition can prevent AA from being implemented properly, especially if those opposed hold positions of power in the organization. For example, a study of three Arizona (U.S.) police departments showed that police captains' opposition to AA hindered the effective implementation of an AA program in hiring, promoting, and retaining female police officers (Allen, 2003).

In addition, AA requires changes in policy and practice that may be difficult to sustain over time, even for employers and managers who are generally supportive of the program. Indeed, research has demonstrated that AA programs have been less successful when they lack formal oversight mechanisms to ensure consistent implementation. Federally mandated AA in the United States had a negligible effect on the representation of female employees during the 1980s, when enforcement was not a priority for the EEOC (Leonard, 1989). Other studies have shown that American (Naff, 1998) and Canadian (Leck & Saunders, 1992) organizations with poorly enforced AA programs hire fewer female employees than do organizations with better-enforced AA. Taken together, these results suggest that AA programs will not succeed on the basis of principle and intentions alone—they require oversight and enforcement to hold organizations accountable to their stated goals and plan to achieve gender equality.

Productivity and Efficiency of Organizations

Critics of AA often contend that the policy limits organizations' ability to conduct their business effectively and efficiently. However, little evidence supports this claim. Research from the United States has demonstrated that AA programs do not impede organizations' efforts to hire well-qualified, high-performing employees. In a representative sample of 3,200 employers in four major metropolitan areas, Holzer and Neumark (1996) found that female AA hires were as qualified for their jobs (in terms of education and skill requirements) as were their male counterparts. The analyses also found no evidence of substantially weaker job performance among female AA hires, compared with all other groups of employees. A review of economic research also found "virtually no evidence of weaker educational qualifications or job performance among females who benefit from AA relative to males, especially within occupational grade" (Holzer & Neumark, 2000b, p. 483).

Research from the United States has also shown that AA programs do not hamper organizations' productivity or performance levels. An analysis of cross-sectional time-series data for police departments in major U.S. cities (collected in 1987, 1990, 1993) found that hiring more female police officers did not produce an increase in unsolved crimes (Lott, 2000). Another study of 24 manufacturing companies with AA programs between 1966 and 1978 showed that the percentage of female employment increased from 25% to 31%. Over this 12-year period, there was no evidence that female productivity was lower relative to that of White men. In other words, no significant efficiency cost was associated with AA (Leonard, 1984b).

Self-Views and Self-Confidence of (Presumed) Beneficiaries

Some women (e.g., Kimura, 1997) have argued that AA and other preferential treatment are stigmatizing for (presumed) beneficiaries. They posit that such institutional solutions foster the impression that disadvantaged groups cannot succeed on their own merit. For instance, when women learn that they may have benefited from gender-based AA in their organization, they may wonder whether they truly deserve their position, or whether the gain was simply due to the preferential treatment.

This attributional ambiguity (see Major, Feinstein, & Crocker, 1994) associated with AA can result in a number of negative psychological and social implications that may hurt women's experiences and outcomes in employment (see also chap. 5, this volume). First, women may question their competence to perform tasks associated with their job. Second, this self-doubt may result in self-handicapping behavior, whereby women shy away from more challenging (and potentially more rewarding) tasks and goals. Third, women's actual task performance may suffer. And fourth, women may experience a higher level of stress and lower well-being. The empirical evidence for each claim is reviewed in the next sections.

Self-Evaluations of Competence

One line of research has used laboratory experiments (with university student participants) to assess the effect of gender-based preferential treatment (AA) on self-evaluations of competence and ability. The most commonly used methodology was developed by Heilman, Simon, and Repper (1987), who placed participants in a group task setting and applied meaningful selection procedures to select a group leader. At the beginning of the session, male and female undergraduate students completed an assessment test and were then ostensibly placed in mixed-gender groups to complete a task. The participant was always selected to be the leader of the task group, and was told that this decision was based either solely on merit (his or her performance on the assessment test) or solely on gender (regardless of score) because the experiment did not include equal numbers of male and female participants. A questionnaire then assessed self-evaluations and desire to remain a leader. The gender-only condition is meant to represent preferential treatment in AA, although this operationalization has been criticized for reflecting an extreme form of AA that is illegal and rarely used (Taylor, 1994).

The original study (Heilman et al., 1987) found that women selected solely on the basis of gender reported more negative perceptions of their own leadership ability and reported a lower desire to persist in the leadership position, compared with women selected solely on the basis of merit. In contrast, this pattern of results was not found for men; the selection criteria made no difference in men's perceptions of their own leadership ability or their desire to persist in the leadership position. This finding has been replicated in other studies using similar experimental paradigms (Heilman, Lucas, & Kaplow, 1990; Heilman, Rivero, & Brett, 1991). Taken together, these results suggest that gender-only preferential treatment has an adverse effect on women's self-views.

The aforementioned research compared the effects of only two selection criteria: gender-only and merit-only. However, many AA strategies can be found in between these two extremes. Thus, Heilman, Battle, Keller, and Lee (1998) compared the effect of five different selection procedures on women's perceptions of their own leadership ability (following the same experimental paradigm as did Heilman et al., 1987): merit only, and one of four possible AA scenarios (preferential ambiguous [gender had unspecified effect on selection process], preferential absolute [woman selected regardless of qualifications], preferential minimum standard [woman selected if her qualifications exceeded the minimum threshold for the position], or preferential equivalent [woman chosen if qualifications were the same as those of the male candidate]). Results showed women to evaluate their own leadership abilities most positively in two conditions: merit only and preferential equivalent. In the remaining preferential treatment conditions, women evaluated their leadership abilities more negatively. Thus, AA strategies that seemed to prioritize gender over merit were most detrimental to women's self-views.

Other experimental studies (using the same paradigm) have not consistently replicated the finding that selection procedure affects women's self-evaluations. Rather, this effect appears to be influenced by (false) feedback about task ability and performance, which is provided to participants before the manipulation of selection procedure. Heilman, Lucas, and Kaplow (1990) found that when women were provided with positive information on task-related ability, their self-perceptions did not differ between the merit-only and gender-only selection conditions. Heilman and Alcott (2001) similarly demonstrated the effect of selection procedure on self-competence ratings only when participants were not given information about their task ability. When women were given (false) feedback about their high task ability, selection procedure did not influence their self-competence ratings. Thus, when women believed they had performed well, the procedure by which they had been selected (gender or merit) did not change their self-evaluations.

Laboratory research on the effects of AA has been criticized on two grounds. First, the operationalization of preferential selection typically does not reflect the legal practice of AA in the workplace. Second, the university students in these samples tend to have very little work experience and thus may respond quite differently than would people who work full-time (see Taylor, 1994). An alternative approach to assessing the effects of AA is to compare employees in organizations that do or do not implement it. Taylor (1994) analyzed responses from the 1990 General Social Survey in the United States, which asked individuals whether their organization implemented any AA or equal opportunity program. Analyses showed no detrimental social psychological consequences of AA, as women in all types of organizations reported the same levels of job satisfaction, work ambition, and psychological well-being. In addition, almost 90% of employed African American and European American women surveyed in a 1995 Gallup Poll indicated that others did not question their abilities because of AA (see Plous, 1996).

At first glance, the results from survey research in the United States appear to be inconsistent with the findings from the experimental studies: The surveys indicate that employed women do not feel stigmatized by AA in their organizations, whereas the lab experiments suggest that the female undergraduates do experience self-doubt. One explanation for these different results may lie in the moderating factor demonstrated in some experimental studies: Women who were provided with positive feedback about their task ability did not report more negative self-evaluations. Employees receive periodic performance evaluations that are generally likely to contain (at least some) positive feedback. Such feedback may explain why the surveyed female employees feel less stigmatized by any (apparent or real) association with AA, compared with the students participating in the laboratory experiments. Future work should directly investigate this process in an organizational context.

Task Selection

Empirical research has considered whether AA and other preferential treatment influences women's choice to undertake harder or easier tasks. In one study (Heilman et al., 1991), male and female undergraduate students were assigned a managerial role in a task group on the basis of merit only, or gender only, following the procedure of Heilman et al. (1987). They were then told to choose from two tasks, one of which was more demanding. On average, women in the gender-only condition chose the less demanding task whereas women in the merit-only condition chose the more demanding task. The selection criteria made no difference to the male participants' choice of task. Thus, extreme AA based solely on gender led women to select less challenging tasks.

The effect of extreme preferential treatment on task selection appears to be moderated by individuals' beliefs about their task ability. Heilman and Alcott (2001, Study 2) provided participants with (false) feedback about task ability before they had been informed of the selection procedure that was used to select them for the leadership position. Results showed that women who were given no information about their task ability chose more challenging tasks in the merit-only condition, relative to the gender-only condition. In contrast, women who were told of their high task ability showed a general tendency to choose more challenging tasks, regardless of the selection procedure (gender-only or merit-only) used to appoint them to the leadership position.

Task Performance

In examining the effect of preferential treatment on actual task performance, various studies have followed Heilman et al.'s (1987) experimental paradigm. Heilman and Alcott (2001, Study 1) showed that women performed worse on a leadership task when they believed they were given a leadership position solely on the basis of gender, rather than solely on merit.

Another study (Brown, Charnasangavej, Keough, Newman, & Rentfrow, 2000) gave female participants one of three explanations for being assigned a leadership role in a group task: gender only, gender and merit, random assignment by coin toss (control condition). Results showed that women who were selected on the basis of merit and gender performed better than did women selected on the basis of gender alone. This is perhaps not surprising: Women chosen partly on merit may have more reason to be confident in their abilities, compared with those chosen on nonmerit criteria. However, this study also found that being selected on the basis of other nonmerit criteria did not have the same debilitating effect: Women chosen randomly performed equally as well as did those who were chosen partly on merit. Thus, the selection criteria of gender alone is unique in undermining women's task performance.

These results are consistent with the concept of stereotype threat, which proposes that individuals who believe that they are the targets of a negative stereotype are likely to underperform in that domain (Steele, 1997; see also chap. 6, this volume). Thus, women who think that they are the beneficiaries of preferential treatment might also think that others perceive them to be undeserving of the position. This belief may be what inhibits their performance on tasks relevant to the position. Ongoing research is focused on identifying the underlying processes involved in stereotype threat, such as anxiety or distraction from the task at hand. In the context of AA, however, it is possible that additional information about task ability or past performance may moderate the effects of preferential selection on future task performance. Future work should address this question.

Stress and Well-Being

Last, a number of studies have considered the effect of being an AA beneficiary on women's stress and well-being. Heilman et al.'s (1998) aforementioned comparison of five selection procedures demonstrated that female beneficiaries report the lowest levels of stress in two conditions: merit only and preferential equivalent. In the remaining three preferential treatment conditions—all of which appeared to emphasize gender more than merit—women reported higher levels of stress. Another study following the same experimental paradigm showed that women selected for a leadership position on the basis of gender report lower levels of positive emotion, compared with women selected on the basis of merit alone. The selection procedure influenced emotional reactions even when women received feedback that their leadership performance had been strong (Heilman & Alcott, 2001, Study 2). Taken together, these results suggest that AA strategies that emphasize gender more than merit have a negative impact on female employees' levels of stress and well-being.

A role-play study with female undergraduates (Nacoste, 1985) highlights a factor that moderates the effect of selection procedure on stress and well-being. Participants were asked to imagine that they had been selected for a position at an organization. The selection procedure was manipulated (gender only, or gender and qualifications), as was the gender equality history of the organization (clear statement of past discrimination or no statement). Participants in the past discrimination condition reported more positive affect when they were selected on the basis of their gender and qualifications, compared with those who had been selected on the basis of gender alone. In contrast, selection procedure did not influence positive affect among participants who were not aware of past discrimination by the organization.

One speculative explanation for these results is that women experience stress about the possibility of being a beneficiary of preferential treatment when they believe they are in an environment that is hostile to their group. In such cases, being identified as an AA beneficiary could invite the accusation that their group is receiving special treatment, and could be accompanied by bias and discrimination. Future work should investigate this effect and its underlying processes more closely.

Perceptions of (Presumed) Beneficiaries

As described in the previous section, women who believe they are the beneficiaries of AA can feel stigmatized by this association with the policy. The question, then, is whether this phenomenon is based solely in women's (internal) self-doubt or in their (external) social contexts as well. Are women perceived, and treated, differently when they are believed to have benefited from AA? In this section I review empirical research on men's and women's attitudes toward female beneficiaries of AA. The studies include both surveys of full-time employed adults and laboratory experiments with university students.

One study surveyed European American men in Chicago and New York City who were employed in a range of occupations and industries (Heilman, Block, & Lucas, 1992, Study 2). Participants were asked to think about a recent nontypical hire in their workplace (e.g., a woman hired for a typically male job) that was at or near their own level of seniority. They were then asked to estimate the likelihood that AA was used to make the hire, and to rate the hired individual on a range of characteristics. Results showed a strong negative correlation between presumed AA and perceptions of competence: Nontypical hires were perceived to be less competent when AA was believed to have been used in the hiring process. The same pattern of results was found for other perceptions of the hire such as talent, skills, and positive interpersonal characteristics. Overall, AA hires were viewed more negatively than were non-AA hires.

One important caveat is that such correlational studies do not permit conclusions about causality. Are individuals believed to be less competent because they are (presumed) AA hires, or are they believed to be AA hires because they are less competent? A series of experimental studies (primarily with student participants) has addressed this question by manipulating the AA status of a target individual (e.g., chosen on the basis of gender or merit) and comparing participants' evaluations of the target in the different conditions.

In one commonly used experimental paradigm, participants were asked to evaluate a target individual (man or woman) who had either received, or was applying for, a specific position. The female target's AA status was manipulated to reflect one of two selection procedures (preferential treatment or merit only), whereas the male target was always selected solely on the basis of merit. Results consistently show that participants evaluated the female AA candidate more negatively than they evaluated the female candidate who was chosen solely on the basis of merit (Dietz-Uhler & Murrell, 1998; Gilbert & Stead, 1999, Study 1; Heilman et al., 1992, Study 1; Summers, 1991). Female AA targets were also perceived to be less competent and more passive than male or female targets chosen solely on the basis of merit (Heilman et al., 1992, Study 1). The differences in perceived competence were amplified when the female target obtained a position that was "typically male" (e.g., electrician) compared with one that was "typically female" (e.g., hospital lab technician; Gilbert & Stead, 1999, Study 1; Heilman et al., 1992, Study 1).

The negative effects of AA on competence perceptions have been consistently shown across various operationalizations of preferential treatment, ranging from hard quotas (Dietz-Uhler & Murrell, 1998) to active consideration of gender (Gilbert & Stead, 1999, Study 1) to a simple nondiscrimination statement (Heilman et al., 1992, Study 1). These findings suggest that female beneficiaries of AA are viewed as less competent (relative to men and women selected solely on the basis of merit) regardless of the specific practices implemented in the AA program. The aforementioned study by Heilman et al. (1998, Study 1) provides more direct evidence for this claim, as it compared perceptions of a female target chosen by merit alone or by one of four preferential treatment procedures. Results showed that the female target was perceived to be more competent in the merit-only condition than in any of the preferential treatment conditions. However, the target selected in the preferential equivalent condition (in which gender and merit were given equal weight) was viewed as more competent than the target selected in any other preferential treatment conditions (in which gender appeared to be more important than merit). This result suggests that the use of the preferential equivalent strategy may limit the negative effects of AA on perceived competence of (presumed) beneficiaries. However, it is important to point out that perceived competence was still lower in this AA condition relative to the merit-only condition.

A final study (Heilman & Welle, 2006) demonstrated that diversity goals can also influence perceptions of beneficiaries' competence. Undergraduate students were provided with one of three rationales for assembling a hypothetical work group: merit, gender diversity, or scheduling convenience. Participants expected female work-group members in the diversity condition to be less competent and less influential than female work-group members in the merit condition or the scheduling convenience condition.

Taken together, the results from these various studies demonstrate that (male and female) individuals view female beneficiaries of AA as less competent and less talented employees who are less entitled to their positions. What happens, however, when individuals receive concrete information about the competence and performance of AA beneficiaries? Do they still assume that AA beneficiaries are incompetent, or do they use this additional information to evaluate AA beneficiaries more positively?

A set of experimental studies has examined these questions by manipulating the information that participants receive about an AA beneficiary's past performance. Results showed that when participants learned about the AA beneficiary's past positive performance, they perceived her as equally competent as male and female targets selected on the basis of merit (Heilman, Block, & Stathatos, 1997; Heilman, McCullough, & Gilbert, 1996). However, when participants learned that the AA beneficiary's past performance was poor, they perceived her to be less competent than male and female targets selected on the basis of merit alone (Heilman et al., 1997). Finally, when no information was provided about past performance (Heilman et al., 1996) or when ambiguous information was provided about past performance (Heilman et al., 1997), participants perceived the female AA beneficiary to be less competent than male or female targets selected solely on merit. Taken together, the results suggest that when no clear, explicit, or objective information is provided about a (presumed) AA beneficiary, the default response is to infer low competence. However, information about an AA beneficiary's past performance can improve individuals' perceptions of her abilities and qualifications.

EVALUATING AND IMPROVING THE EFFECTIVENESS OF AFFIRMATIVE ACTION

Although the past 30 years have seen clear progress in women's employment aspirations and educational achievement, structural barriers in organizational policy and practice have impeded women's progress in employment. Such systemic obstacles are not easily overcome by sheer will or individual achievement alone—a point made here not to disempower women but rather to emphasize that institutional discrimination requires structural and collective solutions (see Crosby et al., 2003). Gender-based AA offers one such solution, whose goal is to move organizations closer to gender equality in the representation and status of female employees. The present chapter reviewed empirical evidence for four specific positive and negative consequences of gender-based AA in employment. This final section integrates these findings to evaluate the general effectiveness of AA and offer recommendations to improve the policy.

Multiple studies in various countries provide unequivocal evidence that AA has successfully increased the representation of female employees in a range of occupations. This outcome of AA builds on, rather than results from, the general societal trend toward gender equality: Organizations with AA have been shown to hire and promote higher proportions of female employees, relative to comparable organizations without AA. Implementing AA also does not disadvantage organizations: Various studies have shown that AA is not associated with decreases in performance or productivity.

In two ways, however, the success of AA has been qualified. First, although the proportion of female employees in organizations has dramatically increased, this number is still lower than the total pool of qualified female applicants in the workforce. Thus, despite 30 years of AA in the United States, full gender equality in employment is still a long way off, particularly at higher levels of management. One explanation is that the implementation of AA is susceptible to human folly. Even in the best-case scenario in which managers demonstrate good-faith intentions to implement AA, the more subtle forms of gender bias may be extremely difficult to identify and correct (see chaps. 5 and 7, this volume). And in the worst-case scenario, employees who are opposed to AA may actively seek to sabotage the program. Thus, a first strategy to improve the effectiveness of AA in achieving its goals is to educate employees and organizations about gender discrimination and the importance of AA.

Another explanation for the less-than-perfect record of AA is that organizations are not held sufficiently accountable to their AA goals and plans. Some countries impose no significant concrete penalties for failing to implement a federally mandated AA program (e.g., Great Britain), whereas others do not consistently allocate sufficient resources to enforcement mechanisms such as audits and investigations (e.g., United States). In addition, no country provides incentives to organizations that implement gender-based AA and achieve their goals. Until such structural (dis)incentives are established and consistently applied, organizations are likely to focus their scarce resources on other aspects of their business, rather than on implementation of AA. Thus, a second strategy to improve the effectiveness of AA is to devote more resources to enforcement and oversight.

A second problem with AA is that it may hurt the well-being and status of female employees once they have entered an organization. AA programs typically set goals for the representation of female employees at each level of seniority. As a result, most AA strategies tend to focus on the selection process, with less attention paid to the beneficiaries of the policy once they are employed by the organization. Female employees may thus have specific negative experiences associated with AA that are not currently addressed by the policy.

For instance, female employees in AA organizations may feel stigmatized by the program because it fosters the impression that women did not achieve their positions through their own merit. Indeed, experimental research has demonstrated that this stigma can have concrete negative implications. In these studies, women who believe they are beneficiaries of AA report lower self-competence ratings, select less challenging tasks, demonstrate lower task performance, and report higher levels of stress. However, the effects of self-competence ratings and task selection are moderated by performance feedback: When women received positive feedback about their performance, they did not exhibit the stigma associated with being a beneficiary of AA. In addition, the effects of AA status on stress and well-being appear to be moderated by the organizational environment: Being a beneficiary of AA was associated with increased stress only in a hostile work environment. The presence of AA did not heighten women's stress in supportive environments.

Experimental research also demonstrates that the stigma experienced by AA beneficiaries is not merely a figment of their imagination. Several studies have found that men's and women's evaluations of (presumed) AA beneficiaries are more negative compared with their evaluations of men and women who have secured their positions solely on their own merit. Information about the target's previous performance is an important moderator here as well: Individuals do not evaluate an AA beneficiary more negatively if they learn that she has performed well. Taken together, the results suggest that AA beneficiaries are assumed to be less qualified and competent, unless concrete and direct disconfirming information is provided.

The results from the lab experiments do not necessarily generalize to the practice of AA in organizations. Survey research has shown that female employees working full-time in AA organizations do not report feeling stigmatized by AA, nor do they report being treated differently because of AA. This finding suggests that the negative consequences of AA for its beneficiaries may not be widespread outside of laboratory settings.

One explanation for this pattern of results lies in the moderating factors identified in the experimental literature (performance feedback and supportive workplace environment). On average, full-time female employees are likely to receive (at least some) positive feedback about their job performance and may have developed a network of social support that helps them cope with the potential stigma of being (perceived as) a beneficiary of AA. This explanation suggests that organizations should do more to develop a more positive work environment for female employees, both individually and collectively. Thus, a third (individual) strategy might be to provide positive feedback about performance. And a fourth (collective) strategy might encourage both formal and informal support networks (e.g., mentoring) for members of underrepresented groups in the organization (see also chap. 10, this volume, for a discussion of the benefits of informal support networks). Taken together, these strategies should improve the effectiveness of AA by reducing the negative consequences for beneficiaries.

SUMMARY

Empirical work in the social sciences provides evidence that AA is effective in moving organizations toward gender equality in the representation of women while allowing them to maintain high levels of performance and efficiency. However, AA has focused primarily on the selection process while devoting less attention to the experience of AA beneficiaries once they are in an organization. Some evidence indicates that women are stigmatized by the association with AA, but these effects seem to be limited outside the experimental lab setting. When AA does produce negative consequences in organizations, research points to specific strategies that may be implemented to blunt the negative effects of the policy. Thus, with increased attention to the experiences of female employees within organizations, AA should become an even more effective strategy in the effort to improve women's status in employment.

REFERENCES

Agars, M. D. (2004). Reconsidering the impact of gender stereotypes on the advancement of women in organizations. *Psychology of Women Quarterly, 28,* 103–111.

Allen, R. Y. W. (2003). Examining the implementation of affirmative action in law enforcement. *Public Personnel Management, 32,* 411–418.

Anderson, B. E. (1996). The ebb and flow of enforcing Executive Order 11246. *American Economic Review, 86,* 298–301.

Blau, F. D., & DeVaro, J. (2006). *New evidence on gender differences in promotion rates: An empirical analysis of a sample of new hires* (Working Paper No. 12321). Cambridge, MA: National Bureau of Economic Research.

Blau, F. D., & Kahn, L. M. (1996). Wage structure and gender differentiations: An international comparison. *Economica, 63*(Suppl. 250), S29–S62.

Brown, R. P., Charnasangavej, T., Keough, K. A., Newman, M. L., & Rentfrow, P. J. (2000). Putting the "affirm" into affirmative action: Preferential selection and academic performance. *Journal of Personality and Social Psychology, 79,* 736–747.

Bruno, A. (1998). *Affirmative action: Recent Congressional and presidential activity* (CRS Report for Congress 97-527 GOV). Washington, DC: Library of Congress.

Collins, G., & Wickham, J. (2002). Experiencing mergers: A women's eye view. *Women's Studies International Forum, 25,* 573–583.

Combs, G. M., Nadkarni, S., & Combs, M. W. (2005). Implementing affirmative action plans in multinational corporations. *Organizational Dynamics, 34,* 346–360.

Crosby, F. J., Iyer, A., Clayton, S., & Downing, R. A. (2003). Affirmative action: Psychological data and the policy debates. *American Psychologist, 58,* 93–115.

Crosby, F. J., & VanDeVeer, C. (Eds.) (2000). *Sex, race, and merit: Debating affirmative action in education and employment.* Ann Arbor: University of Michigan Press.

Dale, C. V. (2005). *Federal affirmative action law: A brief history* (CRS Report for Congress, Order Code RS22256). Washington, DC: Library of Congress.

Darity, W. A., Jr., & Mason, P. L. (1998). Evidence on discrimination in employment: Codes of color, codes of gender. *Journal of Economic Perspectives, 12*(2), 63–90.

DeArmond, S., Tye, M., Chen, P. Y., Krauss, A., Rogers, D. A., & Sintek, E. (2006). Age and gender stereotypes: New challenges in a changing workplace and workforce. *Journal of Applied Social Psychology, 36,* 2184–2214.

Department of Justice Canada. (2006). *Employment Equity Act.* Retrieved January 17, 2007, from http://lois.justice.gc.ca/en/showtdm/cs/E-5.401

Dietz-Uhler, B., & Murrell, A. J. (1998). Evaluations of affirmative action applicants: Perceived fairness, human capital, or social identity? *Sex Roles, 38,* 933–951.

Equal Opportunities Commission. (2006a). *Facts about women and men in Great Britain 2006.* Retrieved July 22, 2008, from www.unece.org/gender/publications/UK/Facts_about_W&M_GB_2006.pdf

Equal Opportunities Commission. (2006b). *History and background of the Gender Equality Duty.* Retrieved July 22, 2008, from http://83.137.212.42/sitearchive/eoc/Default7a73.html?page=20216&theme=print

Equal Opportunities Commission (2006c). *Overview of the Gender Equality Duty*. Retrieved July 22, 2008, from http://www.bath.ac.uk/hr/equalities/gender/overviewofthegenderequalityduty.doc

Equal Opportunity for Women in the Workplace Agency. (2000). *Compliance guidelines*. Canberra, Australia: Commonwealth Government of Australia.

Equal Opportunity for Women in the Workplace Agency. (2006). *About EOWA: Overview of the Act*. Canberra, Australia: Commonwealth Government of Australia.

French, E. (2001). Approaches to equity management and their relationship to women in management. *British Journal of Management, 12*, 267–285.

Gilbert, J. A., & Stead, B. A. (1999). Stigmatization revisited: Does diversity management make a difference in applicant success? *Group & Organization Management, 24*, 239–256.

Great Britain. (2006a). *Equality Act 2006*. London: Stationery Office.

Great Britain. (2006b). *Explanatory notes to Equality Act 2006*. London: Stationery Office.

Hadley, K. (2001). *And we still ain't satisfied: Gender inequality in Canada: A status report for 2001*. Toronto, Ontario, Canada: The National Action Committee on the Status of Women and CSJ Foundation for Research and Education.

Harrison, D. A., Kravitz, D. A., Mayer, D. M., Leslie, L. M., & Lev-Arev, D. (2006). Understanding attitudes toward affirmative action programs in employment: Summary and meta-analysis of 35 years of research. *Journal of Applied Psychology, 91*, 1013–1036.

Harvey, E. B., & Blakely, J. H. (1993). Employment equity goal setting and external availability data. *Social Indicators Research, 28*, 245–266.

Heilman, M. E., & Alcott, V. B. (2001). What I think you think of me: Women's reactions to being viewed as beneficiaries of preferential selection. *Journal of Applied Psychology, 86*, 574–582.

Heilman, M. E., Battle, W. S., Keller, C. E., & Lee, R. A. (1998). Type of affirmative action policy: A determinant of reactions to sex-based preferential selection? *Journal of Applied Psychology, 83*, 190–205.

Heilman, M. E., Block, C. J., & Lucas, J. A. (1992). Presumed incompetent? Stigmatization and affirmative action efforts. *Journal of Applied Psychology, 77*, 536–544.

Heilman, M. E., Block, C. J., & Stathatos, P. (1997). The affirmative action stigma of incompetence: Effects of performance information ambiguity. *Academy of Management Journal, 40*, 603–625.

Heilman, M. E., Lucas, J. A., & Kaplow, S. R. (1990). Self-derogating consequences of sex-based preferential selection: The moderating role of initial self-confidence. *Organizational Behavior and Human Decision Processes, 46*, 202–216.

Heilman, M. E., McCullough, W. F., & Gilbert, D. (1996). The other side of affirmative action: Reactions of non-beneficiaries to sex-based preferential selection. *Journal of Applied Psychology, 81*, 346–357.

Heilman, M. E., Rivero, J. C., & Brett, J. F. (1991). Skirting the competence issue: Effects of sex-based preferential selection on task choices of women and men. *Journal of Applied Psychology, 76,* 99–105.

Heilman, M. E., Simon, M. C., & Repper, D. P. (1987). Intentionally favored, unintentionally harmed? Impact of sex-based preferential selection on self-perception and self-evaluations. *Journal of Applied Psychology, 72,* 62–68.

Heilman, M. E., & Welle, B. (2006). Disadvantaged by diversity? The effects of diversity goals on competence perceptions. *Journal of Applied Social Psychology, 36,* 1291–1319.

Holzer, H., & Neumark, D. (1996). *Are affirmative action hires less qualified? Evidence from employer-employee data on new hires* (Working Paper No. 5603). Cambridge, MA: National Bureau of Economic Research.

Holzer, H., & Neumark, D. (2000a). What does affirmative action do? *Industrial and Labor Relations Review, 53,* 240–271.

Holzer, H., & Neumark, D. (2000b). Assessing affirmative action. *Journal of Economic Literature, 28,* 483–568.

Human Resources Development Canada. (2006a). *Overview of Employment Equity.* Retrieved March 9, 2007, from http://www.hrsdc.gc.ca/en/lp/lo/lswe/we/legislation/guidelines/doc1.pdf

Human Resources Development Canada. (2006b). *Compliance.* Retrieved March 9, 2007, from http://www.hrsdc.gc.ca/en/lp/lo/lswe/we/legislation/guidelines/doc2.pdf

Jackson, S. E. (Ed.). (1992). *Diversity in the workplace: Human resources initiatives.* New York: Guilford Press.

Kimura, D. (1997). Affirmative action policies are demeaning to women in academia. *Canadian Psychology, 38,* 238–252.

Konrad, A. M., & Linnehan, F. (1995). Formalized HRM structures: Coordinating equal employment opportunity or concealing organizational practices? *Academy of Management Journal, 38,* 787–820.

Kravitz, D. A., Harrison, D. A., Turner, M. E., Levine, E. L., Chaves, W., Brannick, M. T., et al. (1997). *Affirmative action: A review of psychological and behavioral research.* Bowling Green, OH: Society for Industrial and Organizational Psychology.

Leck, J. D., & Saunders, D. M. (1992). Hiring women: The effects of Canada's employment equity act. *Canadian Public Policy, 18,* 203–220.

Leck, J. D., St. Onge, S., & Lalancette, I. (1995). Wage gap changes among organizations subject to the Employment Equity Act. *Canadian Public Policy, 21,* 387–400.

Leonard, J. S. (1984a). Employment and occupational advance under affirmative action. *The Review of Economics and Statistics, 66,* 377–385.

Leonard, J. S. (1984b). Antidiscrimination or reverse discrimination: The impact of changing demographics, Title VII, and affirmative action on productivity. *The Journal of Human Resources, 19,* 145–174.

Leonard, J. S. (1989). Women and affirmative action. *Journal of Economic Perspectives*, 3, 61–75.

Lott, J. R. (2000). Does a helping hand put others at risk? Affirmative action, police departments, and crime. *Economic Inquiry*, 38, 239–277.

Major, B., Feinstein, J., & Crocker, J. (1994). Attributional ambiguity of affirmative action. *Basic and Applied Social Psychology*, 15, 113–141.

Molyneux, M., & Razavi, S. (Eds.). (2002). *Gender justice, development, and rights*. New York: Oxford University Press.

Nacoste, R. W. (1985). Selection procedure and responses to affirmative action: The case of favourable treatment. *Law and Human Behavior*, 9, 225–242.

Naff, K. C. (1998). Progress toward achieving a representative federal bureaucracy: The impact of supervisors and their beliefs. *Public Personnel Management*, 27, 135–150.

O'Donnell, V., Almey, M., Lindsay, C., Fournier-Savard, P., Mihorean, K., Charmant, M., et al. (2006). *Women in Canada: A gender-based statistical report*. Ottawa, Ontario, Canada: Statistics Canada.

Office of Legislative Drafting and Publishing. (2004). *Equal Opportunity for Women in the Workplace Act 1999*. Canberra, Australia: Attorney-General's Department.

Office of the Status of Women. (2003). *Women in Australia*. Barton, Australia: Department of the Prime Minister and Cabinet.

Plous, S. (1996). Ten myths about affirmative action. *Journal of Social Issues*, 52, 25–31.

Reskin, B. F. (1998). *The realities of affirmative action in employment*. Washington, DC: American Sociological Association.

Robinson, R. K., Seydel, J., & Douglass, C. (1998). Affirmative action: The facts, the myths, and the future. *Employee Responsibilities and Rights Journal*, 11, 99–115.

Sass, T. R., & Troyer, J. L. (1999). Affirmative action, political representation, unions, and female police employment. *Journal of Labor Research*, 20, 571–587.

Spann, G. A. (2000). *The law of affirmative action: Twenty-five years of Supreme Court decisions on race and remedies*. New York: New York University Press.

Steele, C. M. (1997). A threat in the air: How stereotypes shape intellectual identity and performance. *American Psychologist*, 52, 613–629.

Summers, R. J. (1991). The influence of affirmative action on perceptions of a beneficiary's qualifications. *Journal of Applied Social Psychology*, 21, 1265–1276.

Szafran, R. F. (2002). Age-adjusted labor force participation rates, 1960–2045. *Monthly Labor Review*, 125(11), 25–38.

Taylor, M. C. (1994). Impact of affirmative action on beneficiary groups: Evidence from the 1990 social survey. *Basic and Applied Social Psychology*, 15, 143–178.

Teles, S. M. (1998). Why is there no affirmative action in Britain? *American Behavioral Scientist*, 41, 1004–1026.

Wallace, M. (2001). Women and workplace training: Power relations positioning "the other." *Women's Studies International Forum*, 24, 433–444.

12

MANAGING DIVERSITY IN WORK GROUPS: HOW IDENTITY PROCESSES AFFECT DIVERSE WORK GROUPS

FLOOR RINK AND NAOMI ELLEMERS

Diversity research originated in the 1960s because of the changing nature of the labor market. The research traditionally focused on the way organizations deal with the growing differences in race, ethnic background, and gender and examined the barriers to equality for women and ethnic minority members (for reviews see Milliken & Martins, 1996; Williams & O'Reilly, 1998). At present, the examination of this issue is still the predominant focus of most studies in this area. In addition, researchers now also aim to link diversity issues to valued group processes and group outcomes.

One central question is whether the presence of diversity is detrimental or in fact beneficial for the functioning of work groups. Research shows mixed results, suggesting that diversity can boost creativity and performance but may also lead to in-group bias and pose a threat to feelings of identification and cohesiveness (Jackson, Joshi, & Erhardt, 2003; Milliken & Martins, 1996). The implication is that there are still many complex questions to answer, both for science and for practitioners in organizations. More recently, scholars have therefore started to move beyond demographic variables and included other group composition differences in their research, such as differences between group members with respect to their knowledge, skills, beliefs, values, or attitudes (Barsade, Ward, Turner, & Sonnefeld, 2000;

Bunderson & Sutcliffe, 2002; Harrison, Price, & Bell, 1998; Hobman, Bordia, & Gallois, 2003; Jehn, Northcraft, & Neale, 1999; Pelled, Eisenhardt, & Xin, 1999; Rink & Ellemers, 2007a). Thus, in group diversity research, the term *diversity* is broadly defined and generally refers to many kinds of individual differences between people who work together in a group or in larger entities (see also Ashkanasy, Härtel, & Daus, 2002; Ivancevich & Gilbert, 2000).

This chapter provides an overview of the most recent theoretical developments addressing the general effects of diversity in the context of work groups. We first point out methodological and measurement issues that might have contributed to the development of different perspectives on the varied effects of diversity on group functioning. Then, we present our social identity framework that questions the commonly held view that social identity and self-categorization processes necessarily imply that diversity tends to be perceived negatively by group members. Finally, we take our reasoning as a point of departure to solve several apparent inconsistencies between the social identity approach and recent theoretical insights in diversity research (i.e., faultline theory and self-verification theory). The primary aim of this chapter is to show that social identity and self-categorization processes can in fact also lead group members to evaluate and use their differences in a positive and effective way. We argue that when group composition is in line with prior expectations and reflects congruency, diversity can—just like similarity—come to define the group and form the basis of a common group identity. Finally, on the basis of our argument, we provide insights into practical implementations of diversity policies that foster a culture of diversity.

TRADITIONAL THEORETICAL PARADIGMS

Diversity research has traditionally referred to two different theoretical approaches to explain either the positive or the negative effects of diversity in organizations: (a) the information decision-making perspective and (b) the social identity and self-categorization perspective. Both approaches tend to examine diversity in terms of the amount of heterogeneity in a group and thus both offer a group level of analysis.

Information Decision-Making Perspective

For a long period, the information decision-making perspective has relied on the trait model to explain the overarching effects of different kinds of demographic differences on group performance (McGrath, Berdahl, & Arrow, 1995). This theoretical model maintains that within work groups, demographic differences, such as those based on gender, ethnicity, or age, lead to more variability in the knowledge that group members possess and in the values and beliefs they have. In turn, it is expected that these underlying differences positively influence group decisions and group outcomes (see also Fiske & Taylor, 1991; Lawrence, 1997; McGrath et al., 1995; Nickerson, 1999). This value-in-diversity reasoning suggests that within demographically diverse groups, the differences in knowledge and the presence of unique insights should have a positive influence on work-group creativity and performance (see, e.g., Cox, Lobel, & McLeod, 1991; Hambrick & Mason, 1984; Jackson, May, & Whitney, 1995; McLeod, Lobel, & Cox, 1996; Milliken & Martins, 1996; Webber & Donahue, 2001). However, the central assumption that demographically diverse group members are actually cognitively different from one another has rarely been empirically tested (Jackson et al., 2003). Moreover, as outlined in the introduction to this chapter, evidence suggests that demographically diverse groups do not by definition outperform homogeneous groups (Ancona & Caldwell, 1998; Harrison, Price, Gavin, & Florey, 2002; Pelled et al., 1999; Wiersema & Bantel, 1992; for a meta-analysis see Jackson et al., 2003).

The Social Identity/Self-Categorization Perspective

The social identity/self-categorization perspective (also referred to as the social identity approach) has been used to predict and understand the negative effects of diversity and focuses on people's initial reactions to and perceptions of group processes (Harrison et al., 2002; Hobman et al., 2003; Jehn et al., 1999; Riordan, 2000). Social identity theory states that, to varying degrees, people derive part of their identity and sense of self from the groups to which they belong (referred to as one's social identity; Tajfel, 1972; Tajfel & Turner, 1986). In addition, self-categorization theory developed by Turner and colleagues (Turner, 1985; Turner, Hogg, Oakes, Reicher, & Wetherell, 1987) proposes that people cognitively categorize themselves into social groups (self-categorization) when they feel that they share relevant features with others from these (in) groups. Researchers have therefore argued that perceived similarity to other group members is most critical for one's self-definition as a group member (van Knippenberg & Haslam, 2003; Williams & O'Reilly, 1998).

Some research indeed demonstrates that demographic diversity results in lower levels of group identification, which has negative effects on the interpersonal relations between group members (see Gruenfeld, Mannix, Williams, & Neale, 1996; Jehn et al., 1999; Nonaka & Takeuchi, 1995). As a consequence, diversity scholars have proposed that, in principle, any kind of difference (but especially visible demographic differences such as gender and race) between group members undermines the basis for shared group membership. However, although researchers have invested a lot of effort in understanding exactly how diversity affects a sense of social identity, research findings are still inconclusive. Even though it has been found that group members dislike differences among them, in some work groups these differences do not threaten members' commitment to and identification with their group (see, e.g., Earley & Mosakowski, 2000; Gruenfeld et al., 1996; Phillips, Mannix, Neale, & Gruenfeld, 2004; Rink & Ellemers, 2007a).

In conclusion, the two focal theoretical perspectives yield contradictory predictions, and empirical evidence from both sides is mixed. As a first step to resolve these inconsistencies in the literature, we point out some measurement issues that might have contributed to the varied effects of diversity on group functioning.

IMPACT OF DIVERSITY

Even though there is general agreement that diversity should influence (a) people's initial responses (e.g. stereotyping, in-group bias), (b) the perception of group processes (e.g., conflict, identification, and commitment levels), and (c) actual group outcomes (i.e., performance, information sharing, task satisfaction), only a handful of studies have examined these three classes of variables simultaneously (Bezrukova & Jehn, 2004; Harrison et al., 2002; Jehn et al., 1999; Pelled et al., 1999; Polzer, Milton, & Swann, 2002). Yet, we argue that it is crucial to do so. Up to now, it has been relatively unclear exactly how group members' initial reactions, group perceptions, and group outcomes mutually influence each other. It is not self-evident that initial reactions by individual members will all have a similar influence on each process variable and that the process variables will consequently affect all group outcome measures in the same way. For example, although the presence of gender differences within a group can activate gender stereotypes that may lower identification or hinder performance (Phillips & Lewin Loyd, 2006), such effects do not always occur. Despite group members' initial negative responses to difference, and despite the problematic group processes that can result from such differences, mixed-gender work groups do not necessarily function less optimally than do same-gender groups when the group members are motivated to exert effort on the group task (Jehn, 1995; Rink & Ellemers, 2006; see also minority influence literature, Moscovici, 1985).

Thus, a first step toward the integration of these different findings would be to (a) develop clear hypotheses concerning the mediating role of initial responses and group processes in the relationship between diversity and group outcomes and (b) tailor dependent measures to these specific predictions.

TYPES OF DIVERSITY

Although the term *diversity* has been used to indicate all kinds of distinctive attributes, this does not necessarily imply that all such differences have a similar effect on work groups (Robinson Hickman & Creighton-Zollar, 1998;

Webber & Donahue, 2001). Researchers have classified diversity attributes into distinct categories on the basis of specific features that might explain how these attributes influence group functioning. The most important classifications of diversity attributes refer to the distinctions made between (a) deep-level versus surface-level diversity, (b) job-related versus non-job-related diversity, and (c) social-category versus informational versus work-value diversity. We first briefly discuss each classification separately.

Surface-Level Versus Deep-Level Diversity

Harrison and his colleagues (2002) introduced a distinction between surface-level and deep-level diversity (see also Milliken & Martins, 1996). Harrison et al. (2002) argued that both surface- and deep-level diversity attributes will have a negative influence on group functioning, but at different moments in time depending on the visibility of these attributes to group members. Surface-level diversity attributes (e.g., demographic differences such as gender, ethnicity, or age) are directly discernible and are therefore expected to mostly influence reactions when group members first start to interact with one another. By contrast, deep-level diversity attributes are generally less easily noticed (e.g., work values, personality, or attitudes) and are predicted to become more problematic over time when group members become aware of them through the exchange of personal non-task-related information (Harrison et al., 2002). This line of reasoning introduces the important notion that diversity attributes are not always perceived as such by group members (see also Harrison et al., 1998, 2002; Hartel & Fujimoto, 1999; Randel, 2002; Riordan, 2000; Strauss, Barrick, & Connerley, 2001; Swann, Polzer, Seyle, & Ko, 2004).

Job-Related Versus Non-Job-Related Diversity

The second way of classifying diversity attributes was introduced by Pelled et al. (1999), who examined the degree to which diversity attributes capture experiences, skills, or perspectives pertinent to the task a group has to perform. Pelled et al. (1999) argued that only job- (or task-) related diversity attributes should optimize the group's performance because these differences can increase the amount of task-related knowledge in a group (Webber & Donahue, 2001). Thus, although the trait model of McGrath et al. (1995) proposes that demographic diversity is indirectly task-related because it leads group members to be cognitively different from each other, Pelled et al. (1999) opposed this (untested) assumption and argued that task-related differences should have a larger and more positive influence on groups than will demographic differences that are not useful for the group (see also Simons, Pelled, & Smith, 1999).

Social-Category, Informational, and Work-Value Diversity

Jehn et al. (1999) also proposed that instead of looking at demographic differences alone, it is important to examine the independent effects of other kinds of diversity on work-group functioning as well (see also Schneider & Northcraft, 1999). They defined differences based on demographics such as race, nationality, or gender as *social-category diversity*, to be distinguished from informational diversity and work-value diversity. *Informational diversity* refers to differences between group members in the kind of knowledge and information that they possess, such as those caused by different educational backgrounds or work experiences. In contrast, *work-value diversity* can be conceptualized as differences in the personal preferences and perspectives that group members may have about important work aspects (such as their personal work goals or work styles; Rink & Ellemers, 2007b).

These three ways of classifying diversity partly overlap with one another and, indeed, we argue that the distinction between social-category diversity, informational diversity, and work-value diversity can largely incorporate the other distinctions (see Table 12.1). As noted by Harrison et al. (2002), social-category diversity essentially contains surface-level diversity attributes that are readily detectable. However, as stated by Pelled et al. (1999), these attributes are generally not directly task-related. That is, although demographic differences tend to be highly visible for other group members, it is relatively unclear how they contribute to the task-related knowledge within a group. As such, demographic differences in themselves are unlikely to influence group processes and outcomes.

Conversely, work-value diversity contains deep-level attributes that are usually hard to detect (Jehn et al., 1999), yet these attributes are related to the task because they indicate what kind of tasks group members personally prefer to perform and how they want to perform them. Finally, we argue that informational diversity, like work-value diversity, is generally less visible than is social-category diversity. Stasser and his colleagues (1985, 1989) repeatedly showed that group members do not directly share their unique information,

TABLE 12.1
Diversity Classification Based on Diversity Typology and Attribute Features

	Attribute features	
Diversity typology	Visibility	Task-relatedness
Social category differences	+	0
Work value differences	−	+
Informational differences	−	+

Note. + indicates the presence of a feature, − indicates the absence of that particular feature, and 0 indicates that the feature is not directly implicated.

even when informed about possible informational differences. Instead, group members focus on shared information. Moreover, informational diversity is also task-related because it directly reflects the amount of available knowledge within a group that can contribute to task performance.

In conclusion, social-category differences, such as gender, are highly visible for group members, although they tend not to be task related, whereas work-value diversity and informational diversity both are less easy to detect but more clearly related to the task. Therefore, the latter two types of differences should in principle be more valuable for a group (see Table 12.1).

In summary, we hope that our overarching diversity classification makes clear that we cannot simply say that categorical, informational, or work-value diversity attributes are mainly positive (as proposed by the information decision-making perspective) or predominantly negative (as argued by diversity researchers with reference to the social identity/self-categorization perspective) for group functioning. This classification can explain why research has, for example, been unable to find consistent effects of gender differences in work groups. In the next section, we refine some of the initial formulations and previous predictions derived from the social identity/self-categorization perspective to present an integrative theoretical framework that can explain this apparent contradiction in the literature and address the complexity of diversity effects.

TOWARD AN INTEGRATIVE THEORETICAL FRAMEWORK

The remainder of this chapter shows that the effect of diversity depends on how it reflects shared norms and expectations in the group. We argue that intragroup differences between group members can either divide the group or form a basis for group identification depending on whether it is a part of the group norm and expected by group members. In the following section we outline the assumptions of the social identity/self-categorization perspective that support our reasoning.

First, as indicated at the start of this chapter, scholars have explained the negative effects of diversity by referring to social identity theory (Jehn et al., 1999; see Tajfel, 1972). They reason that group members need to be similar to each other on important dimensions to value their group membership and to feel emotionally attached to the group. However, the social identity approach also outlines the consequences of social categorization and identification processes for the cognitive, affective, and behavioral responses of individual group members (Haslam, 2001; Turner, 1999). In other words, a central tenet of the social identity perspective is that perceived similarity not only forms a basis for categorization and identity processes but can also develop as a result of these same processes (Tajfel & Turner, 1979; for extensive reviews on the use of social identity perspective in an organizational context see Ashforth & Mael, 1989; Haslam, 2001; Hogg & Terry, 2000). In this way, once individuals perceive themselves as members of a group, they will also perceive themselves as categorically interchangeable with other in-group members. This process of cognitive self-stereotyping is referred to as *depersonalization* (Turner, 1985) and leads group members to see themselves as embodiments of the most important group characteristics. Depersonalization causes individuals to behave according to the stereotypical and common beliefs of their group (group prototypes) and has been shown to produce shared group norms, cohesiveness, and increased cooperation within the group (Hogg & Terry, 2000, p. 123; Turner, 1999). From this, we infer that within groups, it should in principle be possible for members who are visibly different from each other to focus on the features that they have in common and to develop a shared group identity. In fact, we argue that in highly diverse groups, members can even come to see the differences among them as a salient feature that unites them as a group, as long as these differences are clearly perceived and considered to be useful to the group. This is the case in diverse work groups in which members are aware that they are explicitly brought together for their unique backgrounds and different kinds of expertise (e.g., international or multidisciplinary groups).

The Importance of Shared Expectations and Clarity

We propose that shared group norms have a relatively strong influence on individual responses, group processes, and the final group performance (Bettenhausen & Murnighan, 1985; Chatman & Flynn, 2001; Ellemers, de Gilder, & Haslam, 2004; Jetten, Postmes, & McAuliffe, 2002). Within small interactive groups, the individual actions of the group members are central to the formation of a common group identity (i.e., inductive identity formation; Postmes, Spears, Lee, & Novak, 2005), and group members generally develop normative expectations of fellow group members and of their group as a whole (Bettencourt, Dill, Greathouse, Charlton, & Mulholland, 1996; Biernat, Vescio, & Billings, 1999). Whereas previous research tended to address the beneficial effects of cooperative norms for group functioning, social identity theorists argue that in principle any kind of norm can reinforce a shared identity of the group and hence strengthen the perception of commonality among group members (e.g., Gellatly & Luchak, 1998; Jetten et al., 2002; Postmes, Spears, & Cihangir, 2001).

This supposition was demonstrated in research by Barreto and Ellemers (2001), who showed that even the induction of a norm of individuality did not endanger group identification, although it did cause group members to display individualistic behavior (see also Hornsey & Jetten, 2004). In addition, Postmes et al. (2005) argued that groups are more likely to accept the expression of individualism when it is clear that in doing so, group members can make a distinct contribution to the group's goals (referring to the concept of organic solidarity developed by Durkheim, 1984; see also Bettencourt & Sheldon, 2001; Rink & Ellemers, 2007a). Consistent with this finding, Foschi and Lawler (1994) argued that groups that allow their members more options as to how to define the social self elicit more positive emotions, and hence elicit more individual attachment to the group. As the expression of individualistic behavior can signal the presence of actual differences within a group, we propose that diversity is not necessarily detrimental for the functioning of work groups, provided that the intragroup differences are evident in a group and also in line with the group's norms (Ely & Thomas, 2001).

In conclusion, social identity theorists have long recognized that people's feelings toward a group as a whole may be distinct from their feelings toward the individual members of that group (Hogg & Abrams, 1988; Prentice, Miller, & Lightdale, 1994; Tajfel, 1982; Turner, 1991). That is, although people may initially prefer to work with similar others on the basis of interpersonal attraction, they can work on joint tasks with different others under the condition that the common group identity (that is based on their common goals) is salient for these group members (e.g., Ellemers et al., 2004; Prentice et al., 1994). Now the question is when can diversity constitute a source of a common group identity and have a positive effect on work-group functioning?

Diversity as a Source for Identification

First, we argue that diversity in itself can become normative for the group only when actual differences between members are indeed perceived as such. Thus, as opposed to Harrison et al. (2002) we believe that it is crucial that the differences among group members become evident in the group, as only clearly visible diversity attributes are likely to be seen as a shared feature among members of the group and may thus become a group-defining characteristic. That is, when work groups cannot easily be defined in terms of interpersonal similarities, clarity about other potential sources of a common identity—such as the awareness that, for example, gender differences among the group members enable them to draw upon unique information and more resources to achieve their common goals—will help give meaning to the group and can indicate how the group members relate to each other (e.g., Oakes, 1987; Rink & Ellemers, 2007a; Scheepers, Spears, Doosje, & Manstead, 2003). It is less likely that group members are able to do so when it is not entirely clear to them to what extent and precisely how they differ from each other.

Second, normative expectations play an important role in how we evaluate fellow group members (see Bettencourt et al., 1996; Biernat et al., 1999). Expectancy-violation theory states that when our expectations of fellow group members are violated (i.e., incongruence), we feel disappointed and evaluate these individuals more negatively than when our expectations are confirmed (i.e., congruence; Bettencourt et al., 1996; Biernat et al., 1999; Heider, 1958; see also Phillips, 2003). Congruency generally elicits instant positive feelings because it enables people to focus on the task, rather than on reconciling their unexpected discrepancies with others (Phillips & Lewin Loyd, 2006; Rink & Ellemers, 2007b). Thus, it is neither similarity nor difference to the self that is essential, but whether the presence of diversity is in line with previous expectations. We therefore argue that when differences are not highly evident from the start, the explicit induction of diversity expectations can lead to congruency and a positive group evaluation (Gruenfeld et al., 1996; Phillips et al., 2004).

Empirical Evidence

We conducted a series of experimental studies to examine our central prediction that clarity and clear expectations about diversity will indeed lead to positive perceptions of decision-making processes (Rink & Ellemers, 2007b). Because diversity is more likely to be valued by group members when they recognize that their mutual differences can be useful for and contribute to the common goals and tasks of the group (see Table 12.1), we initially focused on the evaluation of informational and work-value differences (Pelled et al., 1999). Participants were led to believe that they had to collaborate with another participant via the computer. We found that in the absence of concrete information about this partner, participants held self-activated expectations that this person would be similar to them in their work goals and work styles. Violation of this expectation resulted in more disappointment than expectancy confirmation. When we externally induced expectations that the partner would be different in this respect, and this indeed proved to be the case, participants reported less disappointment and more commitment toward collaboration than when previous expectations were violated (i.e., when the partner who was expected to be different turned out to be similar to the self). Thus, in general, people expect others with whom they have to work to be similar to the self. However, in line with our theoretical framework, we show that when people do expect to differ from their collaboration partners, they are more likely to benefit from diversity. In fact, task-related similarities can even be evaluated relatively negatively when these are unexpected.

As indicated in the introduction, the influence of demographic (categorical) differences—such as gender diversity—on group functioning and identity formation tends to be more complex. On the one hand, the presence of such differences will be noticed relatively easily and might therefore help people to develop a clear conception of these differences as characteristic for the group to which they belong (Jehn et al., 1999). On the other hand, it may be less evident to group members how such differences are related to common group goals, regardless of whether gender differences are highly evident to group members. We therefore argued that social category differences are most likely to have a positive influence on work groups when (a) these differences actually reflect and are congruent with task-related differences (as is assumed by the trait model; McGrath et al., 1995) and (b) this is made explicit to the group members.

In the next study, we therefore examined whether gender differences play a role in the extent to which people expect other informational or work-value differences between themselves and their collaborating partner (Rink & Ellemers, 2006). Our hypothesis was that a man and a woman who work together will most likely expect the other to be different in task-related ways. Gender research has shown that people often have stereotypical trait expectations of women different from those they have of men (e.g., Berger, Ridgeway, Fisek, & Norman, 1998; Carli, LaFleur, & Loeber, 1995; Thomas-Hunt & Phillips, 2004). The work of Eagly and colleagues on the social role theory of gender differences indicates that such gender-based expectancies can play an important role in how people react toward and evaluate women in a work situation (Eagly & Karau, 2002; Eagly, Karau, & Makhijani, 1995). Yet, so far it remains unclear whether people also develop gender-based expectations about more neutral, nonstereotypical informational and work-value differences. Moreover, as we examine diversity in a group context, some researchers have argued that regardless of demographic differences in gender, people also have the tendency to develop similarity expectations of others they work with on the basis of their joint group membership (Bettencourt et al., 1996; see also Miller & Marks, 1982). Thus, we aimed to examine whether people will indeed expect congruence between gender and other, more task-related attributes of their collaborating partners. Moreover, we investigated whether a confirmation of this gender-based expectation would influence further reactions of group members toward each other and toward their collaboration.

To test these predictions, we led participants to believe that they had to collaborate with a same-gender partner or a partner of the other gender. The results of this study showed that participants who had to interact with a same-gender partner expected this person to be similar to the self in task-related ways, whereas those who had to interact with a partner from the other gender expected this person to be different in how he or she wanted to approach the task. When these expectancies were confirmed, participants felt relatively little disappointment, developed a clear image of the partner, and felt committed toward future collaboration. However, when expectancies were violated (i.e., when a same-gender partner unexpectedly turned out to have different work values), participants responded relatively negatively to the collaboration. This study indicates that people prefer congruence over incongruence and would rather work with a partner from a different demographic group (e.g., the other gender) who also differs from the self in terms of task-related features than with a partner from a different demographic group (e.g., the other gender) who unexpectedly turns out to be similar. In this way we showed that people also expect a link between gender- and task-related differences and offered further evidence for our argument that people are more likely to respond positively to diversity when differences are in accordance with expectations.

In conclusion, although the general idea remains that shared group features and group identification are important for benefiting from differences within the group, our common norm argument proposes that feelings of attachment and positive interpersonal relations within a group may be rooted in the very fact that group members expect to differ from each other, and consider their mutual differences as a feature they share that is prototypical for their group. Thus, people can still perceive a shared identity that connects them to each other and feel attached to the group regardless of their actual differences. We show that this is the case in mixed-gender groups when it is clear to the group members that their gender differences align with more underlying (or deeper) task-related informational and work-value differences that can help the group obtain its common goals.

THEORETICAL INTEGRATION

In the previous sections we defined the key issues that inform diversity research and introduced a theoretical framework based on the social identity/self-categorization perspective. Our next goal is to connect this framework to important notions of two other highly important new theoretical approaches that are used to explain the mixed and complex effects of diversity on groups, namely (a) the use of the concept of *faultlines* to examine the influence of diversity on group functioning and (b) the moderating role of *interpersonal congruence* in the effects of diversity on group processes. Although each approach has yielded valuable theoretical insights into the effects of diversity, they take different directions and their precise implications of diversity for social identity processes are unclear (see also Haslam & Ellemers, 2004). Our aim is to show that our integrative social identity theoretical framework can incorporate these new theoretical developments as well as form the basis for novel predictions that can be tested in empirical research.

Faultline Theory

The concept of group faultlines was first introduced by Lau and Murnighan (1998, 2005). They stressed the importance of group dynamics and the composition of multiple demographic differences among group members, in addition to the extent to which group members perceive dissimilarity among them. They defined group faultlines as hypothetical dividing lines that may split a group into subgroups on the basis of one or more converging diversity attributes (Lau & Murnighan, 1998, p. 328). The extent to which faultlines actually cause a group to split into subgroups (the strength of a faultline) depends on the number of diversity attributes in a group that are visible to group members and the extent to which individual group members are able to classify themselves into categories based on these attributes. For instance, a group of four people consisting of two female psychology students and two male law students (converging differences) will have a stronger faultline (based on gender and study major) than will a group of four people consisting of one female and one male psychology student and one female and one male law student where the same number of differences emerge but cross-cut each other. This reasoning implies that two groups that may seem identical in terms of the number of diversity attributes present are not necessarily similarly affected by these attributes. Rather, the argument is that the effects of diversity attributes depend on the potential for faultlines within each group.

On the basis of literature on coalition formation (see, e.g., Murnighan & Brass, 1991), faultline scholars argue that when subgroups emerge (along demographic faultlines), members are likely to experience more conflict within the group as a whole and are less inclined to use their different knowledge and backgrounds to enhance group performance (e.g., Bezrukova & Jehn, 2004; Thatcher, Jehn, & Zanutto, 2003). Yet, on the basis of our social identity analysis of norm-congruency, we argue that confirmed expectations and a convergence of differences should lead group members to consider how their unique characteristics relate to joint actions and common goals (Earley & Mosakowski, 2000). Clarity about diversity should enhance their ability to deal with the differences between them and help them maintain a sense of common identity.

Work based on the social identity perspective by Hornsey and Hogg (2000) shows that under certain conditions, the emergence of subgroups is not necessarily detrimental (and can even be beneficial) for groups. Subcategorization reduces group cohesiveness and causes subgroup resistance only when members identify more strongly with their subgroup than with the group as a whole (Brewer, 1991). However, this is not necessarily the case when the more inclusive and binding identity of the superordinate group remains equally salient for these group members (Hornsey & Hogg, 2000; see also the common in-group identity model, Gaertner, Dovidio, & Bachman, 1996). This situation can be achieved by mutually acknowledging and respecting the overall group goals and distinctions between the subgroups (Barreto & Ellemers, 2002). Too much focus on the overall group can threaten subgroup distinctiveness, causing subgroup members to resist inclusion in the larger group (see the dual-categorization model; e.g., Brown & Wade, 1987;

Gonzales & Brown, 2006; Hewstone, 1996), whereas sole identification with the subgroup most likely will have the result that subgroup members no longer consider themselves to be a part of the superordinate group and will be less likely to make an effort for the benefit of the collective (e.g., van Leeuwen, van Knippenberg, & Ellemers, 2003). In sum, these findings seem to suggest that the balance between subgroup and superordinate group identification determines whether group members show subgroup biases and lose their motivation to work for the group as a whole.

In conclusion, we argue that a social-cognitive analysis of subgroup relations can provide a good understanding of the conditions under which potential faultlines become activated or when they might instead remain passive and not lead to subgroup formation. We propose that active faultline alignment based on diversity attributes will be least detrimental for group processes and outcomes when group members are able to cherish both identities simultaneously. On the basis of our argument, we predict that this situation will most likely happen when intragroup differences constitute an essential part of the overall group identity and when these differences of other members are needed to attain the common group goals. At the same time, subgroup members can preserve their distinctiveness when diversity in itself is accepted by and considered normative for the group as a whole.

Self-Verification

A second promising line of diversity research has been developed by Swann, Milton, and Polzer (2000; see also Polzer, Milton, & Swann, 2002; Swann et al., 2003; Swann, Polzer, Seyle, & Ko, 2004). According to Swann et al. (2003), one important factor that increases the likelihood that group members will share their differences with one another is the extent to which the group promotes or enables self-verification. In a field study, they showed that diverse groups valued diversity more when group members searched for, and attained, confirmation of their self-views (Polzer et al., 2002). Self-verification is expected to give people a sense of predictability and control over the situation. It gives them more knowledge of how to behave in a group and makes people feel more confident about how others are likely to react to them.

However, the question remains as to how group members achieve self-verification. For self-verification to occur, perceivers should be able to individuate their fellow group members, that is, to perceive group members as distinct individuals with unique characteristics. In line with our argument, Swann et al. (2004) argued that individuation (and self-verification) is more likely to occur in heterogeneous groups in which members are clearly distinct from one another. Yet, it can also lead to the conclusion that a shared group identity and perceptions of commonality are at odds with the extent to which these group members are able to see themselves and each other as unique individuals. As we described earlier, we propose that feelings of identification can go hand-in-hand with the acceptance and even effective use of differences among group members, as long as these differences are clear, expected, and considered useful for the group. When diversity is considered to be a part of the norms of the group, group members can display normative group behavior that is in accordance with their self-views, that stimulates them to engage in self-verification processes, and that will lead them to share their unique knowledge in the group.

In the previous sections we defined the key issues that inform diversity research and introduced a theoretical framework based on the social identity perspective with the aim of clarifying some of the seemingly inconsistent findings in this area and connecting some of the important notions of the present theoretical approaches that are used to explain the effects of diversity on group functioning. In the final part of this chapter, we discuss the practical implications of our argument.

PRACTICAL IMPLICATIONS AND CONCLUSION

During the past decade, organizations have increasingly realized the importance of managing diversity—particularly differences in gender, ethnicity, and age—in work groups. The two most common ways for organizations to deal with a diverse workforce are (a) to explicitly portray diversity as an important and valued part of the organizational culture and (b) to invest in formal diversity training programs (Jackson et al., 2003). The organizational culture provides the context in which diverse groups have to operate, and therefore employees will, at least to some extent, be inclined to adhere to the organization's culture (Chatman, Polzer, Barsade, & Neale, 1998; Hogg & Terry, 2000). From this reasoning, one could infer that when an organizational culture values diversity and emphasizes the importance of equality for women and other minorities (e.g., by declaring the importance of diversity and equality in their official mission statements), individual employees within such organizations will be led to adapt this culture (Ely & Thomas, 2001). Likewise, diversity training is based on the idea that organizations represent collections of individuals and therefore focus on changing individual attitudes toward diversity (Bezrukova & Jehn, 2001). So, both measures can help individuals to personally accept diversity within their organization. However, it is not yet clear whether individual training actually influences the extent to which diversity is expected and functional at the work-group level. In fact, work groups often develop strong norms on their own that change one's personal beliefs and can deviate from the organizational culture (Brickson, 2000). If such work groups do not embrace diversity, it is still difficult for individual group members (e.g., women) to counteract stereotypes or to freely express their unique opinion, without running the risk of being considered deviant.

In sum, on the basis of our framework, we argue that both strategies pay perhaps too little attention to the powerful social dynamics that can arise within work groups (Jackson et al., 2003, p. 822). One clear and practical message that can be derived from our theoretical argument is that future interventions of organizations and managers should take the group-level characteristics into account when trying to understand or influence the impact of diversity on group functioning (see the actualizing social and personal identity resources model, commonly known as ASPIRE; Haslam, Eggins, & Reynolds, 2003). For instance, organizations could introduce diversity training designed for work groups that are focused on changing existing group norms. In addition, such training should underline equality and the value of diversity for reaching the common goals of the group. Organizations can also influence the acceptance of diversity at the group level when new work groups are composed. First of all, managers could explicitly choose to form highly diverse groups and make it evident that each member (regardless of their majority or minority status) can offer a unique contribution to the group's performance. Second, as people are generally inclined to develop expectancies of others on the basis of their categorical membership (e.g., on the basis of gender; see Study 3 discussed earlier), managers should monitor and—if necessary— adjust such expectations in newly formed work groups.

In conclusion, by introducing the common norm argument, we hope to have made clear that a different reading of the social identity approach can provide theoretical insights into the circumstances under which diversity can have a positive influence on groups. For gender differences, this positive influence occurs when these differences are expected by group members and when it is evident how they relate to underlying task-related diversity attributes. In this situation, male and female group members are able to form a clear conception of their group and remain committed to future collaboration (Rink & Ellemers, 2007b). We therefore propose that categorical diversity (in gender, ethnicity, race) does not necessarily undermine feelings of group identification, and can in fact even form the basis for these feelings as well as for the development of group norms.

REFERENCES

Ancona, D. G., & Caldwell, D. F. (1998). Rethinking team composition from the outside in. In M. Neale, E. Mannix, & D. Gruenfeld (Eds.), *Research on managing groups and teams: Composition* (Vol. 1, pp. 21–38). Stamford, CT: JAI Press.

Ashforth, B. E., & Mael, F. (1989). Social identity theory and the organization. *Academy of Management Review, 14,* 20–39.

Ashkanasy, N. M., Härtel, C. E. J., & Daus, C. S. (2002). Diversity and emotion: The new frontiers in organizational behavior research. *Journal of Management, 28,* 307–338.

Barreto, M., & Ellemers, N. (2001). You can't always do what you want: Social identity and self-presentational determinants of the choice to work for a low-status group. *Personality and Social Psychology Bulletin, 26,* 891–906.

Barreto, M., & Ellemers, N. (2002). The impact of respect versus neglect of self identities on identification and group loyalty. *Personality and Social Psychology Bulletin, 28,* 629–639.

Barsade, S. G., Ward, A. J., Turner, J. D. F., & Sonnefeld, J. A. (2000). To your heart's content: A model of affective diversity in top management teams. *Administrative Science Quarterly, 45,* 802–836.

Berger, J., Ridgeway, C. L., Fisek, M. H., & Norman, R. Z. (1998). The legitimation and delegitimation of power and prestige orders. *American Sociological Review, 63,* 379–405.

Bettencourt, B. A., Dill, K. E., Greathouse, S., Charlton, K., & Mulholland, A. (1996). Evaluations of ingroup and outgroup members: The role of category-based expectancy violation. *Journal of Experimental Social Psychology, 33,* 244–275.

Bettencourt, B. A., & Sheldon, K. (2001). Social roles as mechanisms for psychological need satisfaction within social groups. *Journal of Personality and Social Psychology, 81,* 1131–1143.

Bettenhausen, K., & Murnighan, J. K. (1985). The emergence of norms in competitive decision-making groups. *Administrative Science Quarterly, 30,* 350–372.

Bezrukova, K., & Jehn, K. A. (2001). *The effects of diversity training programs.* Unpublished manuscript, Solomon Asch Center for the Study of Ethnopolitical Conflict, University of Pennsylvania, Philadelphia.

Bezrukova, K., & Jehn, K. A. (2004). *Examining ethnic faultlines in groups: A multimethod study of demographic alignment, leadership profiles, coalition formation, intersubgroup conflict and group outcomes.* Manuscript submitted for publication.

Biernat, M., Vescio, T. K., & Billings, L. S. (1999). Black sheep and expectancy violation: Integrating two models of social judgment. *European Journal of Social Psychology, 29,* 523–542.

Brewer, M. B. (1991). The social self: On being the same and different at the same time. *Personality and Social Psychology Bulletin, 17,* 472–482.

Brickson, S. (2000). The impact of identity orientation on individual and organizational outcomes in demographically diverse settings. *Academy of Management Review, 25,* 82–101.

Brown, R. J., & Wade, G. (1987). Superordinate goals and intergroup behaviour: The effect of role ambiguity and status on intergroup attitudes and task performance. *European Journal of Social Psychology, 17,* 131–142.

Bunderson, J. S., & Sutcliffe, K. M. (2002). Comparing alternative conceptualizations of functional diversity in management teams: Process and performance effects. *Academy of Management Journal, 45,* 875–893.

Carli, L. L., LaFleur, S. J., & Loeber, C. C. (1995). Nonverbal behavior, gender, and influence. *Journal of Personality and Social Psychology, 6,* 1030–1041.

Chatman, J. A., & Flynn, F. J. (2001). The influence of demographic heterogeneity on the emergence and consequences of cooperative norms in work teams. *Academy of Management Journal, 44,* 956–974.

Chatman, J. A., Polzer, J. T., Barsade, S. G., & Neale, M. A. (1998). Being different yet feeling similar: The influence of demographic composition and organizational culture on work processes and outcomes. *Administrative Science Quarterly, 43,* 749–780.

Cox, T., Lobel, S., & McLeod, P. (1991). Effects of ethnic group cultural differences on cooperative and competitive behavior on a group task. *Academy of Management Journal, 34,* 827–847.

Durkheim, E. (1984). *The division of labour in society.* London: Macmillan.

Eagly, A. H., & Karau, S. J. (2002). Role congruity theory of prejudice toward female leaders. *Psychological Review, 3,* 573–598.

Eagly, A. H., Karau, S. J., & Makhijani, M. G. (1995). Gender and the effectiveness of leaders: A meta-analysis. *Psychological Bulletin, 1,* 125–145.

Earley, P. C., & Mosakowski, E. (2000). Creating hybrid team cultures: An empirical test of transnational team functioning. *Academy of Management Journal, 43,* 26–49.

Ellemers, N., de Gilder, D., & Haslam, S. A. (2004). Motivating individuals and groups at work: A social identity perspective on leadership and group performance. *Academy of Management Review, 28,* 459–478.

Ely, R. J., & Thomas, D. A. (2001). Cultural diversity at work: The effects of diversity perspectives on work group processes and outcomes. *Administrative Science Quarterly, 46,* 229–273.

Fiske, S. T., & Taylor, S. E. (1991). *Social cognition* (2nd ed.). New York: McGraw-Hill.

Foschi, M., & Lawler, E. J. (1994). *Team processes: Sociological analyses.* Chicago: Nelson-Hall.

Gaertner, S. L., Dovidio, J. F., & Bachman, B. A. (1996). Revisiting the contact hypothesis: The induction of a common ingroup identity. *International Journal of Intercultural Relations, 20,* 271–290.

Gellatly, I. R., & Luchak, A. A. (1998). Personal and organizational determinants of perceived absence norms. *Human Relations, 51,* 1085–1102.

Gonzales, R., & Brown, R. (2006). Dual identities in intergroup contact: Group status and size moderate the generalization of positive attitude change. *Journal of Experimental Social Psychology, 42,* 753–767.

Gruenfeld, D. H., Mannix, E. A., Williams, K. Y., & Neale, M. A. (1996). Group composition and decision making: How member familiarity and information distribution affect process and performance. *Organizational Behavior and Human Decision Processes, 67,* 1–15.

Hambrick, D. C., & Mason, P. A. (1984). Upper echelons: The organization as a reflection of its top managers. *Academy of Management Review, 9,* 193–206.

Harrison, D. A., Price, K. H., & Bell, M. P. (1998). Beyond relational demography: Time and the effects of surface and deep-level diversity on group functioning. *Academy of Management Journal, 41*, 96–107.

Harrison, D. A., Price, K. H., Gavin, J. H., & Florey, A. T. (2002). Time, teams, and task performance: Changing effects of surface- and deep-level diversity on group functioning. *Academy of Management Journal, 45*, 1029–1045.

Härtel, C. E. J., & Fujimoto, Y. (1999). Explaining why diversity sometimes has positive effects in organizations and sometimes has negative effects in organizations: The perceived dissimilarity openness moderator model [CD-ROM]. Pleasantville, NY: Academy of Management.

Haslam, S. A. (2001). *Psychology in organizations: The social identity approach*. London: Sage.

Haslam, S. A., Eggins, R. A., & Reynolds, K. J. (2003). The ASPIRE model: Actualizing social and personal identity resources to enhance organizational outcomes. *Journal of Occupational and Organizational Psychology, 76*, 83–113.

Haslam, S. A., & Ellemers, N. (2004). Social identity in industrial and organisational psychology: Concepts, controversies and contributions. *International Review of Industrial and Organizational Psychology, 20*, 39–118.

Heider, F. (1958). *The psychology of interpersonal relations*. New York: Wiley.

Hewstone, M. R. (1996). Contact and categorization: Social psychological interventions to change intergroup relations. In C. N. Macrae, C. Stangor, & M. R. C. Hewstone (Eds.), *Stereotypes and stereotyping* (pp. 323–368). London: Guilford Press.

Hobman, E. V., Bordia, P., & Gallois, C. (2003). Consequences of feeling dissimilar from others in a work team. *Journal of Business and Psychology, 17*, 301–325.

Hogg, M. A., & Abrams, D. (1988). *Social identifications: A social psychology of intergroup relations and group processes*. London: Routledge.

Hogg, M. A., & Terry, R. (2000). Social identity and self-categorization processes in organizational contexts. *Academy of Management Review, 24*, 121–140.

Hornsey, M. J., & Hogg, M. A. (2000). Assimilation and diversity: An integrative model of subgroup relations. *Personality and Social Psychology Review, 4*, 143–156.

Hornsey, M. J., & Jetten, J. (2004). The individual within the group: Balancing the need to belong with the need to be different. *Personality and Social Psychology Review, 8*, 248–264.

Ivancevich, J. M., & Gilbert, J. A. (2000). Diversity management: Time for a new approach. *Public Personnel Management, 29*, 75–92.

Jackson, S. E., Joshi, A., & Erhardt, N. L. (2003). Recent research on team and organizational diversity: SWOT analysis and implications. *Journal of Management, 29*, 801–830.

Jackson, S. E., May, K. E., & Whitney, K. (1995). Under the dynamics of diversity in decision-making teams. In R. A. Guzzo & E. Salas (Eds.), *Team effectiveness and decision making in organizations* (pp. 204–261). San Francisco: Jossey-Bass.

Jehn, K. A. (1995). A multimethod examination of the benefits and detriments of intragroup conflict. *Administrative Science Quarterly, 40,* 256–282.

Jehn, K. A., Northcraft, G. B., & Neale, M. A. (1999). Why differences make a difference: A field study of diversity, conflict and performance in workgroups. *Administrative Science Quarterly, 44,* 741–763.

Jetten, J., Postmes, T., & McAuliffe, B. J. (2002). We're all individuals: Group norms of individualism and collectivism, levels of identification and identity threat. *European Journal of Social Psychology, 32,* 189–207.

Lau, D. C., & Murnighan, J. K. (1998). Demographic diversity and faultlines: The compositional dynamics of organizational groups. *Academy of Management Review, 23,* 325–340.

Lau, D. C., & Murnighan, J. K. (2005). Interactions within groups and subgroups: The effects of demographic faultlines. *Academy of Management Journal, 48,* 645–659.

Lawrence, B. S. (1997). The black box of organizational demography. *Organizational Science, 8,* 1–22.

McGrath, J. E., Berdahl, J. L., & Arrow, H. (1995). Traits, expectations, culture, and clout: The dynamics of diversity in work groups. In S. E. Jackson & M. N. Ruderman (Eds.), *Diversity in work teams: Research paradigms for a changing workplace* (pp. 17–45). Washington, DC: American Psychological Association.

McLeod, P. L., Lobel, S. A., & Cox, T. H. (1996). Ethnic diversity and creativity in small groups. *Small Team Research, 27,* 248–264.

Miller, N., & Marks, G. (1982). Assumed similarity between self and other: Effect of expectation of future interaction with that other. *Social Psychology Quarterly, 45,* 100–105.

Milliken, F. J., & Martins, L. L. (1996). Searching for common threads: Understanding the multiple effects of diversity in organizational groups. *Academy of Management Review, 21,* 402–433.

Moscovici, S. (1985). Social influence and conformity. In G. Lindzey & E. Aronson (Eds.), *The handbook of social psychology* (Vol. 2, pp. 347–412). New York: McGraw-Hill.

Murnighan, J. K., & Brass, D. J. (1991). Intraorganizational coalitions. *Research on Negotiation in Organizations, 3,* 283–306.

Nickerson, R. S. (1999). How we know—and sometimes misjudge—what others know: Imputing one's own knowledge to others. *Psychological Bulletin, 125,* 737–759.

Nonaka, I., & Takeuchi, H. (1995). *The knowledge-creating company.* New York: Oxford University Press.

Oakes, P. J. (1987). The salience of social categories. In J. C. Turner, M. A. Hogg, P. J. Oakes, S. Reicher, & M. S. Wetherell (Eds.), *Rediscovering the social group: A self-categorization theory* (pp. 117–141). Oxford, England: Basil Blackwell.

Pelled, L. H., Eisenhardt, K. M., & Xin, K. R. (1999). Exploring the black box: An analysis of work group diversity, conflict, and performance. *Administrative Science Quarterly, 44,* 1–28.

Phillips, K. W. (2003). The effects of categorically based expectations on minority influence: The importance of congruence. *Personality and Social Psychology Bulletin, 29*, 3–13.

Phillips, K. W., & Lewin Loyd, D. (2006). When surface and deep-level diversity collide: The effects of dissenting group members. *Organizational Behavior and Human Decision Processes, 99*, 143–160.

Phillips, K. W., Mannix, E. A., Neale, M. A., & Gruenfeld, D. A. (2004). Diverse groups and information sharing: The effects of congruent ties. *Journal of Experimental Social Psychology, 40*, 497–510.

Polzer, J. T., Milton, L. P., & Swann, W. B., Jr. (2002). Capitalizing on diversity: Interpersonal congruence in small work groups. *Administrative Science Quarterly, 47*, 296–324.

Postmes, T., Spears, R., & Cihangir, S. (2001). Quality of decision making and group norms. *Journal of Personality and Social Psychology, 80*, 918–930.

Postmes, T., Spears, R., Lee, A. T., & Novak, R. J. (2005). Individuality and social influence in groups: Inductive and deductive routes to group identity. *Journal of Personality and Social Psychology, 89*, 747–763.

Prentice, D. A., Miller, D. T., & Lightdale, J. R. (1994). Asymmetries in attachments to groups and to their members: Distinguishing between common-identity and common-bond groups. *Personality and Social Psychology Bulletin, 20*, 484–493.

Randel, A. E. (2002). Identity salience: A moderator of the relationship between group gender composition and work group conflict. *Journal of Organizational Behavior, 23*, 749–766.

Rink, F., & Ellemers, N. (2006). What can you expect? The influence of gender diversity in dyads on work goal expectancies and subsequent work commitment. *Group Processes & Intergroup Relations, 9*, 577–588.

Rink, F., & Ellemers, N. (2007a). Diversity as a source of common identity: Towards a social identity framework for studying the effects of diversity in organizations. *British Journal of Management, 18*, 17–27.

Rink, F., & Ellemers, N. (2007b). The role of expectancies in accepting task-related diversity: Do disappointment and lack of commitment stem from actual differences or violated expectations? *Personality and Social Psychology Bulletin, 33*, 842–854.

Riordan, C. M. (2000). Relational demography within groups: Past developments, contradictions, and new directions. In G. R. Ferris (Ed.), *Research in personnel and human resources management* (Vol. 19, pp. 131–173). Greenwich, CT: JAI Press.

Robinson Hickman, G., & Creighton-Zollar, A. (1998). Diverse self-directed work teams: Developing strategic initiatives for 21st century organizations. *Public Personnel Management, 27*, 187–200.

Scheepers, D., Spears, R., Doosje, B., & Manstead, A. S. R. (2003). Two functions of verbal intergroup discrimination: Identity and instrumental motives as a result of group identification and threat. *Personality and Social Psychology Bulletin, 29*, 568–577.

Schneider, S. K., & Northcraft, G. B. (1999). Three social dilemmas of work force diversity in organizations: A social identity perspective. *Human Relations, 52,* 1445–1467.

Simons, T., Pelled, L. H., & Smith, K. A. (1999). Making use of difference: Diversity, debate, and decision comprehensiveness in top management teams. *Academy of Management Journal, 42,* 662–673.

Stasser, G., Taylor, L. A., & Hanna, C. (1989). Information sampling in structured and unstructured discussions of three- and six-person groups. *Journal of Personality and Social Psychology, 57,* 67–78.

Stasser, G., & Titus, W. (1985). Pooling of unshared information in group decision making: Biased information sampling during discussion. *Journal of Personality and Social Psychology, 48,* 1467–1478.

Strauss, J. P., Barrick, M. R., & Connerley, M. L. (2001). An investigation of personality similarity effects (relational and perceived) on peer and supervisor ratings and the role of familiarity and liking. *Journal of Occupational and Organizational Psychology, 74,* 637–657.

Swann, W. B., Jr., Kwan, V. S. Y., Polzer, J., & Milton, L. P. (2003). Fostering group identification and creativity in diverse groups: The role of individuation and self-verification. *Personality and Social Psychology Bulletin, 29,* 1396–1406.

Swann, W. B., Jr., Milton, L. P., & Polzer, J. T. (2000). Should we create a niche or fall in line? Identity negotiation and small group effectiveness. *Journal of Personality and Social Psychology, 79,* 238–250.

Swann, W. B., Jr., Polzer, J. T., Seyle, D. C., & Ko, S. J. (2004). Finding value in diversity: Verification of personal and social self-views in diverse groups. *Academy of Management Review, 29,* 9–28.

Tajfel, H. (1972). Social categorization. In S. Moscovici (Ed.), *Introduction à la psychologie sociale* (Vol. 1, pp. 272–302). Paris: Larousse.

Tajfel, H. (1982). Instrumentality, identity and social comparisons. In H. Tajfel (Ed.), *Social identity and intergroup relations* (pp. 483–507). Cambridge, England: Cambridge University Press.

Tajfel, H., & Turner, J. C. (1979). An integrative theory of intergroup conflict. In W. Austin & S. Worchel (Eds.), *The social psychology of intergroup relations* (pp. 33–47). Monterey, CA: Brooks/Cole.

Tajfel, H., & Turner, J. C. (1986). The social identity theory of intergroup behavior. In S. Worchel & W. G. Austin (Eds.), *The psychology of intergroup relations* (pp. 7–24). Chicago: Nelson-Hall.

Thatcher, S. M. B., Jehn, K. A., & Zanutto, E. (2003). Cracks in diversity research: The effects of diversity faultlines on conflict and performance. *Group Decision and Negotiation, 12,* 217–241.

Thomas-Hunt, M. C., & Phillips, K. W. (2004). When what you know is not enough: Expertise and gender dynamics in task groups. *Personality and Social Psychology Bulletin, 30,* 1585–1598.

Turner, J. C. (1985). Social categorization and the self-concept: A social cognitive theory of group behaviour. In E. J. Lawjer (Ed.), *Advances in group processes: Theory and research* (Vol. 2, pp. 77–122). Greenwich, CT: JAI Press.

Turner, J. C. (1991). *Social influence*. Milton Keynes, England: Open University Press.

Turner, J. C. (1999). Some current issues in research on social identity and self-categorization theories. In N. Ellemers, R. Spears, & B. Doosje (Eds.), *Social identity: Context, commitment, content* (pp. 6–34). Oxford, England: Blackwell.

Turner, J. C., Hogg, M. A., Oakes, P. J., Reicher, S., & Wetherell, M. S. (1987). *Rediscovering the social group: A self-categorization theory*. Oxford, England: Basil Blackwell.

van Knippenberg, D., & Haslam, S. A. (2003). Realizing the diversity dividend: Exploring the subtle interplay between identity, ideology and reality. In S. A. Haslam, D. van Knippenberg, M. Platow, & N. Ellemers (Eds.), *Social identity at work: Developing theory for organizational practice* (pp. 61–77). New York: Taylor & Francis.

van Leeuwen, E., van Knippenberg, D., & Ellemers, N. (2003). Continuing and changing team identities: The effects of merging on social identification and ingroup bias. *Personality and Social Psychology Bulletin, 29*, 679–690.

Webber, S. S., & Donahue, L. M. (2001). Impact of highly and less job-related diversity on work group cohesion and performance: A meta-analysis. *Journal of Management, 27*, 141–162.

Wiersema, M. F., & Bantel, K. A. (1992). Top management team demography and corporate strategic change. *Academy of Management Journal, 35*, 91–121.

Williams, K. Y., & O'Reilly, C. A., III. (1998). Demography and diversity in organizations: A review of 40 years of research. In B. M. Staw & L. L. Cummings (Eds.), *Research in organizational behavior* (Vol. 20, pp. 77–140). Greenwich, CT: JAI Press.

AUTHOR INDEX

Numbers in italics refer to listings in the references.

SUBJECT INDEX

321

Barriers to professional development, *continued*
  leadership–gender stereotype incongruity, 29–30
  mentoring opportunities, 244
  negative effects of affirmative action, 13
  network formation, 12–13
  new challenges for women, 14–15
  resistance to affirmative action implementation, 266
  social identity processes, 13
Boards of directors, women members of
  company financial performance and, 156–157
  lack of, attributed to lack of commitment, 154
  patterns and trends, 4, 21
Bryant, Gay, 5
Burlington Industries v. Ellerth, 173, 174, 175
Burlington Northern v. White, 174
Bystander harassment, 179

Canada, 262, 266
Civil Rights Act, 207, 260
Clinton, Hillary, 73, 89
Collective action. *See* Resistance and collective action
Communal beliefs, 23–24, 26, 27, 31–32, 35–36, 86
Communication skills, leadership stereotypes, 25
Competence
  affirmative action effects on coworker perceptions, 272–274, 275–276
  affirmative action effects on self-evaluation for, 267–269, 270, 275
  perceived personal warmth and, 14–15, 78–80, 89
  perceptions of working mothers, 79
  stereotype content model, 76–78, 79
  task performance of affirmative action beneficiaries, 270–271

Competitiveness
  leadership stereotypes, 25
  stereotype content model, 77–78
Control
  gender stereotypes, 23
  stereotype threat moderated by locus-of-control beliefs, 137
Corporate officers, gender patterns and trends, 4, 21, 52, 74, 154, 172
Correspondent inference, 25
Cultural intelligence, 228, 245, 249

Decision making, leadership stereotypes, 25
Department of Labor, U.S., 5–6
Dependent-care support, 203–204
Depersonalization, 288
Descriptive beliefs, 22–23
Development
  effects of stereotype exposure in socialization experiences, 10, 140
  gender stereotypes and domain involvement, 126–131
Disciplinary behavior, leadership stereotypes, 25
Discrimination
  against token employees, 52–53
  based on stereotype incongruity, 29–30
  in benevolent sexism, 87
  as cause of gender gaps in employment, 100–101
  current patterns and trends, 99–100
  current perceptions of, 3–4
  future prospects for women in leadership roles, 38–41
  group identification and, 60–62
  indicators of, 15–16
  institutional factors, 257–258
  legal prohibitions, 260, 262–264
  obscured by advancement of few, 8, 15
  patronizing behavior, 86–87
  positive effects of recognizing victimization, 107, 115
  public recognition, 3

Gender identity, ambivalent sexism theory, 81
Gender–stress–disidentification model
evidence for, 162–164
implications of research findings, 165
outcomes of workplace stress in, 162
theoretical basis, 154, 161
Glass ceiling
conceptual origins, 5, 49
current relevance, 4–5, 6, 7, 9, 49
definition, 5
evolution of attitudes and beliefs, 3–4, 5–6
salient issues in current workplace, 6–13
sexual harassment and, 171–172
See also Senior positions in organizations, women in
Glass cliff
conditions of precariousness, 158–159
corporate appointment practice as evidence of, 156–157
definition, 6
gender–stress–disidentification model, 162–164
implications for organizations, 165
outcomes for women, 160–161
risks for women, 10–11, 155
stress of, 159–160
women's departure from professional development caused by, 154
Glass door, 10, 144–145
Glass escalator concept, 6, 30
men in traditionally feminine occupations, 53
Glass slipper, 6
Glass walls, 6
Government role in work–life policy development and implementation, 216–217
Great Britain, 263–264
Group processes
ambient sexual harassment effects, 179
depersonalization, 288
in-group favoritism, 75
intergroup power relations, 75–76, 82–83

organizational disidentification outcomes, 161
recognition of discrimination, group identification and, 115
sexual harassment risk factors, 186–190
status beliefs, 74–75
stereotype content model, 76–78
stress effects on organizational identification, 160
subgroup formation, 293–294
See also Diverse work groups; Resistance and collective action; Social identity theory

Hiring. See Recruitment

Implicit association, 129–130
Income gap
family responsibilities and, 202
part-time work and, 206
patterns and trends, 99, 257
Informational diversity, 286–287
Internalization of stereotypes
affirmative action effects, 13
in childhood socialization, 10
gender socialization in domain involvement, 128–129
subtle sexism effects, 9, 113–115, 117
Interpersonal interaction
evaluation of fellow group members, 289–290
gender stereotypes, 23, 24
group identification effects, 283–284
mentoring relationships, 244–246
social identity theory, 50–52
sociohistorical factors in relationships among minority women, 237–240
surface-level and deep-level diversity, 236, 285
trust based on perceived commonality, 236–237
See also Networks, social and professional

Job satisfaction
ambient sexual harassment effects, 179

Mentoring, *continued*
    self-assessment for bias, 144
    in social networks, 244–246
Meritocracy beliefs
    effects of discrimination on well-
        being and, 110
    explanations for gender inequality,
        103, 104
    subtle sexism and, 117
    tokenism and, 54
Middle-level management, 37, 201
Minority women
    discrimination experiences, 229
    mentoring relationships, 244–246
    networking strategies, 241–244
    potential costs of networking,
        246–247
    progress for women in general and,
        55, 201
    representation in senior positions,
        201, 229
    role of social networks, 228, 229
    shortcomings in research on, 230
    social group status alignment versus
        ethnic group alignment,
        236–237
    sociohistorical factors in relation-
        ships among, 237–240
    tempered visibility, 242–243
Motivation and commitment
    effects of glass cliff positions, 161, 165
    gender difference studies, 100
    lack of women in senior positions
        attributed to, 100, 153–154,
        165
    mentoring tactics to overcome
        stereotype effects, 144
    stereotype threat effects, 132–133
    task selection behaviors of affirma-
        tive action beneficiaries,
        269–270

Negativity bias, 79–80
Networks, social and professional
    among lawyers, 229
    benefits, 227, 229
    career network mapping, 232, 251

costs and risks, 246–247
    cross-cultural, 12, 228–229, 248–250
    cross-cultural research design, 231–232
    dimensions, 227
    gender patterns, 240–241
    intentional diversity in, 243–244
    mentoring relationships in, 244–246
    minority women and, 228, 229, 230
    rationale for corporations, 228
    role of trust in, 234, 247–248
    shortcomings in research, 230
    social capital linkage, 228, 234–235,
        250
    social group status alignment versus
        ethnic group alignment,
        236–237
    social identity and, 230, 233–237
    sociohistorical factors in relation-
        ships among minority women,
        237–240
    strategies for women's advancement,
        12–13
    structural and functional patterns,
        240–244
    tripartite cross-cultural model,
        233–234
Nonverbal behavior
    misperception of dominance behav-
        iors, 88–89
    power relations and, 88

Occupations, female-dominated
    leadership stereotypes, 30
    patterns and trends, 34
    sex segregation in workplace, 34
    social network characteristics, 241
    token males in, 53
    women managers in, 34
Occupations, male-dominated
    confirmation of stereotypes by obser-
        vation of gender representa-
        tion in, 129–131, 139–140
    cultural stereotypes, 10, 125–126
    early socialization shaping women's
        choices, 126–129
    men's reactions to women's advance-
        ment in, 59–60

prestige positions, 74

risk of sexual harassment of women in, 185, 186, 187–188

sexual harassment risk for women in, 172

social network characteristics, 240–241

stereotype threat and women's performance in, 131–138

strategies for diffusing stereotype effects on women's career choices, 139–144

training programs to advance women in, 257–258, 259

women's presence in, 52

Oncale v. Sundowner Offshore Serv., Inc., 174

Optimistic outlook, 108

Page, Clarence, 73

Part-time work, 34, 205–206

Paternalism, 81

Paternalistic prejudice, 77, 79, 82

Patronizing behaviors, 86

Pelosi, Nancy, 49–50

Pennsylvania State Police v. Suders, 174, 175

Perceptions of equality and discrimination

affective reactions, 58–60

benevolent sexism effects, 83

causal attributions of equity advances, 64, 65

comparison of past and present conditions, 51–52, 55–57, 60–61, 62, 63–64

current discrimination, 14, 101

current statistical evidence, 4, 21

expectations of future progress, 64–65

focus of comparison for disadvantaged groups, 56–57

gender differences in, 57

gender inequality attributed to women's choice, 153–154, 206–207

group identification and, 60–62

implications for collective action, 62–65

implicit association, 129–130

indicators of positive change, 14

inequality obscured by advancement of few, 8, 15, 60, 66

levels of analysis for, 4, 15–16

limitations of statistical analysis, 15–16

new challenges for women, 14–15

organizational outcomes, 60, 61–62

resistance to work–life policies, 214–216

self-fulfilling attributions for gender equality, 103–104

sex stereotyping of leadership, 31–37

since introduction of glass ceiling concept, 3–5, 6

social role expectations, 32–35

sources of reports of discrimination and, 112

tokenism effects, 7–8, 51–52, 53–54, 60–61, 62–63

Personal qualities

contemporary leadership concepts, 35–37

gender stereotypes, 23, 24

individual differences, 110

negativity bias, 79–80

protective factors in discrimination experience, 108, 110

sexual harassment perpetrators, 183–184

stereotype threat buffers, 137

victim-vulnerability theory of sexual harassment, 182

warmth, perceived managerial competence and, 14–15

Pity, 77

Prejudice

aversive, 102

mentor self-assessment, 144

resistance to work–life policies, 214–215

See also Discrimination; Sexism; Stereotypes; Subtle sexism

Prescriptive beliefs, 23

Prestigious occupations and positions, 74

Problem solving, leadership stereotypes, 25

Productivity of organizations, affirmative action and, 266–267
Professional development
    career flexibility policies, 206–207
    cause of gender gaps in, 100–101
    early socialization shaping domain involvement, 126–129
    effects of cultural stereotypes for women in male-dominated fields, 10
    effects of leadership stereotypes for women in traditionally female fields, 30
    effects of sexual harassment, 171–172
    effects of stereotype exposure in socialization experiences, 10
    gender inequality attributed to women's choice, 153–154, 206–207
    glass cliff effects, 154
    glass escalator concept, 6, 30
    stereotype threat effects on career choice, 138–139, 144–145
    strategies for diffusing stereotype effects on women's career choices, 139–144
    token employees, 52–53
    women choosing to opt out, 154–155
Protective factors
    certainty of attribution for discrimination experience, 109
    education about stereotype effects, 143–144
    group identification, 115
    meritocracy beliefs, 110
    optimistic outlook, 108
    sexual harassment, effect of organizational policies against, 188–189, 190
    from stereotype threat effects, 136–137

Queen bee syndrome, 85

Racial and ethnic minorities. *See* Minority women
Racism, 102
Recruitment, affirmative action in, 259

Resistance and collective action
    benevolent sexism effects, 83
    hostile response to counternormative behaviors, 87–88
    perceived effectiveness and likelihood of continuing, 64–65
    perceptions of equality and, 62–64
    to protect privileged status, 65–66
    recognition of barriers to, 65
    subtle sexism and, 115–116, 117
Retirement, 209
Reverse discrimination claims, 59
Role models, 140, 212

Same sex sexual harassment, 175
Segregation by gender in workplace, 34
Self-esteem
    responses to workplace integration, 59–60
    strategies for countering stereotype effects, 140–141
    subtle sexism effects, 106–107, 109
    vulnerability to discrimination effects on well-being, 110–11
Self-evaluation
    affirmative action policy outcomes, 267–269, 275
    depersonalization in group identity, 288
    effects of negative outcomes on domain attachment, 138
    mentor's, for gender bias, 144
    others' expectations and, 128–129
    stereotype threat buffers, 137–138
    See also Self-esteem
Self-verification in group processes, 294–295
Senior positions in organizations, women in
    inequality obscured by advancement of few, 7–8, 15, 60, 66
    lack of, attributed to lack of commitment, 153–154, 165
    patterns and trends, 4, 21, 74, 100, 172, 201
    perceived personal warmth, 14–15
    persistence of gendered experiences, 10

racial and ethnic differences, 229
women choosing to opt out, 154–155
See also Boards of directors, women
members of; Corporate officers, women; Glass ceiling;
Glass cliff; Management,
women in
Sense of humor, 137
Service economy, 34
Sexism
benevolent, 81, 83–84, 87
as cause of gender gaps in employment, 100–101
changes in expression of, 101–102
hostile, 81, 83–84, 87–89
See also Ambivalent sexism theory;
Subtle sexism
Sexual behavior
ambivalent sexism theory, 81
hostile sexism and, 87–88
misperception of dominance behaviors, 88–89
Sexual Experiences Questionnaires,
176–177
Sexual harassment
affirmative defense to claims of,
174–175
ambivalent sexism theory, 87–89
approach and rejection goals, 181
assessment instruments, 176–177, 184
contextual factors, 173, 180, 186–190
definitions, 11
effect of organizational policies and
leadership against, 188–189,
190
effects on witnesses, 179
glass ceiling and, 171–172
in hostile work environment, 174
laboratory research, 184–185
legal conceptualizations, 173–176,
190–191
outcomes, 11, 172–173, 179–180
perpetrators and targets, 179–186, 192
person X situation model, 180
power-threat theory, 182
prevalence, 11, 177–178
preventive and protective factors, 183

psychological definitions, 173, 176
quid pro quo, 174
risk and protective factor model, 190
routine activities theory, 182
same sex, 175
sex-role spillover model, 180
sociocultural model, 180–181
strategies for preventing, 191–192, 193
victim-vulnerability theory, 182
Sexual Harassment in the Workplace, 172
Social capital
creation in social networks,
234–235, 250
mentoring outcomes and, 244
role of networks to increase, 12
significance of, 227
social network linkage, 228
Social dominance theory, 82
Social identity and social identity theory
affective reactions to perceived
inequality, 58–60
barriers to diversity, 13
conceptual basis, 50, 229–230
depersonalization and, 288
diverse work groups and, 283–284,
287–288
diversity as source of group identification, 289–292
faultline theory, 292–294
focus of comparison for disadvantaged groups, 56–57
of gender inequality, 50–52
group identification outcomes of
equity perceptions, 60–62, 185
likelihood of collective action, 62–64
mentoring outcomes, 244
networking strategies of minority
women, 241–244
queen bee syndrome in, 85
self-verification processes in, 294–295
social comparison in, 50–51, 230
social networking and, 230, 233–237
strategies for creating culture of
diversity, 13
tokenism effects, 54
Social identity-based impression management, 230

implications for collective action,
62, 63–64
perceptions of current equity conditions, 55–57
recognition of effects of, 65
social identity theory, 51–52
Tokenism
effect on intergroup comparisons,
52–53
group identification effects, 60–62
implications for collective action,
62–63
inequalities obscured by, 8, 15,
51–52, 53–54
meritocracy beliefs and, 54
negative effects on efforts to reduce
inequality, 8
outcomes for token employees,
52–53
recognition of effects of, 65
Training programs
affirmative action in, 257–258, 259
diversity training, 295–296
Transformational leadership, 36–37
Trust
perceived commonality and, 236–237
in social networks, 234, 247–248

Warmth, personal
perceived managerial competence
and, 14–15, 78–80, 89
perceptions of working mothers, 79
stereotype content model, 76–78, 79
Working mothers, 79

Work–life policies
backlash response within company,
215–216
barriers to, 203, 217
career flexibility, 206–207
within corporate diversity strategy,
214
cultural contexts, 210
current attitudes of workers,
208–209
dependent-care support, 203–204
effectiveness, 11–12, 203
flexible work arrangements, 203,
205–206, 210–211
gender equality linkage, 210
goals, 202
government policies and, 216–217
historical development, 203,
207–208, 209
ideological resistance, 214–215
leadership for effective implementation, 212–213
manager and employee training for
implementation of, 213
organizational culture and, 211–212
policy underlife, 213
rationale, 11, 204–205
strategies for effective implementation, 210–218
strategies for improving, 12
technological support, 204
temporary leave, 204
utilization patterns, 210–211
Work-values diversity, 286–287

ABOUT THE EDITORS

Manuela Barreto obtained her PhD in social psychology from the Free University, Amsterdam, the Netherlands. Her dissertation, which focused on social identity and strategic processes as motivators of pro-group behavior, earned an honorary mention from the Society for the Psychological Study of Social Issues. Dr. Barreto was an associate professor in social and organizational psychology at Leiden University, the Netherlands, and is now a research fellow at the Centre for Social Psychology and Intervention of the University of Lisbon, Portugal. She has been awarded several prizes and prestigious research grants. Her research interests and publications focus on the psychology of the disadvantaged, exemplified by her work on identity respect, reactions to prejudice and discrimination, and the psychology of concealed identities.

Michelle K. Ryan obtained her PhD from the Australian National University and is currently a senior research fellow at the University of Exeter. She holds a 5-year academic fellowship from the Research Council of the United Kingdom and a large grant from the Economic and Social Research Council. She is a member of the Centre for Identity, Personality and Self in Society and works within a social identity framework, specializing in research about gender and gender differences. She is a consulting editor for the *British Journal of Social Psychology* and *Social Psychology*.

Michael T. Schmitt first became involved in social psychological research on gender and sexism as an undergraduate at James Madison University in Harrisonburg, Virginia, working under the supervision of Arnie Kahn and Ginny Andreoli-Mathie. Dr. Schmitt received his PhD from the University of Kansas, where he was mentored by Nyla Branscombe. As a graduate student he received a Fulbright Scholarship to conduct research and study at the University of Amsterdam. Currently, Dr. Schmitt is an assistant professor in the psychology department at Simon Fraser University in Burnaby, British Columbia. His research examines how people respond to inequality between groups, such as inequalities based on ethnicity, gender, nationality, or sexuality.